PEACEKEEPING
IN THE ABYSS

PEACEKEEPING
IN THE ABYSS

BRITISH AND AMERICAN PEACEKEEPING
DOCTRINE AND PRACTICE AFTER THE COLD WAR

Robert M. Cassidy

PRAEGER

Westport, Connecticut
London

Library of Congress Cataloging-in-Publication Data

Cassidy, Robert M., Ph.D.
   Peacekeeping in the abyss : British and American peacekeeping doctrine and practice
after the Cold War / Robert M. Cassidy.
      p.   cm.
   Includes bibliographical references and index.
   ISBN 0–275–97696–3 (alk. paper)
   1. United States—Armed Forces—Foreign countries.   2. Great Britain—Armed
Forces—Foreign countries.   3. Intervention (International law).   4. Peacekeeping forces.   I.
Title.
   JZ6377.U6C37   2004
   355.3'5—dc21   2003045787

British Library Cataloguing in Publication Data is available.

Library of Congress Catalog Card Number: 2003045787
ISBN: 0–275–97696–3

First published in 2004

Praeger Publishers, 88 Post Road West, Westport, CT 06881
An imprint of Greenwood Publishing Group, Inc.
www.praeger.com

Printed in the United States of America

The paper used in this book complies with the
Permanent Paper Standard issued by the National
Information Standards Organization (Z39.48–1984).

10 9 8 7 6 5 4 3 2 1

CONTENTS

Acknowledgments

I thank Professors Dick Shultz, Robert Pfaltzgraff, and Jay Parker. Without their support, patience, and mentorship, this effort would not have come to fruition. A special thanks goes to Professor Shultz who regularly advised me on this project. My gratitude also goes out to several members of the Department of Social Sciences at the United States Military Academy: Brigadier General Dan Kaufman, for allowing me to pursue this research; Colonel Jay Parker and Lieutenant Colonel Cindy Jebb, for being flexible and encouraging in support of my research while teaching full time. I also owe a special thanks to John Nagl for his continuous insights and advice, which included reading and commenting on the manuscript. Finally, I thank my steadfast wife, Chris, who accepted many additional burdens during this effort, among them, taking care of our young twins when I was away doing research.

PREFACE

This book explains British and American military strategic cultural preferences for the use of force and examines how these preferences influenced both the development of the first post–Cold War peace operations doctrine and the conduct of operations in Bosnia and Somalia.

Because the end of the Cold War represented a massive structural change in the international system, accompanied by an increase in UN Security Council resolutions and peace operations, military doctrine for peace operations lagged behind policy. In fact, the British and U.S. militaries deployed to Bosnia (Operation Grapple) and Somalia (Operation Restore Hope) without doctrine for those types of operations. These militaries, therefore, relied on Cold-War era low-intensity-conflict (LIC) doctrine and their military cultural preferences for the use of force. Doctrine was, however, developed concurrently with the conduct of these two operations—some draft and final versions were distributed to the field before these operations ended. As a result of a lag and as a result of feedback from operations Grapple and Restore Hope, cultural preferences and culturally filtered lessons from those operations also manifested themselves in the new doctrine.

For a long time I have been interested in understanding why the U.S. military has not often done operations other than big wars well. The U.S. military operation in Somalia, though initially a humanitarian operation, essentially metamorphosed into an urban counterinsurgency against the strongest warring faction. Like its deeply embedded reaction to Vietnam, the lesson that the U.S. military brought away from Somalia was—"No more Somalias." However, with ongoing asymmetric (counter-guerrilla) conflicts in Afghanistan and Iraq, and with the U.S. Army in the process of "transformation," this book is salient because it examines the American military cultural preferences for big wars and its capacity to change to meet the higher probability of asymmetric conflicts in the future.

MILITARY STRATEGIC CULTURE AND DOCTRINE

Whoever fights monsters should see to it that in the process he does not become a monster. And when you look long into the abyss, the abyss also looks into you.[1]
—Friederich Nietzsche

INTRODUCTION

In 1992 the British forces that entered Bosnia and the American forces that entered Somalia were truly stepping into an abyss. Bosnia was a multiethnic state that was beginning to implode, with its perceived ethnic groups lining up to kill each other based on which alphabet they used and depending on the architectural design of their places of worship. Bosnia suffered from a chronic case of heterogeneity, bad history, and bad leaders. The bad leaders were the real monsters in Bosnia—by espousing ethnic politics and instrumental perfidy, the local thugs guaranteed that Bosnia would spiral downward into an abysmal and savage conflict. Nor was Somalia suffering from a dearth of monsters. The local warlords there cared more about preserving their personal power and expanding their clans' fiefdoms than they cared about the fates of thousands of their women and children who were dying from starvation. The scope of crises in both failed states impelled the British and American governments, as well as several other United Nations (UN) members, to do something under the aegis of the UN to mitigate the human suffering.

That *something* would be the armed escort of humanitarian relief in the midst of ongoing conflicts within these two collapsed states. Absent any existing military doctrine for this type of operation, one can postulate that the British Army in Bosnia and the U.S. Army in Somalia would rely on Cold-War era low-intensity-conflict (LIC) doctrine as well as their embedded cultural preferences about the use of force in operations short of war. Indeed, the British Army and the American Army developed new doctrine during operations in Bosnia and Somalia—the two armies even disseminated draft manuals and the final versions of peace support operations (PSO) doctrine to the field before these operations ended. In addition to the fact that military doctrine lagged behind the massive structural changes in the security environment that attended the end of the Cold War, military cultural change lagged even further behind. Military strategic cultural preferences and culturally filtered lessons from British Army operations in Bosnia and U.S. Army operations in Somalia also manifested themselves in the first editions of post-Cold War doctrine.

Casualty aversion or acceptance in the context of peacekeeping, along with its corollary of force protection, is but one example of a military cultural characteristic that sets the U.S. Army apart from the British Army. After December 1995, when the NATO-led Implementation Force (IFOR) deployed to Bosnia to implement the Dayton Accords, U.S. Army soldiers were required to remain in full battle rattle—weapons, Kevlar helmets, and body armor. British and other European soldiers, however, carried weapons and wore only berets. In other words, U.S. soldiers were postured and attired for combat while the British were outfitted for peacekeeping. This disparity in force protection posture reflected the U.S. commanders' aversion to risking casualties. British commanders viewed IFOR as a peace operation while American commanders viewed it as combat, going in "dukes up," armed for combat. Interestingly, the U.S. soldiers in IFOR who wore full battle uniform earned themselves the epithet "ninja turtles" from some of the European allies in IFOR.[2]

Purpose

The purpose of this book is to explain British and American military strategic cultural preferences for the use of force and to analyze how these preferences influenced both the development of the first post–Cold War peacekeeping doctrine and the conduct of operations in Bosnia and Somalia. This study lies at the intersection of international relations, military history, and military strategy. It should be of interest to those people concerned with strategic studies, military innovation, and peace operations because it looks past the realist notion of rational and unitary state actors to explain the more idiosyncratic causes for the development of two different doctrinal approaches to peacekeeping. According to Ken Waltz, the father of neorealism, if important discontinuities occur within a system whose structure remains constant, then, the causes of these discontinuities lie at the state level. However, the obverse must also be true—if continuities remain within a system whose structure has transformed, then the reasons for these must be found inside the state. This book thus examines the sub-state concept of military strategic culture as an explanatory variable for two different versions of peace support operations (PSO) doctrine in Britain and the United States.[3]

Scope of the Problem

The end of the Cold War witnessed more cooperation in the Security Council and an upsurge in intrastate conflict. As a result, there was a rapid increase in the scope of United Nations security-related activity in the immediate post–Cold War era. The new vitality of the UN Security Council also encouraged a large amount of energy and literature that supported the notion of more forceful peace operations wherein the lines between peacekeeping and peace enforcement VII were blurred. To complicate matters more, these nontraditional missions, involving the nonpermissive or semipermissive use of multinational forces sanctioned by the international community, were subsumed within an expanding and confusing taxonomy of gray-area missions. More significantly, the mandates and doctrinal guidelines for such operations were confusing and incongruous, sometimes combining peacekeeping, peace enforcement, humanitarian action, and disarmament in ways that often brought about disastrous results. Somalia and Bosnia are but the most glaring examples.[4]

Because moral and political factors often impelled the Security Council to act prior to the development of new national doctrines for the gray area, many states embarked on these new enterprises within the context of a doctrinal void or lag. As the numbers and types of peace operations increased in the 1990s, national governments and regional organizations did subsequently develop policies and devise doctrines to meet the new challenges. The British and the Americans, along with other European allies, did hold meetings and seminars to discuss and coordinate emerging doctrines. Notwithstanding the coordination between the U.S. and British doctrine writers, however, their two first post–Cold War editions of PSO doctrine reflected two distinct sets of cultural preferences and thus represented two different conceptual approaches to peacekeeping: the American doctrine reflected a more forceful approach whereas British doctrine rested closer to the lower end of the spectrum of intensity. Figure 1.1 depicts where these two doctrines lay concerning consent and the use of force. Force and consent are inexorably linked to each other in practice; the level at which these two factors are applied is legally derived from Chapters VI and VII of the UN Charter. The operational and doctrinal approaches to the amount of force used and to the maintenance of consent determine the very essence of the operation: the application of decisive force and the loss of consent, coupled with the concomitant perception of partiality, is war. The obverse is not.[5]

The Relevance of Doctrine

Why study doctrine as an explanatory variable? Doctrine is salient because it is central to how militaries execute their missions—it is how we operate. Doctrine, therefore, is an authoritative expression of a military's fundamental approach to fighting wars and influencing events in operations other than war. It should establish a framework of common understanding and action that informs the deci-

Figure 1.1
PSO and Two Distinct Approaches to Consent and the Use of Force

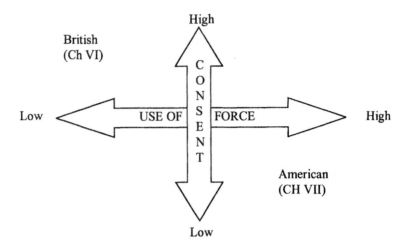

sion-making process. As an overarching statement, military doctrine must be precise enough to guide specific operations yet versatile enough to address the diversity of the global security environment.[6] However, according to retired Brigadier Gavin Bulloch, even when it is published, official doctrine often lags behind events. Despite the British Army's extensive experience in counterinsurgency during this century, "relatively little has been recorded as official doctrine in military publications." The British Army has, however, taken note of the similarities between its traditional approach to counterinsurgency and its doctrinal procedures for peace support operations.[7]

Moreover, to be successful in military campaigns, it is essential that the doctrine be appropriate for the operational milieu. Barry Posen had this to say about doctrine: "by the political and military appropriateness of the means employed, a military doctrine affects the security of the state that holds it." Posen also maintains that military doctrine can damage the security interests of a country if that doctrine fails to adapt to changes in the international security landscape. Military doctrine will also injure the security interests of the state if it does not provide statesmen with the tools needed to pursue the aims of national strategy and foreign policy. History is replete with examples of states and armies that helped defeat themselves with unsound doctrines. What's more, because the post–Cold War security environment engenders more ambiguity and more uncertainty, doctrine must be relevant to a wider variety of threats and operations in order to be effective.[8]

For militaries to be successful in these nontraditional operations they must adapt their doctrines to meet the exigencies of a range of PSO—their doctrines should be congruent and be designed to adequately address the principles and tenets required to achieve success in complex and volatile intrastate emergencies. Not only was there no common international doctrine for the members of the UN, but, even among major allies (NATO) with similar war-fighting doctrines, significant doctrinal differences still existed in PSO despite five years of a high multinational tempo in these operations. The first post-Cold War PSO doctrinal manuals of these two militaries seemed to reflect the cultural-historical propensities of these states toward war and operations short of war. This study will examine the humanitarian operations (a subset of PSO) in Somalia and Bosnia and it covers the period from 1990 to 1995. In 1990, the U.S. Army published its last Cold-War era LIC manual and in 1995 the British, along with other European militaries, relinquished the United Nations Protection Force (UNPROFOR) role for the NATO-led IFOR.

PARAMETERS AND DEFINITIONS

The emphasis of this study primarily rests at the operational level where strategic aims are translated into military action. It is at the operational level where commanders plan and conduct major joint and combined operations. Even still, the operational level is not delimited by the size of the force or by the echelon of the headquarters. Size notwithstanding, if a military force is being used purposely to attain a strategic objective, then it is being employed at the operational level. The operational level is the critical nexus between strategic goals and tactical execution. Finally, although these operations are almost always joint and combined, this research focuses principally on the doctrine of the land-force components. The land forces in each country are responsible for developing doctrine for peace operations and hostilities short of war, doctrine that subsequently forms the conceptual core of joint doctrine in this area.

Before going directly to the concept of military strategic culture, it is necessary to clarify some underlying concepts in the fields of anthropology and organizational theory. Clifford Geertz explains cultural anthropology as the study of "the machinery individuals and groups of individuals employ to orient themselves in a world otherwise opaque." Culture, then, is not so much an experimental science in search of laws; instead, it is an interpretive science in search of meaning. In other words, culture is not something to which causality can be readily attributed, but it is a context in which patterns of behavior can be intelligibly described. In sum, Geertz identifies culture as the "ordered cluster of significant symbols" that individuals and groups of individuals use to make sense of life.[9]

Moving from the anthropological to the political sphere, Lucien Pye maintains that political culture is "the product of both the collective history of a political system and the life histories of the individuals currently making up the system." Political culture provides meaning and structure to the political realm the same way that culture adds meaning and coherence to the social sphere. Political culture comprises only those central but widely shared beliefs and "patterns of orientation" that give form to the political process. Moreover, Sidney Verba argues that the most important characteristic of political culture is that it is a "patterned set of orientations toward politics in which specific norms and general values are mutually related." What's more, both Pye and Verba maintain that a study of political culture must address both the historical development of the system as a whole and the life experiences of the individuals who currently comprise its core. This is because political culture is learned.[10]

On the other hand, Edgar Schein fuses behavior studies and anthropology to arrive at an explanation of organizational culture. According to Schein, we must first ascertain whether a given set of people has had enough common history and stability to allow a culture to form. Some organizations will not have an organizational culture because of either no common history or frequent turnovers. Other organizations will have deep cultures because of shared intense experiences or a long shared history. Schein maintains that culture is "what a group learns over a period of time as that group solves its problems of survival in an external environment and its problems of internal integration." Schein offers a five-fold definition of culture: (1) it is a pattern of basic assumptions; (2) it is invented, discovered, or developed by a given group; (3) it learns to cope with its problems of external adaptation and internal integration; (4) it has worked well enough to be considered valid; and (5) it is taught to new members as the correct way to perceive, think, and feel in relation to those problems. In sum, the consistency and strength of a culture stem from group longevity, stability, intensity of experiences, mechanisms for learning, and the clarity of assumptions espoused by its core leaders.[11]

Moreover, Jeff Legro postulates that military culture is "assessed according to the ideas and beliefs about how to wage war that characterize a particular military bureaucracy." Empirical and measurable indicators include internal correspondence, planning documents, memoirs, and regulations. Likewise, Alan Macmillan offers a succinct definition of strategic culture: "a unique combination of geographic setting, historical experiences, and political culture which shapes the formation of beliefs about the use of force." However, the organizational cultures of the military services are particularly strong because these bureaucracies have a closed-career principle—members spend their careers almost exclusively in these organizations. One expert explains, "the services recruit and indoctrinate new members around their core mission and its requirements, thus ensuring cultural continuity across generations." Military organizations also promote career personnel to higher levels with only a limited external veto and no real external competition. Thus, their cultures are institutionalized by the military and internalized by its professionals. Organizational (military) culture influences organizational behavior significantly but not always positively.[12]

Because mission identity is an important part of a military's self-concept, military organizations will seek to promote core missions and to defeat any challenges to core-mission functions. Even if other missions are assigned, if the organization perceives them as peripheral to its core mission, then it will reject them as possible detractions from its core focus. Moreover, cultural change occurs in terms of "cultural epochs" that normally range in length from just a decade to as long as a century.[13]

Several years ago, a group of RAND scholars concluded that: "the beliefs and attitudes that comprise organizational culture can block change and cause organizations to fail." These authors explain that culture often originates from successes in an organization's history: what worked in the past is repeated and internalized; what didn't work is modified or rejected. If the organization survives, historically successful approaches are internalized and gradually transformed into "the way we think." What's more, this study asserts, military planners must consider the impact of culture—although it frequently operates outside the realm of observable causation, it can be a powerful and potentially counterproductive influence on behavior. The RAND report recommends a comparative approach: "comparisons with other armies can highlight different approaches to the preparation and conduct of warfare, some of which may be culture based." Finally, this study arrived at two important conclusions: first, cultural change requires a significant amount of time—the study determines five years as the minimum time to inculcate a major cultural change; second, major cultural change must come from the top—leaders at the highest levels must unambiguously back the change.[14]

In another study, Williamson Murray argues that military leadership can better influence doctrinal innovations through long-term cultural changes. He contends that the cultural values of a military organization are the most crucial when it comes to innovation. However, these values are the most difficult thing to change. Murray defines military culture as: "the sum of the intellectual, professional, and traditional values of the officer corps." Thus, culture plays an important role in how the military responds to the external environment. Moreover, Murray explains, past traditions are one part of military culture that can frequently block innovation—successful approaches were often worked out on earlier battlefields, at significant cost. As a result, military cultures "tend to change slowly in peacetime."[15]

This study defines military strategy as the art and science of employing the armed forces of a state to secure the aims of national policy by the application of force or threat of force. In war, military strategy encompasses the identification of strategic objectives, the allocation of resources, decisions on the use of force, and the development of war plans. Moreover, organizational culture is the pattern of assumptions, ideas, and beliefs that prescribe how a group should adapt to its external environment and manage its internal structure. Finally, military strategic culture is a set of beliefs, attitudes, and values within the military establishment that shape collective (shared) preferences of how and when military means should be used to accomplish strategic aims. It is derived or developed as a result of historical experience, geography, and political culture. Core leaders perpetuate and inculcate it, but it is most pronounced at the operational level because when armies have met with success in war, it is the operational techniques and the operational histories by which enemies were defeated, which are consecrated in memory.[16]

CASE SELECTION

These two cases were selected because they represent the most significant examples of immediate post–Cold War peace operations that involved each of these two militaries. Moreover, although these militaries were operating under the auspices of combined task forces, in most cases, each military applied its unique national doctrine within sectors assigned by national command. Consequently, one would expect each military to exhibit distinct predilections about using force in different sectors with differing results. Moreover, from a military strategic culture perspective, these countries have objective features in common (i.e., geographic insularity) which might be interesting to test. Although the United States is a superpower and Britain is a middle power, their trans-Atlantic link, their roles in NATO, and their key roles as permanent members of the UNSC have contributed to some similarity in their approaches to international security.

This book traces the development of doctrine by each of these national militaries through the two cases. This book examines scholarly works, memoirs, policy statements, after action reports, and doctrinal publications. It also relies on interviews and personal accounts to trace the development of doctrines in the first half-decade after the Cold War. Where archival sources are already in existence, this dissertation will employ archival sources. This study recognizes the influence of budget constraints but treats them as exogenous to the causal link between new tasks and new doctrine. Moreover, since force structure derives from military doctrine, it lies beyond the scope of analysis. Likewise, this research treats technology as an exogenous factor since its integration and use are shaped by cultural preferences. Because the doctrinal approaches to consent, impartiality, and the use of force play a central role in these types of operations, these factors will be examined throughout each case as well. One policy implication of this research is to arrive at recommendations for improving the ability to alter culturally bounded barriers to effectiveness in nontraditional missions. This may help better develop doctrinal approaches in the future.[17]

ASSUMPTIONS

Given that this study examines a five-year period of significant change in the security environment, accompanied by an upsurge in PSO, my first assumption is that a "cultural lag" in both organizations will lead to continuity in doctrinal approaches. The notion that cultural change is very slow and incremental is prevalent in the literature. In fact, most of the literature maintains that cultural change takes at least a generation. This study borrows and revises two assumptions from Downie's work on institutional learning, with the qualification that his notion of "institutional memory" is a significant part of, if not synonymous with, organizational culture. One assumption is that change to an organization's culture is a precondition for doctrinal change. Moreover, since military doctrine is dependent on military culture, another assumption is that substantive changes in military doctrine may indicate cultural change. In other words, changes in military doctrine can reflect military cultural change. Likewise, continuity in doctrine may indicate cultural continuity.[18]

METHODOLOGY

Barry Posen has asserted that the development of doctrine is an outcome of both international and national variables: "it represents the state's response to the constraints and incentives of the external world, yet it encompasses means that are in the custody of military organizations." Posen seems to agree with the notion that both systemic and subsystemic factors affect why and how states deal with international security issues. What's more, Alexander George stipulates that "it is the task of theory to identify the many conditions and variables that affect historical outcomes and to sort out the causal patterns associated with different historical outcomes." George also maintains that the method of focused and controlled comparison of a few case studies has become a legitimate approach that can contribute to theory development. With this in mind, this research will employ George's comparative framework to focus selectively on culture and the development of PSO doctrine. It will use a qualitative approach, with structured question sets to guide the inquiry into doctrine and military strategic culture.[19]

In conjunction with the focused comparison method, I will employ "process tracing" to uncover and analyze cause-effect links in the development of this doctrine—linkages that connect the independent and dependent variables. Specifically, I will use process tracing to look for observable evidence in the form of explanatory or intervening variables to help explain the development of different doctrine in this area. This research will enlist some of Johnston's methodology to trace military strategic culture from its sources, through the socialization process, to the beliefs and assumptions held by key people who influenced the development of subsequent doctrine in this area. This book also traces the adaptation of doctrine in these two countries beginning with the impetus of the paradigm shift in 1990-1991 and continuing through the American and the British operations in Somalia and Bosnia, respectively. Finally, this study will compare and contrast the first cut of these doctrines to determine where they still diverge and converge.[20]

This book seeks to answer several key questions about military culture and peacekeeping doctrine. First, how did each doctrine change and what variables shaped these changes? Second, how did each new doctrine approach consent, impartiality, and the use of force? Third, do military strategic cultures help account for different approaches to peacekeeping doctrine. In other words, this work attempts to find out whether organizational preferences represent the intervening variable between the changing roles and demands for the use of military force (independent variable) and the outcome—a PSO doctrine for training and operating in a new milieu (the dependent variable).

There are three sets of questions that help focus this comparison of military strategic culture and doctrine. The first question (intervening variable) set draws on the literature in this area to extrapolate questions that help discern military strategic culture. The purpose of the second question set (intervening variable) is to assess U.S. operations in Somalia and British operations in Bosnia for continuity or change and to identify manifest cultural characteristics. The third question set (dependent variable) serves to compare the two doctrines and to determine continuity and change as well as similarities and differences in national approaches to the use of force—it is applied to the last Cold War era doctrines in 1990 and earlier, then first post–Cold War doctrines in 1994.

Independent Variable

The end of the Cold War—a sea change in the structure of the international system—was the catalyst for a change in doctrine because it transformed the international security environment. The shift in the distribution of capabilities precipitated an upsurge in UN-authorized peace operations for at least two reasons: more harmony and cooperation among the Permanent Five members of the Security Council; and more instability and conflict with the end of bipolarity.

Although it is fairly self-evident that absolute bipolarity ended with the collapse of the Soviet Union, there is still no consensus on the emerging structure of the international system. John Mearsheimer and Ken Waltz would agree, however, that the end of bipolarity equates to greater instability throughout the system. In 1993, Christopher Layne referred to a "unipolar" moment in which the United States would remain the pole in a unipolar system only until the first decade of the twenty-first century. According to Layne, this "geopolitical interlude" will ultimately give way to multipolarity. His premise about the demise of unipolarity is simple: "states balance against hegemons, even those like the United States that seek to maintain their preeminence by employing strategies based more on benevolence than coercion." Indeed, the fact that the United States has been playing the role of globo-cop during the last decade lends credence to a unipolar structure. Notwithstanding the unipolar versus multipolar arguments, all of these authors seem to agree that the end of the bipolar era was a harbinger of tumult.[21]

Likewise, the sea change in the distribution of capabilities translated into more cooperation between the two former Cold War adversaries in the UN Security Council. The improved situation in the Security Council in the late 1980s and early 1990s impelled a "near-explosive growth in the number and scope of missions." For example, through 1994 there were twenty-six UN-Security-Council-authorized operations whereas in 1988 there were only five operations. In personnel numbers, this amounted to 9,700 UN military personnel deployed around the world in 1988 compared to over 73,000 in 1994. A significant and unfortunate consequence of the increase in missions was that the UN Secretariat, the Security Council, and force contributors were not well prepared by experience to respond very promptly to the exigencies that arose in places such as the former Yugoslavia, Somalia, and Rwanda. The aforementioned discussion, then, seems to confirm the presence of the independent variable.

Intervening Variable (Question Set 1): What are the military strategic cultures of the U.S. and British armies?

1. How have geography and history affected the shared experiences of each military establishment?
2. Which functional roles are valued (core) in these military strategic cultures?[22]
3. Which functional roles are considered to be detractors to the cultures' central purpose (peripheral)?[23]
4. What is each military strategic culture's self-concept about the efficacy of force?[24]
5. How does each culture deal with technology and casualties?[25]
6. What is the preferred organization (combat formation) of each military strategic culture?

Intervening Variable (Question Set 2): How did military strategic cultural characteristics manifest themselves in the case studies?

1. Did the civilian leaders or the military leaders drive the approach and were civil the military components integrated?
2. Were institutional predilections for the use of force manifested?
3. What was the role of casualties?
4. Was there any indication of a reliance on technology?

Dependent Variable (Question Set 3): The aim of this question set is to determine if the PSO doctrines developed by the British and the U.S. armies were appropriate.[26] This question set relies partially on the principles of PSO as articulated in John Mackinlay's extensive study of the subject (A Guide to Peace Support Operations).[27]

1. How and where do the two militaries categorize peace operations?
2. How much doctrinal literature is dedicated to war-fighting and how much is dedicated to peace operations?[28]
3. How did these doctrines define peace operations and what principles underpin the doctrine for conducting these operations?[29]
4. How does the doctrine approach consent, impartiality, and the use of force?

CHAPTER ORGANIZATION

Chapter 1 defines the concepts of organizational culture and military strategic culture, deriving a synthesized and observable framework for this as a variable. This chapter will also delimit the scope of analysis and determine the three standard question sets to be used for a focused comparison of both the intervening and dependent variables.

Chapter 2 analyzes and explains the military strategic culture of Great Britain. It will rely on a military-strategic culture question set to arrive at generalizations and conclusions about the British Army's propensities for using force. It begins with a historical survey of 19th and 20th century manifestations of national preferences and performance in wars, small wars, and other intrastate conflicts. Although military strategic culture includes land, naval, and air forces, the army is the principal focus since most characteristics stem from its ability to be successful on the ground.

Chapter 3 analyzes and explains the military strategic culture of the United States. It will rely on the same methodology employed in Chapter 2 but the aim is to discern preferences and attitudes about force in the U.S. military.

Chapter 4 compares and contrasts the operations other than war (OOTW) doctrine that existed at the end of the Cold War.

Chapter 5 applies the second question set to analyze how U.S. military strategic cultural characteristics manifested themselves in Somalia. This chapter will also review the lessons learned there and examine how they were incorporated into the newer doctrine.

Chapter 6 also examines how British military strategic cultural characteristics were manifested in Bosnia during the UN Protection Force (UNPROFOR) phase (1992–1995).

Chapter 7 compares the first post–Cold War peace operations doctrines of the two armies for continuity and change. It also identifies where the doctrines converge and where they still diverge insofar as force and consent are concerned.

Chapter 8 explains and links causal variables, synthesizes the different components of the research design, and arrives at inferences and policy implications for the use of force in humanitarian and peace support operations.

SUMMARY

This work will represent a unique contribution to the field because it studies two separate national military doctrines and focuses the analysis on one extremely complex operation. These non-traditional missions represent a challenge for our forces and they have comprised the preponderance (in the types) of mission tempo for these two countries since the Cold War ended. More specifically, since 1945 the American Army's conduct of LIC/OOTW has been conspicuously unimpressive because of its focus on the big-war concept. The British conduct of small wars, on the other hand, has generally been more successful. According to one scholar, the British army's organizational culture exhibits a propensity for doctrinal adaptation partially as a result of many years of colonial policing. Moreover, in this era of seemingly intractable and dirty wars where the aim is often postconflict peace-building [nation-building] instead of the destruction of enemy forces, the ability to adapt military institutions to new ways of using force is more important than ever.[30]

Even so, one military author correctly asserts that, historically, these small dirty wars are the norm and big wars are the exception:

The things lumped together today as operations other than war are not new. Americans in uniform have been doing them since 1775, and these little wars, these OOTWs, have been the rule between the exceptional spasms we normally call wars. We have fought ten major wars, lasting a total of about thirty-eight years, since 1775. But over the span of that same two-plus centuries, the United States conducted hundreds of other combat missions, and the men (and some women) killed in small wars are just as dead as those killed in big ones.[31]

If nontraditional conflicts occurred more frequently in the past and if the past 10 years are any sort of harbinger for this century, then we should find a way to do them better. What's more, by comparing military strategic culture during a short period of relative peace, this study can also test for cultural lag. While events in Somalia and Bosnia have been the focus of many previous articles and research projects, none of them adopted this approach. By tackling this particularly difficult category of operation through two national lenses, this work's aim is to provide a theoretical analysis and causal explanation for the variations in these doctrines. The success or failure in adapting and changing doctrine to meet the exigencies of PSO will also lead to policy recommendations to help redress organizational problems which impede the development of appropriate doctrine. The last section of this chapter reviews the literature on military and strategic culture.[32]

LITERATURE REVIEW

This is a review of the scholarship that examines culture as an explanatory variable for the behavior of state organizations. This study looks at a broad array of works on strategic, political, military, and organizational culture in order to extrapolate and synthesize key concepts for a theoretical framework. The outline for reviewing the strategic culture scholarship relies on Alistair Johnston's critique of the three generations of strategic culture theorists.

However, two important works preceded the first generation strategic-culture theorists. Graham Allison's *Essence of Decision* and Morton Halperin's *Bureaucratic Politics and Foreign Policy* examine some of the sub-systemic variables that later emerge within the context of strategic culture theory. Allison's organizational process paradigm explains state behavior as the outputs of large organizations operating according to "standard patterns of behavior." The behavior and choices of large organizations (i.e., the military) within the government are constrained by previously established standard operating procedures (SOP). Moreover, Allison explains, most SOPs are embedded in the norms and basic attitudes of the organization. Thus, routines and attitudes constrain organizational decisions and behavior—the behavior is in turn characterized by limited flexibility and incremental change.[33]

Likewise, Halperin looks at the essence of governmental organizations and its influence on decision-making and foreign policy. According to Halperin, organizational essence is "the view held by the dominant group in the organization of what the missions and capabilities should be." Corollaries are preferences about the type of knowledge, expertise, and experience members of the organization should have. Moreover, career officials attach a high priority to controlling their own resources in order to preserve their organizational essence. According to Halperin, this leads to typical trends in the standpoints of the organization. For example, each military service might support foreign policies that justify the force structure it believes are necessary for the essence of the service.[34]

The first generation work on strategic culture emerged in the late 1970s and early 1980s; it stemmed from the works of Jack Snyder, Ken Booth, David Jones, and Colin Gray. This work challenged the acultural and ahistorical system-based assumptions of the structural-realist paradigm that characterizes states as utility-maximizing and functionally undifferentiated units. Instead, these works argued that strategic choices were constrained by differences in states' predominant strategic preferences, or cultures, which emanate from the early formative experiences of the state. Moreover, these preferences are influenced to some extent by the cultural, political, and cognitive characteristics of the state and its elites.[35]

In a 1977 study Snyder first used the term "strategic culture" in the context of nuclear strategy and limited war. However, he quite accidentally triggered many subsequent works by authors who used the term differently than Snyder claims to have intended it to mean.

As a result of the socialization process, a set of general beliefs, attitudes, and behavioral patterns with regard to nuclear strategy has achieved a state of semi-permanence that places them on the level of "culture" rather than mere "policy." However, attitudes may change as a result of changes in technology and the international environment. However, new problems are not assessed objectively. Rather, they are seen through the perceptual lens provided by the strategic culture.[36]

Nonetheless, after much scholarship was written in the interim, Snyder seemed to either clarify or reverse his original conception of the term. In 1990, he asserted that it had become uncertain as to which differences could be ascribed to the peculiarities of strategic culture. He then clarified that the term culture had been intended to explain differences in the domestic or international situations facing the strategists of different states. Snyder explains his notion of strategic culture: once a distinctive approach to strategy is embraced, because of the processes of socialization and institutionalization, the approach tends to persist, despite changes in the environment that gave rise to it.[37]

In his 1979 *Strategy and Ethnocentrism*, Ken Booth criticized the rational policy model for characterizing states as Pavlovian dogs that respond mechanically to military stimuli. According to Booth, states respond to strategic catalysts according to national styles and idiosyncrasies: "the dogs of war, when unleashed, may sometimes exhibit Pavlovian behavior, but they also have a pedigree." He maintains that the "rational actor" is culture-dependent in two ways: first, cultural traits may prevent groups from considering as acceptable certain options which nevertheless maximize utility; second, strategists tend to project their own cultural values when thinking about the rational behavior of others. Moreover, culture also shapes how states conceive of the utility of force. Booth argues that the utility of military power can only be determined within a national framework: "it is the balance between aggregate value and aggregate costs as felt by a particular national group." He offers this pithy phrase: "war is an extension of culture, as well as politics."[38]

What's more, in 1990 Booth affirmed what he considers to be the salient aspects of strategic culture. His concept refers to national traditions, attitudes, values, patterns of behavior, and particular ways of adapting to the international security environment. The strategic culture of a nation stems from its history, geography, and political culture; it aggregates the patterns of behavior of the political elite, the military establishment, and public opinion. Although strategic culture is persistent over time, the culture and its constituent elements are not immutable either. However, Booth maintains, those components which deserve the label "cultural" are inclined to outlive all changes except for major changes in the international environment, military technology, and domestic structures. In sum, strategic culture helps influence but does not determine how a state interacts with other states on security issues.[39]

David R. Jones has also examined the concept of strategic culture in analyzing Soviet foreign and military policy. According to Jones, the primary elements that constitute any national culture are the state's nature and geography, the ethnic culture of its people, and its history. A second set of elements emerge from the above: Jones characterizes these as the "social-economic and governmental-administrative structures deemed appropriate to the environment." In addition, Jones identifies the "available technological base" as a significant element for developments in many spheres, including the military. The primary and secondary factors result in the creation of a third network of elements that directly influence a state's political and military culture. In this third set of elements, Jones includes the network of political-military institutions and the patterns of military-political interaction that parallel those elsewhere but also exhibit unique national characteristics.[40]

According to Jones, Snyder's narrow focus on a presumed nuclear strategic culture essentially ignored other important elements, and Snyder reduced Russia's historical legacy to only the Soviet lessons learned during World War II and the Stalinist party-military relations. However, Jones argues, any analysis of Soviet strategic culture must recognize the merger of the Soviet experience with the military culture that existed before the Russian Revolution. The attention that Soviet military historians paid to the lessons of Imperial Russia's wars testifies to the relevancy of pre-Soviet military culture to its contemporary strategic culture. In other words, if the Russian military perceives that its history and military methods are distinct, despite transnational organizational parallels, the Russian approach to basic issues of security policy and military practice is likely to reflect this perception of distinctiveness.[41]

Colin Gray, also among the first generation of strategic culture theorists, maintains that American strategic culture derives from the many uniquely American experiences such as geography, civic culture, political culture, and way of life. Gray derives the idea of a "national style" from American strategic culture, propounding a particularly American way in strategic affairs. He offers a threefold hypothesis: first, there is an American strategic culture which stems from geopolitical, historical, economic, and other influences; second, strategic culture provides the environment in which elites ponder and decide on strategy; and third, an understanding of this distinctively American strategic style can help explain the behavior of decision-makers. Gray describes a number of uniquely American "strategic cultural legacies" that have shaped America's behavior: "continental insularity and isolation from truly serious security dangers; the conditioning effect of living with weak, non-threatening neighbors on one's frontiers; the experience of taming an expanding frontier; the enduring impact of fundamentalist religious beliefs; and the strategic meaning of constituting a nation of immigrants." He makes two particularly salient points about U.S. strategic culture: the United States has come to over-rely on its ability to mobilize technology and know-how; and it has come to delude itself with the notion of American omnipotence which stems from a long historical experience of success against third-class opponents and near-total security provided by two oceans. Gray thus concludes that American strategic culture is "astrategic," resulting in "oscillation between under- and over-preparedness."[42]

Carnes Lord, on the other hand, divorces the technical, organizational, and operational aspects of the conduct of war from his concept of strategic culture. In "American Strategic Culture," Lord focuses on the "fundamental assumptions governing the constitution of military forces and the ends they are to serve." He describes strategic culture as the habits and practices of thought according to which military force is organized and used by a society in the pursuit of its political aims. Lord then lists the elements which are the operative components of strategic culture: the geopolitical setting; international relationships; political culture and ideology; military culture; civil-military relations and their bureaucracy; and weaponry and military technology. Of particular salience, are Lord's propositions concerning political and military culture: liberal democracies view war as essentially abnormal and are disinclined to adequately prepare for war in advance; and the military history of a state shapes its strategic culture. In addition, he asserts that civil-military relations can have a significant effect on strategic culture.[43]

For example, if the civilian leadership dominates the military excessively, it can encourage passivity and the haphazard use of military forces for unsuitable purposes. On the other hand, Lord, maintains that inadequate civilian control can lead to military-bureaucratic domination of strategy and to the pursuit of agreeable military objectives that are inconsistent with the state's broader political interests. He also contends that the island-continental power distinction (geopolitical setting) affects a state's fundamental strategic approach as well as its force structure and size. For island powers, the requirements for national defense are intermittent: these powers tend to rely on naval and militia forces rather than land forces. After describing the other operative components of strategic culture, Lord focuses on four elements which significantly shape American political-military culture: (1) the role of the offensive; (2) approaches to land warfare; (3) the idea of deterrence; and (4) the process of strategic planning and decision-making. He postulates that the United States' political-military culture and geopolitical setting have formed a national strategic culture that is essentially defensive. However, Lord qualifies, although this culture exhibits a tendency toward the defensive at the strategic level, it exhibits a propensity for the offensive at the operational and tactical levels.[44]

Consequently, Johnston criticizes the first generation strategic culture for its definitional problems and its methodological difficulties. For one thing, if technology, organizational culture, political culture, geography, historical experiences, and national character are all subsumed within the concept of strategic culture, then what is not an explanatory variable for behavior? These very unwieldy amorphous definitions leave very little room for nonstrategic cultural explanations of state behavior. Moreover, it is very difficult to create a process for observing strategic culture. According to Johnston, the first generation leaves the following questions unanswered: Why are certain periods deemed to be formative sources of strategic culture and others not? How is strategic culture transmitted through time? Where do scholars look for repositories of strategic culture?[45]

The second generation looks at strategic culture as an instrument of political hegemony in the area of strategic decision-making. Johnston associates only one scholar with the second generation—Bradley S. Klein. According to Klein, strategic culture is "the way in which a modern hegemonic state relies on internationally deployed force." His concept encompasses a state's war-making approach that is manifested by its military institutions and its traditional strategies for the use of air, land, and sea forces. However, Klein argues, it also stems from a state's armaments and technology infrastructures. Strategic culture is about a country's geopolitical position and its relations with allies and enemies. It helps determine how a state delimits where or when the use of military force is warranted. Klein explains that strategic culture emerges from a network of economic and diplomatic international practices that involve a country overseas and constrain its options within the domestic political economy.[46]

Making this concept harder to discern and measure, Klein claims that strategic culture is "embedded in a looser set of cultural relations that infuse any society and that display a constitutive role in the making of political-military strategy." In his conception, strategic culture involves the acceptable ways in which a state can employ force legitimately against presumed enemies. This is the distinguishing attribute of the second generation: it is an instrumentalist perspective that sees culture being used by elites in a declaratory strategy to legitimize the authority of those in charge of strategy. Klein maintains that while actual strategy (operational) may focus on war fighting, declaratory strategy is packaged to be culturally acceptable, depicting a distinct range of plausible and implausible options for the use of force.[47]

Moreover, Klein describes American strategic culture as a "power projection" culture, referring to the U.S. ability to project its military forces well beyond its borders. According to Klein, this power projection approach is defined by the capacity to deliver tremendous destruction abroad in a clean and surgically precise fashion, all the while allowing the public to remain morally satisfied that this delivery is defensive in nature. Klein converges with the first generation scholarship in that he underlines the near-free security that America was afforded for two centuries as a result of its geopolitical insularity and its low-threat neighbors. The American strategic approach has been shaped by the culture of a country which has always gone to war "over there"—a culture whose cities have never been bombed, which has never experienced the immediate impact of mechanized warfare, and whose land has never been overrun or occupied by modern armies. In sum, Klein sees strategic culture as the hegemony of strategists over the American way of war: the strategists articulate a strategy which is consistent with a traditional American political-military strategy (defensive) and which is characterized by terms such as "deterrence" and "arms control." They thereby garner public support for a militarized state while their actual operational strategy is based on a counterforce offensive plan.[48]

Johnston criticizes the second generation because it presents a causal decoupling between strategic culture and behavior: since state behavior is determined by the hegemonistic strategists, strategic options are shaped by their interests rather than by strategic culture. Thus, Johnston contends, it is plausible that states have different declaratory strategies while their operational doctrines are actually similar. It is not therefore certain from the second-generation literature whether strategic discourse influences behavior. An instrumentalist approach to strategic culture suggests that the elites who make decisions rise above the cultural restraints that they manipulate. As a result, the utility of strategic culture as an explanatory variable is tenuous here since the second-generation literature is unclear on cross-cultural differences in operational strategy.[49]

On the other hand, the third generation examines organizational culture, military culture, and political-military culture as independent variables and denounces realist notions as inadequate in explaining strategic choice. According to Johnston, this generation offers a more diverse and rigorous conceptualization of cognitive independent variables as well as a tighter focus on specific strategic decisions. What's more, these definitions of culture exclude behavior as a component and therefore avert some of the tautological traps of the first generation. Otherwise, the most recent definitions of military and strategic culture are similar to the definitions offered by the first generation. Stephen Peter Rosen, Elizabeth Kier, Jeffrey Legro, and Yitzhak Klein are among the most cited third generation strategic culture theorists.[50]

In "Military Effectiveness: Why Society Matters," Stephen Rosen examines cross-cultural differences in the capacity to generate military power. Rosen narrows his focus down to two independent variables: a state's predominant social structure and the extent to which a state's military organizations separate themselves from their societies. The dependent variable is military capability—the amount of defensive and offensive military power that a state can generate. By exploring social structures, Rosen aims to explain why countries from different cultures have different military capabilities. Moreover, he maintains, since social structures may or may not vary across cultural boundaries, this approach can also help explain why countries from different cultures have similar capabilities. According to Rosen, social structures are easier to discern than the subjective beliefs of the elites who devise strategy. Social structures can be studied in reproducible ways because they have observable behavioral indications with which people associate.[51]

However, Rosen's definition of social structure seems as amorphous as the first generation's definitions of strategic culture. He describes social structure as a broad term that encompasses such elements as social classes, caste organization, tribes, and occupational specialization. Moreover, Rosen specifies that purely functional social structures are not necessarily products of culture whereas tribal and caste social structures can be more closely connected to culture. His concept of social structure is broad enough to include family-oriented structures, class structure, village-based structures and many other phenomena.[52]

Rosen presents five propositions about social structures and military capabilities. First, social structures affect the attitudes of individuals toward each other within the society as well as within the organizations that emerge from that society. Second, when military organizations are: small relative to society; physically isolated from their society; temporally disconnected from society by long service of soldiers and officers in the military away from society; and psychologically separated from society as the result of inculcated professional habits, then military organizations are less likely to mirror the structures of the larger society.[53]

Third, Rosen claims that the social structures that lead to divisiveness in the society at large can reduce the military power that can be generated from a given quantity of material resources. Fourth, "the social structures in the political unit also affect the amount of military power that can be generated if those social structures are divisive and the divisions are replicated within the military." Fifth, when military organizations do not reflect the structures of society, this can cause the civilian leadership of that society to distrust the military, thereby affecting the military power of the state. Rosen offers two corollary reasons for this military-society gap: either because the military membership is drawn from sub-groups who are not representative of the whole society or because the military organization is socialized by discipline and training to operate within structures which are not shared by the society.[54]

Rosen's approach is germane to this research because his causal linkages do not rely on the attributes or assumptions particular to one set of cultures. His model can be applied to specific cultures and military organizations to generate propositions about behavior that can be studied empirically. Rosen recommends a comparative study where cases should be selected in which the social structures in a given state and civil-military relations vary somewhat over time. Moreover, he suggests, "cases should also be developed in which two societies with similar social structures have armies that display different degrees of separation from their societies, to assess the interaction of military organizational structures and social structures and strategic behavior."[55]

On the other hand, Elizabeth Kier specifically examines the impact of culture on the development of military doctrines. In "Culture and Military Doctrine," she postulates that choices between defensive and offensive military doctrines are best explained from a cultural perspective. Kier presents a twofold proposition. First, military doctrine is seldom a scrupulously designed response to the international security environment. She contends that elites' beliefs about the role of the military in society guide civilian decisions about the organization of military forces. Moreover, Kier maintains that civilian policy-makers must first answer their concerns about the internal domestic distribution of power before they address international incentives. These elite decisions thus determine force structure and force structure constrains subsequent doctrinal developments.[56]

Kier's second claim is that military organizations do not intrinsically prefer offensive rather than defensive doctrines. As she notes:

Military organizations differ in how they view the world and the proper conduct of their mission, and these organizational cultures constrain choices between offensive and defensive military doctrines. In particular, the military's organizational culture guides how it responds to constraints set by civilian policy-makers. Understanding variations in organizational behavior requires an analysis of cultural characteristics and of how these characteristics shape militaries' choices between offensive and defensive doctrines.[57]

These two propositions lead to her contention that civilian decisions seldom determine doctrine. In other words, by setting the budget and determining force structures, the civilian elites sets the constraints; however, it is how a military's organizational culture interprets these limitations that shapes the development of doctrine. Organizational culture shapes its members perceptions and decisions: Kier asserts that this is particularly true within military organizations where there are powerful assimilating mechanisms.[58]

Kier defines organizational culture as "the set of basic assumptions and values that shape shared understandings, and the forms or practices whereby these meanings are expressed, affirmed, and communicated to the members of an organization." She separates the elements of a military's organizational culture into two parts: the attitudes and values that are germane to the military's relationship with its external environment; and those values that affect the internal function of the organization. To ascertain the culture of the military, Kier examines the following questions: "What is the military's relationship with the state? Does it feel accepted and valued by dominant political actors? Similarly, what skill-set does the officer corps value: do they model their behavior on the modern-day business manager or the warrior and heroic leader?"[59]

Furthermore, Kier notes, it is important to study what beliefs are viewed as deviant in the organization and to determine what it is about such beliefs that are inconsistent with the organization's culture. She also points out that since all militaries do not share the same collection of ideas or experiences about the use of force, not all militaries would react similarly to the same constraints established by civilian decision-makers. Kier is also careful to explain what her notion of military culture does not include. Military culture does not embody a general set of beliefs that all militaries share—all military organizations do not have the same admixture of beliefs and attitudes in common. Nor is her concept of military culture the same as strategic culture—the military culture is not analogous to national character. A military culture may engender some aspects of the civilian society's culture, but this is not necessarily so. Military culture denotes the collectively held beliefs within a particular military organization.[60]

Finally, one of Kier's most salient concepts is her explanation of the causal relationship between military culture and doctrine. In the 1930s, she concludes, the French army did not develop a defensive doctrine because its culture valued defensive doctrine—this would be outcome-driven behavior. The organization did, however, harbor a set of beliefs that limited its possible courses of actions. One of these beliefs was that conscripts were not trainable for the offense. Thus, when French civilian policy-makers decided on a conscript army, the army opted for a defensive doctrine because it was consistent with its cultural assumptions about the value of short-term conscripts.[61]

Kier also justifies the explanatory value of her methodology. Her approach to culture allows for changes in doctrine (the dependent variable) despite continuity in the military culture (the intervening variable). Although the organizational culture remains relatively stagnant, the constraints set by technology and domestic politics (the independent variables) change. Thus the organization continues to think consistent with its culture and integrates external changes into its established concept of doing business. Though doctrine (the dependent variable) may change, military culture (the intervening variable) stays the same. In both France and Britain, Kier concludes, "each army's culture remained relatively static, yet doctrines shifted radically, from offensive prior to World War I to defensive prior to World War II." Kier examines how the British and French armies' organizational cultures incorporated changing exogenous variables to explain the development of doctrine.[62]

Also studying the World War II period, Jeffrey Legro examines culture and the use of force during war. In particular, Legro contends that the organizational cultures of state bureaucracies can create plans and capabilities that do not necessarily correspond to the international security environment. He compares organizational culture and the traditional realist model as variables to explain state preferences on the use of force in World War II. According to Legro, "military organizational cultures deserve attention in understanding restraint in war because of the central role

the armed forces play in national decisions on the use of force." In the context of
military bureaucracies, Legro explains, culture is significant because it influences
organizational perceptions, aims, and capabilities in ways that contradict the expectations of other noncultural approaches to organizations. He focuses on two central
issues: (1) the influence of organizational culture on bureaucratic orientation and (2)
how bureaucratic priorities influence national preferences and policy.[63]

Legro defines the concept of organizational culture as "collectively held assumptions, ideas, and beliefs that prescribe how a group should adapt to its external environment and manage its internal structure." According to Legro, culture
serves as an aid for collective perception and problem solving, like the way a theoretical model can help organize intellectual thought. Moreover, culturally influenced actors tend to discount exogenous factors that contradict existing beliefs. As
a result, he claims, militaries do not consistently adopt war-fighting strategies appropriate to a given strategic situation. Despite efforts, such as military exercises,
Legro explains, to test the effectiveness of war-fighting doctrine, cultural tenden-
cies tend to produce conclusions that reinforce existing beliefs instead of critically
assessing them.[64]

What's more, Legro highlights the material consequences of cultural inclinations. Culture has an impact on which capabilities receive the allocation of resources. He maintains that "collective beliefs dictate which enterprises are
inherently better and should receive support." Thus, organizations will not channel resources to approaches that are incompatible with their cultures, depriving
those areas of funding and attention. Culture therefore determines resource decisions that subsequently tend to strengthen the viability of cultural predilections
notwithstanding their suitability to the strategic environ-ment. Legro's work
demonstrates that culture is influenced by many factors, including technology;
the domestic and international arenas; and individuals. According to Legro, culture has analytical utility because it can be an autonomous force that is not easily
reduced to its many constituent parts.[65]

Legro emphasizes another important point—culture is often resistant to exogenous pressures to change. In other words, organizational cultures do not tend to
functionally adapt, even when the costs of not adapting outweigh the benefits.
This is a tendency, not an absolute, Legro points out. Militaries do adapt and even
learn, particularly during instances of crisis and rapid changes that dramatically
disprove the viability of the extant culture. However, one of Legro's central claims
is that "culture often persists even when in conflict with environmental circumstances." He also examines when organizational culture is particularly salient as a
variable that shapes state behavior.[66]

Legro argues that a culture's influence varies with its organizational salience. Organizational salience, moreover, comprises three dimensions: (1) the degree to
which the organization has monopoly power on expertise; (2) the complexity of the
issue; and (3) the period available for action. First, when a single organization has all
the expertise and is without competitors, organizational inclinations are not curbed
because there is less pressure to change. Second, Legro maintains, the complexity of

issues affects the extent to which expert knowledge is needed for decisions. Thus, when the problems are more complex, organizational preferences will be more pronounced because the senior civilian authorities will be less inclined to oversee the operation. Third, the amount of time available for decision making can also have an impact. When decision-making cycles are truncated, there is little time for adjusting predetermined procedures. Legro posits that all these attributes point to the increased salience of military culture in decisions on the use of force.[67]

Legro's study also presents a proposition relevant to my research on military strategic culture and doctrine. Legro posits that "states are likely to prefer restraint in a particular combat type when its use is antithetical to the war-fighting culture of their military bureaucracy." Conversely, he maintains, when the organizational cultures of their militaries are compatible with the particular method of employing force, states are more likely to favor that use of force. Legro points to the important role organizational culture plays in shaping organizational priorities, perception, and capabilities in ways unaccounted for by non-cultural approaches. His bottom line is "those means compatible with the dominant war-fighting culture will be developed and advocated by the military, those that are not will suffer neglect." What's more, since unique cultures are rooted in particular military services, state preferences on the use of force should vary over time and across issues areas, reflecting the influence of the culture as its organizational salience increases and dercreases.[68]

Finally, this article is helpful in contributing some useful measures and methodology. Legro evaluates organizational culture by examining the war-fighting beliefs and attitudes that are embedded in particular military organizations. According to Legro, a review of available internal correspondence, planning documents, exercise after action comments, and the memoirs of individual members all provide measurable variables. These multiple sources help capture a picture of the legitimate beliefs that underpin the organization. In addition, Legro submits that his is not a "post-hoc tautological explanation" because organizational cultures, in particular military cultures, are frequently quite discernible and can be assessed independent of outcomes.[69]

Yitzhak Klein takes a different approach in "A Theory of Strategic Culture." Instead of focusing on the sources of strategic culture, Klein examines how strategic culture influences objective-oriented activity. Although strategy involves using force in pursuit of political objectives, the abandonment of political objectives in favor of the perceived exigencies of the battlefield is a recurring theme in the history of war. Klein's notion of strategic culture emerges from this dichotomy between the requirements of policy and the demands of the battlefield. He defines strategic culture as "the set of attitudes and beliefs held within a military establishment concerning the political objective of war and the most effective strategy and operational method of achieving it." According to Klein, an analysis of strategic culture must evaluate the quality of the strategy it produces and, thus, it must determine how well that strategy matches means with ends.[70]

Klein's paradigm for strategic culture depicts a three-tier hierarchy that, from top to bottom, connects the concepts of military-political doctrine, strategy, and operations. Military-political doctrine identifies the political objectives of war: it emanates from a thorough interpretation of the national interest and is determined by the state's political leadership. Moreover, Klein explains, the choice of political objectives derives from some conception about the nature of war and its proper role in international relations. Strategy, on the other hand, identifies military objectives whose achievement will directly support the attainment of political aims—it designs campaign plans to achieve military objectives. Klein's model also looks at the operational level, where strategic goals are translated into force compositions and executable missions. This hierarchical linkage of core concepts is what constitutes Klein's notion of strategic culture: "the choice of what to fight the enemy for and how to fight him for it."[71]

However, Klein makes a key qualification—even though his conceptual model for strategic culture is hierarchical, in practice the higher levels don't necessarily determine the content of the lower levels. In other words, strategy and operations may have their own constraints and logic that may stem from factors which have little to do with policy and to which policy must adapt itself. What's more, Klein maintains, "the military planner does not simply choose an abstract strategic objective that seems to suit his doctrinal goal; he looks for a strategy that he believes will work, or else he informs his political superiors that their goals must be revised." Every strategic plan is therefore given an operational feasibility test: a realistic check to see if the capabilities of available forces match the strategic requirements. This leads to one of Klein's most salient points: the operational level of thought is a critical element of strategic culture because it can exert an immediate and even subliminal impact on strategic thought.[72]

However, Klein warns, operational habits can limit a military bureaucracy's ability to adapt and implement new strategies when changing political situations require it. In large and complex militaries, it takes much time to develop new operational capabilities to fulfill new strategic goals. In addition, experience at the operational level is an important element in the remembered history that armies draw on in determining their role in the next war. Consequently, the inertia of operational habits exerts a counteracting impact that travels up the strategic-cultural hierarchy to influence how strategy and policy are devised. Klein contends that military establishments are the bearers of strategic culture because they are charged with identifying the military objectives of war and devising the means of achieving them. These establishments affect the formation, changes, and use of strategic culture. He also asserts that the effect of strategic culture is most pronounced at the operational level. When armies have been successful in war, it is the operational techniques and the operational histories, by which enemies were defeated, which are consecrated in memory. Klein explains that operations remain the sole purview of military establishments. As a result, military establishments seem to be his most prominent source for examining strategic culture.[73]

In sum, Klein explains that when studying strategic culture, analysts should make extensive use of the professional literature of the military establishment, to include official manuals, policy statements, scholarly literature, and memoirs. However, he cautions, much of the military literature contains ideas that are never reflected in strategy, ephemeral ideas which are in fashion one decade and unpopular the next. Therefore, he maintains, it is important to focus on those concepts that actually emerge in military policy, strategic plans, and operational training.[74]

Johnston offers a critique of the third-generation literature and he makes some general observations about all the strategic culture literature. First, Johnston claims that the third generation avoids an important aspect in the second-generation organizational-culture literature: the notion that symbolic (declaratory) strategy may not have any causal effect upon operational doctrine. Also in some instances, military doctrine is the dependent variable, which raises the unexamined question: are declared and operational doctrines different? Furthermore, the literature on strategic/military culture-related concepts arrives at two disparate conclusions: either, a state's culturally embedded beliefs about war-fighting constrain the strategic options of policy-making elites (first/third generation arguments) or, strategic culture is instrumentalized to obscure or validate strategic decisions that are made in the interests of domestic and international hegemons (second generation argument).[75]

Johnston recapitulates the common definitional threads in the strategic-culture literature: culture comprises shared assumptions and rules that oblige a degree of order on individual and group conceptions about their relationship to their social, organizational, or political environment. Moreover, Johnston maintains, "cultural patterns and behavioral patterns are not the same thing: in so far as culture affects behavior, it does so by limiting options and by affecting how members of these cultures learn from interaction with their environment." Although multiple cultures can reside within one society, generally, there is a predominant culture whose bearers are interested in maintaining the status quo. According to Johnston, a definition of strategic culture should be falsifiable or at a minimum, discernible from non-strategic culture variables. It should also explain that strategic culture provides elites with a particularly ordered set of strategic choices from which predictions about behavior can be derived. Strategic culture should also be observable in strategic-cultural objects and traceable over time.[76]

Before defining strategic culture, Johnston makes a simple assumption: "strategic culture, if it exists, is an ideational milieu which limits behavioral choices." He also assumes that from these constraints we should be able to derive some expectations about strategic choice. Johnston defines strategic culture as an integrated "system of symbols that acts to establish pervasive and long-lasting strategic preferences by formulating concepts of the role and efficacy of military force in interstate political affairs, and by clothing these conceptions with such an aura of factuality that the strategic preferences seem uniquely realistic and efficacious." Johnston also develops some observable and traceable indicators for assessing strategic culture.

His notion of strategic culture is twofold: "the first consists of basic assumptions about the orderliness of the strategic environment, that is, about the role of war in human affairs (inevitable or aberrant), about the nature of the adversary and the threat it poses (zero-sum or variable sum), and about the efficacy of the use of force (about the ability to control outcomes and to eliminate threats, and the conditions under which applied force is useful)." These assumptions form the core of Johnston's strategic-culture paradigm. The second part of Johnston's approach comprises assumptions about what strategic options are the most effective for dealing with the security environment. Johnston's bottom line is that the main observable measure of a strategic culture is a limited and ranked set of strategic preferences that is consistent across the objects of analysis and consistent across time. Thus, Johnston explains, his method of ranking is not necessarily affected by changes in noncultural variables such as threat, technology, or organization.[77]

In addition, Richard Duncan Downie published a book that examines institutional learning and low intensity conflict doctrine. In *Learning from Conflict*, Downie focuses on doctrinal continuity and change as a result of the relationship between a changing security landscape that necessitates change and the military's ability to adapt, based on the timing of its cyclical institutional learning process (intervening variable). More specifically, Downie contends that changes in U.S. Army doctrine can serve as observable measures of institutional learning. Two assumptions underpin Downie's approach: (1) change to an organization's institutional memory is a precondition to institutional learning; and (2) military doctrine is "useful representation of the U.S. Army's institutional memory."[78]

According to Downie, an organization's "conventional wisdom," as reflected in norms, SOPs, and doctrine that are widely accepted and practiced, constitutes an organization's institutional memory. To be sure, his conception of institutional memory is very close to the notion of military culture. Downie defines institutional memory as "what old members of an organization know and what new members learn through a process of socialization." Institutional memory, Downie explains, does not change quickly or easily and it can perpetuate doctrinal continuity even when the doctrine leads to suboptimal performance. He defines institutional learning as "a process by which an organization uses new knowledge or understanding gained from experience or study to adjust institutional norms, doctrine, and procedures in ways designed to minimize previous gaps in performance and maximize future success." Downie's work is salient and relevant to this work because it examines how organizations either learn and act to change their doctrine or don't learn and retain outmoded doctrine.[79]

As a final footnote, this literature review has not included every significant contribution to the areas of strategic and military culture. For example, the organizational theory aspects in Barry Posen's *The Sources of Military Doctrine* obviously had some influence on post-1984 approaches to organizational culture. Moreover, John Shy examined the experiential elements of American military culture as early as 1971—his work will be important in my analysis of American military culture. Stephen P. Rosen's article in 1988 and subsequent 1991 book, *Winning the Next*

War, were consulted but not reviewed because his work in 1995 was more germane to my research. Deborah Avant's *Political Institutions and Military Change* and Murray and Millett's work, *Military Innovation in the Interwar Period*, were also examined but they were also excluded from this review. Avant's book will be helpful in comparing the military-cultural characteristics of the British and American armies since it examines the U.S. Army in Vietnam and the British Army during the Malayan Emergency. Likewise, the Murray and Millett study of military innovation during the interwar years will be useful in analyzing British and American military culture. In addition, I conferred with and examined the work of a colleague who did his doctoral work in a related area of study.[80]

The value of this literature review, then, is that it offers a breadth of approaches that have examined strategic and organizational culture as explanatory variables that can supplement or supplant traditional realist/systemic explanations. A general and distilled definition of strategic culture that emerges from this corpus of literature is: a set of preferences, values, and beliefs that bounds the rational choices of the acculturated. Taken in sum, this body of literature seems to validate the utility of culture as an explanatory and causal variable in the field of security studies. The literature also highlights the tautological risks that inhere in a cultural approach. To be sure, a variable that subsumes almost everything risks explaining nothing. However, in aggregate, this literature offers a rich foundation from which new scholarship can build.

NOTES

1. Friedrich Wilhelm Nietzsche, *Beyond Good and Evil*, Book IV, trans. Helen Zimmern (1886), 146 in *Bartlett's Familiar Quotations* (Franklin Electronic Bookman, 1998).

2. Walter E. Kretchik, "Force Protection Disparities," *Military Review* 77 (July–August 1997): 73 and 77.

3. Kenneth N. Waltz, "Reflections on Theory of International Politics: A Response to My Critics," in *NeoRealism and Its Critics*, ed. Robert O. Keohane (New York: Columbia University Press, 1986), 329. Kenneth N. Waltz, *Theory of International Politics* (New York: McGraw-Hill, Inc., 1979), 71.

4. Articles 41 and 42 under Chapter VII of the UN Charter allow for peace enforcement—this is generally the use of economic sanctions and/or the threat or use of force to restore international peace and security. Peacekeeping emerged as an ad hoc remedy to the impasse that emerged in the UN Security Council as a result of the Cold War and the veto. Peacekeeping is generally conducted under Chapter VI of the UN Charter—it is a military operation undertaken to help maintain peace and security but without enforcement powers. Marrack Goulding coined the term "gray-area operations" to describe a host of operations that lie between traditional peacekeeping and peace enforcement. See Marrack Goulding, "The Evolution of United Nations Peacekeeping," *International Affairs* 69 (1993): 461.

5. Richard Smith, "The Requirement for the United Nations to Develop an Internationally Recognized Doctrine for the Use of Force in Intra-State Conflict," *Occasional Paper No 10* (Camberley, U.K.: Strategic and Combat Studies Institute, 1994), 17; and Bi-MNC Directive, *NATO Doctrine for Peace Support Operations* (Brussels: Supreme Headquarters Allied Powers Europe, 1995); and *The Army Field Manual Volume 5, Operations Other Than War Part 2, Wider Peacekeeping* (London: HMSO, 1994), 2-2-2-4.

6. *CFP 300, Canada's Army* (Kingston: Chief of the Canadian Defence Staff, 1995), 5-5; *Emploi des Forces Terrestres dans l'Action des Forces Armees* (Metz: French Doctrine and Training Command, 1996), 0-5; *FM 100-5, Operations* (Washington, D.C.: U.S. Army, 1993), 1-1; *Army Doctrine Publication Volume 1, Operations* (London: HMSO, 1994), 1A-2; Gavin Bulloch, "The Development of Doctrine for Counter-Insurgency—the British Experience," *The British Army Review* 111 (December 1995): 21, 24; John Mackinlay, "War Lords," *RUSI Journal* 143 (April 1998): 24.

7. *CFP 300, Canada's Army* (Kingston: Chief of the Canadian Defence Staff, 1995), 5-5; *Emploi des Forces Terrestres dans l'Action des Forces Armees* (Metz: French Doctrine and Training Command, 1996), 0-5; *FM 100-5, Operations* (Washington, D.C.: U.S. Army, 1993), 1-1; *Army Doctrine Publication Volume 1, Operations* (London: HMSO, 1994), 1A-2; Gavin Bulloch, "The Development of Doctrine for Counter-Insurgency—the British Experience," *The British Army Review* 111 (December 1995): 21, 24; John Mackinlay, "War Lords," *RUSI Journal* 143 (April 1998): 24.

8. Barry R. Posen, *The Sources of Military Doctrine: France, Britain, and Germany Between the World Wars* (Ithaca, NY: Cornell University Press, 1984), 16.

9. Clifford Geertz, *The Interpretation of Cultures* (New York: Basic Books, 1973), 5, 11, 14, 363.

10. Lucien W. Pye and Sydney Verba, eds. *Political Culture and Political Development* (Princeton, N.J.: Princeton University Press, 1965), 8–10, 550.

11. Edgar Schein, "Organizational Culture," *American Psychologist* 45 (February 1990): 111.

12. Jeffrey W. Legro, "Culture and Preferences in the International Cooperation Two-Step," *American Political Science Review* 90 (March 1996): 127; Alan Macmillan, "Strategic Culture and National Ways in Warfare: the British Case," *RUSI Journal* 140 (October 1995): 33 (33–38); and James M. Smith. "USAF Culture and Cohesion: Building an Air Force and Space Force for the 21st Century," *INSS Occasional Paper 19* (Colorado Springs, CO: USAF INSS, 1996), 11–12.

13. Smith, 11–12.

14. James Dewar et al., *Army Culture and Planning in a Time of Great Change* (Santa Monica, CA: RAND, 1996), 2–3, 8, 42.

15. Williamson Murray, "Armored Warfare" and "Innovation: Past and Future" in *Military Innovation in the Interwar Period*, eds. Williamson Murray and Allan R. Millett (NY: Cambridge University Press, 1996), 23 [footnote], 309, and 313.

16. Russell F. Weigley, *The American Way of War* (Bloomington: Indiana University Press, 1973), xvii; Jeffrey W. Legro, "Military Culture and Inadvertent Escalation in World War II," *International Security* 18 (Spring 1994): 112; Schein: 111; Elizabeth Kier, "Culture and Military Doctrine: France Between the Wars," *International Security* 19 (Spring 1995) 66; Yitzhak Klein, "A Theory of Strategic Culture." *Comparative Strategy* 10 (1991): 5–6, 10, 13; Legro, "Culture and Preferences in the International Cooperation Two-Step:" 118, 121; Macmillan: 33; and Carnes Lord, "American Strategic Culture." *Comparative Strategy* 5 (Fall 1985): 273–74.

17. Gary King, Robert O. Keohane, and Sidney Verba, *Designing Social Inquiry* (Princeton, NJ: Princeton University Press, 1994), 47.

18. Richard Duncan Downie, *Learning from Conflict: The U.S. Military in Vietnam, El Salvador, and the Drug War* (Westport, CT: Praeger, 1998), 23.

19. Posen, 38; and Alexander L. George, "Case Studies and Theory Development: The Method of Structured, Focused Comparison" in *Diplomacy: New Approaches in History, Theory, and Policy*, ed. Paul Gordon Lauren (NY: MacMillan, 1979), 44, 49, 57, 61–62.

20. Steven Van Evera, *Guide to Methodology for Students of Political Science* (Cambridge: Defense and Arms Control Studies Program MIT, 1993), 33; King, Keohane, and Verba, 225. Alistair Johnston, *Cultural Realism: Strategic Culture and Grand Strategy in Chinese History* (Princeton, N.J.: Princeton University Press, 1995), 37. John Nagl, D.Phil Queens College, Oxford provided advice and recommendations on a sound methodological approach to this topic.

21. Kenneth N. Waltz, *Theory of International Politics* (New York: McGraw-Hill, 1979), 163–169; John J. Mearsheimer, "Back to the Future" in *The Cold War and After*, eds. Sean M. Lynn-Jones and Steven E. Miller (Cambridge, MA: MIT Press, 1997), 141–42; Stephen Van Evera, "Primed for Peace" in *The Cold War and After*, 220; Christopher Layne, "The Unipolar Illusion" in *The Cold War and After*, 246–47.

22. See Don Snider, "An Uninformed Debate on Military Culture," *Orbis* 43 (Winter 1999): 4. Dr. Snider explains the functional approach to military culture—this approach examines those elements of military culture that derive from the purpose or tasks for which societies maintain militaries. This research also focuses on the functional aspects of military culture.

23. Kier: 70.

24. Alistair Johnston, "Thinking About Strategic Culture," *International Security* 19 (Spring 1995): 46.

25. See Harvey M. Sapolsky and Jeremy Shapiro, "Casualties, Technology, and America's Future Wars," *Parameters* 26 (Summer 1996): 119–27; and Karl W. Eikenberry, "Take No Casualties," *Parameters* 26 (Summer 1996): 109–18.

26. Appropriate, successful, and effective are all rather subjective and relative terms. However, although diverse missions comprise the realm of LIC/OOTW, a general corpus of principles has emerged from a legacy of experiences in operations short of war, to include peace operations. To be appropriate, doctrine in this area should help promote two central aims: (1) to integrate military, political, economic, and social objectives, moving them toward the desired strategic outcome; and (2) to gain and maintain support of the indigenous population.

27. John Mackinlay, ed. *A Guide to Peace Support Operations* (Providemce, RI: Thomas J. Watson Institute for International Studies, 1996), 25–29. John Mackinlay is considered one of the prominent experts in the field of peacekeeping.

28. Legro, "Culture and Preferences in the International Cooperation Two-Step:" 118; and Posen, 14. (Posen also asserts that force posture and the type of weapons in inventory serve as evidence of military doctrine).

29. Legro, "Culture and Preferences in the International Cooperation Two-Step:" 118; and Posen, 14.

30. John A. Nagl, "Learning to Eat Soup with a Knife," *World Affairs* 161 (Spring 1999): 197–98.

31. Dan P. Bolger, *Savage Peace: Americans at War in the 1990s* (Novato, CA: Presidio Press, 1995), 106.

32. Russell F. Weigley, *History of the United States Army* (Bloomington, IN: Indiana University Press, 1984), 562. Weigley maintains that our performance in Vietnam suffered conspicuously due to the persisting post-1945 dilemma of preparing for a European war although smaller wars requiring more agile forces were more likely to occur.

33. Graham T. Allison, *Essence of Decision: Explaining the Cuban Missile Crisis* (New York: Little, Brown, and Company, 1971), 67–68, 83, 91.

34. Morton H. Halperin, *Bureaucratic Politics and Foreign Policy* (Washington, D.C.: The Brookings Institution, 1974), 28, 51, 58.

35. Alistair Johnston, "Thinking About Strategic Culture," *International Security* 19 (Spring 1995): 34.

36. Jack Snyder, *The Soviet Strategic Culture: Implications for Limited Nuclear Operations* (Santa Monica, CA: RAND, 1977), v.

37. Jack Snyder, "The Concept of Strategic Culture: Caveat Emptor" in *Strategic Power USA/USSR*, ed. Carl G. Jacobsen (New York: St Martin's Press, 1990), 4.

38. Ken Booth, *Strategy and Ethnocentrism* (New York: Holmes and Meier Publishers, Inc., 1979), 23, 64, 74–76.

39. Ken Booth, "The Concept of Strategic Culture Affirmed" in *Strategic Power USA/USSR*, ed. Carl G. Jacobsen (New York: St. Martin's Press, 1990), 121.

40. David R. Jones, "Soviet Strategic Culture" in *Strategic Power USA/USSR*, 37.

41. Ibid., 36.

42. Colin S. Gray, "National Style in Strategy," *International Security* 6 (Fall 1981): 22–24, 27–29, 33, and 45.

43. Carnes Lord, "American Strategic Culture," *Comparative Strategy* 5 (Fall 1985): 273–74.

44. Ibid.: 273–74, 276–77.

45. Johnston: 37.

46. Bradley S. Klein, "Hegemony and Strategic Culture: American Power Projection and Alliance Defence Politics," *Review of International Studies* 14 (1988): 136.

47. Ibid.

48. Ibid.: 138–39.

49. Johnston: 36–37.

50. Ibid.: 38.

51. Stephen Peter Rosen, "Military Effectiveness: Why Society Matters," *International Security* 19 (Spring 1995): 6–7.

52. Ibid.: 24–26.

53. Ibid.: 28–29.

54. Ibid.: 29–30.

55. Ibid.: 30.

56. Elizabeth Kier, "Culture and Military Doctrine: France Between the Wars," *International Security* 19 (Spring 1995): 66.

57. Ibid.

58. Ibid.: 68–69.

59. Ibid.: 69–70.

60. Ibid.: 70.

61. Ibid.: 80.

62. Ibid.

63. Legro, "Culture and Preferences in the International Cooperation Two-Step:" 118–23.

64. Ibid.

65. Ibid.: 123.

66. Ibid.: 124.

67. Ibid.

68. Ibid.: 125.

69. Ibid.: 127.

70. Yitzhak Klein, "A Theory of Strategic Culture," *Comparative Strategy* 10 (1991): 5–6; 10.

71. Ibid.: 10–11.

72. Ibid.: 11–12.

73. Ibid.: 13.

74. Ibid.: 14.

75. Johnston: 43.

76. Ibid.: 46–47.

77. Ibid.: 46.

78. Downie, 20–24.

79. Ibid., 5, 22–25, 34.

80. Barry R. Posen, *The Sources of Military Doctrine: France, Britain, and Germany between the World Wars* (Ithaca, NY: Cornell University Press, 1984); Stephen P. Rosen, *Winning the Next War: Innovation and the Modern Military* (Ithaca: Cornell University Press, 1991); John Shy, "The American Military Experience: History and Learning," *Journal of Interdisciplinary History* 1 (Winter 1971); Deborah Avant, *Political Institutions and Military Change* (Ithaca: Cornell University Press, 1994); Williamson Murray and Allan R, Millett, *Military Innovation in the Interwar Period* (New York: Cambridge University Press, 1996); and John Nagl, "Learning to Eat Soup with a Knife: British and American Army Counterinsurgency Learning During the Malayan Emergency and the Vietnam War," Ph.D diss., Oxford University, 1997, 10.

BRITISH MILITARY STRATEGIC CULTURE—THE CARDWELLIAN CONUNDRUM

A [military] philosophy grows from the minds and hearts, social mores and customs, traditions and environment of a people. It is the product of national and racial attributes, geography, the nature of a potential enemy threat, standards of living and national traditions, influenced and modified by great military philosophers, like Clausewitz and Mahan, and by great national leaders like Napoleon.

—Hanson W. Baldwin[1]

Beliefs and attitudes, unlike tanks and rockets, cannot be directly observed. Their existence and content has to be inferred from sources such as strategic behavior and writings and military manuals.

—Alan Macmillan[2]

INTRODUCTION

These quotes aptly point to the principal aim of these next two chapters: to ascertain the beliefs and attitudes within the British and American armies that shape their collective preferences toward the uses of force (military strategic culture). In order to limit this aim to a manageable scope, Chapters 2 and 3 trace the development of these two cultures from the American War of Independence onward. This war is a suitable starting point since it captures both armies locked in a struggle: a great power fighting a limited war against a fledgling nation fighting an unlimited war. It is in part an arbitrary place to start, but it is also germane because the two armies' experiences in small wars have shaped their preferences about force. The American Revolution witnessed some of the American Army's best unconventional war fighting ever, and it revealed some of the difficulties Britain would face if its colonial opponents did not choose to fight on British terms. It was also characteristic of the problems that both armies would face when they brought superior military might to bear against ostensibly inferior militaries, in other words, in asymmetric conflicts.[3]

The British Army's strategic puzzle in the American War of Independence was also a harbinger of perplexity for both armies during subsequent asymmetric conflicts, the Boer Wars and the Vietnam War, being the most notable. These chapters reveal something that now seems axiomatic: great powers lose small wars when their opponents refuse to fight them conventionally. Asymmetry of capability, then, poses this question: can, and how, do great powers adapt their military organizations to successfully prosecute small wars, or operations other than war, successfully? Small wars are not big, force-on-force, state-on-state, conventional, orthodox, unambiguous wars in which success is measurable by phase lines crossed or hills seized. Small wars are counterinsurgencies, low intensity conflicts, peace operations, and complex humanitarian emergencies, where ambiguity rules and success is not necessarily guaranteed by superior firepower.

The American Revolutionary War is also an appropriate starting place because it goes back far enough to get a deep understanding of these two military strategic cultures and because it captures a very formative century in shaping how the British and American armies prefer to use force. The rebellion in America was unprecedented because a conflict between an ideologically motivated insurgent population and a metropolitan state 3,000 miles away had never before been seen. But for a long time the British Army acted as though it was conducting the kind of limited war it had successfully fought since 1689. However, many of the strategic lessons of its past wars were inappropriate to the situation in North America in the late 18th century. These lessons, though, were the only guides the British Army had as precedents.[4]

These two chapters are long, but necessarily so, because they capture the essences and preferences of these two organizations as they evolved over time. In fact, these chapters are central to the book because they identify cultural predilections that should help explain the more observable doctrinal outputs and operational behavior examined later in the shorter empirical case study chapters. Moreover, the titles of these two chapters capture the essence of these two cultures and merit explanations. The moniker "the Cardwellian conundrum" stems from Edward Cardwell's 19th century attempts to reform British Army policy. Cardwell tried to solve imperial Britain's strategic conundrum—how to organize and prepare the British Army for two roles simultaneously: policing a huge empire and winning conventional wars in Europe. Although many of Cardwell's reforms did not solve this puzzle, his reforms had a lasting influence on the British Army's capacity for and attitudes toward conventional wars in Europe. On the other hand, Chapter 3, the Uptonian Paradox is a contradiction engendered by the 19th century oracle of American military thought, Emory Upton, who had a lasting influence on American military attitudes. Since the end of the 19th century, Upton's thinking has contributed to this contradiction: the U.S. Army has embraced a Clausewitzian military philosophy on the one hand; but, on the other hand, it seems to eschew Clausewitz's overarching maxim that subordinates the military instrument to political purposes. The U.S. Army exhibits this tendency when it tries to prescribe its preferred paradigm for war to its civilian leadership.[5]

A comparison of British and American military strategic cultures reveals similarities and differences as well as contradictions and dilemmas. For a substantial portion of their history, both the British and Americans had in common a geographic-strategic advantage afforded by their insularity. In addition, the democratic political cultures of these two states also shared an aversion to standing armies. In fact, the Americans inherited this aversion both from British political culture and from Britain's military policies in her North American colonies. Both countries have faced a historical dilemma between a militia and a regular army. In addition, in an uncanny coincidence, both armies established general staffs around 1903–1904. Both armies also have over one hundred years experience fighting asymmetric conflicts against indigenous tribes. What's more, after a century (19th) of unqualified successes in small wars, the two armies fought peripheral wars that were successful yet Pyrrhic at the turn of the century—the British Army fought the Boer Wars and the American Army fought the Spanish-American War. However, the U.S. Army's culture was shaped more significantly by the Civil War—the most conventional and symmetric war it fought in the 19th century—rather than the host of asymmetric and unorthodox campaigns it prosecuted against indigenous peoples. On the other hand, British Army culture was shaped more by its host of asymmetric [small] wars of the 19th century than it was by its one conventional and symmetric conflict of the post–Napoleonic period—the Crimean War.[6]

The 19th century experience of imperial policing fixed the regiment as the British Army's valued organization, and fighting a varied host of indigenous warriors in adverse environments made the British Army adaptable, locally. On the other hand, although the U.S. Army spent most of the 19th century fighting against unconventional Indian warriors, its culture was shaped most indelibly by its Civil War experience. It seemed to develop a preference for total wars of annihilation, it became enamored of the Prussian Army Model as well, and it embraced Clausewitz, although it didn't seem to grasp Clausewitz's overarching concept of military subordination to civilian policy. Moreover, the one instance when the British Army faced a European power in a symmetrical and conventional war after Waterloo—the Crimean War—it showed itself poorly prepared. Thus, the 19th Century experience of both armies reveals no small degree of irony: the European army exhibited a predilection and a capacity for non-European small wars—it viewed conventional European war as aberrant; and the non-European army's thought and attitudes focused on the Civil War and European models for war—it perceived its 19th century counterinsurgency campaigns against the American Indians as aberrations.[7]

Although the officer corps in both countries operated under democratic civilian control, the differences in military experiences between Great Britain and the United States in the period before World War I were fundamental. For the U.S., according to Janowitz, "because its colonial areas were capable of political integration, and because its boundaries kept expanding, the military tasks of internal security and foreign policy were entwined." On the other hand, in England, the military was excluded from internal security functions as of the last Jacobin uprising in 1745. As it was exempted from an internal security function, the British Army did not operate under the assumption that its principal task was to force British standards of conduct on unfriendly states. As a result, the British Army was able to carry out a variety of political objectives; and, whether it was engaged in continental Europe or on colonial policing expeditions, the British Army was accustomed to tasks with limited objectives.[8]

However, after the Spanish-American War, the United States Army had to prepare for the eventuality that it might have to fight a major war in the future. As Janowitz explained, "the frontier function had disappeared, and the internal police function was in effect, separated from the strategic military one." American military leaders then had to realize that the frontier operational code was no longer appropriate to their tasks. "The operational code and the professional self-image were no longer universally based on a philosophy which considered war inevitable, implicitly punitive, and fought for self-evident objectives."[9]

Explaining the United States' failure in Vietnam, Michael Vlahos provides a poignant contrast of the military strategic behaviors of the United States and Britain: the [U.S.] foreign policy and defense policy elites "prosecuted a brushfire war as would Garnet, Wolseley, or Kitchener, but they did so with a draft army of civilians." However, the Vietnam War, unlike the British experience, could not continue as long as necessary because "there was no tough, professional, all-but-impressed clutch of battle-hardened regiments to battle the Ashanti or the Zulu." The Americans, he asserts, "do not go to war unless it is a revolutionary, liberating, all-embracing struggle for reform."[10] What's more, for most of the 20th century, both Britain and the U.S. faced similar strategic dilemmas: to prepare for war on the European continent or to tailor their militaries to cope with crises that were peripheral to, but not unrelated to the great power confrontation in Europe.[11]

One of the most fascinating findings was a strategic-historic reversal in capabilities: America as a fledgling state started off doing unconventional operations well but as it moved toward and achieved great power status, it started doing these operations poorly; on the other hand as Britain approached the apogee of its great power status, it did asymmetric operations poorly (the Peninsular War notwithstanding) since it started out with vastly inferior numbers relative to the French; but after its decline as a great power, it did these operations better. Interestingly, the Americans, confronted with a strategic paradox of unlimited aims and limited means, were compelled to adopt a Fabian strategy against the British during the War of Independence. "The strategy of Fabius was not merely an evasion of battle to gain time, but calculated for its effect on the morale of the enemy." According to Liddell Hart, the Roman general Fabius knew his enemy's military superiority too well to risk a decision in direct battle; therefore, Fabius sought to avoid it and instead sought by "military pin-pricks to wear down the invaders' endurance." Thus,

Fabius' strategy was designed to protract the war with hit-and-run tactics, avoiding direct battles against the enemy's superior concentrations.[12]

Likewise, George Washington avoided decisive set-piece battles against the superior British forces, and instead, wore down the British forces, physically and psychologically, by concentrating against British outposts and piecemeal detachments. Consequently, from the Peninsula Campaign onward, when the British fought against European conventional militaries, they exhibited a Fabian predilection. Conversely, from the Civil War onward, against conventional and unconventional enemies, the Americans abandoned Fabian strategy and embraced a Jominian-Clauswitzian strategic admixture that amounts to decisive and overwhelming force, always.[13]

The British difficulties in North America and the American difficulties with small wars after it emerged as a great power may also be explained by the supposition that great powers lose small wars. There are two qualifications to this generalization: if the native forces (inferior numbers/weapons) fight on the terms of the great power; and if the great power successfully manages to limit (by internal or external factors) the conflict and fight on the terms of the native guerrilla. The first exception is evidenced in the British Army's 19th century colonial wars and the American Army's wars against the Plains Indians. The second exception is more rare—the U.S. approach to the Huk Rebellion in the Philippines and the British experience in Malaya being clear-cut examples. During the American War for Independence, for example, the fledgling army defeated a European great power's superior army because Washington was able to use conventional tactics in an unorthodox manner to concentrate against British Army weakness in the North. Also, Nathanial Greene successfully used a combination of conventional and unconventional methods to fight the British in the South. Since asymmetry characterized the relationship between the American Army and the British Army, both Washington's and Greene's methods were correct in that they avoided open battle against the superior British Army. On the other hand, most of Britain's colonial opponents in the 19th century, up to and including the Battle of Omdurman, fought the British Army on its terms and inevitably lost.[14]

However, in the 20th century indigenous forces adopted Fabian/Maoist strategies, fueled by nationalist/communist ideologies, to challenge and defeat the superior numbers and technology of the colonial powers. In fact, the post–World War II historical record shows that military and technological prowess is a very unreliable indicator for the successful outcome of small wars. In Algeria, Cyprus, Aden, Morocco, Tunisia, Indochina, and Vietnam, indigenous nationalist forces achieved their political objectives through armed confrontation against big powers that had overwhelmingly superior conventional military forces. After analyzing the Battle of Omdurman and the Italians' war in Abyssinia, both instances where European forces decimated indigenous forces, Mao Tse-tung observed that defeat is the inevitable result when native forces fight against modernized forces on their terms. As Andrew Mack explains, symmetric wars are total wars wherein the struggle is a zero-sum one for survival by both sides—the world wars being an example. On the other hand, an asymmetric struggle implies that the war for the indigenous insurgents is total but it is inherently limited for the great power. This is because the insurgents pose no direct threat to the survival of the great power since they lack an invasion capability. Moreover, for the great power in an asymmetric situation, full military mobilization is neither politically possible nor considered necessary. The disparity in military capabilities is so great and the confidence that military power will predominate is so acute that victory is expected [5]

However, not only does superior conventional military strength not guarantee victory, but, under certain conditions it may undermine it. Since the insurgents lack the technological capacity to destroy the external power's military capability but nonetheless have unlimited political aims such as independence, they must look to the political impact on the metropolis. Ironically, at the apex of their great power status, both Britain and the U.S. lost asymmetric struggles against ostensibly inferior military forces: the British lost to America in the War of Independence and the Americans lost to the Vietnamese in their war for independence. Moreover, both the 18th century American Army and the 20th century North Vietnamese Army (and Vietcong) faced strategic paradoxes in that they embraced unlimited political ends but possessed limited military means. [16] In this context, Henry Kissinger's explanation of the U.S. failure in Vietnam cogently captures the essence of asymmetric conflict and great powers:

We fought a military war; our opponents fought a political one. We sought physical attrition; our opponents aimed for our psychological exhaustion. In the process, we lost sight of one of the cardinal maxims of guerrilla warfare: the guerrilla wins if he does not lose. The conventional army loses if it does not win. [17]

In other words, according to Mack, "the insurgents must retain a minimum degree of invulnerability" to avoid defeat; and to win they must be able to impose a continual aggregation of costs on their adversaries. From a strategic perspective, the rebels' aim must be to provoke the great power into escalating the conflict. This in turn will incur political and economic costs on the external power—these are the normal costs of war such as soldiers killed and equipment destroyed—but over time they be seen as too high when the security of the great power is not directly threatened. The direct costs of lives and equipment lost only gain strategic importance when they achieve the indirect results of psychologically and politically amplifying disharmony in the metropolis. Domestic criticism in the great power will therefore increase as battle losses and economic costs escalate against adversary that poses no direct threat to its vital interests. As Mack reiterates, "in a limited war, it is not at all clear to those groups whose interests are adversely affected why such sacrifices are necessary." Equally salient is the fact that the need to risk death will seem less clear to both conscripts and professional soldiers when the survival of their country is not at risk. This consideration is germane to both counterinsurgency and peace support operations, when great powers employ modern militaries in less developed areas.[18]

Mack highlights another paradox that helps explain why powerful states lose small wars: "Mao and Giap have repeatedly emphasized that the principal contradiction which the imperialist army must confront on the ground derives from the fact that forces dispersed to control territory become spread so thinly that they are vulnerable to attack." What's more, if the imperial power concentrates its forces to overcome this vulnerability, then other areas are left insecure. A massive increase in metropolitan forces can help resolve this operational contradiction but it also immediately increases the domestic costs of the war. Conversely, if the great power wants to placate domestic opposition by withdrawing some forces, the contradiction at the operational level becomes more acute. Any effort to address one contradiction will exacerbate the other. Even as early as the American War for Independence, Nathanial Greene was able to exploit this paradox against the British Army. In fact, Greene's descriptions of his doctrine were uncannily similar too some of Mao's axioms. For example, Greene said "there are few generals that has run oftener, or more lustily than I have done" whereas Mao offered "the ability to run away is the very characteristic of the guerrilla." What's more, Mao explained that, if the "enemy advances, we retreat; enemy halts, we harass; enemy tires, we attack; enemy retreats, we pursue." Greene simply said "we fight, get beat, rise and fight again."[19]

Therefore, at the near-apex of British hegemony, the British Army in America was confounded by the "principal contradiction" that characterizes asymmetric struggles. Weigley captures this situation:

The British had fallen entrapped into the dilemmas of a war of posts conceived as a counter to a guerrilla campaign. Their posts had never been numerous enough really to control the country, because partisan raids on the smaller posts had compelled them to consolidate into fewer and fewer garrisons. But the garrisons too few to check the partisans' marauding, were themselves too small against a reasonably strong field force.[20]

Thus, the American "strategy of erosion" against the British was not unlike both Mao Tse-tung's and Henry Kissinger's prescriptions for guerrilla victory. Washington's strategic purpose was to break, or erode, the resolve of the British government through gradual and persistent engagements against peripheral detachments of the British Army. The Americans, on the other hand, conducted a strategic defensive and "did not lose" by preserving their inchoate army. Washington's army was so weak compared to the British Army that it could not even pursue a battlefield attack in the tactical realm because his soldiers could not win. Yet, the Americans' political objectives—to expel the British Army and secure independence— were total. To find a way out of this contradiction, Weigley explains, "Washington's hopes had to lie mainly not in military victory but in the possibility that the political opposition in Britain might in time force the British Ministry to abandon the conflict." Likewise, local nationalist forces in the post–World War II period won against opponents with overwhelmingly superior military capabilities by not losing—indigenous forces protracted the conflicts and increased the costs (economic and political) for the great power. The weaker military forces accomplished this by refusing to confront the modernized armies on their own terms and by instead resorting to unorthodox approaches. Greene and Giap were both able to overcome their strategic paradoxes in asymmetric struggles by such methods.[21]

THE BRITISH ARMY

The British excelled in small-unit, anti-guerrilla warfare as they did in other aspects of counterinsurgency. History had given them an army that was relatively small and decentralized, and therefore ideally suited to such warfare. Since Britain is an island nation, the navy and not the army has been its first line of defense. Distrusted and under-funded, the junior service was thus relatively unaffected by the revolution in size and organization experienced by continental armies during the nineteenth century.[22]

Since the Royal Navy has always been the principal defense against invasion, the British Army has for most of its history been perceived as a small professional long-service force serving mainly overseas, out of sight and out of mind. However, the real dilemma for British strategy has lain in the choice between the defense of its global empire and its commitment to continental European security. Chandler and Beckett summarize this dilemma: "the notion of the Army being a projectile fired by the Royal Navy has been an attractive one over the centuries but the pull of European conflict has always effectively proved too great to avoid and a commitment to European defense has been central to the Army's role since the Paris agreements of 1954." Moreover, since history and geography have compelled the British Army to meet a broad array of challenges, often with limited resources, its performance has sometimes exhibited the constraints imposed by tradition. Notwithstanding, the British Army has been very successful over the course of its existence—the only major war it lost was the American War of Independence.[23]

However, after 1850 the industrial revolution spread to continental Europe and the United States. As a result, the impact of technology on naval power degraded the security that an insular geography had once afforded Britain for free. Before, this century, Britain rarely committed her own forces to major operations in Europe, preferring instead to underwrite her allies with the income from her prosperous colonial trade. "As late as 1890 it was possible for a British general to say that England was split between those who adhered to the tradition of Wellington and those who wished to make the army a profession." England was safe behind a sea barrier at home while she pursued a policy abroad of colonial expansion and of foreign trade based on naval supremacy. As a result, Britain developed the professional standing of naval officers while it was slow to see the need to professionalize the officer in the army. Britain's officers, at the turn of the century, were "gentlemen first, landed gentry almost always, professionals almost never."[24]

It is likely that no other country in modern history has aggregated as broad an experience in counterinsurgency in its client states of the less developed world as Britain did during its long devolution of empire. The British Army never had an overarching manual for colonial tactics. After much experience in imperial polic- ing, the British devised a basic approach to both rural and urban insurrection that, when applied properly, served to reduce the level of violence to manageable pro- portions. The British understood that military tactics alone were of little use in counterinsurgency unless they were integrated with the political tactics. As Bell explains, military tactics that had been refined over a generation of men with dif- fering experiences could be learned and applied but could not be effective unless those tactics were used in the context of a political formula to isolate the rebels from the population. The British Army realized and was sensitive to both the ulti- mate power of the Cabinet and the political aspects of revolt. The military recog- nized that the bounds of political strategy and action were delimited in London, based on advice from and not as a result of the direction of the General Staff. Not- withstanding, the British Army always sought the authorization to pursue the in- surgents with a robust campaign that was centralized under one command (ideally that of a military officer) and unrestricted by local authorities.[25]

The two world wars precipitated three strategic realities for Great Britain: loss of great power status; divestment of empire; and a larger, more permanent role for her Army in Europe. Britain faced the task of trying to balance her reduced eco- nomic power with both her security requirements in Europe and the maintenance of empire. The result, French maintains, was "a piecemeal disengagement from the responsibilities of empire accompanied by a series of small colonial wars which extended over thirty years." By the 1950s, however, many of the factors that had once contributed to British military superiority beyond Europe were fading away. Britain's obligations in NATO required her to forward deploy a large por- tion of her defense forces in Europe. What's more, international norms and princi- ples (i.e., the UN Charter) increasingly proscribed the use of force to maintain colonial possessions. The 1967 Healey decision to abandon bases east of Suez marked the end of Britain's role as an imperial military power. "In 1965–66, one member in four of the armed forces had been deployed outside Europe. The corre- sponding figure in 1973–74 was only one in ten." From 1969 on, however, the British Army's focus in training and deployments was still bifurcated between a commitment to Europe and the possibility of conventional war and LIC in North- ern Ireland and peacekeeping in Cyprus.[26]

Since the end of the Cold War, the British Army has shifted closer to a doctrin- ally based maneuver-oriented approach to the conduct of operations. In 1991, it fought a short high-intensity war in the Persian Gulf with the U.S. and other allies. It has also contributed to most of the UN sanctioned peace operations in the 1990s. In fact, the first British Army over-arching doctrinal manual (*ADP Volume 1, Op- erations*) published after the Cold War ended was written in close concert with and paralleled U.S. Army *FM 100-5, Operations*. Doctrinal publications and manuals have also merged to reflect the changes after the Cold War, dealing anew with doc-

trine for operations short of war. Moreover, according to BG (Ret.) Gavin
Bulloch, the British Army has noted the similarities between Military Assistance
to Civil Authorities (MACA), counter-insurgency, and peace support operations
on behalf of the UN.[27]

THE INFLUENCE OF GEOGRAPHY AND HISTORY

> The history of the British Army, then, is the history of the institution that the British
> have always been reluctant to accept that they needed.
>   —Correlli Barnett[28]

This reluctance was possible because of Britain's geographic advantage as an
island state. Even when Britain found it necessary to raise expeditionary forces to
tip the balance of power on the continent, the British Army in its expeditions to the
continent has always enjoyed an advantage not available to continental armies: it
could run away. For continental states, long borders with other powerful states
made the role of armies central to national survival. The histories and geographies,
for example, of Germany and France confer primacy on their armies for national
security. On the other hand, up until the latter part of the 19th century, the British
Navy had played this central role, assuring British survival. However, this is not to
say that the "blue-water myth"[29] has much credence when Britain has had to wield
its weight as a great power on the continent. According to Correlli Barnett, the
"blue-water" myth has been popular in Britain because it offers a way of winning
big wars on the cheap: "it offers victory over powerful opponents without the need
for a large field army." To the chagrin of strategists and budgeteers, however, Britain's history with continental wars over the last several centuries dispels this myth.
British intervention on the continent has only been decisive when Britain has
fielded large armies, committed for the duration and willing to fight major battles
against continental enemies.[30]

Thus British military strategic culture has been characterized by a cycle not unfamiliar to the U.S. Army experience: "instead of continuous development of a national army, as on the continent, there is a succession of sudden expansions to meet
particular emergencies, followed by a relapse into peacetime stagnation and national neglect." This approach to military policy, pitfalls notwithstanding, was a
luxury afforded only to insular great powers, and only until the middle of the 20th
century. The central dilemma for British military policy has been the choice between defense of global empire and involvement on the continent; but since the
Paris agreements of 1954, a commitment to NATO has been a big part of the British Army's role. Although Hew Strachan explains that the British Army developed
a more continental ethos in the 1970s and 1980s, colonial legacies still remained
relevant. In 1991, British troops and ships were still deployed in 25 different locations around the globe. In fact, the end of the Cold War witnessed a reassertion of
Britain's role beyond Europe. Britain agreed to contribute two divisions to
NATO's new Rapid Reaction Corps, a unit whose parts were more likely to see,

and actually did see, service outside of NATO's traditional area. In fact, Britain's 1992 Defense White Paper reasserted a global role for the British Army.[31]

However, the British were averse to any type of permanent army for several centuries. According to Ian Roy, "the lesson of the Civil War and the Cromwellian Interregnum is that large standing armies, the high taxes which are needed to pay for them, military government, and ambitious generals who intervene in politics, are anathema to the British and foreign to the British State." Thus, the experience of the Civil War and Cromwell's rule imbued both the English political elite and the public with "a profound distaste for armies and a sharp nose for any whiff of military involvement in civil government." Two additional factors encouraged an aversion to large standing armies in Great Britain: low soldiers' pay and the quartering of soldiers in the homes of civilians. With little or no money, soldiers behaved two ways: they acted like armed thugs among the population, often refusing to pay for services; or, they moonlighted with civilian jobs. Moreover, billeting soldiers in private housing soured civil-military rapport as it was often impossible for the homeowners to oblige the impoverished soldiers to pay their keep.[32]

The neglect of Great Britain's army is also attributable in part to its insularity—as an island nation, British survival had never really been threatened by anything more significant than tribal conflict with the Welsh and Scots. While continental states relied on armies to secure their existence, Britain relied upon its navy for security. What's more, since Britain had a long-standing naval tradition, its people could not understand why they should have to pay professional soldiers to do what had always been done by amateurs, since the Norman Conquest. "Any such institution as a standing army was regarded as entirely unnecessary, and in fact the whole history of the British army reflects this attitude." "Completely neglected in peacetime yet expected to achieve miracles in war, the only periods of progress or reform were during or immediately after an emergency when, through no fault of its own, the army had been unable to meet all the demands made on it."[33]

Britain lies adjacent to, but not contiguous to, European continent populated by peoples whose culture has "no more in common than our own than has that of countries founded by men of our stock in such inconveniently distant parts of the world as North America, the Antipodes, and even Southern Africa." According to Yardley and Sewell, Britain's fundamentally maritime strategy took shape between the 15th and 18th centuries, when the main concern became the maintenance of a fleet that could defeat any other power. The Royal Navy thus became the priority of effort, receiving the most money and attention. Once Britain acquired a trading empire with colonies and bases for the fleet, she required garrisons to protect them. Britain would deploy infantry battalions from home, and later from British India, to man the garrisons and serve as armed policemen. Thus, unlike other armies of Europe, imperial policing became the main task of the British Army. Moreover, since Britain's territorial security depended on her insularity, her policy was also to balance against whatever hegemon was seeking to dominate Europe. Britain did this by supporting coalitions of rival states with money and troops. So long as Britain was safe from invasion, the British could afford to engage in prolonged warfare with every confidence in victory. "The regiments of an army could be created and disbanded as necessary around a nucleus of permanent troops, and the Army needed to be no larger than was necessary to demonstrate Britain's commitment to her allies." Thus, the British Regular Army evolved as a disparate group of individual regiments, accustomed to isolated locations and long service. By the middle of the 19th century, the regular army saw 80 percent of its troops stationed abroad, with imperial policing, as well as occasional internal policing, dominating its development.[34]

The late professionalization of the British Army officer was another salient factor in the development of British military strategic culture. Recognizing the need for professionalism, the British Army established the Staff College in 1858. However, in actuality it was merely an annex to Sandhurst until 1870 and the absence of a General Staff until the early 20th century mitigated its effectiveness anyway. The Cardwell reforms were the next major attempt at reform. The dilemma presented by the exigencies of imperial warfare and continental warfare was theretofore addressed on an ad hoc basis until Edward Cardwell became the Secretary of State for War in 1868. When Cardwell took office the British Army comprised long-service troops that were appropriate for the imperial demands but who provided almost no reserve for future expansion. "Cardwell brought the number of troops overseas into balance with those at home, reduced the terms of service from 20 years to six years with the regular army and six years with the reserves, and reorganized the infantry regiments of the line. Linking the battalions, with one at home for every one overseas, was in many respects a brilliant solution to meet both the needs of empire and the potential exigencies in Europe.[35]

Insofar as these reforms influenced the British Army's military strategic culture, the War Office Act of 1870 and the Localization Act of 1872, were the most salient. The War Office Act clarified and centralized the relationship between the Secretary of State for War and the commander-in-chief of the Army by subordinating the latter to the former. However, this reform did not really help professionalize the Army until after 1894 when the chief of the Army Lord Cambridge, who impeded the implementation of meritorious promotions, retired. What this act ultimately did, though, was to centralize civilian control over the Army and thus make the Army more responsive to the policy decisions of its civilian masters. The Localization Act, on the other hand, was designed to improve the effectiveness of home defense battalions while also generating from the home units trained replacements for imperial policing battalions. This act established 66 territorial districts, each of which would man two line battalions, two militia battalions, and several volunteer units. Although this act did improve the efficiency of the home units, it did not fulfill the purpose of providing adequate replacements for colonial battalions. According to French, this would only have worked if there had been parity between the number of line units at home and those overseas. However, a host of small colonial wars in the 1870s helped create an asymmetric situation wherein 59 battalions were at home and 82 battalions were overseas. Moreover, home battalions were often cannibalized to keep imperial units manned, thereby reducing home battalions to skeletons.[36]

The organization of the British Army that resulted from the Cardwell Reforms of 1870–1872 was one geared toward colonial policing rather than large-scale conventional war in Europe. The Crimean War in 1854–1855, the Indian Mutiny in 1857, and the German Army's performance in the Franco-Prussian War all helped generate impetus for serious reform of the British Army. The less than stellar performance by the British Army in the Crimean War highlighted the shortcomings of a colonial army sent to fight a European war. The Indian mutiny, on the other hand, increased the military burdens of empire—if Britain wanted to gain control of India and minimize the threat of further rebellion, it needed to increase its reliance on British garrisons and reduce its dependence on indigenous troops. In addition, British observers of the wars of German unification noted that those wars were won by large conscript armies and the proliferation of such armies throughout Europe were bound to reduce the potential of the smaller British Army. Secretary of State for War Edward Cardwell consequently initiated four major reforms: the centralization of Army policy under the secretary of state; the abolition of purchase; the introduction of short service enlistment to enable the formation of a new army reserve; and the localization of the home army so that each regiment was assigned a specific geographic area where it could recruit and where it was affiliated with local forces.[37]

Although Cardwell's reforms were brilliant conceptually, there were problems with them in practice. For example, the amorphous array of battalions that represented the home army was suitable only for providing drafts for and rotating with overseas units. Moreover, launching any protracted expedition overseas tended to throw the system out of whack. Also, as stated elsewhere, Cardwell's system mandated homogeneity among linked battalions—this definitely constrained the British Army in carrying out both of its two roles because it could either be organized to do imperial policing or continental warfare but not both. In the aftermath of the Boer War debacle, Secretary of State for War Hugh Arnold-Foster tried to implement a permanent fix to the imperial-continental dichotomy by establishing a long-service army for imperial policing and a short-service army that could serve as home defense as well as an expeditionary force on the continent in the event of war. Winton argues that this was a viable solution but it was anathema to the Army Council and to Edward VII—it was offered on a trial basis but abandoned in 1905 when Campbell-Bannerman's liberal government took office.[38]

Explaining the success of the British Army until the 1830s, French attributes it to the British Army's superior discipline, organization, and tactics rather than to superior technology or numbers. French also refutes the common perception that it was the Cardwell Reforms that enabled the British Army to win a series of late 19th century colonial wars and to meet the security needs of the empire. He cites reasons other than the Cardwell system that explain the British Army's successes. For one, Britain's colonial wars did not stir much opposition at home because they were cheap in terms of lives and monetary outlays. This he attributes to the fact that colonial expeditions were normally small—between 1815 and 1899, the largest deployment comprised a force of 35,000 sent to Egypt in 1882. Moreover, the diversity of both Britain's 19th century colonial adversaries and of the terrain where the British Army fought precludes generalizations about the conduct of colonial campaigns. It is important to point out, however, that the whole nature of the British Army's 19th century colonial wars differed markedly from the more ideologically driven insurgencies that the British Army would face in the 20th century. The British Army's approach to colonial warfare was much more orthodox and conventional in the 19th century, partly because many of its colonial enemies tended to fight the British Army on its terms.[39]

The Battle of Omdurman in 1898 represented both the culmination and the apotheosis of Britain's 19th century style of colonial warfare. This battle for the Sudan in September witnessed 11,000 Dervishes killed compared to 48 British killed; by fighting the British European-style, "the Dervishes invited the British to indulge their own preconceptions of what constituted proper combat." Kitchener's army, equipped with rifled artillery, 20 machine-guns, and breech-loading rifles, decimated the Dervish army, which had opted to attack the entrenched British by frontal assault, in human waves. There were, however, some common elements to these campaigns. Whether the British Army was fighting the Arabi Pasha, the Zulus, the Ashanti, the Pathans, or the Afghans, the British normally assumed the strategic offensive as early as possible because they worried that if they delayed too long that it would encourage others to join the opposition. The British Army also preferred battle in the open because it was the best way to translate its superior discipline into the largest possible casualties for the enemy. The British Army could maintain soldiers in the field indefinitely and apply continuous pressure until attrition wore down their enemies.[40]

The Battle of Omdurman also represented one of the last effective horse cavalry charges in history. For his success, Kitchener received the Dervish commander's bleached skull and a peerage from Queen Victoria while the British Army rested on its laurels. The British regulars espoused the old Wellingtonian aphorism that "her Majesty's enemies would always come in the same way and be dispatched the same old way." However, as Bolger points out, the battle was anachronistic even as it occurred and, unfortunately, it encouraged the British Army to continue fighting the way it preferred instead of the way it should. "The eventual corrective measures had to be lubricated by a generous application of British blood."[41]

The Boer War, contrariwise, was the harbinger of a more difficult and cunning approach to insurgent warfare, one in which indigenous opponents would prove unwilling to fight the British Army European-style. The tenacious Boers elected not to be Dervishes or Ashanti or Zulus and they fought their own style of war on the hills and plains of South Africa from 1899–1902. As Kitchener later observed, "the Boers are not like the Sudanese who stood up to a fair fight. They are always running away on their little ponies." Although British horse soldiers continued to operate in World War I, the ways of the Union Brigade at Waterloo or the Heavy Brigade at Balaclava had outlasted their usefulness. To defeat the Boers, it would take a complete purge of senior British commanders, additional troops, an over-haul of the British Army, and concentration camps for Boer families.[42]

The fallout from the Boer War provided the next impetus for reform, and as a result the General Staff was established in 1904 as a necessary addition to the Staff College. In fact, in his memoirs the first Chief of the General Staff, Neville Lyttleton, remarked that "I have seen or taken part in the development of our Army from an occupation to a profession."[43] In 1904, the British government took a significant step toward reform with the Esher Report. The Esher Committee analyzed the ineffectiveness of a military bureaucracy that had been built piecemeal since 1660. This report laid down the foundations of the War Office organization and general staff system that has endured essentially to the present. Correlli Barnett referred to the recommendations of the Esher Report as "the reconstruction of the brain of the Army on clear functional lines." The substantive recommendations and consequent reorganization that resulted from the Esher Report were the creation of an Army Council, a general staff, and the division of departmental responsibilities inside the War Office on clearly defines and logical principles. The Army Council would provide a single collective body to review and decide questions of policy in place of the amorphous responsibilities of the War Secretary. Moreover, the Secretary of State for War was placed unambiguously in charge—all military policy recommendations to the Crown would go through him, thus consummating civilian and parliamentary control of the Army. The creation of the Army Council and the general staff also necessitated the elimination of the post of Commander-in-Chief of the Army. As a result, the last incumbent Commander-in-Chief was removed in 1904 and responsibility for preparing the Army for war was vested in the new post of Chief of the General Staff (CGS). The creation of a general staff also gave the Staff College at Camberley a new sense of purpose—the residual traces of the old dry curriculum were swept away in favor of practical training in different staff duties in the field. The end result of the Esher Report recommendations was that the British Army was instilled with a sense of professional purpose not witnessed in peacetime since the days of the Commonwealth.[44]

The dilemma between a continental commitment and an imperial commitment played a significant role in shaping the British Army culture. The debate between proponents of either a purely naval strategy or a strictly continental strategy dominated military policy for most of this century. It finally culminated in favor of a continental strategy after Defense Secretary Dennis Healey announced in 1967 that Britain would abandon her mainland bases east of Suez. Northern Ireland, however, continued to require a commitment and other commitments, for example Cyprus, emerged. This dilemma created a duality in British military policy whereby Britain had to balance and shift resources for the Navy and Army, between an imperial approach with naval preeminence and a continental commitment requiring a larger Army. David French refers to this dualistic approach as a "mixed paradigm" and he attributes it to Paul Kennedy, G. S. Graham, and Michael Howard. In fact, French relies on another lucid explanation:

A commitment of support to a Continental ally in the nearest available theater, on the largest scale that contemporary resources could afford, so far from being alien to traditional British strategy, was absolutely central to it. The flexibility provided by sea power certainly made possible other activities as well: colonial conquest, trade war, help to allies in Central Europe, minor amphibious operations, but these were ancillary to the great decisions by land, and they continued to be so throughout the two world wars.[45]

Moreover, Howard maintains, when Britain did depend solely on naval strength, it was due to strategic exigencies rather than a matter of choice. French joins Howard, Graham, and Kennedy in challenging B. H. Liddell Hart's conception (prescription) of Britain's way of war. Liddell Hart argued that a "distinctively British practice of war" engendered a strategy of mobility and surprise, best achieved through the employment of the Royal Navy. He argued for a return to the "traditional and successful maritime strategy," one that avoided a commitment of large land forces to wars of attrition and instead relied on the Navy for empire maintenance. "By our practice we safeguarded ourselves where we were weakest, and exerted our strength where the enemy was weakest." Liddell Hart asserted that three centuries of experience in warfare had proved this maritime "practice" to be sound. On the other hand, Corelli Barnett argues that this one-dimensional notion of the "British way in warfare" is flawed strategically: "the Navy can and has assured British survival; but is only a limited instrument of national policy in Europe or in the interior of any other continent." In all but one of the six wars Britain fought against France, French points out, in addition to the Royal Navy, Britain also needed the support of continental allies to balance against France.[46]

"It is easy to ignore, or to discount as historical curiosity, the decennial invasion scares which swept the British Isles during the nineteenth century." However, it was not self-evident that the insular invulnerability on which British policy had depended for so long could survive each new wave of technological change that the century had witnessed. "It is certainly doubtful whether the Army had faced the implications of, for the first time in a generation, transforming itself from a small professional force concerned primarily with imperial policing into a cadre to train and command a conscript force of over a million strong to take part in large-scale continental warfare." Even after the Franco-Prussian War many leaders in Britain still viewed France as the hegemon in Europe and believed that it was in Britain's interests to keep a distance from the continent. However, after Britain's weaknesses were revealed in the Second Boer War in 1899–1902, Britain made efforts to end her isolation from European affairs through a series of diplomatic arrangements. Another important outcome of the Boer War was a renewed push for military reform. One of the most important reforms was the creation of a General Staff system based on the Prussian model. The change abolished the position of commander-in-chief and replaced it with a new Army Council comprising seven members.[47]

When Richard Haldane became the Secretary of State for War in 1905, his challenge was to continue military reform and reduce expenditures. He restructured and standardized military organizations and manuals throughout the Empire and he created an expeditionary force of seven divisions. Haldane also reorganized the volunteers into a new Territorial Force of 14 divisions, transformed the old militia into a special reserve to reinforce the expeditionary force, and streamlined the command and control of the infantry regiments. By any measure, Haldane's feat was not insignificant. Only a few years after the Boer debacle, Britain, historically a dominant naval power, had acquired a formidable Army at a decreased cost. Subsequently, Britain employed this new Army in its leading role of fighting a war against the major European land power of the day. Yardley and Sewell help explain the unprecedented character of World War I for Britain. "It was a total war in which, for the first time, much of a nation's private industry was mobilized toward the single aim of victory, and airships attacked concentrated civilian targets." "Fundamentally, it was a war of attrition where being a winner was less important than not being a loser." One of the most salient lessons of World War I for the British was that the cost of victory had been too high: nearly a million soldiers were killed in action. The end of the war saw the British Empire larger than any time in history and the possibility of an early return to fight in Europe seemed remote.[48]

The British Army existed in an extremely antimilitary environment from 1920 until early 1939. On the one hand, Liddell Hart's polemical concept of a "traditional British way in warfare" emerged as an attractive alternative to revisiting the bleeding the British had suffered in World War I. Hart's limited liability concept was a strategic approach that relied on naval supremacy and a small army for attacks on the periphery. Such an approach, Hart maintained, had historically allowed Britain to avoid the heavy casualties that accompany continental war. Moreover, it was this "traditional" approach that had enabled Britain to influence the outcome of continental conflicts during the same time that it was creating a global empire. On the other hand, all the political parties rejected the experience of World War I and the literati's novels and war reminiscences reinforced antiwar and antimilitary attitudes. By the mid-1930s, Murray explains, "much of the educated population in Britain fervently believed that nothing was worth the price of war."[49]

The result was a hostile environment for the British Army at the very time when the international security environment was becoming increasingly menacing. From the mid-1930s, Army leaders identified Germany as the most probable enemy and they recognized that such a conflict would require a commitment of troops to the continent. However, the willingness of the government and the nation to expend resources on defense remained minimal. To make matters worse, the British Army's sister services received priority for equipment, personnel, and training. Moreover, when Chamberlain came to power in 1937, he completely embraced Hart's concept of "limited liability." After a series of defense reviews, the Chamberlain government essentially stated that Britain would not commit an army to the continent under any circumstances. As a result, work to prepare the Army for a continental role halted and the government assigned the following priorities to the Army: (1) to protect the home islands; (2) to secure trade routes; (3) to garri-

son the empire; and (4) to cooperate for the defense of British allies but only after it
had addressed the first three priorities. Moreover, the government described the
Army as a general-purpose force, a vague term that made it difficult to requisition
equipment or supplies for any theater of operation.[50]

According to Murray, the political environment had a significant impact on the
British Army's willingness and ability to confront the issues about war on the continent. For one, the political guidance did not direct the Army to focus on war in
Europe since the government indicated that the Army would not be used there under any circumstances. On the other hand, when the Army finally received political direction to prepare for war on the continent, the government demanded that it
accept a huge number of conscripts and create a mass army. To complicate matters, military reformers like Fuller and Hart who should and could have helped innovate doctrine and forces, had so vilified the Army leadership during the interwar
years that that leadership was hardly amenable to Fuller's and Hart's ideas on the
eve of war.[51]

Moreover, Harold Winton agrees with Murray that social and political indifference impeded the development of armored warfare in Britain. But Winton adds
military conservatism and the imperial defense mission to the list of obstacles.
Winton defines military conservatism as "the tendency to preserve existing military institutions and practices" and he acknowledges that this conservatism clearly
played a role in the development of doctrine leading up to World War II. The cavalry's attachment to horses and its determination to have a cavalry officer command the Mobile Division is another facet of military conservatism. It was also
Montgomery-Massingberd's desire to preserve the cavalry as a branch that played
a significant role in his decision to use the cavalry as the core of the Mobile Division. However, according to Winton it was neither the antimilitary milieu nor military conservatism that were the major obstacles to the development of multiple
armored divisions in the interwar years. The principal obstacle was a historical focus on the imperial defense mission and an Army organized primarily for imperial
defense with its bulk comprising 136 infantry battalions.[52]

Winton is unambiguous in this finding: "Of these various factors, the imperial
defense mission was the single most significant impediment to the development of
armored formations. So long as the Army's primary mission was to garrison the
Empire, armored divisions were of little utility." The organization of the British
Army that resulted from the Cardwell Reforms of 1870–1872 was one geared toward colonial policing rather than large-scale conventional war in Europe.[53] As
highlighted earlier, the Cardwell system mandated a one-for-one matchup of units
deployed garrisoning the empire and units in Britain for home defense (war in Europe). Winton, moreover, argues that the principal effect of the imperial policing
mission, coupled with the Cardwell system, was to almost completely rule out the
creation of a large organization for armored warfare. The Tank Brigade was in actuality an add-on to the Cardwellian British Army and it could be maintained only
by maintaining a commensurate number of armored car companies overseas.
However, the colonial defense mission assigned to the overseas armored compa-

nies was entirely unrelated to the Tank Brigade's mission for war in Europe. What's more, "vehicles that worked well on English roads and in English climates often did not perform well on Indian roads in Indian climates." Nor were men trained for mechanized warfare in Europe necessarily well suited for imperial policing.[54]

During the period leading up to World War II, therefore, several military strategic and political cultural factors combined to influence Britain's strategic response to the German threat. First, the British Army's cultural preferences, especially the regimental system, impeded innovation in armor operations and slowed transition to larger formations. Second, British political culture was averse to direct or frontal approaches, largely as a result of exorbitant British casualties during World War I. Third, Liddell Hart, although marginalized in the intra-institutional innovation debate, wrote books and articles prescribing an indirect/Fabian British strategic approach that certainly influenced British military thought. Finally, Churchill himself had been an advocate of Fabian strategy since his time in the Admiralty during World War I. He, consequently, was amenable to Liddell Hart's prescriptions for British strategy vis-a-vis continental Europe. More fundamentally, however, all of these factors resulted in one strategic reality in 1940—any confrontation in Europe between German forces and British forces would be an asymmetric one.[55]

Between 1941 and 1944 American and British strategists discussed their differing views on the right approach to defeat Germany. The unwavering position of the Americans was to assault the main armed strength of the German's (the main enemy) directly and to destroy that strength as soon as possible. The British strategists, on the other hand, argued for a more indirect approach that would aim at and exploit the relative weak points of the German's Fortress Europe, for example, in the Mediterranean. The British approach favored waiting for a substantial degradation in the German defenses before striking where the Germans were the strongest. The differences in strategic approaches between the British and the Americans became evident as early as the 1941 ABC Conference where the British put forward the idea of an indirect attack in the Mediterranean and against Italy. During the summer of that year, the British argued for "probing soft spots by mobile, hard-hitting armored forces operating on the periphery of German-controlled territory and eventually striking into German itself, rather than large-scale ground action to meet the full power of the German military machine." According to Matloff, this approach was consistent with Britain's insular position, its maritime traditions, and its experiences with continental wars, (notwithstanding World War I) which were wars of attrition and opportunity. In fact, Matloff's description of Britain's strategic approach World War II offers a cogent explanation of the essence of British military strategic culture: "It was a compound of military and political factors, of British military experience in the first World War and Dunkirk, and of Prime Minister Churchill's predilections."[56]

After World II War neither the political nor the military leaders of the United Kingdom shrank any longer from a continental commitment. "They had learned their lesson; though it was not until 1954, ten years after the Normandy landings, that a final, binding commitment was undertaken to maintain substantial British armed forces on the continent in time of peace." At the end of World War II the British Army comprised three million men scattered all over the world. It was inevitable that the British Army would be reduced in size—the total strength of the postwar Army was 305,000 but by1951 it was increased by 100,000 due, in part, to the Korean War. The postwar Army was also a conscript Army as a result of the 1947 National Service Act—it remained so until 1963 when it became an all-regular Army. For the British Army, the period 1945–1970 was a "transitional phase whereby the Army lost its overseas role and gained one in Europe; when it fought small wars but became ever more focused upon" the defense of mainland Europe; and "when it lost its large number of conscripts, reverting to a small regular force to be expanded by reservists and Territorial Army volunteers in time of war." "Although both the Heath and Thatcher governments attempted to retain a vestigial world role for the Army, the Army's ability to intervene in conflicts outside Europe was strictly limited."[57]

Several key lessons emerged from the British Army's experience of major war prior to the Korean War: (1) The Army lacked a formal doctrine for war and tended toward intellectual indifference; (2) The decentralized regimental system was well suited to imperial policing, and in particular helped to promote a strong esprit de corps, but it was less well suited to modern warfare. In particular, the regimental system impeded combined arms cooperation and standardized procedures for training and operations; (3) The Army focused on the tactical level of war and it paid little attention to the strategic or operational levels. However, this did not necessarily translate into tactical competence—instead the Army's tactics were often simple and unimaginative compared to the best continental armies; (4) The Army demonstrated a distinct preference for set-piece, attritional battles, emphasizing artillery and infantry; and (5) The Army almost invariably fought its major wars as part of a coalition. Although Britain proved skilled at the strategic and political dimensions of coalition warfare, it was not always successful at the military-operational level."[58]

What's more, the Korean War seemed to reaffirm the British way of warfare. "The British fought according to traditional methods, adapting them as required, rather than developing a coherent body of ideas in advance of war which covered both training and operations."[59] The British Army's experience in the Korean War highlighted several issues. First, despite the large size of the British Army and of the threats consequent to the Cold War, the Army had difficulty finding the forces for Korea and it was not prepared for war. The war in Korea revealed the Army's difficulty in responding promptly and in strength to major overseas crises.[60]

Between 1950 and 1955 significant new developments began to influence the military policies of Britain. The creation of NATO and the emergence of the "Lisbon Goals" to put 90 divisions in Europe eliminated the possibility of a smaller occupation force there. During the same period, the Korean War reinforced U.S. arguments for large armies. However, it was the requirements of Britain's empire that decisively pointed to the need for a conscript army in peacetime. The Malayan campaign kept thousands of British troops occupied in countering the Communist insurgency and as soon as the campaign approached a successful end, the Mau-Mau rebellion in Kenya and the E.O.K.A. crisis in Cyprus occurred. Initially, empire maintenance simply required numbers, more troops to act as reinforcements for the police in Palestine or to conduct punitive anti-bandit operations in Eritrea. However, on the Malay Peninsula, for the first time, the British Army confronted a guileful opponent trained in the Maoist model of guerrilla strategy. Soon the troops were learning the counterinsurgency trade on the ground. For example, the Far East Land Forces training center in Malaya developed a coherent philosophy of counterinsurgent warfare and trained every arriving officer and soldier before they began jungle operations. In Kenya, British officers and soldiers operated for long periods in the forests, using unconventional techniques against an unconventional enemy.[61]

However, although the advent of nuclear weapons and the emergence of Maoist guerrilla warfare were both transforming the character of military operations, no real changes in the training of the British Army at home came about. As Gwynne Jones explains, "the training and doctrine of the British Army in 1955 were still essentially that of a nation in arms, dedicated to the principle of unlimited war fought by massive forces and only reluctantly discarding the organization and tactics of El Alamein and the Normandy beaches." Moreover, Gwynne Jones asserts, the 1956 Suez campaign, notwithstanding the political fallout, unambiguously demonstrated that the British Army was unable to get the right forces in place on time. The implicit basis of the 1957 White Paper was that British overseas commitments would gradually be eliminated. The new professional Army was to be concentrated into a strategic reserve in England: a small, mobile, hard-hitting force. "This belief, based on a mistaken reading of the strategic effects of constitutional advance in the colonies, remained an article of official faith for about five years."[62]

By the early 1960s, British Army tactics and training were absorbing the valuable lessons of its wide experience in counterinsurgency. Past experience demonstrated that success in counterinsurgency depended on first-rate political and military intelligence, effective modalities for integrating the political and military spheres, and the training of local forces. In its "Cold-War role," the British Army, Gwynne Jones asserts, "achieved an enviable expertise, partly because of its imaginative use of the lessons of the past, and partly because operations of this type were quite its favorite occupation."[63] British soldiers adopted a very pragmatic approach to colonial warfare. "The British, of course, could draw on a very substantial body of experience—greater than any other colonial power—and their rather ad hoc attitude toward fighting colonial campaigns reflected its length and diversity."[64] The 1980's witnessed a significant change in the British Army's approach to high intensity warfare. The impetus for this change was twofold: first, by the early 1980s the political priority of forward defense and the reliance on the early use of nuclear weapons were no longer tenable; and second, Sir Nigel Bagnall, through strength of personality and intellect, was able to push reforms through within the British Army.[65]

During the Persian Gulf War (Operation Granby for the British Army), the 1st British Armored Division fought a war of maneuver with a coherent plan of operations, in close cooperation with the Americans, and drew heavily upon the doctrinal ideas developed in the 1980s and the idea of doctrine itself. Again in this war, the British approach revealed an emphasis on flexibility. "Whether this is a conscious decision or one forced upon the Army by financial limitations and poor planning is, to some extent unimportant because the result is the same: the British Army has responded to crises by adapting what it has rather than by advanced preparation."[66] As a result of the end of the Cold War, the focus of British defense policy shifted "to what was termed wider security interests," so the Army came to be seen as increasingly important in roles ranging from humanitarian assistance in Bosnia to high intensity war in the Gulf.[67]

VALUED (CORE) FUNCTIONAL ROLES

It is characteristic of the older military establishments that there methods are rooted in the past, addicted to usage and tradition, and influenced by organizational patterns that often owe more to administrative convenience and instinctive conservatism than to the requirements of efficiency in battle.[68]

The success of British counter-insurgency has stemmed from a combination of fortuitous circumstances and historical development that produced a military establishment well-suited to combating internal unrest. Out of this favorable context, the British developed methods and more importantly, principles upon which these methods were based.[69]

During the Napoleonic Wars Britain was faced with a strategic dilemma since it had a superior navy but an army inferior to the French Army. "If, because of the Royal Navy's supremacy, the British Isles were invulnerable to invasion, Britain's geographic seclusion and the defeat of her continental allies left her facing impotency on the strategic level, too." Britain could pluck at the periphery of Napoleonic Europe but she could not roll back Napoleon's forces alone. This asymmetric situation on land, therefore, compelled Britain to adopt a Fabian strategy against the French Army in Spain. Wellington's methods in the Peninsular War were uncannily similar to the methods that Nathanial Greene had employed in the Carolinas against the British during the American Revolution. Wellington recognized Napoleon's superiority too well to risk a decisive battle, so he indirectly used "pin-prick" attacks in order to induce the French to concentrate against him while the Spanish guerrillas consolidated control over the Spanish countryside, attacking French outposts and lines of communication.[70]

In the Peninsular War, Britain's most significant impact was in aggravating the Spanish insurgency against French occupation and encouraging the source of it. "Rarely has she caused a greater distraction to her opponents at the price of so small a military effort." The presence of the British Expeditionary Force (BEF) facilitated success but Wellington's battles were materially the least effective part of his operations. The overwhelming majority of French losses were as a result of Spanish guerrilla operations. Wellington was successful in harrying the French and making the countryside a desert where the French forces could not sustain themselves. He fought very few battles during the five years of campaigning on the peninsula. The initial purpose of the BEF, in other words, was for 26,000 British soldiers to distract 100,000 French soldiers from the main theater of war in Austria. "Wellington's greatest influence came through his threats rather than his blows. For, whenever, he threatened a point, the French were forced to draw off troops thither, and thus give the guerrillas greater scope in other districts." For example, in 1810 the French had 350,000 troops deployed in Spain but could only use 90,000 of them to attempt invading Portugal because the rest had to be used for counterinsurgency and to guard their lines of communications (LOC). Wellington's force, by 1810, comprised 50,000 troops.[71]

Although the French forces were far superior in numbers, they were unable to concentrate against Wellington's combined Anglo-Portuguese force because Spanish guerrillas compelled the French to disperse in order to protect their vulnerable LOC. Logistics was also a problem for Napoleon's forces—they were accustomed to living off the land but Spain was too poor to support any large foraging army. The Royal Navy, on the other hand, supplied Wellington's forces. The Iberian Peninsular represented a theater ideally suited to Britain's naval supremacy and small army—it was surrounded by water on three sides and the Navy both convoyed ships to supply the BEF and prevented the French from moving men and supplies around the coast.[72] David French sums up the Peninsular War cogently:

The Peninsula gave the British one of the best opportunities they ever had to exploit their sea power. The navy prevented the French from moving men and supplies around the coast and compelled them to use roads which were subject to attacks from Spanish guerrillas. The guerrillas made possible Wellington's survival by supplying him with much valuable intelligence and preventing the French from concentrating their superior numbers and crushing his field army.[73]

Wellington's campaign on the peninsula, by the end of 1812, had liberated Portugal and southern Spain, prevented Napoleon from using 29 ships of the line sealed in Cadiz harbor, and compelled Napoleon to divert a large part of his army to wage a fruitless war of attrition.[74] Substitute Wellington for Fabius and Marshall Massena for Hannibal in the following excerpt from Liddell Hart's *Strategy* and the analogy becomes uncanny: "Hovering in the enemy's neighborhood, cutting off stragglers and foraging parties, preventing them from gaining any permanent base, Fabius remained an elusive shadow on the horizon, dimming the glamour of Hannibal's triumphal progress."[75]

However, the circumstances created by Wellington's success on the Peninsula and subsequent victory at Waterloo "profoundly affected the development of the

British Army, both positively and negatively, for much of the nineteenth century." Because Britain's hegemony was to remain unchallenged for almost four
decades of peace in Europe, the Army was marginalized, compared to the Royal
Navy, as an instrument of foreign policy. Its preparedness to fight a large-scale
land war deteriorated and it commanded little public attention. The improbability of foreign invasion even diminished the Army's importance as an instrument
of home defense. Faced with an economizing parliament and an indifferent public, the British Army was left to run itself with minimal interference. This, Peter
Burroughs explains, had deleterious consequences: "Here the collective memory
of victory over the French exerted a detrimental influence, since it strengthened
and legitimized the forces of habit and torpor so ingrained in the operations and
ethos of an authoritarian, hierarchical institution." What's more, Burroughs argues, complacency and traditionalism were not subjected to the test of battle until the Crimean War because in the many small wars of the period, "British
numbers, discipline, and firepower were usually sufficient to secure comforting
victories."[76]

During the 18th century, moreover, fighting in the colonies was not peripheral
to Britain's war efforts in Europe but central to them. Colonial operations were
not separable from European war because Britain's opponents outside Europe
were not indigenous peoples but rival imperial powers: in 1739 Britain fought
Spain for control of the West Indies; the Seven Years War saw Britain fighting
France for control of North America and India; and Britain's break with the
American colonists lured France into a renewed struggle with Britain for maritime control of the Atlantic. In the 19th century, the pattern changed as no serious European challenge to Britain's colonial hegemony emerged until the 1880s.
The British Army then fought its 19th century battles against the native populations of Britain's Asian and African possessions. The British Army's central role
during the 19th century was to "ensure security, stability, and consolidation of
empire."[77]

The British Army's 19th century experience of colonial wars had a significant
influence on the British military strategic culture as it evolved into the 20th century. The British way in war as embodied in the campaigns of the three Victorian
heroes, Roberts, Wolseley, and Kitchener, reflected essentially all the British
people knew of war. "It was in fact a highly specialized form, which contrasted
sharply with war as fought between great industrial powers." The British approach
emphasized small scale instead of large scale, the soldier rather than the system,
and small casualties and easy victories instead of prolonged fighting and heavy
losses. But small wars against savages really could not test an army, as evidenced
by the British Army's problems in the Boer Wars and its experiences in the world
wars. These colonial victories created a dangerous perception in Britain, that wars
were "distant and exotic adventure stories, cheaply won by the parade- ground
discipline of the British line."[78]

According to Eliot Cohen, "one reason for the success of British small wars has
been Britain's development of a military manpower system uniquely suited to

such conflicts." In the early 19th century, British statesmen created a regimental system that was quasi-tribal in which officers and enlisted men served together over extended periods of time, rotating between overseas and home assignments. Moreover, the regimental system provided an "emotional substitute" for the sense of public approval relied on by the U.S. military. Another reason for the success of the British Army in small wars, Cohen explains, has been Britain's "near-exclusive reliance on volunteer professional soldiers rather than draftees or reservists." Cohen maintains that regular soldiers are more adept at the challenging types of operations that inhere in small wars. What's more, the use of volunteer professionals to fight low intensity but protracted conflicts mitigates domestic political constraints since they are not unwilling participants.[79]

Hew Strachan explains that in the 20th century it was also Britain's empire, and not Europe, that had been the more continuous element in soldiers' experiences. The years between the world wars reinforced the idea that war on the continent was an aberration rather than a norm. In the interwar years, the British Army was conducting imperial policing from Palestine to the northwest frontier of India. Although Strachan points out that the theory of war since 1945 has been Eurocentric, the practice of war has not: counterinsurgency in the 1950s and colonial withdrawal in the 1960s shaped the careers of senior British Army officers who were still serving in the 1980s. "Even as the 20th century draws to its close," Strachan argues, "Britain's recent military experience has more in common with its colonial past than with the Army's declared commitment to Europe." The persistent low-intensity conflict in Northern Ireland was viewed as the last stage of imperial withdrawal. In addition, the Falklands Islands War in 1982 was also limited in scope as far as geography and means were concerned.[80]

The British Army in 1918 as well as 1945 was able to resume its role in imperial policing. It was also significant that after 1918, the British political and military establishment was determined to never again sacrifice the British Army in a continental role. The imperial style in which the Army had been cast before 1914 had been modified and not transformed by Haldane's creation of a European expeditionary force and the concept of depending on territorial as well as regular Army reserves to support it. In 1939, the rapidly assembled BEF deployed to France less well equipped, armed, and trained in every way. Moreover, the memories of World War I casualties, coupled with an emphasis on imperial policing between the wars, ensured that the British commanders of World War II were required to husband their manpower. According to one scholar, the imperial perspective of and a need to avoid high casualties led Churchill to prefer any peripheral and indirect (Fabian) approach to a direct European one.[81]

By the end of the World War II, large numbers of British soldiers and colonial policemen had equal familiarity with the actual conduct of guerrilla warfare. Many of the techniques involved in a politico-military insurgency, particularly of guerrilla warfare, were merely adaptations of traditional rebel tactics against which the British had often fought in their imperial past. In addition to its experience in this area, "the British advantage laid in a tradition of flexibility, based upon the fact that throughout the colonial policing campaigns of the past they had been forced to make do with only limited resources." "Global responsibilities had spread a relatively small volunteer army thinly on the ground and precluded the maintenance of a strategic reserve, while financial parsimony had made the soldiers aware of a need to husband their supplies of ammunition and equipment." Therefore, once the British were confronted with a revolt, they were more likely to take a low profile response, using their armed forces sparingly and searching for solutions that did not necessitate large expenditures of men or materiel. Moreover, "the wide range of threats to imperial rule and the different geographical conditions encountered, produced a constant need to adapt responses to fit local circumstances and avoided the development of a stereotyped theory of policing."[82]

Thus by 1945, as the British faced a host of threats to their rule or influence, they already possessed three important characteristics for low intensity conflict: experience, appropriate military skill, and flexibility. The British Army during this period never compiled an elaborate theory to which it rigidly adhered, but "a series of responses which, when adapted to fit specific conditions, proved successful in maintaining at least a measure of political stability." The pattern of British counterinsurgency was therefore well established, founded upon flexibility and experience and comprising the key components of political primacy, appropriate military response, and isolation of the guerrillas.[83]

The key to the British Army's success in counterinsurgency conflicts was its integrated civil-military approach. Civilian officials remained in control of emergencies and were responsible for the broader political strategy and for propaganda. The British Army operated under civilian control and accepted the requirement of employing minimum force. Moreover, even though a preference for large-scale operations can be discerned in the early phases of its campaigns, the British Army tended to be flexible, adapting to meet local circumstances. The British Army was flexible enough to switch to small-unit operations with decentralized control after it became evident that large-scale sweeps did not succeed. A similar pattern emerged in the subsequent British Army experience in Northern Ireland. According to Colin McInnes, "the civil authorities remained in control; minimum force was generally used; new tactics were constantly developed and tactical control devolved; close relations were established with the police; and finally the Army recognized that it could not resolve the conflict on its own, but that a broader-based political strategy was required.[84]

Thus, the British approached insurgency with the critical assumption that insurgency was not principally a military problem. "If necessary soldiers would be brought in to bolster the police, but the soldiers would always be acting in aid to the civil power and would be bound, like the police themselves, to use only that degree of force" that was essential to restore order, and should never exceed it. "Close cooperation between colonial administrators who implemented reform, police who maintained order, and soldiers who fought the insurgents was essential." According to Thomas Mockaitis, these operations required a degree of decentralization of command and control, "which was further encouraged by the tendency of the insurgents to operate in small, highly mobile bands." Moreover, British success in counterinsurgency is also attributable to a society that had created an Army "ideally suited to counter-insurgency and to cultural attitudes about how that Army might be used." The character of the British Army, Mockaitis contends, also set it up for success in counterinsurgency operations.[85]

Success in countering guerrillas requires the ability to deploy small units on an area basis and to decentralize command and control. However, conventionally minded officers and armies are usually averse to such dispersion because they have been taught to mass and concentrate their forces. The British, though, had a somewhat unconventional army. The British Army's history of imperial policing made internal security the norm and conventional war the exception. Operating with a regimental system also facilitated decentralization: "The British were used to deploying smaller units throughout the empire for extended periods, which enabled these units to mesh with the civil administration and police within an area." What's more, Ian Beckett maintains, Charles Callwell's 1899 *Small Wars: Their Principles and Practice* played a significant role in capturing the lessons learned from the imperial experience of the 19th century. Callwell was able to discern several principles of counterinsurgency; although some became less relevant in the context of 20th century insurgencies, others had lasting relevance for the British Army's role in LIC.[86]

Callwell's extensive use of historical examples as a way of suggesting lessons was also significant since this was also a characteristic of the traditional British approach to the study of counterinsurgency. Charles Gwynn's 1934 *Imperial Policing* followed in the footsteps of Callwell and derived lessons from the revolts in Amritsar in 1919 to Cyprus in 1931 to demonstrate the principles of minimum force, firm action, civilian control, and the integration of civilian and military efforts. After 1945, the British Army faced a new form of insurgency "firmly based on political revolutionary ideology and often eschewing direct military action against security forces for political indoctrination among the population." The fundamental versatility of the traditional British approach assured that what were by then accepted tenets of military subordination, use of local resources, intelligence gathering, and a recognition of the need to divorce active insurgents from their local supporters were very adaptable to unique conditions and generally effective in maintaining at least a modicum of political stability, even against the pressure of fervid nationalism or communist revolutionary challenges.[87]

The British Army fought its post–World War II campaigns in predominantly rural conditions, varying from jungle conditions (Malaya, Kenya, Borneo, Guyana, Dhofar) to desert conditions (Palestine, Muscat and Oman, Radfan, Kuwait). The most salient common characteristic of these campaigns was how successful the British Army was in conducting small-scale and medium-scale operations. The British Army helped bring about favorable political outcomes for Britain. In almost every case of devolution, the newly independent states allowed the British Army to retain facilities in their countries. According to Michael Dewar, the British were successful in small wars because they were willing to fight like their indigenous adversaries. For example, in Malaya and Borneo, the British Army fought the guerrillas not with air power and artillery but by inserting small patrols that operated like the insurgents. The Army used stealth and cunning and on the few instances when bombers or artillery were employed they were remarkably unsuccessful.[88]

What's more, in assessing British Army attitudes in the post–World War II period, Correlli Barnett observed that the British Army's social structure, its values, and its way of life survived the years 1939-1960 with surprisingly little change. The British officer corps was still dominated by the "gentleman." It remained essentially a working-class Army officered by the upper classes. The continued power of regimental loyalties signified that the British Army had survived the social revolutions of the mid-20th century with its traditions in tact. The counter-guerrilla struggle in Malaya lasted from 1948 to 1960 and "it ended with the only victory won by a Western power against practitioners of revolutionary warfare." The British fought this war like their guerrilla opponents, with limited resources, and adapting themselves to living and fighting deep in the jungle for long periods and with minimum supplies. They outfought and outsmarted the Communist insurgents at their own game of camping, ambush, and jungle tracking. Notably, the insurgents' ability to live off the local population was undermined by resettling villagers in model villages under government protection. In fact, in all the operations during the British retreat from empire, the Army's techniques of riot control avoided unnecessary shooting and the systematic brutality that characterized the experiences of other armies in similar situations.[89]

The British Army's campaign in Malaya was in many ways the archetypal counterinsurgency campaign, although it took several years to adopt a good counterinsurgency strategy and 12 years total to ultimately defeat the guerrillas. Although regular troops, aircraft, and sophisticated equipment played no small part in defeating the insurgents, the British could not have achieved success without the support of the indigenous population—the Federal Army, the Home Guard, the Police Force, the Malayan Chinese Special Branch, and a preponderance of the civilian population. Military measures, Emergency Regulations, and winning hearts and minds together defeated the Communist insurgents. The British defeated the guerrillas in Malaya because the British Army was willing to beat them at their own game. All in all, in Malaya the British Army lost 509 soldiers and the insurgents lost 6,710 of its 12,000 members killed.[90]

Notwithstanding the Korean War and the Falklands, almost all the campaigns the British Army fought during the Cold War were counterinsurgency in character. "Of all the former colonial powers, the British experience in counter-insurgency is probably the richest." The British Army's experiences in small wars had been gained over a long period when the Empire was established, maintained, and devolved. According to one scholar of British Army history, however, even the strategic focus on Europe after 1967 and the shift to a maneuver-oriented doctrine in the 1980s did not detract from the British Army's cultural affinity for operations other than war. Dr. John Stone maintains that the Northern Ireland commitment pulled manpower toward the imperial policing mission, with tankers and artillery-men functioning as infantry since there was nobody to take their places.[91]

In August 1969, the British Army was called in to give military aid to the civil power in Northern Ireland. The troops' initial task was to protect the Catholics in Londonderry. However, after the Provisional IRA split from the IRA, it aimed to kill as many British troops as possible in order to influence British public opinion to force the British government to pull its troops out. The Provisional IRA adopted tactics that were a mixture of terror and guerrilla warfare. They were so successful that the traditional IRA decided to join the shooting and ambushed an Army patrol in May 1971. However, in spite of recent counterinsurgency experiences in Kenya, Malaya, Cyprus, and Aden, the British Army was unsure of an approach. It initially alienated most of the Catholic community with its policy of internment without trial and bad intelligence—imprisoning the wrong people. This went from bad to worse, however, when on a day early in 1972, which came to be known as "Bloody Sunday," the Parachute Regiment killed 13 men and wounded 13 others. In March 1972, the British dissolved the Ulster Parliament and implemented direct rule from Westminster. The British Army was subsequently compelled to recon-sider its intelligence methods and training—Frank Kitson reexamined and revised tactics and improved training facilities. After 1975 the British Army successfully contained the Troubles by improving its tactics and making its intelligence opera-tions more sophisticated. Moreover, the Army was employed to support civil po-lice efforts, which remained primary. This was a Corporal's War, with great responsibility place on young NCOs. As a result of Northern Ireland, the British Army has unique experience in urban patrolling, covert surveillance, and bomb disposal. Until 1995, the commitment to Northern Ireland occupied about 18,500 British soldiers, of which 11,500 were regulars and 6,000 comprised the Ulster Defense Regiment.[92]

Colin McInnes asserts that British military culture "would suggest certain conti-nuities in underlying approach between colonial insurgency and Northern Ireland because of deep-seated beliefs and attitudes held by the Army as a result of its histor-ical experiences, despite the different pressures unique to the Army's role in the province." Gavin Bulloch and Thomas Mockaitis also support this assertion. Ac-cording to Bulloch, "the experience of numerous small wars has provided the British Army with a unique insight into this demanding form [counterinsurgency] of con-flict." Mockaitis adds: "although the hey day of British counter-insurgency ended with the Malayan Emergency in the 1960s, the examples of Oman and Northern Ire-land suggest that the principles upon which it is based are as valuable today as they were 30 years ago." Succinctly stated, the British principles for counterinsurgency are: (1) minimum force; (2) civil and military cooperation to win support of the pop-ulation; and (3) decentralization of command and control, which is nurtured by the regimental system and creates initiative in junior leaders.[93]

Hew Strachan sustains this notion of continuity and maintains that the low in-tensity function of the British Army remained central even after the Healey deci-sion to withdraw the British military from east of Suez. According to Strachan, even though this decision was thought to have settled the dilemma between Europe and empire in favor of the continent, colonial legacies remained. Institutions of the British Army have been shaped far more by colonial continuities than by the intense but infrequent periods of continental warfare. Moreover, the periods between major European wars have not been characterized by peace, but by continuous fighting in imperial wars in the 1840s, 1890s, 1920s, 1950s, and 1970s. John Strawson also emphasizes the influence of Northern Ireland in perpetuating the British Army's experiences and attitudes about low intensity conflict: "Despite subsequent distractions like the Falklands Islands and the Gulf, we should not underestimate the profound influence of Ulster on soldiers' lives." This apparently endless commitment called much of the tune. According to Strawson, this commitment conditioned training, movement, deployment, logistics, and morale. It shapes the soldier's life.[94]

In sum, "only the British have enjoyed notable success in counter-insurgency." Against the Communist insurgents in Malaya, the Mau Mau in Kenya, and the EOKA nationalist insurgents in Cyprus, the British Army successfully defeated indigenous movements. What's more, the British Army was involved in two post-imperial campaigns: from 1970 to 1975, British soldiers advised the Sultan of Oman's armed forces against Dhofari nationalists; and it conducted internal security operations in Northern Ireland from 1969 to 1995. The lessons derived from the British Army's earlier campaigns helped influence its response to these more recent insurgencies. According to Mockaitis, Frank Kitson successfully applied insights he gained during the Mau Mau emergency in Kenya to Belfast in the early 1970s where he commanded British troops. Although much of the official British doctrine was not formulated until the last quarter of the 20th century, it built on experience gained doing imperial policing in the Middle East, India, and Ireland during the first three quarters of the century.[95]

MARGINALIZED (PERIPHERAL) FUNCTIONAL ROLES

Anti-tribal warfare and population control required small, lightly equipped units operating over large areas in relative isolation from one another. These missions exposed many men to hostile fire and helped develop bravery and individual fighting skills. They fostered, however, neither the ability to handle large formations nor the development of the heavier equipment, especially the artillery, needed for European warfare.[96]

Britain's military experience during the 19th and 20th centuries was not predominantly European. In only 35 years of the 200-plus years since 1792 has Britain fought continental forces—in the Napoleonic Wars, in the Crimea, and in the two world wars. And yet in almost none of the intervening periods have British soldiers not been engaged in operations and not suffered casualties. Britain's historic practice has been colonial and imperial. The organizational culture of the British Army thus reflects its experience—sound and successful integration of civil and military policy in colonial policing—and this experience has been essentially extra-European. During its Malay campaign, British Army leaders "shared a common conception that the essence of the organization included colonial policing and administration." When a conventional approach failed, the British Army was able to create an organizational consensus that change was needed: political solutions, in addition to purely military ones, were within its reach. One scholar on British Army culture elucidates: "an innovative and varied past created a culture amenable to the changes required to defeat a complex opponent in a new kind of war."[97]

Even so, the culture and organization that made the British Army amenable to changes required to successfully counter insurgencies or control internal unrest also made it very difficult for the British Army to prepare, innovate, and successfully conduct symmetric/conventional wars in Europe. The conventional wars that the British fought against continental powers—the Napoleonic, Crimean, and World Wars—testify to a mediocre record in this operational milieu. Although the British Army was ultimately victorious in all of these wars, it embarked on each one unprepared in size, doctrine, or mindset. Even during the Napoleonic Wars, the British Army found itself on the inferior side of an asymmetric relationship and was therefore compelled to use an unorthodox (indirect) approach to gain a foothold on the Peninsula, combining a Fabian conventional strategy with guerrillas to disperse and overextend the French. Moreover, the Crimean War and World War I underscore the problems the British Army faced when operating outside of its principal imperial defense role. The British Army, in size, organization, and doctrine, certainly was not prepared for conventional war against Germany in 1940. The history of the British Army's thus reveals a culture whose attitudes, experiences, and preferences see major wars as the exception, or aberration, and LIC as the norm.

Between 1815 and 1914, imperial policing dominated the British experience and the Crimean War was the only instance of major war against a continental power. David French offers a germane observation of the British Army's experience there: "The Crimean War was an aberrant experience for the Victorian armed forces. They were not designed to fight a first-class European power on the Continent."[98]

At the end of the 19th century, moreover, the British Army fought colonial wars against the Boers, a quasi-European power using guerrilla tactics, and very nearly lost. "In 1899 the British expected a short, cheap and victorious conflict." But the British Army began the war without a strategy and its operations were hampered by an inadequate number of trained staff officers. The Boer Wars demonstrated that the Cardwell system could not supply the manpower needed to wage even a large colonial war.[99]

The British Army was believed to be in top-notch shape in 1899. However, it was organized to fight small colonial wars throughout the Empire, not to fight a major war. Its last major war against an adversary of comparable power had been the Crimean War, which, although ultimately successful, was somewhat of a fiasco for the British Army. Moreover, campaigns that had been fought since the Crimean War had not required the mobilization of large formations for any one region; rather, small garrisons were deployed throughout British territories. When the Boer War broke out in 1899, the British Army considered itself to be more than a match for a bunch of farmers. After all, it had conducted more than 30 successful campaigns against a variety of rebellions in Egypt and throughout the Empire. Whatever the British thought of the Boer Army, it had been carefully designed for the conditions of South Africa. The Boers had an efficient mechanism for mobilizing their citizen army in which all able-bodied men between 16 and 60 had to be available for military service. Boer training was so good in fact that the British Army was as surprised by Boer marksmanship as by the Boers' speedy movement into seemingly inaccessible positions.[100]

During the Boer War, it required 400,000 British troops to defeat about 70,000 Boer soldiers, without reserves. Boer tactics were developed to prevent casualties and they preferred the ambush to other methods. The Boers also carefully studied the terrain upon which they would fight, marking it for range. A typical Boer engagement technique was to lie in wait on a hill under cover of large stones and initiating fire with smokeless powder that did not reveal their positions. If the Boer position was threatened, the Boers would run to their ponies behind the hill and withdraw out of range. The British Army in South Africa became painfully aware of the cunning and skill of the Boer fighters during its first major operation in December 1899. During what became known as "Black Week," the Boers defeated the British Army in three separate engagements resulting in British losses of 3,700 men and 12 Royal Artillery guns. These losses were partially the result of underestimating Boer capabilities: one column blindly marched into an ambush because its commander didn't deem it necessary to use cavalry as forward security against the Boers; another commander launched a night attack without conducting reconnaissance and fell into a Boer trap; the third element attacked entrenched Boers across open ground.[101]

However, even after the creation of a general staff and the Haldane reforms, at the beginning a World War I the British Army was not capable of fighting a major war on the continent. "Doctrinally, the British Army before 1914 was poorly prepared, as its major experience of war since the Crimea had been colonial wars, of which the latest was in South Africa." After the Boer Wars, the infantry improved its shooting skills and field craft, but new doctrine did not emerge. "Indeed, there was no institution through which the Army could engage in serious thinking about war before 1914, and army manuals were often written by poorly prepared staff—thus one officer before 1914 found himself writing three manuals at once: one on infantry training, the songbook of the British Army, and the handbook of the 4.5-inch gun!" Leadership and staff work above the regimental level were also inadequate.[102] Although the British Army improved its performance from 1914 to 1918 and subsequently played a major role in winning the war, "there was a yawning chasm between Britain's chosen strategy and her actual military organization or long-term planning." According to Peter Simkins, even though the BEF was committed to fight in a continental war, the implications of that commitment had not been thoroughly considered and no plan existed for raising a mass army or expanding ammunition production.[103]

Harold Winton offers a cogent explanation of the obstacles to preparing the British Army for World War II: "units organized primarily for imperial defense were simply no longer suitable for the demands of modern war on the Continent." In the context of preparing for conventional war in the 1930s, for example, Winton identifies military conservatism, social and political indifference, and the imperial defense mission as principal obstacles to mechanization and armored warfare. However, Winton argues, "the imperial defense mission was the single most significant impediment to the development of armored formations." This is because armored formations were of little utility to an Army whose primary mission was to garrison and police the empire. As a result, the British Army entered World War II significantly under prepared, vis-à-vis the Wehrmacht.[104]

The British approach to World War II, consequently, was an admixture of political, economic, and military factors, of caution stemming from the exorbitant casualties of World War I, and of the Prime Minister's strategic preferences.[105] Maurice Matloff sums up the British viewpoint:

The British concept of how to defeat Germany early became apparent. Essentially, they proposed relying on blockade, bombing, subversive activities, and propaganda to weaken the will and ability of Germany to resist. The emphasis would be on mobile, hard-hitting armored forces operating on the periphery of German-controlled territory rather than on large-scale ground action in confrontation with the full power of the German military machine. No vast armies of infantry as in the First World War would be needed. This whole approach was in accord with The Churchillian theory of waging war on the Continent with a peripheral strategy, a concept he had developed after the searing British experience between 1914 and 1918.[106]

Thus, acutely sensitive to the losses of World War I, the Britain relied on its navy and air force, adopting a peripheral (indirect/Fabian) strategy to hit Germany on the fringes of the Continent and to slowly dissipate Germany's strength. Its strategy also called for the support of the occupied countries through arms and subversion. Liddell Hart, in fact, traces the growth of subversion and partisan warfare to the deep impression that T. E. Lawrence had made on Churchill. After Dunkirk, Churchill employed guerrilla warfare as a counterweapon. Essentially, the British had to adopt this indirect approach out of exigency: "it was tailored to suit scattered interests, a small-scale economy, and limited manpower for ground armies."[107]

Likewise, the Korean War saw the British Army's imperial defense culture influence it approach to major war. According to Colin McInnes, Korea reaffirmed five themes that characterize the British Army's approach to conventional war. Those themes were: "that it lacked a formal doctrine for war; that the regimental system promoted a strong esprit de corps but was poorly suited to large unit operations and combined arms cooperation; that the Army focused on the tactical level of war; that it preferred attritional set-piece battles to maneuver warfare; and that it invariably fought wars as part of a coalition, often working well at the political and strategic levels, but perhaps less well at the military-operational level." While the regimental system helped sustain British Army morale during the winter of 1950, the disadvantages of the regimental system were also evident, with operations conducted as a series of battalion or brigade-sized actions instead of one coherent division or corps concept of operation. What's more, the British Army had difficulty finding the forces for Korea and was not prepared for war.[108]

Three decades later, the British Army of the 1980s was still not a product of sustained, rational planning. Rather it was developed in a "higgeldy-piggeldy fashion often in reaction to, rather than in anticipation of, the wars it had been called on to fight."[109] For the British Army, the Persian Gulf War was the first occasion since World War II that it had employed an armored division in battle and it was the first time that the ideas of maneuver warfare that had been developed in the 1980s were put into practice. In fact, it is one of the few examples of the British Army being involved in a high intensity war since 1945, and the only example of an entire British armored division being used in battle after the Second World War. During the post–World War II period, the scope of the British involvement in the Persian Gulf War was matched only by Suez.[110]

SELF-CONCEPT ABOUT USING FORCE

Since at least 1945, the basic principle of minimum force has underpinned the British Army's approach to operations short of war. In 1961 the situation in Georgetown, Guyana did not escalate because the British troops did not overreact. In 1967 in Aden General Tower did not re-occupy Crater right away because it would have required significant force, probably including 76mm armored car guns. In Londonderry and Belfast, Northern Ireland, the British Army did not immediately storm the "No-Go" areas because it would have required maximum force. Moreover, the Yellow Card (rules of engagement) limitations imposed on British soldiers in Northern Ireland laid down very strict conditions for when a soldier was authorized to use deadly force.[111]

Initially, the principle of minimum force did not apply to insurgency but to all situations up to and including riots. However, in the aftermath of the Indian massacre at Amritsar in 1919, this principle was also applied to most forms of internal unrest except those types of antiguerrilla operations that approximated conventional combat. According to Mockaitis, the Hunter Committee, which investigated the Amritsar massacre in 1919, discovered what the United States discovered a half-century later in Vietnam: "The employment of excessive measures is as likely as not to produce the opposite result to that desired." Restraint, or circumspect selectivity on when to use force, is essential to succeed in counterinsurgency operations because they require security forces to hit the insurgents without harming the population at large. "Amritsar profoundly affected the attitude of British officers toward internal conflict and encouraged a steady evolution of the principle of minimum force to include every form of disturbance from riot to revolution."[112]

In fact, a quick recapitulation of the Amritsar incident helps illuminate why it was so central in embedding the minimum-force principle in British Army culture. In April 1919, Brigadier General Dyer ordered his men to open fire on a crowded assembly in the Jallianwala Bagh in Amritsar. Within ten minutes the soldiers expended 1,650 rounds, killing 379 and wounding over 1,200. Dyer did not have a martial-law imprimatur when he acted but he did have the authorization of the deputy commissioner of Amritsar to use force "if necessary." The official inquiry into this massacre had limited the military's responsibility in cases of civil disorder and found that Dyer had violated the principle of minimum force. As a result, the interwar Army came to embrace the notion that military force was only to be used as an instrument of discrimination and restraint. Sir Charles Gwynn's *Imperial Policing*, published between the wars, also argued that minimum force was a *sine qua non* of counterinsurgency operations. Moreover, the British Army's experience in Ireland in 1919–1921 and Palestine in 1946, wherein it focused more singularly on military measures and where it used greater force, proved unsuccessful. "It had seen the situation in military terms: in looking for an enemy it had gone some way toward creating one."[113]

Consequently, minimum force became a central principle in the British approach to intrastate conflicts, to include peace operations. Until the events at Amritsar in 1919, the principle of minimum force was applicable only if the uprising was still under the control of the civil authorities. Until Amritsar, if the civil authorities had handed the situation over to the military, the principle of minimum force was no longer necessary. However, after Amritsar, the principle of minimum force was codified in the Manual of Military Law and remained embedded in the British approach to intrastate emergencies. This principle was also clearly manifest in Malaya where the British response to the Communist insurgency reflected its colonial traditions: "tight integration of civilian and military authority, minimum force with police instead of army used when possible" and a predilection for the use of "small, highly skilled troops in well-planned operations rather than [the] massive use of large numbers and heavy firepower."[114]

TECHNOLOGY AND CASUALTIES

The military establishment is marked by the same cultural lag and the same reluctance to adopt new technological innovations as is industrial enterprise. But the cultural lag of the military has had more dramatically disastrous effects, since the consequences of warfare are quick and deadly.[115]

Technology is treated as exogenous to this study's concept of military strategic culture, but its development and evolution is something that both the British and Americans have had to respond to and harness according to their cultural preferences. In fact, it was naval technology that helped Britain create and sustain Pax Britannica. It was also naval technological developments that precipitated the decline of British naval supremacy in the second half of the 19th century. Consequently, advances in naval technology finally eliminated Britain's virtually free security afforded by insularity. Again, it was technology that Britain turned to try to maintain the last vestiges of great power status. Whether it was the steam-propelled naval ship, the tank, or the nuclear missile, British military strategic culture harnessed it or failed to harness it in consonance with its preferences for the employment of force. In other words, according to Hew Strachan, while geography has been a key determinant in British military policy, technology has been strategically neutral. Technology has not undermined Britain's relationship between geography and strategy as much is sometimes imagined. In fact, Strachan, argues, technology has been more of an asset than a hindrance, facilitating rapid air and sea deployment and allowing Britain to quickly concentrate troops for home defense.[116]

Michael Dewar asserts that it was a lack of high technology that helps account for some of the British successes in counterinsurgency. "In both Malaya and Borneo and indeed in the Radfhan and Dhofar it was usually the shortage of helicopters that forced commanders to seek an option more suited to the terrain rather than go for the easy solution of insertion by helicopter." The British Army has achieved a significant degree of success in operations other than war because of limited resources and, concomitantly, a more limited reliance on massive technological superiority. By employing small units and small unit tactics without a significant amount of air or artillery support, the British seemed to meet with success more often than the Americans who tended to do the obverse in their operations other than war.[117]

Moreover, advances in naval technology and then air force technology impelled Britain's strategic focus toward the continent as they both helped undermine Britain's natural strategic advantage, thereby making stability on the continent more germane to British security. A trade-off for rejecting conscription and maintaining a small Army has been the reliance on advanced technology as a substitute. Britain relied on the Dreadnought at the beginning of the 20th century, the bomber in the 1930s and 1940s, and nuclear missiles since 1957 to support her twofold pursuit of colonial and maritime roles while retaining the façade of relevance as a great power. "Such weapons specifically targeted the enemy's civilian population, even if indirectly through blockade." However, the effectiveness of targeting civilian populations is refutable. The contributions to victory of the Dreadnought during World War I and the bomber during World War II have been controversial. What's more, the acquisition of high technology during periods of peace has meant that Britain has had to tax more heavily.[118]

During the Korean War, British troops were clearly under-equipped, particularly by U.S. standards. British equipment tended to be inferior to American: the British 25-pounder gun was not as good as the American 105mm, for example.[119] In addition, during the Persian Gulf War, the British Army's equipment and logistics support came in a poor second to that of the U.S. capabilities. However, whereas the U.S. Army emphasized materiel supremacy, the British Army seems to have struck more of a balance between the importance of men and materiel. This is not to say that equipment is unimportant to the British Army; rather it is to say that the Army's historical experience has led it to develop an approach to war that emphasizes more of a balance between human and materiel factors.[120]

On the other hand, the British elites, public, and military seem not to be averse to casualties during operations not in defense of vital interests. The British experience in Northern Ireland had the most immediate influence on the casualty issue—the British public was more conditioned to casualties as a consequence of a thirty-year commitment that resulted in over 2000 casualties. However, the British perspective on casualties stems from a long history of neglect and lack of visibility of the Army. A former British officer used the ageless aphorism—"when you take the King's shilling, you accept the consequences"—to help explain the casualty question. This expression dates back to the 17th century and the new model Army—it refers to the method by which the dredges of British society were recruited (impressed into the army). Recruiters would scour the bars to find potential soldiers and entice them into signing up by buying them beers. At the bottom of the pint was a shilling—if the citizen drank the beer and took the shilling, he accepted the consequences of being a soldier in the British Army.[121]

Almost two centuries of colonial policing ensured that the British Army continued to be deployed to far-flung locations from which casualties were not very visible to the British public. What's more, a British officer with five tours in Northern Ireland, explained that "we never adopted the view that we needed to minimize casualties." While all good generals seek to minimize casualties, the British Army and public does not seem to get to worked up over them. Moreover, the Ministry of Defense did not even keep an accurate tally of killed and wounded British soldiers over the 30 years it spent conducting operations in Northern Ireland. However, most officers and academics cite over 2000 casualties of which over 600 were killed—about a battalion's worth. Richard Connaughton also pointed out that the British Army only had one casualty-free year between the end of World War II and the end of the Cold War.[122]

DEFINING AND CENTRAL ORGANIZATION

"The key to understanding the Army's culture is the regimental system. The Army still makes the regiment the focus of emotional attachment and individual loyalty. For them [senior British officers] the regimental system represents a cluster of attitudes rather than a specific structure."[123] In addition to geographic and historical factors, the structure and values of the Army also contribute to British military strategic culture. The most salient of the British Army's organizational features is the regimental system. The Army's separate regiments engender two cultural values—respect for tradition and particularism. These values, moreover, derive from the value that the British place on continuity and from the relative stability of British society. The infantry and cavalry regiments trace their lineage way back to their origins and seek to maintain an esprit particular to that heritage. As Winton elucidates, "the inculcation of regimental histories, the wearing of distinctive uniforms, the formation of regimental associations, and the appointment of regimental colonels commandant made the individual feel much more part of his regiment than the Army at large." Although difficult to prove, British soldiers justify the centrality of the regiment with the proposition that loyalty to the regimental family makes British soldiers continue to perform effectively under duress when otherwise they would not. On the other hand, the family spirit embodied by the regiment is not conducive to military innovation. "The regimental system tends to perpetuate established procedures, narrow men's outlooks, and, most significantly, complicate organizational change."[124]

Yardley and Sewell most succinctly, yet comprehensively, explain the nature of the British regimental system. Individual soldiers identify with the regiment as their clan or tribe. The regiment is associated with one special role instead of being an integrated combined arms unit. Regiments generally have an affiliation with a particular region in the United Kingdom and one or more Territorial Army (TA) units may share their regimental identity. There is a body of sacred history, a host of sacred possessions, a special dress code, and a rigid hierarchy wherein individuals clearly know their place. The origins of this hierarchy are considered feudal, with the social organization and regimental practices and traditions generally reflecting those of old England. The royal link is sustained and regiments have developed very arcane customs. In fact, Yardley and Sewell explain that it was during the period between 1870 and 1914 that the regiment as apotheosis, as this century knows it, was realized. "Sadly, it was also the same period in which Britain's transition from a rural county-based society to an urban, technological society was completed, and in which the nature of warfare changed as small colonial conflicts gave way to clashes on a titanic scale."[125]

The regimental system is a significant component of British military strategic culture and it was certainly a variable in influencing the Army's ability, or inability, to meet its bifurcated strategic demands. The regimental system can help account for the absence of militarism in England. Strachan defines militarism two ways: the Army's intervention in civilian politics or a veneration of the military beyond the exigencies of warfare. Partly as a result of continual overseas service, Britain has had a professional regular Army that has remained separated from civilian society. Moreover, since loyalties in the British Army are alleged first to the regiment rather than the Army at large, the Army has tended not to act a unified front in a political context. In other words, loyalties that lie first and foremost to individual regiments have essentially precluded the Army from acting as one voice, and as a result, have made it in some ways less threatening, and more responsive, to civilian leadership. Loyalty to regiment is inculcated from the very beginning of an officer's career when the individual regiment is a powerful influence in molding an officer, helping him make the transition from civilian to military life and from school house to profession. "Through the regiment's mess, through it distinctive traditions, through its paternalism, the officer's loyalty is directed towards" the regiment as an institution rather than the British Army.[126]

World War I as a harbinger of massive industrialized warfare between divisions, corps, and armies, should have for all intents and purposes been the death knell of the regimental system. World War I made it clear that the Cardwell system was not successful in balancing British Army resources and training between Britain's dual strategic requirements of imperial policing and countering continental powers aspiring to hegemony. However, World War I buttressed the centrality of the regiment in two emotional ways. When the British Army expanded from its 161 regular infantry battalions extant in 1914 to it wartime peak of 1,750 battalions, the new battalions were attached to existing regiments. Therefore, virtually every family in the country was related to someone who had served with an infantry battalion associated with a regiment, with its history, tradition, and distinctive cap badges. The result of adding a hugely increased number of battalions without increasing the number of existing regiments was to propagate the regimental spirit from the old British Army to the widest scope. Secondly, the war more closely linked nationalities to the regiments. The adjutant general's policy of assigning personnel by nationality into nationally affiliated regiments reinforced the national identities of the regiments, and further ensconced the regimental system as a subculture of the British Army. For example, in 1914 Scots comprised 42 percent of the Scot Guards whereas by 1918 Scots comprised 63 percent of that regiment.[127]

Williamson Murray argues that the regimental system stifled both the development of a coherent corpus of doctrine and technological innovation. "The British Army remained tied up within its regiments and separate constituencies of infantry, cavalry, and artillery. Of the three, the cavalry displayed the most resistance to new ideas and technology." In 1927 and 1928, the British Army conducted experimental maneuvers with tanks, and the results were very encouraging for the wider potential for armored warfare. In fact, the experimental armored force achieved huge successes against the traditional cavalry and infantry units. However, Montgomery-Massingberd, the general in charge of the command that sponsored the maneuvers, chose to emphasize how the successes of the armored formations were having a negative impact on the traditional branches. Instead of arguing for the creation of a new armor force, Montgomery-Massingberd argued that motorization should take place throughout the whole Army. His arguments, together with the shortage of resources, deactivated the experimental armored force until 1931. Although maneuvers continued in the 1930s, the tale of British armor development for the decade was a tale of missed opportunities. The chiefs of the imperial general staff in the 1930s tied the development of armor to the traditional cavalry and infantry branches while exhibiting little interest in pursuing the potential of armor. In fact, in the late 1930s the British Army leadership decided not to increase armor forces by expanding the Royal Tank Regiment but to motorize the cavalry instead. In justifying their decision not to increase armored forces, the Chiefs of Staff essentially asserted that it would be an imprudent time to disturb an institution that has valuable traditions.[128]

The fact that the British Army became a servant of the empire during the inter-war period partly justified the reassertion of the regiment—colonial policing again validated the regimental system in the infantry and the cavalry. However, World War II revealed the flaws in the Cardwell regimental system: the needs of the whole army dictated that men were posted to under-strength units notwithstanding regimental links; and a narrow military education as defined by the experiences and expectations of regimental life may have contributed to operational level inep-titude during the North Africa campaigns of 1941–1942. During the Korean War the disadvantages of the regimental system were also evident: the British clearly preferred to operate at brigade and battalion level, and indeed for the first critical months of the war operated as independent brigades. Even when the Common-wealth Division was established, operations tended to be thought of more in terms of a series of brigade or battalion-sized actions rather than the entire division oper-ating under a coherent and unified concept of operation. Also, Williamson Murray asserts that the insularities of the regimental system and its concomitant influence on British Army culture created a parochial anti-intellectualism that impeded an understanding of operations beyond the battalion level and that derided intellec-tual professionalism. [129]

Notwithstanding, in 1957 when Duncan Sandys new defense policy included measures to cut the conventional forces and abolish conscription, the army's se-nior leadership equated the regiments with the essence of the army as a whole and fought to defend it. By making the needs of the army equal to the needs of the regi-ments, these senior officers politicized the regiment. Sir Gerald Templar, Chief of the Imperial General Staff between 1956 and 1958, was a key figure in this fight. Templar himself was shaped by the regimental system and imperial policing—his own regiment, the Royal Irish Fusiliers, had been scheduled to be disbanded in 1921 but was saved by a compromise that enabled it to continue as a single-battal-ion regiment. Sitting out most of World War II due to a serious injury, Templar's reputation was made in Malaya where small units (battalion-size regiments) were most adaptable and best suited for prolonged counterinsurgency operations in the jungle. "As in the nineteenth century and between the wars, the empire gave the single-battalion regiment a tactical and administrative relevance it could not sus-tain in European warfare." What's more, even though the British Army shifted fo-cus toward European war in the 1970s and 1980s, defense of the regimental persisted, as officers who had reached the top of the Army in the 1970s and 1980s had earned their spurs under Templar. [130]

"That Britain possesses not an army but a collection of regiments is a truism which has long outlived the obvious reasons for the system itself." Even by 1990–1991, when the Ministry of Defense released its post–Cold War review, "Options for Change," leaving to the Army the decision on which regiments re-main and which amalgamate, the Army failed to address the broader questions of its shape and size. The Army Board continued to espouse the single-battalion regi-ment even though lessons from NATO and the Persian Gulf War pointed to the de-sirability of thinking in terms of larger formations and of the Army as a whole. Not surprisingly, the then chief of the general staff and his successor were both products of the regimental system (Gurkhas and Green Howards) as was the chief of the United Kingdom Land Forces (Gloucestershire Regiment). One can infer that their regimental loyalties did not predispose them to support a fundamental restructuring that threatened the regiment. The institution's justification for this unusual reversal of priorities was, that "the regiment, by virtue of the fierce loyalties which it generated, was the receptacle of the Army's history and traditions, and was therefore the bedrock of the Army's morale and fighting qualities." Since the end of the Cold War, the combinations of reductions in number of units and troops has driven the British Army to orient contingency planning along the lines of reinforced brigade structures.[131]

Although the 20th century witnessed the advent of mass armies and combined arms formations of divisions and corps, the continued importance of imperial garrisoning to Britain continued to confer a functional validity on the infantry regiment that was disappearing elsewhere. The battalion was an appropriate load for a troop ship, a sensible organization for a colonial outpost, and a reasonable component unit of the relatively smaller sized regimental formations used for imperial policing. What's more the separation of imperial regiments from the home society through overseas service made the regiment more that just a military unit. "It saw itself as an enlarged family, a self-contained community, with its own welfare arrangements, its own recreation and sports." By the end of the 20th century it became the focus of the British Army's political activity. Officers and soldiers were readily enticed into defending their regiments because most of their professional careers were centered on the regiment. They also understood the value of regimental symbols, badges, and uniforms as instruments to rally support from the wider community.[132]

Corroborating the centrality of the regiment to the British Army' culture, another scholar observes that "the much discussed, yet never properly and comprehensively researched regimental system can still be placed at the heart of British military cultures and subcultures." Every officer and soldier held and holds a stake in his regiment, serving and retired. Undoubtedly, according to Mileham, the regimental system saw its heyday between 1871 and 1958. The regimental system's finest moment was in August 1914 when the Kitchener battalions and territorial battalions were provided an instant identity and war-fighting history. Some argue that the regimental system held the British Army together during its most trying period, at a time when it comprised the highest number of citizen soldiers in its history. Without doubt, Mileham explains, the British Army's strength once laid in the regimental system. However, it no longer does because power has shifted to the central institutions like Sandhurst and the Staff College.[133]

CIVIL-MILITARY RELATIONS

In Britain, there was always a fear of the threat to civil liberties that might accompany the presence of a large standing army. The British Army's long-time role in the aid of civil authorities certainly contributed to this fear. The Army acted as a constabulary until the middle of the 19th century and despite its relative small size and frequent deployment overseas, there has always been friction between civilian and soldiers. In addition, the unrepresentative demographic composition that the Army engendered under a mostly voluntary enlistment system also alienated the British Army from society. However, compared to other armies, the British Army has been mostly apolitical—no officer has been dismissed since 1764 for his political views. In another scholarly work, Deborah Avant explains why the patterns of preferences and professionalism developed differently in the British and American armies. In sum, she argues that because, although they are both insular liberal democracies, the British Army professionalized with a large degree of civilian oversight while the U.S. Army professionalized with very little civilian oversight.[134]

The reason for this, Avant argues, is because civil military relations were institutionalized very differently in each country. In Britain, changes in the 19th century centralized control over making policy in the Cabinet. The British Army, then, was responsible basically to one institution and its development converged with civilian preferences. In the United States, on the other hand, the system of checks and balances institutionalized divisions among the civilian leadership. Civilian institutions, therefore, were as occupied with monitoring one another as much as the military. Also, different institutions in the U.S. have different electoral concerns and policy preferences, based on different constituencies. This, and distrust between civilian branches of government in the U.S. influenced the mechanisms the civilians chose to control military organizations and resulted in a more autonomous Army that was less malleable to changes that were inconsistent with its operational code.[135]

As a result, Avant argues, the U.S. Army was better able to pursue its professional and political interests than the disorganized British Army in the 19th century. More specifically, U.S. Army officers were able to embrace the deductive notions of military science (based on the Prussian model) that were popular among military circles because civilian leaders decided to grant the military autonomy over their professional development. However, in Britain civilian leaders closely supervised the professionalization of the military. Military leaders interested in and capable of meeting Britain's diverse security issues were rewarded, and adaptability became a central characteristic of the Army's professionalization. Notwithstanding, professionalism was impeded in the British Army before the 1870s because of the way civilian leaders chose to control the Army. Deborah Avant attributes this to a pattern of political competition that led to the purchase of commissions and to an unstructured education system in the British Army. "Having failed to control the highly organized Army after the English Civil War, Parliament's strategy for controlling the Army was to staff it with leaders representative of Parliament, that is gentlemen of the land." Social class was the principal qualification for officership and military education was not deemed necessary. Since officers identified themselves with their social class and not the Army, this strategy reduced the possibility that the Crown could employ the Army against the Parliament. Parliament's strategies for guaranteeing that the British Army would not act against it, therefore, prevented the Army from developing strong cultural preferences. The outcome was an unprofessionalized Army with very mixed leadership.[136]

Consequently, in 1870 the Cardwell reforms simultaneously centralized all control of military policy within the Cabinet and initiated the professionalization of the British Army. These reforms essentially removed the Crown's last vestiges of control over the Army, abolished the purchase system, and instituted a new system of service and reserves. Although these reforms were a harbinger for a more professionalized Army, they also gave the Parliament and the Cabinet, the structure of which unified civilian rule, more complete control over military policy. After 1870, according to Avant, "the ease with which the Cabinet could intervene in military policy affected the development of military professionalism in Britain."[137]

There were three main schools of thought in the British Army at this time: the "traditionalists" were suspicious of the Cardwell reforms and rejected the need for professionalization; the "continentalists" endorsed the need to professionalize but, much like the reformers in the U.S., they were enamored of the Prussian system and they strove to develop a military scientific strategy based on the Prussian experience; and there were the "imperialists," who also embraced the need for reforms and drew lessons from the continent but, who tended to adapt these lessons to address the immediate concerns facing the British Empire. Although the continentalists were involved in implementing the Cardwell reforms, their standing diminished in the latter part of the 19th century and they had very little impact on military policy. The continentalists became less relevant because they failed to focus on the roles and requirements of an imperial army. Conversely, the imperialists had much more influence on military policy in Britain during the last part of the 19th century.[138]

According to Avant, the imperialist school adopted a critical attitude toward lessons from the Prussian experience, embraced an approach which gave primacy to the Army's roles of colonial policing and home defense, and exhibited a progressive attitude toward officer education and technical innovation. Moreover, since politicians in the War Office promoted military leaders who adopted the policies that were congruent with the civilian interpretations of Britain's strategic requirements, the imperialist school had the most influence in shaping the British Army's policies and preferences during the last part of the 19th century. Avant's most salient point is that Army purists (continentalists) were not able to autonomously determine their preferred paradigm of war because, unlike the American Army, the British Army developed its culture under the close scrutiny of Cabinet civilians. The War Office rewarded Army officers who advocated a more flexible doctrine, one that focused on Britain's varied and immediate strategic demands. The fact that the civilians could easily replace officers who did not respond to the Cabinet's preference for a flexible Army (capable of carrying out a variety of roles) created incentives. Unified civilian control and oversight caused the Army to be responsive to civilian concerns, concerns focused on the management of empire. As a result, a uniquely British approach that emphasized adaptability emerged. As the British military-strategic culture further evolved at the end of the 19th century, it exhibited less resistance to change and less affinity to massive force and the offensive than did the U.S. Army.[139]

CONCLUSION

Before examining American military strategic culture and comparing it to that of the British, in the next chapter, it is necessary to summarize some of the key inferences arrived at in this chapter. Figure 2.1 summarizes the salient characteristics of British military strategic culture. First, history and an insular geography have helped shape a pragmatic and indirect British approach to strategy. Second, imperial policing, intrastate security, and counterinsurgency have been considered normal roles for the British Army. LIC (or OOTW) has dominated the British Army experience and the Army has embraced LIC as central to the institution. Next, although the British Army has been successful in almost all of its conventional wars, for the historical, cultural, and organizational reasons elaborated in this chapter, for most of its history the British Army has viewed its expe-

Figure 2.1
The Military Strategic Culture of the British Army at the End of the Cold War*

Characteristic	British Army
Geography/History	Insular/Pragmatic/Indirect
Central Roles	Imperial Policing/Intrastate (LIC)
Peripheral Roles	Expeditionary/Continental
Self-Concept about Using Force	Minimum/When Required (Fabian**/Patience)
Technology/Casualties	Reliance but Limited/Not Averse
Defining Organization	Regiment
Civil-Military Relations	Centralized civilian control; integrate political with military; Clauswitizian in subordination of military to civilian policy; responsive to policy change

* The idea for a figure like this was borrowed from John Nagl's outstanding work in "Learning to Eat Soup with a Knife: British and American Counter-Insurgency Learning during the Malayan Emergency and the Vietnam War" (Unpublished Ph.D. dissertation, Oxford University, 1997), 91. John Nagl's advice and discussions were very valuable in helping me with this chapter.

** The term "Fabian" connotes an indirect strategic use of force and stems from the Roman general Quintus Fabius Maximus who defeated Hannibal in the Second Punic War by the avoidance of decisive battles. See Liddell Hart, *Strategy*, 26–27.

ditionary role to fight on the Continent as aberrant and peripheral. Imperial policing, and subsequently internal security/counterinsurgency, have been the mainstay of British Army operations. Likewise, the regimental system has proved responsive and adaptable to the exigencies of intrastate operations. However, as Winton explained, imperial policing and the regimental system were impediments to preparing for conventional conflicts on the Continent. The regimental system is embedded in British Army culture.

Additionally, years of experience in low intensity conflicts and counterinsurgency have over time imbued the institution with certain principles about the use of force in such operations. As a result, the British have wholeheartedly accepted that they should use minimum force and only when required. The British Army also seems to exhibit more perseverance or patience when it comes to protracted internal security problems—this is probably attributable to a tradition of operating in small, autonomous units in isolated and far away places. The British approach to casualties, moreover, is best described as a "stiff-upper-lip" attitude: a history of taking a limited number of casualties in remote places for unclear reasons has made the British more tolerable of casualties. This is not to say that the British Army does not try to avoid casualties, only that it does not seem to be averse to them. The British also exhibit a tendency to rely on and harness new technology to their advantage. However, due in part to a history of limited resources for the Army, the British Army has not come to over rely on technology as a be-all and end-all solution. In term of civil-military relations, the British system is more centralized and therefore better able to exercise control over the military. Likewise, throughout history, the British Army has been more responsive to changes that were directed by Parliament. Finally, the British have demonstrated an ability to conduct integrated civil-military operations, at least in the context of intrastate emergencies.

NOTES

1. Hanson W. Baldwin, *The New York Times*, Magazine Section, 3 November 1957, 13, quoted in Morris Janowitz, *The Professional Soldier* (New York, N.Y.: The Free Press, 1960), 278.

2. Alan Macmillan, "Strategic Culture and National Ways in Warfare: The British Case," *RUSI Journal* 140 (October 1995): 34.

3. "Asymmetric Conflict" is conflict wherein a numerically and technologically superior military force faces an inferior one. Implicit is that one is a great power and the other is not. However, history shows that the force with inferior combat power can win with the right strategy, see Andrew Mack, "Why Big Nations Lose Small Wars," in *Power, Strategy, and Security: A World Politics Reader*, ed. Klaus Knorr (Princeton, NJ: Princeton University Press, 1983), 128–133.

4. David French, *The British Way in Warfare: 1688–2000* (London: Unwin-Hyman, 1990), 67.

5. These are inferences from many works but Russell F. Weigley, *Towards an American Army: Military Thought from Washington to Marshall* (New York: Columbia University Press, 1962) and Harold R. Winton, *To Change an Army* (Lawrence, KS: University Press

of Kansas, 1988) are good points of departure for gaining an understanding of the influences of Upton and Cardwell.

6. Weigley, *Towards an American Army*, vi–x; and French, xi–xvii. These are but two of the many works I rely on to distill these general observations.

7. These generalizations emerge from facts internalized after from reading Russell F. Weigley, *The American Way of War: A History of United States Military Strategy and Policy* (Bloomington, IN: Indiana University Press, 1973); Weigley, *Towards an American Army*; Russell F. Weigley, *History of the United States Army* (New York: Macmillan Publishing Company, Inc., 1967); Correlli Barnett, *Britain and Her Army: 1509–1970* (New York: William Morrow and Company, 1970); David Chandler and Ian Beckett, eds. *The Oxford History of the British Army* (New York: Oxford University Press, 1996); and French, *The British Way in Warfare*.

8. Janowitz, 263.

9. Ibid.

10. Michael Vlahos, "The End of America's Postwar Ethos," *Foreign Affairs* 66 (Summer 1988): 1100.

11. Eliot A. Cohen, "Constraints on America's Conduct of Small Wars," *International Security* 9 (Fall 1984): 152.

12. B. H. Liddell Hart, Strategy, 2nd ed. (New York: Praeger, 1967), 26–27. The term "Fabian" connotes an indirect strategic use of force and stems from the Roman general Quintus Fabius Maximus who defeated Hannibal in the Second Punic War by the avoidance of decisive battles. Also see B. H. Liddell Hart, *The British Way in Warfare* (New York: The Macmillan Company, 1933), 97.

13. Weigley, *The American Way of War*, 5–15; 18–34; and French, 96–97; 116–18.

14. Weigley, *The American Way of War*, 5–15; 18–34; Mack, "Why Big Nations Lose Small Wars," 132; Edward Spiers, "The Late Victorian Army," in *The Oxford History of the British Army*, 198–210.

15. Mack, 126–27, 132; and Spiers, "The Late Victorian Army," 198–210.

16. Mack, 128, 130, 132–33; Weigley, The American Way of War, 18; and French, 66–68.

17. Henry Kissinger, "The Vietnam Negotiations," *Foreign Affairs* 47 (January 1969): 214.

18. Mack, 136–39.

19. Ibid., 138–39; and Weigley, *The American Way of War*, 36.

20. Weigley, *The American Way of War*, 34.

21. Ibid., 5 and 15; and Mack, 145–46.

22. Thomas R. Mockaitis, *British Counterinsurgency, 1919–60* (New York: St. Martin's Press, 1990), 146.

23. French, xiii–xiv; and David Chandler and Ian Beckett, eds., "Introduction," in *The Oxford History of the British Army*, xv–xvi.

24. John Winthrop Hackett, *The Profession of Arms* (London: Times Publishing Company Limited, 1962): 36–37.

25. J. Bowyer Bell, "Revolts Against the Crown: The British Response to Imperial Insurgency," *Parameters* 4 (1974): 31, 40–41.

26. French, 215–16, 220–21.

27. Gavin Bulloch, "The Development of Doctrine for Counter Insurgency—the British Experience," *The British Army Review* Number 111 (December 1995): 24; and Colonel Richard P. Cousens, United Kingdom Liaison Officer to the United States Army Training and Doctrine Command, Telephone interview by author, Medford, MA., 10 March 1997.

28. Barnett, *Britain and Her Army*, xviii.

29. This "blue-water" perspective of maritime power argues that small bodies of British troops fighting limited campaigns in distant theaters against a detachment of a continental enemy isolated by the Royal Navy have a disproportionately large effect on a war; much larger than direct British intervention in a continental campaign. See Barnett, xix.

30. Barnett, xviii–xix.

31. Ibid., xix; Chandler and Beckett, xv; and Hew Strachan, "The British Way in Warfare," in *The Oxford History of the British Army*, 408.

32. Ian Roy, "Towards the Standing Army, 1485–1660" in *The Oxford History of the British Army*, 45; and John Childs, "The Restoration Army, 1660–1702" in *The Oxford History of the British Army*, 54, 57, and 60–61.

33. Jock Haswell, *The British Army: A Concise History* (London: Book Club Associates, 1977), 9.

34. Michael Howard, *The Continental Commitment* (Bristol, Great Britain: Western Printing Services Ltd., 1972), 9; Michael Yardley and Dennis Sewell, *A New Model Army* (London: W. H. Allen and Co., 1989), 13–15.

35. Winton, 9–10.

36. French, 133, 138–40.

37. Winton, 9 and 232; Colin McInnes, *Hot War, Cold War: The British Army's Way in Warfare 1945–1995* (Washington, D.C.: Brassey's, 1996), 115; French, 133, 138–141, 144; and Peter Burroughs, "An Unreformed Army," in , *The Oxford History of the British Army*, 185.

38. Winton, 9–10.

39. French, 141–43.

40. Ibid. and Daniel P. Bolger, "The Ghosts of Omdurman," *Parameters* 21 (Autumn 1991): 28–30.

41. Bolger: 31.

42. Bolger: 31; and Kitchener's quotation is from Hew Strachan, *European Armies and the Conduct of War* (London: George Allen and Unwin, 1983), 84, quoted in "The Ghosts of Omdurman:" 31.

43. Lyttleton is quoted in Winton's *To Change an Army*, 11.

44. Barnett, 359–61, 367.

45. Michael Howard, *The Causes of War and Other Essays* (London: Temple Smith, 1983), 180, quoted in David French's *The British Way in Warfare: 1688–2000*, xvii; French, 220; and Macmillan: 34.

46. Howard, *The Causes of War and Other Essays*, 180, in David French's *The British Way in Warfare: 1688–2000*, xvii; Macmillan: 34; French, xvii; B. H. Liddell Hart, *When Britain Goes to War: Adaptability and Mobility* (London: Faber and Faber Limited, 1935), 41; Barnett, 149, 187–88.

47. Michael Howard, *The Continental Commitment*, 25 and 131; Yardley and Sewell, 17.

48. Yardley and Sewell, 17–20.

49. Williamson Murray, "Armored Warfare: the British, French, and German Experiences" in *Military Innovation in the Interwar Period* , eds., Williamson Murray and Allan R. Millet (New York: Cambridge University Press, 1996), 9–11.

50. Ibid., 9–10.

51. Ibid., 12.

52. Winton, 225–26, 229–30.

53. Ibid., 9 and 232; McInnes, 115; David French, 133, 138–141; and Peter Burroughs, "An Unreformed Army," in *The Oxford History of the British Army*, 185.

54. Winton, 174 and 230. In 1931 British Army Chief of the Imperial General Staff Milne authorized the creation of the First Brigade, Royal Tank Corps by joining up the only four tank battalions in the British Army. This sole British armored brigade's purpose was to test tank maneuver concepts and became known as the Tank Brigade.

55. See Winton, French, Chandler and Beckett, Liddell Hart, *When Britain Goes to War: Adaptability and Mobility;* and B. H. Liddell Hart, *The British Way in Warfare* (New York: The Macmillan Company, 1933).

56. Russell F. Weigley, *Eisenhower's Lieutenants, Volume I* (Baltimore: Johns Hopkins University Press, 1981), 10; and Maurice Matloff, "The American Approach to War: 1919–1945," in *The Theory and Practice of War*, ed., Michael Howard (New York: Praeger, 1966), 234.

57. Howard, *The Continental Commitment*, 146. McInnes, 4. Michael Dewar, *Brushfire Wars: Minor Campaigns of the British Army since 1945* (London: Robert Hale, 1990), 15.

58. McInnes, 30.

59. Ibid., 49.

60. Ibid., 49–50.

61. Alun Gwynne Jones, "Training and Doctrine in the British Army Since 1945," in *The Theory and Practice of War*, 315–316, 318.

62. Ibid., 319 and 325.

63. Ibid., 325–326.

64. Keith Jeffrey, "Colonial Warfare 1900–39," in *Warfare in the Twentieth Century: Theory and Practice*, eds., Colin McInnes and G. D. Sheffield (Winchester, MA: Unwin Hyman, Inc., 1988), 31.

65. McInnes, 74–75.

66. Ibid., 111–12.

67. Ibid., 4.

68. Gwynne Jones, 313.

69. Thomas R. Mockaitis, "Low-Intensity Conflict: the British Experience," *Conflict Quarterly* (Winter 1993): 14.

70. David Gates, "The Transformation of the Army 1783–1815," in *The Oxford History of the British Army*, 157–58; and B. H. Liddell Hart, *Strategy*, 2nd ed. (New York: Praeger, 1967), 26–27, 110–11, 115–17.

71. Liddell Hart, *Strategy*, 110–11 and 114–17; and French, 111.

72. French, 111–13; and Liddell Hart, *Strategy*, 110–11 and 115–17.

73. Ibid., 111–13; and Ibid., 110–11 and 115–17.

74. French, 113.

75. Liddell Hart, *Strategy*, 27.

76. Burroughs, 161–62.

77. Strachan, "The British Way in Warfare," 403–4.

78. Barnett, 324.

79. Cohen: 172–73.

80. Strachan, "The British Way in Warfare," 404–5.

81. Anthony Verrier, *An Army for the Sixties* (London: Secker and Warburg, 1966), 61–62.

82. John Pimlott, "The British Army: the Dhofar Campaign, 1970–1975" in *Armed Forces and Modern Counter-Insurgency*, eds., Ian F.W. Beckett and John Pimlott (New York: St. Martin's Press, Inc., 1985), 16–19.

83. Ibid., 19 and 24.

84. McInnes, 182.

85. Mockaitis: 8 and 10; and Thomas R. Mockaitis, "A New Era of Counter-Insurgency," *The RUSI Journal* 136 (Spring 1991): 75.

86. Mockaitis, "Low-Intensity Conflict: the British Experience:" 11; and Ian Beckett, "The Study of Counter-Insurgency: A British Perspective," *Small Wars and Insurgencies* 1 (April 1990): 47–48.

87. Beckett: 48–49.

88. Dewar, 180–81.

89. Barnett, 487–89, 484–85.

90. Dewar, 43–44.

91. Dewar, 15; and John Stone, email correspondence, London, King's College, 26 July 1999.

92. John Strawson, "The Thirty Years Peace," in *The Oxford History of the British Army*, 350–52.

93. McInnis, 149–50; Gavin Bulloch, "Military Doctrine and Counter-Insurgency: a British Perspective," *Parameters* 26 (Summer 1996): 4 ; and Mockaitis, "A New Era of Counter-Insurgency:" 75–76.

94. Hew Strachan, "The British Way in Warfare," 408–409; and Strawson, 348.

95. Thomas R. Mockaitis, "A New Era of Counter-Insurgency:" 75.

96. Winton, 8.

97. Hew Strachan, "The British Way in Warfare," 403; and John Nagl, "Learning to Eat Soup with a Knife," *World Affairs* 161 (Spring 1999): 195.

98. French, 145.

99. Ibid., 154–55, 159.

100. Emanoel Lee, *To the Bitter End* (New York: Viking Penguin Inc., 1985), 27–28; 37–38.

101. Lee, 43; and Jock Haswell, *The British Army: A Concise History* (London: Book Club Associates, 1977), 111.

102. Tim Travers, "The Army and the Challenge of War 1914–1918," in *The Oxford History of the British Army*, 210, 212–13.

103. Peter Simkins, "The Four Armies 1914–1918," in *The Oxford History of the British Army*, 236.

104. Winton, 231, 225, and 232.

105. Maurice Matloff, "Allied Strategy in Europe, 1939–1945," in *Makers of Modern Strategy*, ed., Peter Paret (Princeton, NJ: Princeton University Press, 1986), 685.

106. Ibid., 684.

107. Ibid., 679 and 685; Liddell Hart, Strategy, 362.

108. McInnes, 49 and 51–52.

109. Yardley and Sewell, 23.

110. McInnes, 77.

111. Dewar, 181–82.

112. Mockaitis, "Low-Intensity Conflict: the British Experience:" 10–11; and Mockaitis, "A New Era of Counter-Insurgency:" 75.

113. Hew Strachan, *The Politics of the British Army* (New York: Oxford University Press, 1997), 166–71.

114. Bulloch, "The Development of Doctrine for Counter-Insurgency—the British Experience:" 21; and John Shy and Thomas W. Collier, "Revolutionary War" in *Makers of Modern Strategy*, 845.

115. Janowitz, 25.

116. Hew Strachan, "The British Way in Warfare," 406.

117. Dewar, 181.

118. Strachan, "The British Way in Warfare," 414–15.

119. McInnes, 52.

120. Ibid., 113.

121. Anthony Forster, interview by author, Manchester, England, 19 December 1999; and Richard Connaughton, telephone interview by author, West Point, New York, 1 April 2000.

122. Connaughton interview; and Trevis interview. Trevis explained that in March 2000, *The Daily Telegraph* ran the casualty lists after its own research revealed more accurate figures than MOD.

123. Yardley and Sewell, 37.

124. Winton, 10.

125. Yardley and Sewell, 38–39, 42–43.

126. Strachan, "The British Way in Warfare," 414–15; and Hew Strachan, *The Politics of the British Army*, 196–97.

127. Strachan, *The Politics of the British Army*, 208–9.

128. Murray, 26–28.

129. Strachan, *The Politics of the British Army*, 211–12; McInnes, 49; Murray, 23.

130. Strachan, *The Politics of the British Army*, 214–18, 223.

131. Strachan, "The British Way in Warfare," 411–14; Strachan, *The Politics of the British Army*, 225–26; and Douglas A. Macgregor, *Breaking the Phalanx: A New Design for Landpower in the 21st Century* (Westport, CT: Praeger, 1997), 89.

132. Murray, 26–28; and Strachan, *The Politics of the British Army*, 232–33.

133. Patrick Mileham, "Ethos: British Army Officership 1962–1992," *The Occasional Number 19* (Camberley, England: Strategic and Combat Studies Institute, 1996), 30–24.

134. Chandler and Beckett, xiii–xiv.

135. Deborah D. Avant, *Political Institutions and Military Change: Lessons from Peripheral Wars* (Ithaca, NY: Cornell University Press, 1994), 21–23.

136. Ibid., 23, 36–37.

137. Ibid., 37–38.

138. Ibid., 38.

139. Ibid., 39–41.

AMERICAN MILITARY STRATEGIC CULTURE—THE UPTONIAN PARADOX

From the Civil War onward, the United States Army won its major wars mainly by overwhelming its enemies with a superior weight of numbers and resources. Superior strength flooded over the enemy's armed forces, eroding them through attrition and finally annihilating them. American soldiers became habituated to the advantages of wielding overwhelming combat power.

—Russell F. Weigley[1]

THE AMERICAN ARMY

Americans faced no serious external military threat for most of their history. Therefore, many Americans could afford to dedicate most of their energy and thought to the pursuit of peace whereas other states devoted such thought and energy to preparing for war. "But the United States won its independence in the course of a global war, found its security threatened for several decades thereafter by other global wars, and then, following the long interval of safety, discovered itself caught up in the global wars of the twentieth century." According to Weigley, a focus on naval power was implicit to a country of large ocean frontiers—this very focus appeared early and persisted. However, the United States is a continental power as well, and U.S. concerns over security have also turned to the establishment of an American Army.[2]

Although the history of the U.S. Army likewise reflects many years of experiences with non-traditional types of conflict, its culture prefers a concept of war akin to its World War II approach to war. For example, the U.S. Army has consistently refused to seriously consider any type of war except a European-style conventional war. "When the U.S. Army has nevertheless had to participate in unconventional, insurrectionary, or guerrilla wars, the experiences have soon been dismissed as aberrant." Long before the Vietnam War, the American Army culture had virtually erased the Philippine Insurrection (1899–1902) from its memory. Ostensibly, it allowed this to happen based on the assumption that the kind of warfare engendered therein (counterinsurgency waged across rugged terrain and in a tropical climate), was not likely to revisit the U.S. Army. Likewise, even though the U.S. Army had a long history of warfare against the Indians, it never bothered to develop a doctrine suited to the particularities of counter-Indian warfare because it diverged from the European style of war.[3]

Similarly, in 1989 Carl Builder observed that the experiences of two world wars have combined to form within the Army a strong perception of the U.S. Army in the role of "defender and liberator of Europe." In the interwar years though, the U.S. Army resumed its role as the government's handyman, patrolling the Mexican borders, quelling veterans' riots, running the Civilian Conservation Corps camps during the Depression, and so forth. However, Builder asserts, the Army's experience in its final and best year of World War II influenced the institution so significantly that it has persisted to the present day. The Army's experiences in Korea and Vietnam have been consigned to the "wrong kinds of wars," disquieting aberrations because they either lacked public support or limited the military's use of force with onerous political constraints. World War II, Builder observes, was an experience the Army liked, the last successful absolute crusade—a self-image very distinct from its subsequent experience during the Cold War. A Weigley aphorism, in fact, alludes to this: "military men are forever preparing to refight the last *satisfactory* war."[4]

However, although the Cold-War U.S. Army focused its force structure, training, and doctrine on fighting the big battle for Central Europe, it conducted a diverse array of missions: constabulary forces in Japan and Germany, a UN "police action" in Korea, a contingency operation in the Dominican Republic, the Sinai peacekeeping commitment, Vietnam, Grenada, and so forth. According to Builder, "none of this long list of duties—for the recent past or the likely future—includes the war toward which the Army has devoted so much of its energies and equipment designs." Although, Builder was not prescient enough to foresee the Persian Gulf War back in 1989, Saddam Hussein provided the U.S. with a war that was perfectly congruous with the Army's favorite paradigm. According to Dan Bolger, the Persian Gulf War gave the U.S. Army what it had longed for since 1945: "it was a war of clear aims, well-defined means, and circumscribed duration, fought in happy concert with many allies." However, Bolger argues, "strategically, operationally, and tactically, this one was a museum piece—exciting, militarily impressive, and in the long run as sterile and unimportant as Omdurman."[5]

In another work, Bolger maintains that World War II and the Persian Gulf War were actually the aberrations in the American Army experience. "The American military's artificially narrow definition of war has never matched the real world or its own heritage of small, ambiguous wars." The preferred American paradigm for war is one that is a declared war against a conventionally organized enemy. The U.S. Army prefers to prepare for wars where its adversaries come to fight division against division, with tanks and jets, the kind of foe that fights fairly, just like Americans do. However, the U.S. Army has experienced about 100 hours worth of what it defines as war (in contrast to "operations other than war" and limited war) since 1945. What's more, the U.S Army's experience in and after Vietnam, coupled with it success in the Persian Gulf War, reaffirmed a propensity for the big-war model. As Eliot Cohen explains, "the American armed forces' understanding of the domestic political context of small wars has been shaped, and in fact distorted, by the experience of Vietnam." U.S. officers, Cohen asserts, were shocked by their military's apparent inability to annihilate an enemy who had less mobility and less combat power. "Accustomed since World War II to a large measure of popularity and respect, the armed services found themselves during the Vietnam era the target of criticism and occasional abuse."[6]

A preponderance of officers in the U.S. Army derived from Vietnam the determination to never again prosecute a war without the degree (full) of public support more characteristic of a world war than a small war. As Michael Vlahos observes: "Ironically, Vietnam brought us back more intently to the myth of World War II, to the restatement of the just war, or as Studs Terkel cunningly sensed, *The Good War*, that it represents." Weigley maintains that Vietnam was America's least successful war and that it was the single most important cause of uncertainty and turbulence for the U.S. Army in the 1970s and 1980s: "the manner in which the war was fought also generated profound misgivings within the service as well as among the American people at large about the possible erosion of the Army's tactical, operational, and strategic skills." After Vietnam, the U.S. Army redoubled its focus on planning and doctrine for war in Europe. Although focusing on Europe helped to ultimately renew the U.S. Army, it also helped recreate an army that was not very agile in the conduct of wars other than the conventional type.[7]

During the 1970s and 1980s, in examining past wars to derive lessons for future conflicts, the U.S. Army generally tended to eschew both Vietnam and Korea as unpleasant anomalies. Revisiting World War II and embracing the recent technological developments of the conventional 1973 Yom Kippur War, the American military hoped that the next war would prove to be like World War II. In fact the principal architect of the first post–Vietnam Army doctrine, General William Depuy, was a product of the U.S. Army's success in World War II and its failure in Vietnam. In describing him, one study observes: "Depuy was skeptical of the relevance of the Korean and Vietnam experiences, except as they reinforced his ideas." Depuy engendered armored warfare, combined arms operations, and he was enamored of the German methods of warfare. It was this experience and these ideas that appeared in the post–Vietnam doctrine, and around which Depuy sought to renew the Army. In addition, the new technology and lethality augured by the Yom Kippur War helped reinforce the fear of Depuy and his assistants that: "Vietnam had been an aberration in the historical trend of warfare, and that the Army had lost a generation's worth of technological modernization there while gaining a generation's worth of nearly irrelevant combat experience."[8]

Added to Depuy's renewed focus on Europe was a book written by Harry Summers that argued that the civilians had screwed up the strategy for fighting Vietnam. Summers highlights in his book the fact that the United States cited 22 different reasons for fighting the war. As a result, political and military leaders could not arrive at a consensus on strategy or properly identify the nature of the war, which according to Summers, would have been the application of overwhelming U.S. conventional force to defeat the North Vietnamese Army. Summers "lessons"' became the predominant school of thought and devolved into, and perpetuated, the "Never-Again-School." Moreover, in the 1980s the Never-Again-School dominated American military strategic culture: it was articulated in the Weinberger Doctrine in the middle of the decade; and it was subsequently embodied by General Colin Powell as the Chairman of the Joint Chiefs of Staff (JCS) at the end of the decade. The "lessons" of Vietnam, coupled with the lessons from the 1983 bombing of U.S. Marines in Beirut, were: the United States should not commit troops without public support; if America does commit the military, it should have clearly defined political and military objectives; the United States should only use force in an overwhelming manner and with the intent of winning; America should only commit force in defense of vital national interests; and the United States should only use military force as a last resort.[9]

However, a scholar examining the U.S. military's performance in low-intensity type conflicts in the 1980s observed that America usually performed them badly. The history of America's involvement in low-intensity conflicts during the 1980s testifies to a litany of military and political failures: the aborted hostage rescue in Iran, the invasion of Grenada, and the bombing of the Marines in Beirut. Nagl explains: "Rather than squarely face up to the fact that Army counter-insurgency doctrine had failed in Vietnam, the Army—and the governments of the 1980s and 1990s—decided that the United States should no longer involve itself in counter-insurgency operations." Instead of resisting change to counterinsurgency doctrine, the more influential groups in the U.S. Army opposed participation in LIC entirely and sought to peripheralize the supporters and doctrine for LIC. Richard Duncan Downie uses the moniker "War is a War" to identify Summers' Never-Again-School. According to Downie, this powerful and predominant group looked to Army big war norms and domestic popular support to avoid involvement in LIC. Consequently, the Weinberger Doctrine codified the criteria that, when followed, essentially proscribed the use of the U.S. military in anything other than its preferred paradigm, conventional mid-intensity conflict in which the United States could exert technological prowess and overwhelming combat power to annihilate the enemy.[10]

In 1989 a former Chairman of the JCS summarized a disquieting aspect of the Weinberger Doctrine:

After we decide to use force, we must rush in there, deal with the situation decisively and emphatically, lose no people, not take long doing it—two weeks to 30 days—destroy our targets completely, and not disrupt American life. Don't reach out through conscription.

Don't upset the stock market. Don't cause undue ripples. Just withdraw and come home after victory.[11]

In addition, the U.S. military's success in the Persian Gulf War was viewed as a vindication of the War-is-a-War and Never-Again-Schools. "The Gulf War, although waged against a Third World country, was a classic conventional war fought along the lines of strategies and tactics developed in World War II, Korea, and the Arab-Israeli wars of the previous four decades, and America's military is very good at conventional combat." Many also thought that the Gulf War had finally expunged the ghosts of Vietnam. As the ground war took shape, in fact, President George Bush claimed, "By God, we've kicked the Vietnam Syndrome once and for all." John Nagl argues, "the Gulf War simply confirmed the Army's Jominian concept of fighting purely military battles with high technology weaponry and overwhelming firepower." Cori Dauber at UNC Chapel Hill explains the significance of the Weinberger Doctrine and the success of the U.S. military in the Gulf War: "Desert Storm is represented by a variety of authors in a variety of venues as being successful precisely because the U.S. military learned—and applied—the appropriate lessons of Vietnam."[12]

THE INFLUENCE OF GEOGRAPHY AND HISTORY

"American ways of war were offshoots of European ways of war, and American strategic thought was therefore a branch of European strategic thought."[13] It is important to emphasize from which European military strategic thinkers the American military tradition stemmed—more so from Napoleon and Jomini than from Clausewitz. From the outset, Weigley explains, "one of the American changes of emphasis was toward less restraint in the conduct of war, in both means and ends, than became characteristic of European war after the close of the Wars of Religion and before the Wars of the French Revolution." Although wars in Europe after 1648 were fought by professional armies for limited ends, the wars between the colonists and the Indians, at least after King Philip's War, were wars of cultural survival fought with absolute aims wherein European restrictions on attacks against the property and lives of noncombatants were frequently disregarded.[14]

George Washington was foremost among those Americans who sought to import European models of war. Washington modeled the Continental Army as closely as possible after the rival British Army and he fought the Revolution as a conventional war with the American prototype of an 18th century professional army. However, since Washington's Army was limited in personnel, resources, and time to train up, he soon realized that committing his troops to open battle against the British would invite disaster. Therefore, after the Continental Army's unsuccessful defenses of New York in 1776 and Philadelphia (Brandywine Creek) in 1777, Washington avoided head-on collisions with the British Army. Acknowledging his limitations, Washington adopted an indirect strategy of attrition whereby he avoided general actions against the British main body but instead concentrated what forces he had against weak enemy outposts and piecemeal detachments. Washington's plan for victory was to keep the Revolution alive by preserving the Continental Army and wearing down the British will to resist with raids against the periphery of its armies. According to Weigley, this "strategy of erosion" stemmed from a strategic paradox: Washington's political objective had to be the absolute removal of the British from the insurgent colonies but his military means were so weak that he had no other alternative than a strategic defensive.[5]

Although Washington tried to approximate 18th century European military orthodoxy with his inchoate Army, he employed an unorthodox and asymmetric approach because of incongruous strategic realities. Washington eschewed guerrilla warfare and he himself did not conduct a guerrilla war. However, the Revolution produced some of the best unconventional warriors and guerrilla fighting in the history of American warfare. In the Northern Department, irregulars helped force the surrender of British Major General John Burgoyne's army at Saratoga by conducting unconventional hit-and-run harassment of Burgoyne's flanks and lines of communication. Moreover, in the Southern Department, Major General Nathanial Greene "developed a capacity to weave together guerrilla operations and those of his regular forces with a skill that makes him not unworthy of comparison with Mao Tse-tung or Vo Nguyen Giap." In part, Greene's strategy stemmed from the shortage of provisions for his regulars and the presence of partisan bands (thanks to British policies that alienated neutral southerners) in the Southern Department. He separated his regular forces into detachments simply because three scattered detachments could subsist more easily off the land than one concentrated force. Moreover, Greene used the guerrillas to impede British movements and supplies long enough to prevent the British from concentrating against his dispersion. But by dispersing, fighting, and running, Greene was able to entice Cornwallis to also violate the principle of concentration, thus making the British in the south more vulnerable to partisan harassment and his regular detachments.[16]

The subsequent course of U.S. history—characterized by a rapid increase in power and resources—curbed any further development of both guerrilla and counter-guerrilla methods. Weigley argues that Greene "remains alone as an American master developing a strategy of unconventional warfare." After the war, the influence of Washington's orthodoxy prevailed. Greene and the other unconventional warriors who performed so well in the Revolution did not play a role in influencing the development of American military strategic culture. "Whenever after the Revolution the American Army had to conduct a counter-guerrilla campaign—in the Second Seminole War of 1835–1841, the Filipino Insurrection of 1899–1903, and in Vietnam in 1965–1973—it found itself almost without an institutional memory of such experiences, had to relearn appropriate tactics at exorbitant costs, and yet tended after each episode to regard it as an aberration that need not be repeated."[17]

In fact, when the Seminole War started, the professional U.S. officer corps was preparing the Army to fight with new skills in campaigns of the conventional European style. It did not serve so well to prepare the American Army for an unconventional, irregular war. The U.S. Regular Army was modeled sufficiently on European and British patterns by 1835 that it was not much better prepared for a guerrilla war against the Seminoles in Florida than Napoleon's army been prepared to fight guerrillas on the Iberian Peninsula. This was true in spite of the experience the Army had gained fighting Indians in the French and Indian War and the irregular campaigns that American soldiers had themselves prosecuted against the British in the American War of Independence. As it turned out, the U.S Army, in its campaigns against the Seminoles, had to learn counter-guerrilla warfare all over again, as the Seminoles adopted an asymmetric approach in Florida. "The Seminoles refused to stake their future on showdown battles but preferred instead to wear out their adversaries by means of raids and terror, and by turning their forbidding homeland itself into a weapon against their foes."[18]

In the first part of the 19th century, moreover, the West Point of Sylvanus Thayer and Dennis Hart Mahan was divorced from the main intellectual trends of Jacksonian America. West Point's isolation allowed it to establish high standards of performance, but the price of isolation was high. Weigley elucidates, "standing apart from American life, American military leaders failed to address themselves to the discovery of military programs in accord with that life." Proud of the performance of the U.S. Army in Mexico and of the professional growth of the regulars, these officers were growing more confident in the prowess of the regular Army. However, they avoided any serious thought about preparing a military policy designed to achieve the greatest effectiveness from an armed citizenry, despite the fact that any major war would have to be waged mostly with militia and volunteers. To be certain, it was unlikely that Jacksonian America would authorize either a larger regular Army or even an expansible army of regular officer cadre. If the professional officers were to lead Americans to war, they would have to lead armed citizens, deficiencies notwithstanding; otherwise they would lack the numbers to fight a serious war. Dennis Hart Mahan was one of the original oracles of American military thought. Mahan received part of his military education in France and his hero was Napoleon. His book, *Outpost*, revealed Mahan's personal preference for the offensive mode of war and the commitment of professional officers to regular troops since no other troops could assure the fulfillment of an offensive role.[19]

In other words, the pre-Civil War U.S. Army culture was divorced from realistic thought about how to fight an American war. "They expected society to adapt itself to their mode of warmaking; they made little effort to adapt their ideas on warfare to American society." Therefore, these officers were ill prepared for the full scope of the Civil War, a total war that witnessed mass armies of armed citizen soldiers waging a war of annihilation for survival. Bruce Catton best captures the totality of the Civil War: "The nation itself had been heated to an unimaginable pitch by three years of war and now it had been put on the anvil and the hammer was remorselessly coming down, stroke after clanging stroke, beating a glowing metal into a different shape."[20] The absolute character of the Civil War would have been anticipated by Clausewitz, but not by the American military's preferred ora military strategy before the Civil War—Jomini. In fact, the Civil War would become the harbinger of a solely American fusion of Jomini's separation of the military from politics and Clausewitz's precept that all wars incline toward the absolute. This fusion would be engendered by Emory Upton, a hero of the Civil War, a protégé of Sherman's, and "the single most influential officer in sealing the commitment of the officer corps to the conservative, professionalist view of war."[21]

After the Civil War, paradoxically, the isolation of the U.S. military was the principal precondition for the development of professionalism. "Withdrawn from civilian society and turning inward upon itself, the U.S. Army came under the influence of reformers like Sherman, Upton, and Luce." They looked abroad for most of their ideas. Upton, in particular, focused on the Prussian military system. In fact, the years between 1860 and World War I saw the emergence of a distinctive professional military ethic in the United States Army.[22]

Emory Upton was the most influential younger officer among the U.S. Army reformers. After the Franco-Prussian War , the U.S. military's reverence for French military institutions abated and U.S. Army officers became interested in the military institutions of Germany and other countries. Sherman, in fact, played a pivotal role in sending Upton on his inspection of foreign militaries in 1870–1871, with instructions for a particular emphasis on German military institutions. Upton's *The Armies of Europe and Asia*, the first study to emerge from his tour, revealed in a comprehensive fashion to American officers the degree to which the U.S. Army was behind its European counterparts in the process of professionalizing. Upton recommended that the U.S. Army establish advanced military schools, a general staff, a system of personnel evaluation reports, and promotion by examination. While Upton studied the experiences of many militaries, he was particularly enamored of German military institutions. Upton contrasted the backward state of American military education with the fact that, in 1866, every Prussian general was a graduate of the Kriegsakademie. Sherman, who thought that the German system of military organization was "simply perfect," agreed with Upton wholeheartedly.[23]

Consequently, Clausewitz was translated into English in 1873 and many articles about Prussian military topics began to appear in the U.S. professional military journals. Huntington maintains that American officers tended to accept the German methods unquestionably and that by the end of the century, American military thinkers fully accepted the German general staff model. Even though American officers frequently misinterpreted and misapplied German military theory, the desire by the U.S. Army to emulate German institutions was an important factor in the development of American military professionalism. Weigley identifies and summarizes the confluence of three factors that explain of professionalization in the U.S. Army's history: (1) As the U.S. Army was left to languish on the frontier, it was impelled to nalize; (2) When Clausewitz was translated to English ng U.S. officers; and (3) the oracle of total war,

Sherman, established the Army's post-graduate professional schools between 1869–1883.[24]

In 1878, Major General Winfield Scott Hancock established the Military Service Institution of the United States, with the purpose of promoting "writing and discussion about military science and military history." In 1879 the *United Service Journal* also began publication. Sherman encouraged these institutions to supplement the school system. In 1881, Sherman established the School of Application for Infantry and Cavalry at Fort Leavenworth. The purpose of the post-graduate school system was to establish a "pyramid of institutions through which the officer could learn the special skills of his own branch of service and then the *attitudes* and principles of high command." The journals and the schools cross-fertilized each other, with the journals affording an outlet for ideas and studies nurtured at the schools. Army officers John Bigelow and Arthur Wagner wrote for these journals and their work had a significant influence in shaping professional attitudes. Bigelow also published a textbook, *Principles of Strategy*, in which he included principles "drawn from Sherman's warfare against civilian populations." Moreover, Wagner, who taught at the Leavenworth school from 1888 to 1904, eventually helped transform Leavenworth into the General Service and Staff College. Wagner was also one of the founders of the Army War College. Wagner admired the excellence of the Prussian military system and he regarded the Prussian school system as a "model for American military schools to emulate."[25]

However, it was Emory Upton who had the most influence in shaping U.S. Army professional attitudes during the late 19th century. For many years, anyone interested in U.S. military history consulted his *Military Policy of the United States* as the standard work in the field. "He argued that all the defects of the American military system rested upon a fundamental, underlying flaw, excessive civilian control of the military." As officers were alienated from the country, they embraced Upton's ideas in the late 19th century. Articles written in the new professional journals that suggested approval of Upton's work became more frequent. According to Weigley, Upton did lasting damage "in setting the main current of American military thought not to the task of shaping military institutions that would serve both military and national purposes, but to the futile task of demanding that the national institutions be adjusted to purely military expediency."[26]

Published after his death, Upton's *The Military Policy of the United States* argued for a strong regular military force. What's more, Sherman endorsed Upton's recommendations for reform, and the U.S. Army embraced *The Military Policy of the United States* in its disputes with the militia advocates. Upton considered the Prussian model to be excellent because of its general staff system, mass army, and freedom from civilian control. For the rest of his life he endeavored to get Congress to implement reforms based on the German Army. All of Upton's recommendations had a single aim—the creation of a modern professional U.S. Army. However, according to Stephen Ambrose, Upton was incapable of realizing that one could not simply graft a European-style professional army onto the American liberal system. This was so, Ambrose explains, b

Upton failed to grasp the interrelationship between the political and military spheres in a democracy.[27]

Upton seemed to misinterpret Clausewitz and to misunderstand the nature of a liberal democracy. In *Military Policy*, he argued that officers alone should be entrusted with directing armies in the field. Moreover, through his vitriol against the Secretary of War, Upton was advocating a complete independence of the Army from civilian control. Enamored of the German war machine, Upton wanted the U.S. Army to achieve a similar status. Upton was willing to let the President retain the title of commander in chief but his remarks about the defects in the Constitution (that encourage the President to assume the character of military commander) bespoke his real intentions. According to Ambrose, Upton renounced the military policy of the United States as one of imprudence and weakness, largely because uninformed civilians dominated the military. In Upton's opinion, the United States needed a professional, expansive, and autonomous Army.[28]

Deborah Avant also emphasizes the influence that Sherman, Upton, and other military reformers exerted on the cultivation of the U.S. Army's cultural preferences. The U.S Army developed a very deductive method for understanding warfare and it stemmed largely from the Prussian "science of war." "The Army objected to the use of the armed forces as a police force (because it was beneath the soldiers vocation) and argued that the Army must always be governed by classic military principles." As a result, Avant asserts, the U.S. Army developed an approach to war that was biased toward decisive and offensive doctrine that was derived from Europe and suitable for the European theater. Moreover, the efforts of Sherman and Upton helped the Army institutionalize an officer educational system that focused on the principles of war and cultivated uniformity of thought. The principles of war, as taught in the educational system of the U.S. Army, led more and more to a rigid conception of war. As in the Prussian Army, the American Army favored the science of war over the art of war, resulting in a stiff adherence to principles and a bias against individual initiative.[29]

U.S. Army leaders were able to professionalize, unencumbered by congressional oversight, because they deliberately formulated proposals for reform that would not require budgetary increases. "Military leaders learned that budgetary requests would prompt congressional scrutiny and acted to shape the development of the military institution without request increases in their budget." Recognizing that the chances for a budgetary increase during the post–Civil War period were unlikely anyway, U.S. Army leaders opted for autonomy to focus on professionalism. As long as the U.S. Army was kept down to a strength of 25,000 men, Congress allowed the West Pointers to develop it as they wished. Developing the professionalism, including the creation of professional institutions, was not that ~nsive. "Sherman, for instance, carefully avoided Congress in setting up the ~~nlication at Leavenworth; he did not wish it to be the subject of legis- to Huntington, Sherman repeatedly stressed to Congress that ~h and Monroe required no extra finding beyond usual

It is also perplexing that in the late 19th century, the U.S. Army embraced the conventional Prussian military system as paragon of professionalism at the same time that the American Army was engaged in the frontier war against the Indians—the most unorthodox of the U.S. Army's 19th-century enemies. According to Robert Utley, the Regular Army was a product of the frontier. In fact, frontier needs prompted the creation of and sustained the justification for a standing army. "Except for two foreign wars and one civil war, frontier needs fixed the principal mission and employment of the Regular Army for a century." Utley considers the frontier employment of the U.S. Army against the Indians to be a paradox: the experience made the U.S. Army unsuited for orthodox war at the same time that its focus on orthodox war made it unsuited for fighting the Indians. The organization of the frontier Army in companies and regiments seemed absolutely conventional in the 19th century context. The Army's system of border outposts was shaped by the frontier and it resembled the (conventional) strategic approach used by the British Army in the American War of Independence. Moreover, although most Army officers recognized the Indian as master of guerrilla warfare, the Army never institutionalized a counter-guerrilla doctrine; nor were there training programs, military schools, or professional literature on how to fight Indians. Utley explains, "lacking a formal body of doctrine for unconventional war, the Army waged conventional war against the Indians."[31]

The conventional tactics offered in Upton's, Casey's, and Scott's manuals were sometimes effective, when the Indians were imprudent enough to give battle on the nonindigenous Americans' terms. However, most persistent campaigns of pursuing the Indians simply broke down the horses and made the troops spend as much time trying to keep themselves supplied as they spent fighting Indians. In fact, according to Utley, U.S. Army leaders viewed Indian warfare as an ephemeral nuisance. In 1876, for example, General Winfield Scott Hancock testified before a congressional committee that the Army's Indian mission was irrelevant in determining the U.S. Army's composition and organization. The generals were partly driven by their desire to place the Army on a more permanent footing than afforded by Indian warfare. They were also sincerely concerned about national defense. Nonetheless, the Army they created was designed for the next conventional war rather than the present unconventional one. Even though the Army conducted the Indian wars conventionally, it was still unfit for conventional war as evidenced by its less than optimal performance in orthodox wars in 1812, 1846, 1861, and 1898. Because its frontier role had the U.S. Army scattered across the continent in small border outposts, units seldom assembled or trained in more than battalion strength.[32]

Utley further explains that a central component of the U.S. Army's 20th century practice can be traced to its frontier mission. The conduct of total war, wherein enemy populations are objects of war "finds ample precedent in the frontier experience." The practice of total war can be found in the Seminole Wars, but Sherman and Sheridan codified it as a deliberate approach against the Indians after 1865. "With the march across Georgia and the wasting of the Shenandoah Val[

models, they set forth in the two decades after the Civil War to find the enemy in his winter camps, kill or drive him from his lodges, destroy his ponies, food, and shelter, and hound him mercilessly across a frigid landscape until he gave up." Weigley also testifies to this approach: as far back as King Philip's War of 1675–1676, the colonists ensured their military victory was complete by extinguishing the Indians as a military force throughout southeastern New England. Moreover, in the fall of 1868 Sheridan chose a strategy against the Indians that reflected his and Sherman's experiences of "carrying war to the enemy's resources and people." Sheridan waged winter campaigns, "striking when the Indians' grass-fed war ponies were weak from lack of sustenance and the Indians' mobility was at a low ebb." Sheridan would then strike against the enemy's fixed camps where the Indians sheltered against the winter weather.[33]

Weigley maintains that essentially every professional officer from Winfield Scott onward—until Schofield, who as commanding general as of 1888 eschewed Uptonian prescriptions for civilian subordination to the military and reasserted civilian supremacy by deferring to the Secretary of War—was convinced that the only way to solve the civil-military relations issue was for the civilian authorities to yield military policy to the military. "Here was still another pernicious fruit of the divorcement which the professional Army had allowed between itself and civilian America." Separated from the civilians and disdainful of them as soldiers, Army officers were not inclined to accept the highest military guidance from citizens whom they perceived to be inept in military matters. Scott, McClellan, Sheridan, and Sherman—all these generals in chief had looked for an Uptonion solution. Moreover, they all helped proselytize among the American officers the dogma that military policy must be left to military men alone. Weigley sums this problem up cogently: "The officer corps had lost sight of the Clausewitzian dictum that war is but an extension of politics by other means." Thus, by the late 19th century the U.S. Army exhibited a reluctance to acknowledge that in war military aims cannot be divorced from political purposes, and that the ultimate decisions rested with the civilian political leaders of the state.[34]

Many of Upton's ideas were implemented under Secretary of War Elihu Root from 1901 to 1903. Root established the War Department Staff—the first high-level coordinating agency responsible for the creation and development of doctrine. The Root reforms also promulgated a coherent system of service schools for the U.S. Army, subsequently the principal sources of applied doctrine. In fact, the first version of what the Army now calls *FM 100-5, Operations*, the official Army manual for overarching doctrine, was published by the War Department in 1905. The 1905 manual, *Field Service Regulations*, the first official manual of general doctrine appeared in successive editions to incorporate the lessons of World War I ...ntinued into the 1920s. Beginning with the establishment of the General ... Root in 1903, during the first half of the 20th century the U.S. Army ... trend toward the emergence of the "massive armed force." ...lopments in the U.S. military paralleled those of the ...ialized states: these militaries "underwent a continuous and consistent transformation, accelerated during World War I and World War II and arrested to varying degrees during peacetime." This transformation encompassed the introduction of modern technology and large-scale managerial techniques that created the mass army and led to the notion and reality of total war.[35]

Root is also credited with the creation of the U.S. Army War College, the capstone to Sherman's school system that Upton had advocated. It continued the study of U.S. military policy and brought to fruition the ideas of Sylvanus Thayer and Dennis Hart Mahan (to foster the study of war and military art). In addition to establishing the general staff and the War College, Root's reforms established the three-battalion infantry regiment but without the skeleton third battalion. Moreover, the Dick Bill of 1903 standardized the state National Guard and put in place modalities to make the Guard measure up to federal standards.[36]

From the turn of the century up until World War I, the focus for American military strategy had been twofold: continental defense and the protection of its Pacific possessions. The first focus was traditional whereas the second part had come about as a result of the U.S. war with Spain in 1898. However, the War Department' plans were based on the Army's primary objective of defending the territorial United States. Since the Navy was the traditional first line of defense and since it was focused on the Pacific, World War I didn't really test U.S. strategic doctrine. However, World War I redirected American strategic planning and set important new precedents. According to Maurice Matloff, "the war rooted in the subconscious of the military planners the idea of a major American effort across the Atlantic." Another new strategic principle that emerged from World War I was the "idea that the imbalance of power on the European continent might threaten the long range national security of the United States and require overseas combat operations in Europe." General Pershing's insistence on employing American forces for offensive combat, open warfare, and breakthroughs, reflected the traditional American military desire for "sharp and decisive wars." U.S. leaders called for a war of mass and concentration and warned against sideshows. As in earlier wars, the U.S. military's aim from the outset was total victory. Saliently, future World War II U.S. Army leaders received their strategic education in Europe during World War I.[37]

After World War I, U.S. war planning reverted to a preoccupation with the Pacific and the defense of the continent. "National Policy, the public mood, and starved budgets put constraints on strategic planning and returned it to earlier channels." The color plans, for example, implied a concept of war that was limited in forces, area, and scope. However, the strategic debate in Europe between the defensive school and the offensive school began to resonate in American military thought. Slowly, Matloff explains, "the offensive overtones in European theory came to be seen as reinforcing American experience and began to seep through the constraints imposed on war planning and on the official doctrinal writings." What's more, Pershing's victories in France seemed to validate the Clauswitzian principles for total war. The 1923 version of the Field Service Regulations (the antecedent to the current 100-5 series) reflected a model of war focused on annihilation: "The ultimate objective of all military action is the destruction of the enemy's armed forces in battle. Decisive defeat in battle breaks the enemy's will to war and forces him to sue for peace." Borrowed from 19th century European theorists and reinforced by the World War I experience, this model of war remained the American approach to war.[38]

In addition, during the accelerated preparation for war in 1939–1941, new developments began to transform U.S. strategic thought and doctrine. There were four particularly significant developments: the shift from color to rainbow plans; the conceptual shift from continental to hemispheric defense; the adoption of a Europe first approach; and the emergence of theories on how to defeat Germany. As early as the ABC Conference in 1941, differences between the American and British approach to strategy began to emerge. Whereas the British argued for an indirect strategy to probe German weaknesses around the periphery of Fortress Europe, the American planners concluded that victory lay in coming to grips with and defeating Germany's ground forces and breaking the German's will to fight. "Vague as they were about preliminary operations," Matloff illumines, "they were already disposed to think in terms of meeting the German armies head on—and the sooner the better." From an institutional perspective, for U.S. strategists World War II was a war of organization, of big planning staffs, and of corporate leadership. What's more, the traditional American separation of political and military policy continued throughout the war and it was buttressed by Roosevelt's focus on unconditional surrender. "No strategic doctrine to relate political and military objectives in a coherent patter," Matloff emphasizes, "emerged before or during the conflict."[39]

America emerged from World War II in a position of uncontested military superiority. According to Henry Kissinger, "the war seemed to have confirmed all traditional American strategic axioms." Notwithstanding its late mobilization, America had in concert with its allies crushed the aggressor; and this victory had been achieved by harnessing and unleashing massive amounts of materiel. However, the onset of the Cold War precipitated a significant and fundamental shift in U.S strategy and force structure during peacetime. NSC 68, in conjunction with the Korean War, "served as a crucial catalyst for the ultimate implementation of the Army's strategic plans in the early 1950s." Before World War II, the U.S. Army had historically been reduced to minimum strength after wars; and immediately after World War II, the Army had again been demobilized in favor of a strategy that relied principally on strategic air power. However, NSC 68 helped the Army fulfill its own organizational agenda for the Cold War, "thereby revitalizing more than just its overall force structure, but providing much of the institutional rationale for more men, more money, and more equipment." NSC 68, coupled with the perceived Soviet threat in the context of the North Korean invasion, suppressed rooted American historical and cultural biases against funding and maintaining a large ground force during peacetime. The Cold War Army had to support strategic policies that spanned the globe and it had to be prepared to meet the massive Soviet arsenal in Europe as well as limited wars on the periphery.[40]

The U.S. Army's participation in World War I was too brief to change the concept of war and strategy that it had developed from the Civil War and that it subsequently nurtured by the study of Civil War campaigns in the interwar period. A concept of war stemming from the final campaigns and results of the Civil War emerged in 1918 when the American military complained about the incompleteness of the destruction of the German army and the Allied victory. At the strategic level, the U.S. military concluded that World War I testified to the impossibility of fire and maneuver because mass armies were too large to have vulnerable flanks. Most American officers thus concluded that the advent of mass armies left the frontal assault as the only course. As a result, during the years leading up to World War II, America's military strategic culture—one manifest in the military school system that it had borrowed from the Prussians, the instructors at those schools, and the scholarly publications associated with those schools—embraced a concept of war based on the Civil War model. America's strategic aim of completely imposing its political aims upon the vanquished, therefore, would be achieved by applying Grant's method of applying overwhelming combat power to destroy the enemy's armed forces and by applying Sherman's approach of destroying the enemy's economic resources and will to fight.[41]

The one exception to this Grantian annihilatory approach to war was the U.S. Marine Corps' *Small Wars Manual*, which expounds on American experiences in Central America, the Caribbean, and the Philippines. It also combined aspects of British and French doctrine for colonial wars. The *Small Wars Manual* emphasized the difference between conventional conflicts and colonial conflicts. What's more, its authors highlighted the necessity of both being sensitive to the handling of the civilian population and of avoiding maximum force because of its tendency to alienate the host population.[42] However, "the 428-page 1940 *Small Wars Manual*, an admirable guide to 'state-of-the-art' counter-insurgency doctrines, had no impact at all on practice." Any American focus on "small wars" disappeared after Pearl Harbor and the 1940 *Small Wars Manual*'s successor in 1949 was only a ten-page pamphlet.[43]

World War II had a significant influence on U.S. military strategic culture. Officers in the American Army had been able to prepare themselves for the transition from a small peace-time Army in 1940 to the World War II Army in part because the U.S. Army had inherited "the traditions and institutions of one great, European-style war of its own: the American Civil War of 1861–1865." According to Weigley, "the Civil War had molded the American army's conceptions of the nature of full-scale war in ways that would profoundly affect its conduct of the Second World War." However, the Civil War legacy was somewhat incongruous to the frontier-constabulary role that dominated the Army's experience until World War I: the experiences on the frontier suggested that mobility was the chief military principle while the memory of the Civil War pointed to massive force as the principal military principle. Reconciling these two principles to arrive at an appropriate military balance, Weigley asserts, was the main problem of metamorphosing the old U.S. Army of the frontier into the new Army of European war.[44]

From the Civil War experience, the U.S. Army inherited a strategic approach that its officers generalized as applicable to all major large-scale wars. Although Grant had continuously tried to turn Lee's flank, the Union Army ultimately destroyed the Army of Northern Virginia by fighting it head-on.[45] Both the Union's superior resources and its aim of unconditional surrender made Grant's strategy of simultaneous offensives on every part of the front an appropriate one.[46] Likewise, in the 20th century, the United States' confidence in its physical power allowed the armed forces to think about the destruction of enemy militaries not by maneuver but by the head-on use of overwhelming power.[47] America's immense resources and overwhelming power would ensure the annihilation of the enemy's war-making capacity and armed forces. With such vast resources, the U.S. military could all the better attack the enemy everywhere along the front line as Grant's Army had done to the Confederate Army.[48]

Subsequently, as the U.S. Army approached World War II, it espoused a clear strategic credo: war is won by destroying the enemy's war-making ability, particularly his armed forces, and maneuver alone will not accomplish this destruction This destruction is to be accomplished by confronting the enemy's main armed forces directly and overwhelming them with superior power. What's more, in the years between the end of World War II and the Korean War, the U.S. Army's doctrine remained essentially that of World War II. The advent of nuclear weapons and the postwar strategic environment made it difficult for the Army to develop doctrine. However, from the Army's perspective land warfare was not obsolete. "A final victory could still be gained only by rather traditional ground operations, and the World War II experience, especially in the European Theater, remained a valid basis for postwar doctrinal development."[49]

It is somewhat ironic, revealing, and disquieting that an institution with more history and experience fighting irregular conflicts of limited intensity than total wars without limits, would have its core culture so profoundly influenced by Sherman, Upton, and the World War II experience. As a result of these factors, the U.S. military strategic culture that emerged is one that ostensibly embraces the Clausewitzian axiom of subordinating military modalities to the political but, in all actuality, is truly Jominian. Instead, the U.S. military, once war breaks out, prefers to fight big conventional wars without limitations and without constraints imposed by its political masters.[50] According to Dunn, the most significant feature of the United States' twelve-year effort in Vietnam is what little impact it has had on strategic thinking in the U.S. Army and Marine Corps. The U.S. was as unprepared in the 1980s as it was in the 1960s to fight a protracted counterinsurgency campaign. For the Army, whose focus had been on the Central Front in Europe, Vietnam was but a large bump on the road to Europe. Many officers say that Vietnam remained unstudied because senior officers felt that in doctrinal terms the Asian experience was irrelevant to Europe.[51]

More recent scholarship also points to the U.S. military strategic cultural tendency to divorce the military from the political: "In the United States, one of the basic assumptions of armed force organization at the national level is that war-fighting is an autonomous sphere." In other words, war is an activity that is to be prosecuted by soldiers without significant interference from politicians. "This is an attitude with deep roots in the organizational culture of the Army."[52]

Examining the American Army and Vietnam, John Nagl explains that the U.S. Army leaders were unambiguously cognizant of the organization's essence: "its core competence was defeating conventional armies in frontal combat. The U.S. Army, Nagl asserts, never arrived at a consensus that a change of approach was dictated by the nature of the conflict in Vietnam. "An unshakable belief in the essence of the organization precluded organizational learning and has continued to preclude consensus on the lessons of Vietnam and on required changes in the organization through the present day." Moreover, Cori Dauber argues that "President Bush's pronouncement at the end of the Gulf War that we had finally kicked the Vietnam syndrome was incorrect: the Weinberger Doctrine is its very apotheosis." To clarify, if the Weinberger Doctrine essentially proscribes any type of intervention outside the preferred paradigm of big war, and if the U.S. political leadership demands action outside of the Weinberger script, then the result can be a half-measured intervention that looks a lot like the interventions—Vietnam and Lebanon—that precipitated the Weinberger rules in the first place. In Dauber's own words: "Perhaps paradoxically, the demand to go in with everything or nothing, juxtaposed with a demand to 'do something,' ends up producing precisely the limited forms of military intervention the Weinberger Doctrine was designed to preclude."[53]

VALUED (CORE) FUNCTIONAL ROLES

"The national American aversion to war is responsible for the all-or-nothing approach; that is to say, total victory over the enemy in an ideological crusade to make the world safe for democracy, or abstention."[54] The American paradigm for war as it emerged after the world wars obtains "a vigorous strategic and tactical offensive under conditions of full domestic mobilization, making use of the full array of military assets that the United States can bring to bear."[55] "An effective use of American military force must forge a bond with World War II and its transcendental heroic imagery." A 1996 RAND study identified five very salient U.S. Army cultural characteristics as impediments to planning and innovation. These characteristics are: a preference for close-combat maneuver; the centrality of the division; a big-war predilection, a big-army mindset; and defense against all enemies, preferably foreign. In elaborating further, this RAND study explains that the big-army mindset is a "relatively recent acquisition, since for much of its history the U.S. Army was both small and generally behind European armies technologically and doctrinally. However, before it even became a large Army it exuded a large army mindset, borrowing technology and doctrine from Europe. It was this predilection that laid the foundation for the development of a big-army mentality during World War II and the Cold War. The U.S. Army became larger and technologically superior to most of its competitors during the Cold War. "The Army's training and development base grew, and contributed truly advanced training techniques and doctrine like 'Air Land Battle' that exploited new technologies at least as effectively as any other army in the world." The Persian Gulf War, the RAND authors assert, simply validated the big-army mindset. However, a culturally embedded big-army mindset, the RAND study concluded, "could represent very expensive impediments to the Army's post–Cold War adjustment."[56]

U.S. Army culture also exhibits a predilection for "big wars." The RAND study explains that an army that prefers big wars "invests its resources to retain in-depth strength in modern, heavy forces rather than a diversity of one-of-a-kind specialized units." It also focuses its training orientation and doctrine on high-technology, high-intensity warfare against the most capable opponent in the world. World War I was the first opportunity for the U.S Army to fight against and with the industrial-age mass armies of Europe; and after that war, the Army's focus centered on the equipment and doctrine for fighting a big conventional war with infantry, armor, and artillery. "The big-war mindset was solidly defined starting with World War II." Although the end of World War II and the advent of the atomic age precipitated a rapid reduction in the size of the Army, the Korean War, and more importantly, a national strategy of graduated response after 1961, gave the Army a mission confronting the largest land forces in the world. As a result, training and preparation for the "big war" became the principal focus. Moreover, the RAND authors argue that Korea and Vietnam—the only small wars the U.S. Army engaged in during the Cold War—may have only strengthened the big-war preference. "Both were seen as failures by both the public and many Army officers, with the latter group often convinced that failure sprang from political constraints on military operations." Both wars thus encouraged the Uptonian biases of the U.S. Army—"what it ought to do was prepare for big wars in which it would have substantial public support and be given the operational freedom necessary to deliver victory."[57]

A statement by the last commander of the U.S. Military Assistance Command Vietnam (MACV), General Fred C. Weyand, is testimony to this "big-war" preference:

War is death and destruction. The American way of war is particularly violent, deadly and dreadful. We believe in using "things"—artillery, bombs, massive firepower—in order to conserve our soldiers' lives. The enemy, on the other hand, made up for his lack of "things" by expending men instead of machines, and he suffered enormous casualties.[58]

Of special salience, however, are the RAND study's conclusions about the U.S. Army's cultural preference for "big wars." The RAND study concluded:

The major risk of a big-war predilection is that the U.S. Army will retain the thinking, infrastructure, and forces appropriate for a large-scale war that may not materialize while failing to properly adapt itself to conduct simultaneous smaller engagements of the type that seem to be occurring with increasing frequency.[59]

This report concluded that a continued cultural preference for big wars may undermine the Army's ability to develop capabilities for: (1) countering insurgencies and terrorism as well as conducting peace operations; (2) suppressing domestic unrest and closing borders effectively; and (3) responding rapidly for small, self-sustaining force elements in crisis situations.[60]

Brian Jenkins, commenting on the Army's concept of war in 1970, explained that the concept had not changed as a result of the U.S. experience in Vietnam:

War is regarded as a series of conventional battles between two armies in which one side will lose and, accepting this loss as decisive, will sue for peace. . . . Our Army remains enemy-oriented and casualty-oriented. War, then, is assumed to be a battlefield where tactics rather than strategy are important; hence, good tacticians are necessary and are promoted.[61]

This same RAND author cogently captured the difficulty that U.S. Army faced by trying to force fit its paradigm for war to Vietnam: "the Army's doctrine, its tactics, its organization, its weapons—its entire repertoire of warfare was designed for conventional war in Europe. In Vietnam, the Army simply performed its repertoire even though it was frequently irrelevant to the situation." In this same study, Jenkins cites an anonymous remark by a senior American officer in Saigon: "I'll be damned if I permit the United States Army, its institutions, its doctrine, and its traditions, to be destroyed just to win this lousy war."[62]

According to Jenkins, an impediment to changing the approach in Vietnam was the attitude exhibited by many that the war in Vietnam was irrelevant to the *institution*. "Many in the military argue against making drastic organizational changes on the basis of experience in Vietnam, since the war there was regarded by many as an aberration. Higher echelon positions tended to be dominated by officers with World War II experience whose concept of future war, the one the U.S. Army had to be prepared for, was a European-style general war. "The war in Vietnam is regarded as an exotic interlude between the wars that really count." Thus, transforming the entire organization to fight it was not desirable. With a certain degree of prescience, Jenkins also asserts: "Much more troubling than our apparent failure in Vietnam is our inability to learn and apply lessons from these failures."[63]

In a recent and unprecedented analysis of U.S. covert operations in Vietnam, Richard Shultz affirms that the American military's preference for conventional wars was a major impediment to developing any meaningful and strategically integrated special operations campaign against North Vietnam. Shultz explains that President Kennedy's demand that the military establish a special warfare capability was an "edict that challenged everything the mainstream military stood for." When Kennedy took office he perceived incongruity between the changing nature of war and the American way of war. The problem was, if the military continued to embrace conventional war alone, it would be least ready for those conflicts that it was most likely to face. Since the essence of the U.S. armed forces had been significantly shaped by the conventional wars of the 20th century, it was very resistant to a different model.[64] Shultz offers this succinct explanation of the U.S. armed forces' perspective on war:

They had been victorious in two world wars and successfully prosecuted a limited war in Korea. In each, conventional forces and strategy had been the answer. As a result, the American military developed a conventional mindset. Technological advances in mobility and firepower only reaffirmed this approach.[65]

Another scholar identifies five elements of the U.S. Army's organizational culture as the "constituent elements of the Army's model of war, a model usually referred to as 'conventional war.' " According to Thomas K. Adams, these elements are: (1) war is an exclusive province of the military; (2) an emphasis on exclusively military skills as the essence of the organization; (3) a focus on the use of force to kill as a general method; (4) a conceptualization of the enemy as the professional military of an opposing state; and (5) an emphasis on a code of institutional and personal conduct based on the chivalric ideal, especially those elements of chivalry defining loyalty and honorable conduct.[66]

Weigley's work confirms the U.S. Army's aversion to conflicts other than the big war paradigm. In 1977, Weigley surveyed the pages of *Military Review*, the U.S. Army's professional journal. For the entire year's (1976) worth of issues, he found almost no critical appraisal of low-intensity conflicts. In contrast, in 1976 there were a preponderance of articles that examined large-scale conventional wars and the World War II paradigm. Likewise, in 1981 and 1982, Weigley also discovered that professional military thought, as reflected in *Military Review* and other professional military journals, pointed to the same conclusion—a focus on World War II-style conflicts with very little critical analysis of Indochina and very little hint at the possibility of small wars in the future. A 1989 survey that examined the 1400 articles published by *Military Review* between 1975 and 1989 discovered only 43 articles dedicated to LIC.[67]

Furthermore, in the late 1970s, the Commandant of the U.S. Army War College arranged for Colonel (Ret.) Harry G. Summers to be assigned there. Impressed with Summers' writing ability, the Commandant assigned him to write a book on Vietnam that used the BDM Corporation study. Instead of using the BDM report, Summers used for his theoretical framework Clausewitz's *On War*. Consequently, the perspective Summers argued in his book *On Strategy: A Critical Analysis of the Vietnam War* was the opposite of the BDM conclusions. Summers concluded that the Army failed in Vietnam because it did not focus enough on conventional warfare. In other words, the U.S. Army's problems in Vietnam stemmed from its deviation from the big-war approach and its temporary and very incomplete experiment with counterinsurgency. Not surprisingly, Summer's book was readily embraced by the Army culture while the BDM report drifted into obscurity. On Strategy has been and remains on the Command and General Staff College

(CGSC), the Army War College, and the official Army professional reading list. A survey of the 1990 CGSC class revealed that only six of 392 students in the class had read the BDM study.[68]

Moreover, just as the end of the Cold War was making a conventional war in Europe improbable, the Persian Gulf War happened. The Gulf War was offered as validation of the American paradigm of war, in contrast to Vietnam:

> In the same way that Instant Thunder had served as a counterpoint to the slow escalation of the Rolling Thunder air campaign in Vietnam, so too did this massive buildup of ground forces signal a rejection of gradualism, of limited force, of the perceived strategic shortcomings that led to the quagmire in Southeast Asia. Encouraged by Powell, Bush embraced—in Cheney's infelicitous phrase—"the don't screw around school of military strategy." A force so formidable as to be invincible would mass in the Saudi Desert, a force so huge that inevitably it contributed to the momentum propelling the nation toward war.[69]

The literature about the Gulf War is replete with the notion that Desert Storm was fundamentally different from Vietnam and that it represents a complete validation of the process of applying lessons learned. According to Dauber, Vietnam has become the central metaphor of American foreign policy. General Colin Powell's words to outgoing President Bush bear testimony also: "Mr. President you have sent us in harm's way when you had to, but never lightly, never hesitantly, never with our hands tied, never without giving us what we needed to do the job." In another chapter, after reflecting on a conversation with General Norman Schwartzkopf, Powell writes "Go in big and end it quickly." We could not put the United States through another Vietnam. Powell regarded the Weinberger Doctrine as a set of useful guidelines, derived from the lessons of Vietnam. While serving as Chairman of the JCS during the Gulf War he saw his task as ensuring that victory would be inevitable by applying Weinberger's criteria.[70]

For those who viewed the American way of war as an innate and unalterable manifestation of our strategic culture and national will, Operation Desert Storm served as validation. After Desert Storm, General Powell published a National Military Strategy that included a list of strategic principles that included "Decisive Force." Decisive Force is, essentially, an addendum to Weinberger's criteria. It is "the concept of applying decisive force to overwhelm our adversaries and thereby terminate conflicts swiftly with a minimum loss of life." Implicit in decisive force, however, is the notion that long conflicts will cause public dissatisfaction with the military, civilian micromanagement, and a critical media.[71]

MARGINALIZED (PERIPHERAL) FUNCTIONAL ROLES

Russell F. Weigley, in describing the U.S. Army of 1835, best captures the U.S. Army's historical approach to LIC.

> A historical pattern was beginning to work itself out: occasionally the American Army has had to wage a guerrilla war, but guerrilla warfare is so incongruous to the natural methods

and habits of a well-to-do society that the American Army has tended to regard it as
abnormal and to forget about it whenever possible. Each new experience with irregular
warfare has required, then, that appropriate techniques be learned all over again.[72]

According to Sam Sarkesian, "in the main, unconventional conflicts do not
easily fit into American cultural precepts or perceptions of the external environment." When attempts are made to design strategy and doctrine for unconventional conflicts, "they become suspiciously similar to conventional factors
disguised as unconventional." Moreover, Sarkesian asserts, "U.S. strategy and
doctrine for unconventional conflicts not only lack a conceptual base, but are divorced from the broader political-psychological dimensions of unconventional
conflicts." For those who attempt to isolate (unconventional) conflicts from the
conflict spectrum, unconventional conflicts are placed on the periphery of serious strategic thinking.[73]

Furthermore, Richard Shultz explains that low intensity conflict lies in the category of indirect strategy and thus differs greatly from the view of war and strategy
that has dominated U.S. military thinking and experience during the 19th and 20th
centuries. The direct (strategy) application of military force dominated U.S. military thinking during and after World War II and has manifested itself in the services' inability to develop strategy and doctrine for the principal type of low
intensity conflict the United States has been involved in insurgency.[74] The United
States has not been very successful in the operations other than war arena. Shultz
explains that conflicts short of conventional war have become more widespread,
but the U.S. Army has had difficulty developing doctrine for them. By the summer
of 1989, the services could still not agree on a new manual for *Military Operations
in Low Intensity Conflict (FM 100-20).*[75]

Nonetheless, "the difference between the United States' approach to Vietnam
and the British Army's approach to counter-insurgency in its numerous campaigns
since 1945 belies the fact that general principles have emerged which are of near
universal applicability when dealing with insurgency." "The most surprising aspect of the American experience with the Huk Rebellion (1946–54) was the apparent failure to apply the lessons where the United States was directly involved in
conflict against communists as opposed to merely advising others to resist it." It
has been argued that the U.S. Army never seriously attempted counterinsurgency
in Vietnam, its lack of flexibility being summed up in the memorable remark attributed to one American general: "I will be damned if I will permit the U.S. Army,
its institutions, its doctrine, and its traditions to be destroyed just to win this lousy
war."[76]

A smug hubris—the disease of victory—infected the Army, as it infected much of the
American government. Victory in World War II had been so absolute, so brilliantly
American, that the notion of losing a war was unthinkable. The formula for triumph in
Europe and the Pacific—superior firepower, superior manpower, superior technology—
seemed prescriptive for any conflict. The dominant characteristics of the senior leadership

of the American armed forces had become professional arrogance, lack of imagination, and moral and intellectual insensitivity. Those characteristics would lead the Army's commanding generals willfully to underestimate their enemies and overestimate their own battlefield prowess. Tragically, the only antidote to the disease of victory was the humiliation of defeat.[77]

The U.S. Army's instincts went back to the American Civil War while the Vietnamese communists drew heavily from Mao's theories of protracted warfare. The U.S. Army was unable to adapt to the kind of war conducted by the NVA and the VC. "By its more conventional response, its strategy of attrition and the unceasing quest for the big set-piece battle, the Army became, in effect, a large French Expeditionary Corps—and met the same frustrations. U.S. Army doctrine focused little attention on unorthodox methods of warfare. "With little interest or recent experience in counter-insurgency on a large-scale—and few recognizable payoffs in annual budgetary allocations or personal career enhancement—the evolving U.S. Army strategy was probably inevitable." The U.S. Army would use a sledgehammer where a screwdriver was more appropriate, while the practice of unconventional war was left largely to the Special Forces.[78]

Unfortunately, as a result of the reorganization of the U.S. Army after Vietnam, its lesson learning was replaced by a realignment of responsibilities and functions and no lesson learning function carried over into the new Training and Doctrine Command (TRADOC). TRADOC, "despite having all the essential ingredients for centralized lesson learning within it, it did not inherit any mission for combat processing." Also, a doctrinal shift back toward big conventional operations (Europe) diminished any residual influence the Vietnam experience-processing system might have exerted. Thus, the U.S. Army, either by default, design, or both, did not institutionalize the lessons from its most recent combat experience in Vietnam. Instead, the Army looked to research and analysis, exercises and field tests, and the historical experiences of World War II to prepare it for what it saw as the next war—a high intensity mechanized war in Europe. Propitiously, the Arab-Israeli War of 1973 served as surrogate laboratory of recent combat experience in the U.S. Army's preferred kind of war. TRADOC studied the lessons of this war very closely and incorporated those lessons into the U.S. Army's doctrine.[79]

Essentially, however, the lesson-learning system and lessons of Vietnam had not been simply forgotten: "The Army cast them aside with the revitalized NATO focus, buried them in the organizational reforms, and considered them unnecessary once the war ended." According to Vetock, the end of American combat in Vietnam by itself would have probably doomed the wartime lesson-learning system, but the Army's postwar organizational and doctrinal changes guaranteed its demise." Even the term, "lessons learned," disappeared from the indexes to Army publications. The war became a concluded event and a matter of history. After January 1973, "whoever sought lessons from the Vietnam War had to look backwards, historically, with the wisdom and burden of hindsight." The Army so diluted the Vietnam experience from its current memory that a 1975 Command and

General Staff College version of *Infantry in Battle* included 62 case studies from the three most recent U.S. wars: greater than 50 percent were about World War II, almost 25 percent were on Korea, and less then 10 percent focused on Vietnam.[80]

However, the U.S. Army's first comprehensive examination of the Vietnam War criticized its doctrine and conduct of counterinsurgency in Vietnam. More importantly, the study reported that the Army had ignored the lessons of Vietnam, had failed to study low-intensity conflict, and needed to correct its inability to conduct counterinsurgency. Published by the BDM Corporation in June 1980 for the Army War College, this study concluded that the U.S. Army still did not know how to do low-intensity conflict because the strategic lesson the U.S. learned from Vietnam was that intervention was to be avoided. The report also maintained that the U.S. military's traditional separation between military and political means significantly hindered the effective employment of military force in accomplishing objectives established by the political leadership. It criticized the American paradigm of war aimed at the destruction of enemy forces while ignoring other complex and relevant political factors. According to one expert on counterinsurgency, the BDM report was essentially an indictment of the U.S. Army's conventional and inappropriate approach to Vietnam. However, this study was shunted aside in favor of an assessment more congruous with the U.S. Army's preferred paradigm.[81]

Another study, completed by Kupperman and Associates, Inc. in 1983, examined a conceptual framework for the U.S. Army and low-intensity conflict (LIC). It also tried to determine whether the Army's organization and doctrine were appropriate for emerging low-intensity missions. The Kupperman Study identified a dilemma confronting the U.S. Army: extended high intensity conventional conflict in Europe dominates the Army's thinking, resource allocation, and doctrine, but it is the conflict least likely to occur. "The low-intensity conflict environment is not one for which the Army is currently prepared." The executive summary of the report asserted that the U.S. Army needed new organization, doctrine, tactics, and equipment "to meet successfully the foreseen challenges at this low end of the violence spectrum." The study also stated that the Army must overcome major external and internal barriers in restructuring to meet the focus of the future.[82]

Eliot Cohen maintains that the most significant limitations on America's capacity to conduct small wars stem from the resistance of the U.S. military to the very idea of participating in such conflicts and from the unsuitability of the American military for fighting such wars. According to Cohen, there is a fivefold requirement to wage small war successfully: expectations, doctrine, manpower, equipment, and organization. However, the U.S. military's understanding of the domestic political context of small wars was distorted by Vietnam. American military officers were shocked and frustrated by the Vietnam experience: they were shocked by the gap that emerged between civil society and the armed forces; they were frustrated by their inability to vanquish an ostensibly inferior third world opponent with firepower and mobility. Since World War II the U.S. military had become used to a large amount of popularity and respect, and it was traumatized by its vilification by large portions of society upon returning from Vietnam. These junior and middle level officers ran the military in the 1980s and 1990s, and in response to their unfair treatment during the Vietnam War, they were determined never to fight a war again without the fullest public support, support more apposite to a World-War-II-type war than a small or unconventional war.[83]

This desire for the fullest popular support has metamorphosed into a conspicuous reluctance to use force at all. However, insistence on massive public support for any use of force and the limitations that define small wars are incongruent. "Small wars are frequently long wars, which require skill and patience to conduct rather than the sudden and massive use of power." The Boer War notwithstanding, a quick review of British history shows that British Army regulars fought many colonial wars without the kind of public backing that was marshaled for the world wars. What's more, the U.S. Army successfully quelled the three-year-long Philippine Insurrection despite persistently vocal opposition back home. In the 1980s, the U.S. military leadership thus developed a set of requirements for popular backing that were unlikely to be met except in the case of a World-War-II style war in Europe. Small wars, by nature, also involve the integration of the political and military spheres. However, "the skills of manipulation which successful coalition warfare in such circumstances requires are not only scarce, but in some measure anathema to the American military." The U.S. military culture's preference to divorce the political problems from the military problems and to handle only military problems both accounts for and stems from its difficulties in Vietnam.[84]

The most important constraint on the conduct of small wars by America, Cohen asserts, is institutional (cultural)—the reluctance of the armed services to prepare adequately for such wars and the inability of the national security apparatus to conduct such wars with finesse. Another lesson the American high command drew from Vietnam was to never again jump into such a protracted low-level war. However, according to Cohen, it was precisely this "Never-Again-Club" mentality stemming from the Korean experience that pushed for the most thoughtlessly inappropriate and extreme approach in Vietnam. The American paradigm for war as it emerged after the world wars obtains "a vigorous strategic and tactical offensive under conditions of full domestic mobilization, making use of the full array of military assets that the United States can bring to bear." But it is not well suited to the challenges of small wars which must be waged under a host of political constraints and frequently require a strategic defensive. For most of the Vietnam War, the U.S. Army fought conventionally, using firepower and technology aggressively and on a scale commensurate with total war but counterproductive in the context of the war it was fighting. In addition, there is not much evidence of institutional learning in the aftermath of Vietnam—the first U.S. Army operations manual (*FM 100-5*) distributed after Vietnam in 1976 engenders principles and tenets that focus only on war in Europe. It emphasized the kind of offensive aggressiveness that characterizes the American method of war.[85]

The U.S. Army's response, to be sure a military cultural one, to its failures in Vietnam was not to institutionalize lessons learned there and create a better doctrinal approach to asymmetric/counterinsurgency type wars. Instead, it eschewed such wars and the concomitant doctrine, focusing almost exclusively on the "big war" in Europe after Vietnam. Its institutional solution to the Vietnam imbroglio, therefore, was "we don't do Vietnams." This is all too evident in its responses to post-Vietnam studies trying to answer the question: what went wrong and how can we do these wars better? Downie does a very good job of recapitulating the U.S. Army's response to a host of official and unofficial postmortem analyses. Army Chief of Staff General Creighton Abrams, the first post-Vietnam Chief, directed the Astarita group to conduct a strategic assessment to determine if a conventional strategy was appropriate to the post-Vietnam security environment. Their Astarita Report shifted the U.S. Army's institutional attention away from the frustrations of Vietnam and focused the Army on readiness and deterrence issues in Europe. "The Army focused on what it could do well—conventional warfare—as opposed to something the Vietnam War proved that the Army could not do well—counterinsurgency."[86]

What's more, Harry Summers, as a central proponent of the Never-Again group, highlighted the need for public support again in 1984: "Never again must the president commit American men to combat without first fully defining the nation's aims and then rallying Congress and the nation for war." In *Masters of War*, Michael Handel also asserts that Summers' *On Strategy* had a very strong influence on the U.S. military's strategic thinking in the early 1980s and on the formulation of the Weinberger Doctrine. However, Summers and his disciples' ideas and lessons were not uncontested. Another less influential subculture emerged, and it derived very different lessons from Vietnam. This school probably has its origins in a group of officers Janowitz labeled "pragmatists:" a small minority of officers who privately refuted the decision to intervene in Vietnam and doubted the appropriateness of the tactics both during the advisory period and the large-scale intervention. "They were doubtful about search and destroy tactics as the basis of an counter-guerrilla campaign." After the Vietnam War and into the 1980s, a more accurate sobriquet for this evolving school would be "LIC Supporters."[87]

In short, Krepinevich and the LIC supporters argue that the U.S. Army failed in Vietnam because it fought the war too conventionally, according to its preferred paradigm for war and not according to the principles and tenets of counterinsurgency. They would also agree with the notion that low-intensity conflicts are far more likely to recur and involve U.S. interests than are big wars. According to Krepinevich, "the Army's conduct of the war was a failure, primarily because it never realized that insurgency warfare required basic changes in Army methods to meet the exigencies of the new conflict environment." In attempting to overlay operational methods that were successful in previous wars, the Army focused on the attrition of enemy forces instead of denying the enemy access to the population. By focusing on perceived civilian failures and contriving criteria like the Weinberger Doctrine, instead of taking a harder look at its own failures, Krepinevich argues, the Army is perpetuating the fiction that its way of war (Concept) remains valid across the spectrum of conflict. On the other hand, LIC supporters learned these lessons: overwhelming force does not always work; military operations cannot be divorced from politics; using military force in pursuit of less than vital national interests is feasible; and gaining and maintaining the support of the indigenous population is central to success.[88]

Another author claims that the lessons the U.S. military captured from Vietnam was don't do them. Kenneth Campbell asserts, the largely successful outcome of the Persian Gulf War demonstrated to U.S. military leaders that Weinberger-Powell Doctrine worked well, thus affirming the Vietnam syndrome instead of kicking it. "Military leaders, therefore, had no intention of putting their Vietnam lessons behind them after victory in the Gulf for the Vietnam disaster taught them well how not to use force." The traditional "can-do" approach of the military prior to Vietnam has been supplanted by a post-Vietnam "no-can-do"' reluctance to use force outside of the American military's preferred paradigm.[89]

In contrast, the Kupperman Study of 1983 asserted that low intensity conflict would be the normal form of conflict in the 1990s. However, the report went on, the U.S. Army was not prepared to conduct LIC and the Army would need to develop doctrine and a force structure that would allow it to win in this environment. The Kupperman Study concluded that the Army was least prepared to fight the most likely form conflict—LIC—and best prepared for the least likely form of conflict—conventional war in Europe. In addition, in 1985 the Joint Low Intensity Conflict (JLIC) final report listed four prevalent themes: "as a nation we do not understand low intensity conflict; we respond without unity of effort; we execute our activities poorly; and we lack the ability to sustain operations." It also highlighted two common trends: though LIC is the most likely threat, the U.S. had no coherent strategy for dealing with it; and the U.S. military continually applied conventional solutions to unconventional challenges. The report asserted that the tendency to think and apply the same prescriptions for deterring and fighting conventional wars to the various forms of LIC was the greatest obstacle to developing an LIC capability. In other words, an over reliance on the traditional structures and approaches to conventional war impeded the development of LIC policy and doctrine.[90]

Of special salience for this study, however, according to David R. Segal and Dana Eyre, after the Vietnam War, "peacekeeping became incorporated at the fringes of doctrinal thinking through its inclusion as part of low intensity conflict. Subsuming peacekeeping within LIC had two deleterious results. First, it marginalized peacekeeping along with LIC. Second, peacekeeping came to be defined as a type of conflict rather than conflict resolution or conflict management. Segal and Eyre argue that "this distorted the perception of peacekeeping and necessary analysis and confrontation with critical issues such as the role of force in peace operations and the difficulties involved in maintaining the linkage between political/diplomatic activities and military activities in peace operations was ignored."[91]

The reasons why LIC/OOTW are marginalized by the American military are summed up best by Dan Bolger: "Americans define war as being waged against a uniformed, disciplined opposing state's armed forces, the sort who will fight fairly, the way the Americans do." Moreover, since 1945 the American military has brutally and successfully annihilated any foe stupid enough to fight it on its terms: force-on-force and tank for tank. For many in the military TWWRND ("things we would rather not do") would be a more accurate moniker for OOTW. "Desert Storm, a magnificent accomplishment, was a thing we would rather do: war by the American definition."[92]

SELF-CONCEPT ABOUT USING FORCE

However, while reluctant to resort to arms, the military does not support limitations or restraints on the nature of force once the decision to employ military means has been made. Over the past twenty years, American military experience has retained and even reinforced the absolutist tradition in the American military culture. . . . Our institutional preference, reinforced by both our national character and our resources, is for total warfare fought for unlimited ends by the complete destruction of the enemy's capacity to resist, including both the enemy's military forces and warmaking capability.[93]

After Desert Storm, General Colin Powell published a National Military Strategy that included a list of strategic principles that included "Decisive Force," also known as the Powell Corollary to the Weinberger Doctrine. Decisive force is "the concept of applying decisive force to overwhelm our adversaries and thereby terminate conflicts swiftly with a minimum loss of life." Implicit in decisive force, however, is the notion that long conflicts will cause public dissatisfaction with the military, civilian micromanagement, and a critical media. Certainly shaped by his Vietnam experience, Powell declared, "once a decision for military actions has been made, half-measures and confused objectives extract a severe price in the form of a protracted conflict which can cause needless waste of human lives and material resources, a divided nation at home, and defeat."[94]

In examining trends in our national military strategy, Samuel Huntington explained the reaction to America's experience in Vietnam: "the belief that if we are going to use conventional force in limited engagements abroad, we had better use it in circumstances where we can win quickly and avoid a slow bleed." Huntington also asserts that the U.S. experience in Vietnam has led the military to become the principal and most vociferous opponent to the employment of military force at all. However, the American preference for maximum and decisive force predates Vietnam by a century. According to Russell Weigley, "the Civil War molded the American Army's conceptions of the nature of full-scale war that would profoundly affect its conduct of the Second World War." The conception that the U.S. Army inherited from the Civil War, applied to World War II, and embraced for most of the Cold War was that "overwhelming American power would assure the annihilation of the enemy's strength." The Army entered the Vietnam imbroglio with the same maximalist predilection for the use of force and, to be sure, this was incongruent with the nature of counterinsurgency and the winning of hearts and minds.[95]

Krepinevich's analysis arrives at a similar observation—the 'Army Concept' comprises two characteristics: a focus on conventional warfare and the reliance on "high volumes of firepower to minimize casualties." However, the U.S. Army's traditional approach to the use of force does not suit it well for LIC, where the emphasis is on minimizing firepower and light infantry formations instead of the massive use of firepower and armored divisions. Weigley asserts that the history of U.S. strategy testifies to an American conception of war that best characterizes American strategists as "strategists of annihilation." In the beginning when America had limited resources there were some strategists of attrition but America's wealth and its adoption of unlimited aims in war abrogated that development, "until the strategy of annihilation became characteristic of the American way of war."[96]

Of the post-Vietnam U.S. Army doctrine for COIN/LIC, counterinsurgency expert Thomas Mockaitis observed "concerning the use of force in COIN: U.S. military doctrine is a curious blend of the British minimum force principle with the American maximalist approach to problem-solving." He paraphrases an excerpt from the 1990 U.S. Army manual for LIC (FM100-20): "in COIN, the government should stress the minimum use of violence to maintain order. At times, the best way to minimize violence is to use overwhelming force." However, Mockaitis asserts, "in no case has the application of overwhelming force produced victory in COIN."[97] Mockaitis sums up the U.S. military strategic cultural problem with the use of force in LIC: "Neither the American political system nor American attitudes are well suited to protracted war. A culture that places great faith in the efficacy of military power to resolve any conflict will have difficulty applying minimum force."[98]

TECHNOLOGY AND CASUALTIES

> We must expend steel and fire, not men. I want so many artillery holes that a man can step from one to the other.
> —General Van Fleet, 8th Army, 1951[99]

In 1991, Samuel Huntington stated that one greatly important of the many U.S. military strategic continuities is "use of our technological capability to maintain various forms of qualitative superiority over our opponent." During World War II, the U.S. military relied on its advanced weapons systems, technological prowess, and stupendous production capacities to enable it to win the war with approximately over ten million Americans under arms. Another author has maintained that U.S. technological superiority was perceived as rendering the U.S. military invincible prior to Vietnam since many Americans viewed Korea as aberrant: it was inconceivable that the U.S. military could fail to establish superiority. The industrial and technological prowess of the United States should have assured victory.[100] In an introspective analysis of our over reliance on technology, Robert McNamara observed the following:

We failed then—as we have since—to recognize the limitations of modern, high-technology military equipment, forces, and doctrine in confronting unconventional, highly motivated people's movements. We failed as well to adapt our military tactics to the task of winning the hearts and minds of people from a totally different culture.[101]

In another study of the evolution of U.S. Army doctrine, one historian postulated this about Vietnam: "firepower became the dominant characteristic of American operations. Maneuver was used primarily for locating and fixing the enemy. By de-emphasizing the infantry assault and concentrating on massive firepower against the enemy, American commanders minimized their losses while maximizing the strength of their forces." This same author observed, that over the long term, the U.S. Army has put more emphasis on the development of new weapons technology than on the development of new doctrine and force structures for employing new technology. "In some instances, this has resulted in new weaponry being grafted onto existing tactical concepts." Over the thirty-year period Doughty studied, the U.S. Army had major increases in firepower. The improvements on the tank, the mechanization of the artillery, the introduction of the armored personnel carrier, and the adoption of the helicopter, all added tactical firepower and mobility. In sum, from 1946 to 1976 the emphasis on fire-power and attrition steadily increased until they became central characteristics of U.S. Army doctrine.[102]

Carnes Lord explains the emphasis on technology and firepower as among the peculiarities of the American style of land warfare: "the heavy reliance on firepower, technology, and logistics support as well as the avoidance of risk, all of which is related to the political imperative to minimize casualties that is characteristic of liberal democratic armies generally." Colin Gray, another expert on defense issues, has argued that "in the twentieth century, the United States, whenever possible, has waged technological war, rather than wars of human (*American*) attrition." U.S. governments have prudently been sensitive to potential American casualties, as is appropriate for a political culture imbued with Lockean ideals of liberty. By way of illustration, in World War II, the American Army would often attempt to clear minefields with excessive artillery barrages whereas the Soviets would use up men and women for the same purpose. Likewise, the ubiquity of the phrase, "why send a man when you can send a bomb or a bullet," testifies to a uniquely American reliance on technology to minimize casualties.[103]

After the Vietnam War, the U.S. directed a large amount of its defense expenditures and energies toward the research and development of new highly technological weapon systems, to the modernization of materiel and forces neglected during the years of the Vietnam war effort, and to the enhancement and upgrading of systems tried and tested during the conflict. Even though this development was not surprising, the BDM study maintained, "it has caused a great number of military leaders and defense analysts alike to question the nation's high-tech approach to defense and its preoccupation with the performance of sophisticated weaponry." The American experience in Vietnam added greater impetus to the development of high technology in defense. This same report concluded while it was not necessary to stop or impede technology's march forward, "it is certainly imperative that a compromise be reached between, on the one hand, the level of sophisticated technology available, and on the other, the present day capabilities of our servicemen."[104]

A reliance on technology to avert casualties has become even more pronounced since the Gulf War, which bestowed a perceptual legacy upon the American people that decisive victory can be achieved at minimal cost. "Pentagon pictures showing the effects of smart weapons led people to think that we really can win with technology." America's "national aversion to bloodletting," moreover, lends the revolution in military affairs (RMA) and the Army's modernization effort (Force XXI) even more appeal. Another author offers a very cogent caveat to the American military's over-reliance on technology:[105]

But in fact, the gee-whiz gizmos of the programs of RMA and the Army's modernization effort, known as "Force XXI," sensors, robots, communications gear, unmanned aircraft, and the like—are best suited for high-intensity conventional warfare. They will be of little use in the broad spectrum of less conventional conflicts, including counterinsurgency, peacekeeping, and peacemaking operations of the sort we have seen in recent years, in such places as Bosnia, Haiti, Somalia, and Lebanon.[106]

Also, Gentry asserts that we should have learned from the Vietnam War that technology by itself does not win wars, "but we have shown a strong collective resistance to learning from history." Another work examining the Weinberger-Powell Doctrine and its influence on post–Cold War peace operations concludes that, "the concern for American casualties has reached a new level." Tolerable levels for casualties in operations for humanitarian interests are zero. What's more, Dauber purports, the new phrase "another Somalia" signifies an operation where any casualties will produce political pressure for withdrawal, whether or not the mission has been completed. The Clinton doctrine on the use of force, in fact, stemmed largely from the Weinberger-Powell Doctrine, modified for peace operations in the aftermath of Somalia. It allowed for the use of limited military means to attain limited political objectives, when important but non-vital interests are involved and when the risks are commensurate with those interests. One implication of the Clinton doctrine, according to Charles Stevenson, is that "U.S. casualties must remain low, even when vital interests are at stake."[107]

DEFINING AND CENTRAL ORGANIZATION

The division is the defining organization of the U.S. Army. It was created on a permanent basis in 1914 subsequent to Army Chief of Staff Leonard Wood's experiment with a maneuver division in San Antonio in 1911. The Stimson Plan, named after Secretary of War Henry Stimson, was the catalyst for the establishment of the three-brigade division in the U.S. Army. Stimson first proposed his plan for four maneuver divisions in 1913 to all the general officers that were stationed within the continental United States. "Some of the older ones still had hesitated before so drastic a departure from what they knew." The 1910 *Field Services Regulations* were revised to reflect the new organization: it defined the division as "a self-contained unit made up of all necessary arms and services, and complete in itself with every requirement for independent action incident to its operations." Robert Doughty's study traces the tactical doctrine of the U.S. Army from 1946 until 1976; it also traces the evolution of the U.S. Army division. And, although strategic requirements, doctrine, and tactics underwent various changes, eliminating the division for the sake of greater dispersion during the "pentomic era," or to more realistically meet the terrain and enemy situations in Vietnam, was almost inconceivable.[108]

Doughty examines the evolution of the Army division over thirty years: from the World War II division through the Korean War; the pentomic division for the nuclear battlefield; the ROAD division through the ostensible "counterinsurgency era;" the short-lived TRICAP division (triple capability); back to the conventional division during the post-Vietnam era; and the Army of Excellence (AOE) of the 1980s. As a counter point, as early as 1945 Major General Jim Gavin concluded that a nuclear battlefield required widely dispersed and relatively autonomous "battle groups, each one capable of sustained combat on its own." Even though it could be argued that abandoning the division for regimental-sized battle groups would have been a better option, five battle groups came to comprise a redesigned division. Moreover, after World War I, in the interwar period, any reorganization of the division was controversial. John Wilson observes, "once that organizational structure [the division] became embedded in both the Regular Army and the reserve components, it became exceedingly difficult to alter it in any way."[109]

By the 1980s, the AOE concept introduced the "light infantry division" (LID), even though the Kupperman study had asserted that the Army's organizational [divisional] structure would not permit it to win in a LIC environment. The study had proposed the creation of regionally oriented light infantry brigades to be trained and equipped under a pilot light infantry division training headquarters. In fact the LID was being designed to augment heavy forces even though it was originally conceived as a LIC organization. One author writing in the mid-1980s argued that the light infantry brigade concept clashed with the U.S. Army's large-unit, division and above emphasis. As a footnote to the centrality of the division, Doughty observed that from 1946-1976, the doctrine for the armor and artillery branched seemed almost static. "For most of the period under study, both performed in essentially the same fashion they had in World War II."[110]

"The combat division is the centerpiece of Army war-fighting doctrine and the focus of its operational plans." The RAND study, *Army Culture and Planning in a Time of Great Change*, identifies "the centrality of the division" as a distinctive characteristic of U.S. Army culture. This study asserts that the division has long been viewed as the "most prestigious Army assignment and the most sought-after organization in which to command troops." U.S. Army divisions comprise the greater part of its combat power; and to some degree, the Army assesses its state of preparedness by the number of divisions it maintains, especially regular Army divisions. "As an artifact of the industrial age, the division has remained continually in existence since before World War I." Although the Army has periodically redesigned the organization of the division, the division as a concept and an organizing principle remains unaltered. Another author who has argued that the division may no longer be relevant makes this conclusion of the Army's post–Cold War "transformation:" "recognizing that the development of American military tactics, doctrine, and war fighting organizations for future conflict has been rendered more difficult because the character of the threat is no longer specified, it is not surprising that the Army's Force XXI program has not resulted in any significant change in the war-fighting structure of Army forces since the Persian Gulf War.[111]

In contemporary Army thinking, the division is still the dominant U.S. Army organization that trains and fights as a team—the division combined arms team is still the centerpiece of the U.S. Army's war-fighting structure and doctrine. Even the creation of Force XXI, a truly innovative and forward-looking concept to fundamentally redesign the Army for information-age warfare, implicitly retains the idea of the division as a basic building block. "The very fact that Force XXI testing revolves around brigade, division, and corps operations suggests that test results will explicitly confirm the division's importance." In fact, somewhat ironically, the cultural resistance to move away from the division to a regimental-sized combined battle group at the and of the 20th century is as strong as was the Army's resistance to transition from regimental operations to divisional operations at the beginning of this century. Macgregor explains how the cultural resistance to eliminating the division can be an obstacle to genuine transformation: "trained and organized for a style of war that has changed very little since World War II, current Army organizational structures will limit the control and exploitation of superior military technology and human potential in future operations."[112]

To the degree that the central role of the Army division stems from cultural preference and resistance rather than a deliberately and comprehensively considered decision, it is likely that the Army may dismiss future changes in technology and the international security landscape, as well as in national security strategy, if those changes precipitate a different organizational centerpiece. With the current division-based force structure, the American Army "continues to reflect the distinguishing features of the industrial age forces that it developed during World War II." Today's Army forces, according to Macgregor, still comprise large industrial era forces capable of massing firepower. Even the first fully digitized division in Texas (Fourth Infantry Division at Fort Hood), with its digitized 70-ton Abrams tanks and digitized infantry fighting vehicles, reveals the coupling of 21st century digital technology with heavy division structure and equipment that has changed little since World War II.[113]

CIVIL-MILITARY RELATIONS

Along with history and geography, political culture and national character certainly influence the development of a military's strategic culture. Although an in-depth examination of U.S. political culture lies beyond the scope of this book, Samuel Huntington's seminal work, *The Soldier and the State*, has civil-military relations as its focus and it provides a cogent starting point for any analysis of U.S. civil-military relations. According to Huntington, "the outstanding historical fact of American civil-military relations has been the extent to which liberal ideology and conservative constitution combined to dictate an inverse relation between political power and military professionalism. Since the creation of the United States government through World War II, Huntington asserts, the Constitution and liberalism remained the constant components of American civil-military relations. This combination delayed the professionalization of the U.S. Army until it was nearly complete in Europe. It also significantly shaped the development of U.S. military strategic culture.[114]

Huntington makes two salient points about liberalism and America. First, "liberalism in the United States has been unchanging, monotonous, and all-embracing." Second, military institutions and military conservatism are anathema to liberalism. What's more, Huntington maintains, the United States' isolation from international politics in the 19th century reinforced the predominance of liberalism. National security was simply a given—there was no need for a philosophy to explain U.S. relations with the rest of the world and to lay down the correct course for national security policy. Internally, the role of power in politics was mitigated by the absence of class conflict; and externally, the role of power in international politics was attenuated by the absence of threats.[115]

Huntington examines the post–Civil War professionalization of the U.S. Army and asserts that the professionalization of the U.S. Army was unique because it was almost entirely the product of a core group of reformers with minimal civilian input. "Professionalism was the creation of an inherently conservative group against a liberal society, rather than the product of a general conservative reform movement within society." The two generations of reformers were distinctly military because they were cut off from contemporary American civilian influence and they derived their ideas from the American Military Enlightenment and from foreign military institutions.[116]

From the second decade of the 19th century until World War II, the United States had very few worries about security—it was a geographic fact. Concerns about civil-military relations were confined to the impact of military institutions upon political values and institutions. However, the changes in America's international political position and the changes in technology that accompanied the aftermath of World War II combined to make security the ultimate goal of policy instead of a beginning assumption. Thus, Huntington asserts, since the beginning of the Cold War and since the emergence of U.S. global hegemony, the principal question has changed. Before World War II the question for America was "what pattern of civil-military relations is most compatible with American liberal democratic values?" After World War II, the central question became "what pattern of civil-military relations will best maintain the security of the American nation?"[117]

However, when the Soviet threat disappeared with the end of the Cold War, other exigencies began to require the use of military force in situations outside its preferred paradigm and antithetical to the Weinberger-Powell prescriptions. A perceived "crisis in civil-military relations" has stirred debate over the military's role in determining how and when force should be used. James Burk poses the question: "How much influence over this debate should be wielded by a military elite that sees itself as a political interest group?" This question is given added salience when one considers that the political values of the U.S. military elite are increasingly homogeneous and incongruent to the political values held by many other elite groups. "Distrustful of the public, yet sure they require public support for any mission abroad, large or small, military and political leaders have become reluctant to deploy armed forces unless the mission appears certain to be a success, quickly achieved at little cost to life."[118]

One principal aim of the 1986 Goldwater-Nichols Act was to enhance effective civilian control over the military's ostensibly autonomous service bureaucracies. Defense Secretary Perry considered the Act "perhaps the most important defense legislation since World War II." It streamlined the military chain of command from the unified CINCs directly to the Secretary of Defense; and although it empowered the Chairman vis-à-vis the service chiefs, it placed him outside the chain of the combat commanders and in an advisory role only for the Secretary. Congress used pellucid language to make this point unambiguous: "the Secretary has sole and ultimate power within the Department of Defense on any matter on which the Secretary chooses to act." The impetus for this was an assessment in Congress' *Defense Organization Report* that "numerous obstacles precluded exercise of effective civilian authority, especially the Secretary of Defense." The efforts of the Secretary, the report observed, were impeded significantly by the absence of "truly independent military advice." As a result of the bureaucratic politics that had characterized the interplay among the Joint Chiefs, there had been an increase in civil-military disagreement and a "highly undesirable lessening of civilian control of the military." The act also prescribed the chain of command: it ran from the President to the Secretary to the CINC; the Chairman and the Joint Chiefs were explicitly removed.[119]

In addition, Goldwater-Nichols sought to improve the quality, training, and education of officers selected to the Joint Staff. Title IV of the act set procedures for the education, selection, assignment, and promotion of joint duty officers. Also, the joint officer standards and incentives established by Goldwater-Nichols have "notably improved the performance of those selected to serve in joint duty assignments." In light of Dr. Snider's observations below, the Goldwater-Nichols, coupled with a diminishing depth of military expertise among civilian leaders and staff, may have actually increased the "organizational salience" of the military. While this does not threaten to undermine civilian control per se, it may nonetheless confer upon the military more leverage when making policy decisions on when and how to use force. This would manifest itself in an observable way if the Weinberger rules prescribed the preferred approach to the use of force and attempted to proscribe uses of force outside that preferred paradigm.[120]

Don Snider posits the following: "individual military decision makers are better prepared to deal with current and future decision-making than are their civilian counterparts." Senior military officers are prepared better because they are better trained and educated because they have had more relevant experiences. "Even in the interface between the Department of Defense and Congress, the military staffs at the Pentagon usually outperform the congressional staffs and those of their analytical support agencies." Finally, in the field, the military is taking the lead in the joint mission and political-military analyses that now precede most operations other than war." Snider postulates, that, the decreasing familiarity with military affairs among the civilian leadership partly accounts for this disparity in expertise. For example, the 104th Congress represented the first time that a majority of the members of Congress have had no military experience. In addition, Snider explains, large numbers of experienced Cold-War era civilians retired in the early 1990s.[121]

In contrast, "more officers than ever before are educated in the policy sciences at the best universities. Military officers are posted more often and remain longer in policy-related assignments, either in the Pentagon or and in the regional joint commands around the globe. The Goldwater-Nichols Act also created highly competent joint specialists to work on high-level staffs within and outside Washington. The first major post–Cold War military operation, the Persian Gulf War, conferred upon the military a renewed esteem and respect for the traditional areas of expertise (mid-intensity conventional operations) for uniformed officers. Very few civilian leaders or staffs are coming to engender that degree of expertise in military affairs. However, no one, not the civilian leaders, nor the military services, have a clear conception of what the military should be able to do or how the military should be structured and equipped for the 21st century.[122]

On the other hand, Deborah Avant asserts that while military advice over the last decade has been reticent and conservative on decisions on the use of force in low-level conflicts, this is not necessarily a crisis but it does reflect a lack of consensus among civilian leaders. "While we do not necessarily want the military to determine security goals, if military hesitancy makes civilian leaders think twice about difficult commitments for which there is not domestic support before the United States is involved, it may be a good thing. In other words, in addition to the disparity in expertise observed by Snider, it is also the absence of a unified civilian strategy-policy front, on how and when the U.S. uses military force, which confers on military advisers additional leverage, or organizational salience. According to Avant, "when civilians disagree, the military has an incentive to act strategically and play civilians off one another in order to gain support for its own preferences." Thus, if the U.S. military's strategic culture has embedded opinions about using force (for example, if it prefers a big-war paradigm over OOTW/peace operations) and civilians disagree on policy, then, military opinions will have more influence and salience. The obverse would be true when "civilian institutions unify power over the control of the military in one branch of government."[123]

In the latter case, Avant explains, civilians can better exercise checks that incentivize military responsiveness and de-incentivize reticence. Therefore, when civilian control is unified, it induces the military to anticipate civilian goals. Avant also attributes the difference between divided civilian control and unified civilian control to the difference between presidential systems and parliamentary systems. "Presidential systems are held to create unwieldy arrangements that do not allow countries to respond effectively to the international system." On the other hand, parliamentary systems enable governments to respond more effectively and quickly to changes in the international security environment. However, Avant cautions, "parliamentary systems purchase efficiency at a cost—they increase the risk of civilian errors." The solution is to marshal civilian consensus about the conditions when responding to LIC threats is important to U.S. security.[124]

Another of Harry Summers' conclusions about the U.S. defeat in Vietnam was, that because no clear political objective was ever formulated, there was a paucity of strategic direction. Even success at the operational level was contributing to a strategy that could never win the war. Summers argued the need for civilian leaders to establish political objectives to enable the armed forces to establish complementary military objectives. Summers' focus on the Army's purely military approach on the battlefield reflected a traditional American preference (Jominian, not Clausewitzian) to wage war unimpeded by civilian interference.[125] Summers' misread of Clausewitz's overarching message is manifested in this now ubiquitous exchange:

> *Colonel Summers:* "You know you never defeated us on the battlefield."
> *North Vietnamese colonel:* "That may be so but it is also irrelevant."[126]

Summers "lessons," however, became the predominant school of thought and devolved into perpetuating the Never-Again-School. What's more, in the 1980s the Never-Again-School dominated American military strategic culture: it was articulated in the Weinberger Doctrine in the middle of the decade; and it was subsequently epitomized by General Colin Powell as the Chairman of the Joint Chiefs of Staff (JCS) at the end of the decade. The "lessons" of Vietnam, coupled with the lessons from the 1983 bombing of U.S. Marines in Beirut, again were: the United States should not commit troops without public support; if America does commit the military, it should have clearly defined political and military objectives; the United States should only use force in an overwhelming manner and with the intent of winning; America should only commit force in defense of vital national interests; and the United States should only use military force as a last resort.[127]

Two particularly germane quotes highlight this dynamic within the U.S. military strategic culture:

My responsibility is to lay out to my political leaders the full range of military options, to let them know what we can do, to let them know how we can solve a political problem, to let them know where I do not believe military force will solve a political problem, and to make them understand all of the consequences of the use of military force.[128]

The current preference of the U.S. military is captured in the Powell corollary to the Weinberger doctrine: the fast, overwhelming and decisive application of maximum force in the minimum time. Such an approach may produce effective, short-term results. It is irrelevant, probably even counterproductive, when matched against the very difficult internal problems that form the underlying problems in target countries.[129]

COMPARISON OF BRITISH AND AMERICAN MILITARY STRATEGIC CULTURES

"A conventional military force, no matter how bent, twisted, malformed or otherwise 'reorganized' is still one hell of a poor instrument with which to engage insurgents."[130] Russell Weigley also addresses both British and American dilemmas of trying to be prepared simultaneously to counter insurgents and wage large-scale conventional war: "for one kind of task, rapid and agile movement in reaching the scene and in campaigning after arrival was at a premium; the other kind of war demanded heavier formations with a capacity for sustained fighting under severe casualties." The British did not resolve this dilemma successfully: "the army was too much structured for and too heavily involved in colonial wars to be a convincing deterrent force or an initially decisive participant in European conflict." In addition, British manpower was limited due to an aversion to the draft, complicating the difficulties with British readiness. However, the Americans did not resolve this dilemma conspicuously well either: "A focus on European war in planning and doctrine—re-doubled since the close of the Vietnam War—has tended to create an army without appropriate agility for unconventional wars—or for rescuing hostages in Iran in 1980."[131]

In sum, this examination of American military strategic culture also points to several generalizations. First, although insular geography also afforded the Americans a degree of cheap security, history and geography shaped American military culture much differently than it did the British. Vast land space, hostile indigenous tribes, and a cataclysmic civil war embedded a direct and absolute approach to war. A salient component of this approach was a perceived or real struggle for survival on the new continent dating back to King Philip's War. What's more, as a consequence of the Civil War and of an adulation of first the French, then the Prussian model of war, the U.S. Army became focused on conventional war (alone) and massive firepower. Moreover, Sherman, Upton, and their disciples, as advocates of the conventional Prussian model, fused it with their total-war-of-annihilation approach in the Civil War and imbued it in the profession through institutions and journals. As a result, anything outside of the core paradigm came to be viewed as aberrant and ephemeral.

In addition, American political culture, vast resources, and values combine to create the view that war is bad and should only be waged as a crusade to achieve victory swiftly and justly. As a result, the notion of war as a last resort but with maximum force evolved. The U.S. Army for most of this century has also embraced the combat division as the preferred combat formation—this is a "no brainer"—the combat division *was* the most appropriate formation for the U.S. Army's favorite kind of war. Also germane, and topical in the context of peace operations, is a U.S. military cultural over emphasis on casualty avoidance and an over reliance on the "silver bullet," or technology. Finally, the aforementioned factors, coupled with the way and context in which the U.S. Army professionalized at the end of the 19th century led to what I have called the "Uptonian Paradox." The contradiction is this: the U.S. military ostensibly worships Clausewitz as the principal philosopher/oracle of war on the one hand, but on the other hand it exhibits a Jominian predilection to divorce the political from the military when the shooting starts. U.S. military strategic culture also, while in no way usurping civilian control of the military ultimately, exhibits a tendency

Figure 3.1
A Comparison of the Military Strategic Cultures of the British and American Armies at the End of the Cold War

Characteristic	British Army	American Army
Geography/History	Insular/Pragmatic/Indirect	Insular+Land/Absolute/Direct
Central Roles	Imperial Policing/Intrastate (LIC)	Conventional/Interstate (MIC-HIC)
Peripheral Roles	Expeditionary/Continental	LIC/PSO
Self-Concept about Using Force	Minimum/When Required (Fabian*/Patience)	Maximum/Last Resort (Decisive Force/Impatience)
Technology/Casualties	Reliance but Limited/Not Averse	Max leverage/to Minimize
Defining Organization	Regiment	Division
Civil-Military Relations	Centralized civilian control; integrate political with military; Clauswitizian in subordination of military to civilian policy; responsive to policy change	Decentralized/more autonomous military bureaucracy; tendency to divorce military from political; Uptonian/Jominian in prescribing conditions when military force should be used

* The term "Fabian" connotes an indirect strategic use of force and stems from the Roman general Quintus Fabius Maximus who defeated Hannibal in the Second Punic War by the avoidance of decisive

to influence or reshape its political masters' views in order to make those views on war congruent with its preferred paradigm for war. Moreover, Vietnam, Harry Summers' book, the Weinberger Doctrine, and Goldwater-Nichols have all helped perpetuate and exacerbate this tendency of the military to prescribe to the civilian elite "what kind of wars we do and don't do."

Figure 3.1 recapitulates the characteristics, some of which are directly traceable to Cardwell and Upton, of British and American military strategic culture. My notions of an Uptonian Paradox and a Cardwellian Conundrum highlight salient characteristics of the American Army's and the British Army's cultural predilections and attitudes about different types of conflict and the use of force. The bottom line is both Cardwell and Upton's ideas and policy prescriptions confined both cultures' capabilities and preferences to a certain kind of war. However, B-52 Arc-light strikes don't win hearts and minds, and foot infantry regiments don't defeat armored divisions.

NOTES

1. Russell F. Weigley, *History of the United States Army* (Bloomington, IN: Indiana University Press, 1984), 577.

2. Russell F. Weigley, *Towards an American Army: Military Thought from Washington to Marshall* (New York: Columbia University Press, 1962), viii–ix.

3. Russell F. Weigley, "Reflections on Lessons from Vietnam," in *Vietnam as History*, ed., Peter Braestrup (Washington, D.C.: University Press of America, 1984), 116.

4. Carl Builder, *The Masks of War: American Military Styles in Strategy and Analysis* (Baltimore, MD: Johns Hopkins University Press, 1989), 38, 185–86; and Weigley, "Reflections on Lessons from Vietnam," 115.

5. Builder, 186–87; and Daniel P. Bolger, "The Ghosts of Omdurman," *Parameters* 21 (Autumn 1991): 34. Bolger refers to the Battle of Omdurman in the Sudan in 1898 as an analogy for the American-led victory against Iraq in 1991. The Battle of Obdurman saw the British handily and brutally defeat their Dervish adversary because the Dervishes decided, as imprudently as Saddam Hussein decided, to fight a European-style conventional war against a European-style army.

6. Daniel P. Bolger, *Savage Peace: Americans at War in the 1990s* (Novato, CA: Presidio Press, 1995), 69–70; Eliot Cohen, "Constraints on America's Conduct of Small Wars," *International Security* 9 (Fall 1984): 167–68.

7. Cohen: 168; and Michael Vlahos, "The End of America's Postwar Ethos," *Foreign Affairs* 66 (Summer 1988): 1101–102, 1105; Weigley, *History of the U.S. Army*, 558, 589.

8. Weigley, "Reflections on Lessons from Vietnam," 115; and Paul H. Herbert, *Deciding What has to Be Done": General William E. Depuy and the 1976 Edition of FM 100-5, Operations*, Leavenworth Paper, No. 16 (Fort Leavenworth, KS: Combat Studies Institute, U.S. Army CGSC, 1988), 21 and 99.

9. Hugh M. Arnold, "Official Justifications for America's Role in Indochina, 1949–67," *Asian Affairs* (September/October 1975): 31 in Harry G. Summers, Jr., *On Strategy: A Critical Analysis of the Vietnam War* (Novato, CA: Presidio Press, 1982), 98; and Stephen J. Mariano, "Peacekeepers Attend the Never Again School," (Unpublished Master's Thesis, Naval Postgraduate School, 1995), 2, 6, 50–51; and Casper Weinberger, "The Uses of Military Power," News Release 609-84 (Washington, D.C.: Office of the Assistant Secretary of Defense for Public Affairs, November 1984). Mariano explains the "ever Again School" as

the core of the post-Vietnam Army culture although it stems from the Korean War experience. It describes the actions that political and military leaders should never again take in the conduct of war and foreign policy—essentially those actions that prevent the military from using overwhelming force in the pursuit of decisive victory, in other words, the World War II model.

10. Loren B. Thompson, ed. *Low-Intensity Conflict: The Pattern of Warfare in the Modern World* (Lexington, MA: Lexington Books, 1989), x; John Nagl, "Learning to Eat Soup with a Knife: British and American Counterinsurgency During the Malayan Emergency and the Vietnam War, Ph.D. Diss., Oxford University, 1997, 252; and Richard Duncan Downie, *Learning from Conflict: The U.S. Military in Vietnam, El Salvador, and the Drug War* (Westport, CT: Praeger, 1998), 167.

11. William J. Crowe, Jr., "What I've Learned," *Washingtonian* 25 (November 1989): 109 in Christopher M. Gacek, *The Logic of Force: The Dilemma of Limited Force in American Foreign Policy* (New York: Columbia University Press, 1994), 270.

12. William Head and Earl H. Tilford, Jr., eds., *The Eagle in the Desert* (Westport, CT: Praeger, 1996), 5, 11; Nagl, 253; and Cori Dauber, "Poisoning the Well: The Weinberger Doctrine and Public Argument Over Military Intervention" (Unpublished Paper, UNC Chapel Hill, 1998), 7–8, 23.

13. Russell F. Weigley, "American Strategy from Its Beginnings Through the First World War" in *Makers of Modern Strategy*, ed. Peter Paret (Princeton, NJ: Princeton University Press, 1986), 408.

14. Ibid., 409.

15. Ibid., 410–12; and Russell F. Weigley, *The American Way of War: A History of United States Military Strategy and Policy* (Bloomington, IN: Indiana University Press, 1973), 5, 15, 18–19.

16. Weigley, "American Strategy from Its Beginnings Through the First World War," 410–11; and Weigley, *The American Way of War*, 18, 23–24, 26, 29.

17. Weigley, "American Strategy from Its Beginnings Through the First World War," 411; and Weigley, *The American Way of War*, 36.

18. Weigley, *The History of the United States Army*, 160–61.

19. Weigley, *Towards an American Army*, 78, 47.

20. Bruce Catton, *A Stillness at Appomatox* (New York: Washington Square Press, 1953), 286.

21. Weigley, *Towards an American Army*, 78, 101.

22. John Winthrop Hackett, *The Profession of Arms* (London: The Times Publishing House, 1962), 38.

23. Samuel P. Huntington, *The Soldier and the State* (Cambridge, MA: The Belknap Press, 1957), 232–35.

24. Ibid., 235; and Weigley, *History of the United States Army*, 272–73.

25. Weigley, *History of the United States Army*, 273–75.

26. Ibid., 278–81.

27. Huntington, 232–34; and Stephen F. Ambrose, *Upton and the Army* (Baton Rouge, LA: Louisiana State University Press, 1964), 96, 122.

28. Emory Upton, *The Military Policy of the United States* (Washington: 1904), 305, 318; and Alvin Brown, *The Armor of Organization* (New York: 1953), 191–92 in *Upton and the Army*, 131–32.

29. Deborah D. Avant, *Political Institutions and Military Change: Lessons from Peripheral Wars* (Ithaca, NY: Cornell University Press, 1994), 27.

30. Ibid, 28–29; Huntington, 226–34.

31. Robert M. Utley, "The Contribution of the Frontier to the American Military Tradition," *The Harmon Memorial Lecture Series Number 19* (Colorado Springs, CO: USAF Academy, 1977), 3–5.

32. Ibid., 5–6.

33. Ibid., 8–10; and Weigley, *The American Way of War*, 19, 159.

34. Weigley, *Towards An American Army*, 167–71.

35. Morris Janowitz, *The Professional Soldier* (New York: The Free Press, 1960), viii; and John L. Romjue, *American Army Doctrine for the Post-Cold War* (Fort Monroe, VA: Military History Office, U.S. Training and Doctrine Command, 1997), 13.

36. Weigley, *Toward an American Army*, 149–50.

37. Maurice Matloff, "The American Approach to War: 1919–1945," in *The Theory and Practice of War*, ed., Michael Howard (New York: Praeger, 1966.), 215–17.

38. Ibid., 219, 223.

39. Ibid., 230, 234–35.

40. Henry Kissinger, "American Strategic Doctrine and Diplomacy," in *The Theory and Practice of War*, ed., Michael Howard (New York: Praeger, 1966), 279; and David T. Fautua, "The Long Pull Army: NSC 68, the Korean War, and the Creation of the Cold War U.S. Army," *The Journal of Military History* 61 (January 1997): 95–98.

41. Russell F. Weigley, *Eisenhower's Lieutenants, Volume I* (Baltimore: Johns Hopkins University Press, 1981), 4 and 7.

42. Keith Jeffrey, "Colonial Warfare 1900–39," in *Warfare in the Twentieth Century: Theory and Practice*, eds. Colin McInnes and G. D. Sheffield (Winchester, MA: Unwin Hyman, Inc., 1988), 38–39.

43. Ibid., 39.

44. Weigley, *Eisenhower's Lieutenants, Volume I*, 2–3.

45. Ibid., 4.

46. Ibid.

47. Ibid., 7.

48. Ibid., 4–5.

49. Ibid., 9–10; and Robert A. Doughty, "The Evolution of U.S. Army Tactical Doctrine, 1946–76," Leavenworth Paper No. 1 (Ft Leavenworth, KS: U.S. Army CGSC, 1979), 2.

50. Bernard Brodie, *War and Politics* (New York: Macmillan Publishing Company, 1973), 10; and Michael I. Handel, *Masters of War: Sun Tzu, Clausewitz, and Jomini* (Portland, OR: Frank Cass and Co. Ltd., 1992), 161. According to Handel, a Jominian approach separates politics and strategy, which are viewed as independent fields of activity. This approach is manifest in U.S. Army, *The Principles of Strategy for an Independent Corps or Army in a Theater of Operations* (Fort Leavenworth, KS: Command and General Staff School, 1936), 19. In an explanation of politics and the conduct of war, this manual explains: "Policy and strategy are radically and fundamentally things apart." It also maintains that strategy starts where politics stops. "All that soldiers ask is that once the policy is settled, strategy and command shall be regarded as being in a sphere apart from politics."

51. Peter M. Dunn, "The American Army: the Vietnam War, 1965–1973" in *Armed Forces and Modern Counter-Insurgency*, eds., Ian Beckett and John Pimlott (New York: St. Martin's Press, Inc., 1985), 99.

52. Thomas K. Adams, "Military Doctrine and the Organization Culture of the U.S. Army" (Ph.D. Diss., Syracuse University, 1990), 27.

53. John Nagl, "Learning to Eat Soup with a Knife," *World Affairs* 161 (Spring 1999): 195; and Dauber, 41–43.

54. James B. Motley, "U.S. Unconventional Conflict Policy and Strategy," *Military Review* 70 (January 1990): 10.

55. Cohen: 168–71.

56. Vlahos: 1105; and James Dewar, Debra August, Carl Builder, et al., *Army Culture and Planning in a Time of Great Change* (Santa Monica, CA: RAND Corporation, 1996), 16, 23–25.

57. Dewar, August, Builder, et al., 26–28.

58. General Fred C. Weyand and LTC Harry G. Summers, Jr., "Vietnam Myths and American Realities," *CDRS CALL* (Ft Leavenworth, KS: U.S. Army CGSC, July–August 1976), 3.

59. Dewar, August, Builder, et. al., 28.

60. Ibid.

61. Brian M. Jenkins, *The Unchangeable War* RM-6278-2-ARPA (Santa Monica, CA: RAND, 1970), 4.

62. Ibid., 3–4.

63. Ibid., 2, 6–7.

64. Richard H. Shultz, Jr., *The Secret War Against Hanoi* (New York: HarperCollins Publishers, Inc., 1999), 269–70.

65. Ibid., 269.

66. Adams, 30.

67. Weigley, "Reflections on Lessons from Vietnam," 115; and Michael J. Brady, "The Army and the Strategic Military Legacy of Vietnam," Master's Thesis, U.S. Army CGSC, 1990, 110.

68. The BDM study concluded that the U.S. Army still did not know how to do low-intensity conflict because the strategic lesson the U.S. learned from Vietnam was that intervention was to be avoided. The report also maintained that the U.S. military's traditional separation between military and political means significantly hindered the effective employment of military force in accomplishing objectives established by the political leadership. It criticized the American paradigm of war aimed at the destruction of enemy forces while ignoring other complex and relevant political factors. See The BDM Corporation, *A Study of the Strategic Lessons in Vietnam, Volume III Results of the War* (Washington, D.C.: Defense Technical Information Center, 1981), Executive Summary, 4-3–4-14, 4-22; Downie, 73; Brady, 250–91; and Department of History, *Officer's Professional Reading Guide* (West Point, NY: United States Military Academy, 1996), 28.

69. Rick Atkinson, *Crusade: The Untold Story of the Persian Gulf War* (New York: Houghton Mifflin Company, 1993), 113.

70. Dauber, 7 and 23; Colin Powell, *My American Journey* (New York, Random House, 1995), 567–68, 487; and Atkinson, 122.

71. Dauber, 7, 23; Powell, 567–68, 487; Atkinson, 122; Colin Powell, "National Military Strategy of the United States" (Washington, D.C.: United States Department of Defense, 1992), 10; and F.G. Hoffman, *Decisive Force: The New American Way of War* (Westport, CT: Praeger, 1996), xii.

72. Weigley, *The History of the United States Army*, 161.

73. Sam C. Sarkesian, "The Myth of U.S. Capability in Unconventional Conflicts," *Military Review* 68 (September 1988): 5–8.

74. Richard H. Shultz, Jr., "Doctrine and Forces for Low Intensity Conflict" in *The United States Army: Challenges and Missions for the 1990s*, eds., Robert L. Pfaltzgraff and Richard H. Shultz, Jr. (Lexington, MA: Lexington Books, 1991), 119–20.

75. Ibid., 127.

76. Ian Beckett and John Pimlott, eds. *Armed Forces and Modern Counter-Insurgency* (New York: St. Martin's Press, Inc., 1985), 7. The quote attributed to the anonymous general is attributed to C. B. Currey, *Self-Destruction: The Disintegration and Decay of the U.S. Army during the Vietnam War* (New York: W. W. Norton, 1981), 60. This is also quoted in *The Unchangeable War*, 3.

77. Rick Atkinson, *The Long Gray Line* (Boston, MA: Houghton Mifflin Company, 1989), 82.

78. Dunn, 84–85.

79. Dennis J. Vetock, *Lessons Learned: A History of U.S. Army Lesson Learning* (Carlisle Barracks, PA: U.S. Army Military History Institute, 1988), 119–20.

80. Ibid., 120.

81. Downie, 71–73.

82. Robert H. Kupperman and Associates, Inc., *Low Intensity Conflict, Vol. 1, Main Report*, AD-A 137260 (Fort Monroe, VA: U.S. Army TRADOC, 1983), iv, vi–vii.

83. Cohen: 165–68.

84. Ibid.: 168–71.

85. Cohen: 170–71, 177; and Andrew Mack, "Why Big Nations Lose Small Wars: the Politics of Asymmetric Conflict," in *Politics, Security and Strategy: A World Politics Reader*, ed. Klaus Knorr (Princeton, NJ: Princeton University Press, 1983), 126–51.

86. Downie, 70.

87. Harry G. Summers, Jr., "Lessons: A Soldiers View," in *Vietnam as History*, ed., Peter Braestrup (Washington, D.C.: University Press of America, 1984), 114; Handel, 160; and Janowitz, xliii. The LIC supporters, among others, would include Larry Cable, Andrew Krepinevich, Richard Shultz, and Sam Sarkesian. Russell F. Weigley, while not necessarily an LIC supporter, certainly identified the mismatch between the American Way of War and counter-insurgency in Vietnam. See Weigley, "Reflections on Lessons from Vietnam," 115–24; and Mariano, 51.

88. Andrew F. Krepinievich, *The Army and Vietnam* (Baltimore, MD: Johns Hopkins Univeristy Press, 1986), 259 and 271; and Mariano, 2.

89. Kenneth J. Campbell, "Once Burned, Twice Cautious: Explaining the Weinberger-Powell Doctrine," *Armed Forces and Society* 24 (Spring 1998): 366–70.

90. Kupperman and Associates, Inc., Executive Summary; and Downie, 75 and 78.

91. David R. Segal and Dana P. Eyre, "The U.S. Army in Peace Operations at the Dawn of the Twenty-First Century," Report (Draft) prepared for the U.S. Army Research Institute for the Behavioral and Social Sciences, 1994, 63–64.

92. Bolger, *Savage Peace*, 69.

93. F. G. Hoffman, *Decisive Force: The New American Way of War* (Westport, CT: Praeger, 1996), 10–11.

94. Dauber, 7, 23; Powell, *My American Journey*, 567–68, 487; Atkinson, *Crusade* 122; Powell, "National Military Strategy of the United States," 10; and Hoffman, xii.

95. Samuel P. Huntington, "The Evolution of U.S. National Strategy" in *U.S. National Security Strategy for the 1990s*, eds., Daniel J. Kaufman, David S. Clark, and Kevin P. Sheehan (Baltimore: Johns Hopkins University Press, 1991), 17; and Weigley, *Eisenhower's Lieutenants, Volume 1*, 3–4, 6–7.

96. Krepinevich, 5; and Weigley, *The American Way of War*, xxi.

97. Thomas R. Mockaitis, "A New Era of COIN," *The RUSI Journal* 136 (September 1991): 77–78. Although Mockaitis' endnote 23 references this excerpt as being from page 2-19, it is actually on page 2-10 of the 1990 manual. See *Field Manual 100-20: Military Operations in Low Intensity Conflict* (Washington, D.C.: U.S. Army and U.S. Air Force, 1990), 2–10.

98. Ibid.: 78.

99. Colin S. Gray, "National Style in Strategy: The American Example," *International Security* 6 (Fall 1981): 38.

100. Huntington, "The Evolution of U.S. National Strategy," 15; Major Albert C. Wedemeyer, War Plans Division, U.S. War Department General Staff cited in *The American Way of War*, 317; and Motley: 10.

101. Robert S. McNamara, *In Retrospect: The Tragedy and Lessons of Vietnam* (New York: Times Books, 1995), 322.

102. Doughty, 38 and 48–49.

103. Carnes Lord, "American Strategic Culture," *Comparative Strategy* 5 (Fall 1985): 280; and Gray: 28–29, 38.

104. The BDM Corporation, 4-9, 4-11.

105. James Gentry, "Military Force in an Age of National Cowardice," *Washington Quarterly* 21 (Autumn 1998): 181–85 .

106. Gentry: 181–85.

107. Ibid; Dauber, 38; and Charles A. Stevenson, "The Evolving Clinton Doctrine on the Use of Force," *Armed Forces and Society* 22 (Summer 1996): 511–12.

108. Weigley, *History of the United States Army*, 334–35; John B. Wilson, *Maneuver and Firepower: the Evolution of Divisions and Separate Brigade* (Washington, D.C.: U.S. Army Center of Military History, 1998), 33–34; and Doughty, 1.

109. Doughty, 16; and Wilson, 415.

110. Kupperman and Associates, Inc., 47; Downie, 75–77; John L. Romjue, *The Army of Excellence: the Development of the 1980s Army* (Fort Monroe, VA: U.S. Army TRADOC Military History Office, 1997), 119; Peter N. Kafkalas, "The Light Infantry Divisions and Low Intensity Conflict: Are They Losing Sight of Each Other?" *Military Review* 66 (January 1986): 18–27 in *The Army of Excellence*, 119; and Doughty, 48.

111. Dewar, August, Builder, et al., 16 and 28–29; Weigley, *The History of the United States Army*, 330–40; and Douglas A. Macgregor, *Breaking the Phalanx: A New Design for Landpower in the 21st Century* (Westport, CT: Praeger, 1997), 50.

112. Dewar, August, Builder, et al., 16, 28–29; and Macgregor, 62, 227.

113. Dewar, August, Builder, et al., 29; and Macgregor, 59.

114. Huntington, *The Soldier and the State*, 143.

115. Ibid., 145.

116. Ibid., 233.

117. Ibid., 2–3.

118. James Burk, ed. *The Adaptive Military: Armed Forces in a Turbulent World*, 2nd ed. (New Brunswick, NJ: Transaction Publishers, 1998), 13–14.

119. James R. Locher, 3rd, "The Goldwater-Nichols Act: Ten Years Later," *Joint Forces Quarterly* 13 (Autumn 1996): 10–12, 16.

120. Ibid.: 14–15. For a definition of "organizational salience" see Chapter 1 and Jeffrey W. Legro, "Culture and Preferences in the International Cooperation Two-Step," *American Political Science Review* 90 (March 1996): 123–25. A military organization's salience, or influence, increases when it has a monopoly on expertise, the problem is complex, and when the decision-making cycle is accelerated.

121. Don M. Snider, "U.S. Civil-Military Relations and Operations Other Than War," in *Civil-Military Relations and the Not-Quite Wars of the Present and Future*, ed. Vincent Davis (Carlisle Barracks, PA: Strategic Studies Institute, 1996), 1–2.

122. Ibid., 2.

123. Deborah D. Avant, "Military Reluctance to Intervene in Low-Level Conflicts: A "Crisis"?" in *Civil-Military Relations and the Not-Quite Wars of the Present and Future*, 20–22.

124. Ibid., 20, 22–24.

125. Summers, *On Strategy*, 142–143; and Mariano, 50.

126. Summers, *On Strategy*, 1; and Mariano, 50.

127. Arnold: 31 in *On Strategy*, 98; Mariano, 2, 6, 50–51; and Weinberger, News Release 609–84.

128. Green Berry Melton, "Sacred Honor: A Biography of General Colin Powell," *Today's Officer*, October 1993, 17 in *Decisive Force: The New American Way of War*, 112.

129. Donald M. Snow and Dennis M. Drew, *From Lexington to Desert Storm: War and Politics in the American Experience* (Armonk, NY: M. E. Sharpe, 1994), 325–26 in *Decisive Force: The New American Way of War*, 114.

130. Attributed to an anonymous U.S. general, cited in Jenkins, *The Unchangeable War*, 6.

131. Weigley, *The History of the United States Army*, 589.

4

EXISTING PEACEKEEPING DOCTRINE AT THE END OF THE COLD WAR

> When there is little time to explore the details of the pressing case, the strategist then is obliged to go with what he knows already and act according to what he judges, and feels to be correct: culture rules.
>
> —Colin Gray[1]

INTRODUCTION

Colin Gray's observation is germane to the immediate post–Cold War period since there really wasn't much extant doctrine in either army that explained how to do the new "middle-ground" or "gray-area" operations such as Bosnia or Somalia.[2] Both armies did have some doctrine but it only seemed to offer techniques and checklists for conducting traditional peacekeeping, for operations such as the Sinai Peninsula or Cyprus. Retired Brigadier Gavin Bulloch, an official doctrine expert for the British Army, offered this observation: "we didn't have any written doctrine for these types of operations in 1990."[3] To put it more emphatically, the former soldier and current academic expert on peace operations, John Mackinlay, explains—"there was a most hellish absence of doctrine" for the middle-ground operations. Moreover, Mackinlay asserts, no "division-one academics really studied peacekeeping during the Cold War because it was unsexy." As a result, there was a dearth of doctrine in the immediate post–Cold War period. Mackinlay offered this simile: the initial British Army approach to Operation Grapple (British operations in Bosnia under UNPROFOR) was "like an orchestra without music."[4]

According to John Ruggie, the absence of doctrine for gray area operations impeded and defeated the UN efforts in Somalia. Under the U.S.-led phase (UNITAF), the operation was authorized to use Chapter VII force to establish a secure environment for humanitarian relief. The U.S. forces' mission statement reflected extant American predilections on the use of force: "an overwhelming force applied decisively over a limited period of time, after which the remaining political and humanitarian tasks would be handed off to the United Nations."[5]

Immediately following the Persian Gulf War, and before the official end of the Cold War (25 December 1991), Britain, the U.S., and France led an international coalition to provide humanitarian relief to hundreds of thousands of Kurds who were caught between Iraq and a hard place, the mountains of northern Iraq. The operation, labeled Provide Comfort by the Americans and Safe Haven by the Brits, seemed to be both a watershed and a harbinger for the 1990s—the decade witnessed the willingness of the major powers to use force inside sovereign states for humanitarian purposes. John Mackinlay explains, operating in the context of ongoing intrastate conflicts was a very different operational milieu for traditional peacekeepers: "instead of patrolling the sterile and defined strips of land between stationary armies, they were required to operate statewide, in huge ill-defined territories, shared by a proliferation of armed factions and ungovernable and traumatized populations."[6] Again, Mackinlay offers some valuable insight into the nature of the challenging missions of the post–Cold War era:

From the vantage point of the military peacekeeper in a spaghetti tangle of confusion, linked interests and multiple involvement, it was important to distinguish the operational features that characterized this new activity, still referred to as peacekeeping, from the less challenging version they experienced in the buffer zones.[7]

The most significant operational difference engendered by a Somalia or a Bosnia was that "the tactical priorities that were fundamental to a traditional war zone were confused by a new dimension." The population itself had become the military objective of the post–Cold War operations. Traditional military objectives, such as the seizure of a terrain feature or a vital node, were now simply the means; the relocation, control, division, and extermination of the people were now war aims. Moreover, conventional combat training and Cold-War-era peacekeeping provided little insight to multinational forces intervening in a conflict situation where civilian populations were the targets, victims, and byproducts of violence. Another UK author drew the same conclusions about doctrine in the early 1990s: the pace of changes in the strategic environment is creating significant challenges for the developers of doctrine. According to Theo Farrell, Western armies found themselves conducting an entirely new type of operation. Although there were similarities between counterinsurgency (COIN) and traditional peacekeeping, the new operations presented a "much more ambiguous and politically sensitive environment than COIN, and at a much greater scale and intensity than peacekeeping." Both Somalia and Bosnia demonstrated that neither the British Army nor the U.S. Army could rely solely on past experience as a guidepost for the new kinds of operations. According to Farrell, however, both armies had to conduct these operations before they "were conceptually prepared to do so."[8]

In spite of the lack of change in published doctrine, evidence of military strategic cultural continuity can be observed from the way LIC/OOTW are conducted.

For example, the American Army and the British Army began their operations in Somalia and Bosnia, respectively, without a published doctrine for "gray-area" operations.[9] The U.S. Army published a new edition of its overarching doctrinal manual (*FM 100-5*) in June 1993 that did incorporate a chapter on operations other than war (OOTW), including peace operations. In addition, the U.S. Army did provide an OOTW extract of the 1992 draft version of the above to the U.S. troops who deployed to Somalia. However, the Americans did not publish *FM 100-23, Peace Operations* until December 1994, months after the United States concluded it operations in Somalia. Moreover, although the British Army began conducting UN-sponsored humanitarian operations in 1992 before the U.S. military deployed to Somalia, the first drafts of the British Army's first post–Cold War peacekeeping manual (*Wider Peacekeeping*) also appeared in 1993. The final draft version of *Wider Peacekeeping* was approved for publication in November 1994.

Notwithstanding, military strategic culture should help explain the two approaches to armed humanitarian operations as well as the doctrine that resulted from those two operations. The American operations (Operation Restore Hope) in Somalia and the British operations in Bosnia (Operation Grapple), by way of lessons learned, influenced the development of peace operations doctrine. Likewise, there were reciprocal influences between the two militaries that stemmed from both the doctrinal processes and from concurrent experiences (in Somalia and Bosnia) of the British and American armies. For example, Theo Farrell and Peter Jakobsen assert that while operating simultaneously in Bosnia, the British learned lessons from the U.S. experience in Somalia. Conversely, Farrell also asserts that the first post–Cold War draft of U.S. Army doctrine (*FM 100-23, Peace Operations*) also reflected some of the more circumspect distinctions between peace enforcement and peacekeeping found in British manual, *Wider Peacekeeping*. In addition, one of the principal U.S. Army TRADOC authors of peace operations doctrine attested to a continuous exchange of ideas, doctrinal concepts, and experiential lessons between TRADOC officers and British doctrine writers throughout the development of *FM 100-23* and *Wider Peacekeeping*.[10]

PURPOSE AND SCOPE

What military doctrine for peace operations did the British and Americans have when they started Operations Grapple and Restore Hope in 1992? How and where did the two militaries categorize peace operations? How much doctrinal literature is devoted to war fighting and how much is dedicated to peace operations? How did these doctrines define peace operations and what principles underpin the doctrine for conducting these operations? How did these two militaries' doctrines approach the factors of consent, impartiality, and the use of force? This chapter's purpose is to answer the above questions by examining the doctrine for peace operations before *Wider Peacekeeping* and *FM 100-23, Peace Operations* were published.

   This chapter focuses on the collective use of military force, sanctioned by the
international community, to penetrate a state's boundaries for ostensibly humanitarian purposes. More specifically, I will examine those operations which conform
to *Type Four* and *Type Five* in Marrack Goulding's typology of peacekeeping:
"operations to protect the delivery of humanitarian relief supplies in conditions of
continuing warfare; and operations deployed in a country where the institutions of
state have collapsed.[11] The principal aim of this type of intervention is to stop a
substantial loss of life and human suffering. For the purpose of clarity and stan-
dardization within this paper, these operations will be subsumed within the single
term, armed-humanitarian operations (AHO).
   The United Nations Charter does not mention the terms peacekeeping, peace
enforcement, or armed humanitarian operations. Chapters VI and VII of the Charter are invoked as the legal bases for authorizing peacekeeping and peace-enforcement missions. However, the range of activities included within the label "peace
operations" in the post–Cold War context have not fit the traditional definitions of
peacekeeping and peace enforcement, blurring the line between war and actions
short of war. Peace enforcement is war fighting: it is the imposition of peace between belligerents who do not at all consent to intervention and who may be engaged in combat activities. The United Nations actions in Korea and Kuwait were
unambiguous examples of enforcement operations.[12] In 1992, approved and published doctrine for both the British and U.S. armies only revealed one doctrinal
category for UN-related missions—peacekeeping. In Chapter I, this study defined
military doctrine as an authoritative expression of a military's fundamental approach to fighting wars and influencing events in OOTW. It should, in other
words, offer a framework of principles and tenets that guide how armies train and
operate.[13]
   According to Richard Duncan Downie, "doctrine is the most observable source
of the Army's standard operating procedures and formal institutional norms." Although "there is no explicit body of informal knowledge that would include informal norms," doctrine does embody the spirit and corpus of unwritten norms and
military thought in a broad sense. Downie considers doctrine to be the best reflec-
tion of the U.S. Army's institutional memory; this study considers Downie's concept of institutional memory to be virtually analogous to military culture.[14]
   Every Chapter VII mandate, however, does not signify a use of force commensurate with war-fighting: Chapter VII can be invoked to legalize intervention in a
failed state where there is an absence of legitimate consent-granting authorities; it
can also be invoked to authorize a robust and credible military presence without
calling for the intervening force to become involved in war-fighting. Traditional
peacekeeping operations under Chapter VI, on the other hand, require the consent
of the parties. Only Chapter VII mandates can authorize intervention in intrastate
affairs, if the Security Council "determines the existence of any threat to the
peace" and "decides" to take measures in accordance with Article 42 of the UN
Charter. Much of the conceptual and doctrinal confusion which inhere in AHO
emanate from two factors: the UN framework was designed to address interstate

conflicts; and the national military doctrines address Chapter VII mandates and the principles of consent, impartiality, and the use of force differently.[15]

While it is clear that civilian policy and diplomacy will ultimately determine the success of any collective intervention, this study focuses on the roles and contributions of the military. Military activity, moreover, is classified into three levels: strategic, operational, and tactical. The emphasis of these chapters primarily rests at the operational level of war where strategic aims are translated into military action. It is at the operational level, that commanders plan and conduct major joint and combined operations. What's more, the operational level is not delineated by the size of the force or by the echelon of the headquarters. Size notwithstanding, if a military force is being used purposely to attain a strategic objective, then it is being employed at the operational level. In addition, in operations short of war, the strategic and tactical spheres are often compacted, since a mistake at the tactical level can undermine strategic aims. The operational level is the critical nexus between strategic goals and tactical execution. Figure 4.1 depicts the relationship between the levels of war.[16]

HISTORICAL BACKGROUND TO BRITISH AND AMERICAN DOCTRINE

After World War II, the British Army soon became involved in counterinsurgency operations, from Palestine to Malaya. However, not until 1949 did the British republish an updated version of *Imperial Policing and the Duties in Aid of Civil Power*, which incorporated the new developments but re-affirmed much of the

Figure 4.1
The Levels of War

STRATEGIC
(national policy and objectives)

OPERATIONAL
(link between strategic objectives
and tactical execution)

TACTICAL
(execute battles
and engagements)

pre-World War II doctrine on counterinsurgency. Moreover, publications that were dedicated to lessons learned in particular campaigns appeared in the early 1950s—the most notable were *The Conduct of Anti-Terrorist Operations in Malaya* (1952) and *A Handbook of Anti Mau Mau Operations* (1954). The scope of British counterinsurgency efforts, however, pointed to the need for a modern form of overarching doctrine. Then in 1957, and in a later revision in 1963, the British published "Keeping the Peace," a doctrinal pamphlet that covered communist insurgencies of the Maoist genre. The British developed very little doctrine during the latter part of the 1960s, until 1969, when it rationalized all its tactical manuals into a series of volumes under the title *Land Operations*. Although the 1969 doctrine included a volume on counterinsurgency, *Counter Revolutionary Warfare*, the British Army only began one of its more recent and salient counterinsurgency operations, Northern Ireland, that same year.[17]

However, even when that manual was revised in 1977 it did not take into account the experience in Northern Ireland. The only real indicator that the British Army learned from its experience in Northern Ireland was the training conducted by units before they deployed there. Units studied enemy tactics and received training by the cadre of units rotating out of Northern Ireland. With a dearth of officially published doctrine on intrastate emergencies, military authors with experience in such operations tried to fill the gap. General Frank Kitson, Sir Richard Thompson, General Clutterbuck, and Colonel Tugwell wrote doctrinal works on "how insurgency and terrorism have developed and offered more up to date principals and guidelines on how to defeat these two types of scourges of the late 20th century."[18]

Since the end of the Cold War, British doctrine has changed, reflecting a more maneuver (American) oriented approach as well as newer contributions to peacekeeping. This is germane for two reasons: (1) the British Army has recognized the similarities between counterinsurgency, military aid to a civil authority (MACA—Northern Ireland), and peace operations during ongoing conflict; (2) when the operations in Bosnia began, the British had no doctrinal publications that incorporated the lessons of Northern Ireland, just lessons handed down from unit to unit. According to a principal author of British doctrine in this area, the British Army had very little by way of published doctrine for its operations under UNPROFOR (Operation Grapple)—it had to "adapt on the hoof."[19]

On the other hand, since 1982 the Air-Land Battle concept had dominated U.S. Army doctrine. Following the publication of the 1982 version of *FM 100-5, Operations*, Air-Land Battle was sanctioned as the fighting doctrine of the Army for the ensuing decade. American Air-Land Battle emphasizes firepower and maneuver and draws heavily on the maxims of Clausewitz. The Air-Land Battle concept was clarified and expanded in 1986 to better balance the offense and defense, to incorporate the operational level of war, and to emphasize the necessity of synchronizing the close, deep, and rear battles. According to one author, "more than any other change of the period [read post-Vietnam], the introduction of Air-Land Battle doctrine marked the renaissance of an Army clear in its purpose and its will to fight and win." Significantly, the U.S. Army saw its success in the Persian Gulf War as validation of this doctrine.[20]

"If doctrine is a vehicle for thinking war through beforehand, those in government service owe it to the country to develop good, comprehensive doctrine for low-intensity conflicts (LIC)."[21] In 1979, none of the current Army "how-to-fight" manuals explained anything about low intensity conflict. However, in the first half of the 1980s, the U.S. Army made good progress in developing doctrinal circulars and pamphlets that addressed the challenge of LIC. In 1985, U.S. Army Training and Doctrine Command (TRADOC) participated in the Joint Low-Intensity Conflict Project (JLIC), which included the Air Force, State, the CIA, and the JCS. Released in 1986, the JLIC study argued that U.S. military doctrine for LIC was not adequate and that the military needed to develop guiding principles for LIC. The report also identified a major problem with LIC—how to define it. Because of the broad range of activities subsumed within LIC, this problem persisted. In fact, the JLIC Project determined that LIC activities should be categorized into four groups: insurgency/counterinsurgency; terrorism counteraction, peacetime contingency, and peacekeeping operations.[22]

Another important bi-service change was the establishment of the Army/Air Force Center for LIC in 1986. The center resided under U.S. Army TRADOC until 1990 when it was moved to the Deputy Chief of Staff for Operations and Plans in 1990. However, The U.S. Army's progress in developing doctrine for low intensity conflict slowed noticeably in the latter half of the 1980s. The delay was partly a result of the increasing fusion of the doctrine and debate into the joint arena, which was an outcome of the Goldwater-Nichols legislation. In addition, the Army was slow to reach consensus on the doctrine internally. The U.S. Army, "focused as it still was, on the combat requirements necessary to win a mid- to high intensity war, was having difficulty with the concept of indirect application of power, which was seen as fundamental to low intensity conflict." The Center for LIC (CLIC) however published *FM 100-20, Military Operations in Low Intensity Conflict* in 1990. The 1990 doctrine delineated, defined, categorized, and offered guiding principles for LIC—its chapter on peacekeeping was the only doctrine the U.S. Army had for peacekeeping when the Cold War ended.[23]

EXISTING BRITISH PEACEKEEPING DOCTRINE AT THE END OF THE COLD WAR

The doctrine available for use by the British Army when it deployed to Bosnia for Operation Grapple I in 1992 was Cold War vintage. The 1988 British peacekeeping doctrine, *The Army Field Manual, Volume V, All Arms Tactics, Special Operations, and Techniques, Part 1, Peacekeeping Operations* (hereafter *PKO*), reflected not so much the most recent British experience in Northern Ireland, but traditional peacekeeping experiences, such as Cyprus. *PKO* was replete with checklists and vignettes on how to set up checkpoints but it didn't seem to cover much in the way of how to deliver humanitarian aid in the midst of ongoing conflict.[24] The overarching British Army manual was the 1989 edition of *Design for Military Operations: The British Military Doctrine* (hereafter *BMD*). The cover of *BMD* states: "the function of the Military Doctrine is to establish the framework of understanding of the approach to warfare in order to provide the foundation for its practical application."[25] In addition, one other manual was germane to British peacekeeping as the decade of the 1990s approached—*The Army Field Manual, Volume I, The Fundamentals, Part 1, The Application of Force* (hereafter *Application of Force*). As overarching operational doctrine drives specific doctrine, this analysis begins with *BMD* and then examines *Application of Force* and *PKO*.

PEACEKEEPING CATEGORIES, TASKS, AND LITERATURE

It is significant that *BMD* devotes one sentence to peacekeeping and refers to the only two PKO where Britain played a significant role. Peacekeeping is one of several missions that are subsumed under the heading "Commitments out of the NATO Area." Under the one bullet on peacekeeping, *BMD* states that elements are deployed "when invited" under a UN mandate (UNFICYP—Cyprus) or under multinational arrangements (MFO—Sinai). Humanitarian tasks are another sub-bullet listed under the same commitments. In addition, *BMD* explains that, "the spectrum of conflict is a general guide to the way in which force is used." However, the manual qualifies, the spectrum of conflict does not refer to peacekeeping operations which aim to prevent the resumption of conflict. By way of comparison, this is very salient since U.S. doctrine identifies peace operations as a subcategory of low intensity conflict. Although *BMD* and U.S. doctrine identify general war, limited war, and low intensity conflict as typologies within the spectrum, the British doctrine only lists two types of LIC—Civil Disorder and Revolutionary Warfare.[26]

Application of Force reinforces this exclusion of PKO from the spectrum of conflict. Chapter 2 of this manual, "The Nature of Conflict," emphasizes the key difference between counterinsurgency (a subset of LIC) and peacekeeping: counterinsurgency operations "are designed to defeat an insurgency and maintain the authority of a legitimate government." Peacekeeping operations, the manual states, aim "to prevent conflict, or its resumption, by the physical separation of hostile elements by a third party to allow negotiations to reach a political settlement." Moreover, *Application of Force* bifurcates peacekeeping into "enforcement action" (it cites the Korean War as an example of this and notes the rarity of such operations) and peacekeeping, which may be authorized by the UN "with the consent of all parties." It lists only two sub-categories of PKO—military observer groups and peacekeeping forces. For an example of the former it cites the UN Military Observer Group India and Pakistan (UNMOGIP) and for an example of the latter it lists the UN Emergency Force in Egypt (UNEF 1, 1956–1967). The next section of the chapter, Section 4—The Spectrum of Conflict, discusses counterinsurgency and civil disorders at length.[27]

Although the British Army has historically been doctrine averse, it is important to note that it had an entire manual dedicated to peacekeeping whereas the American Army had only one chapter in its LIC manual devoted to peacekeeping. The stated aim of the Brits' *PKO* is to elucidate how observer missions and peacekeeping forces operate—how they are trained, controlled, and supported. Once again, reflecting continuity and connectivity to *Application of Force*, PKO focuses almost exclusively on peacekeeping rather than enforcement (Chapter VII of the UN Charter, Article 45—"enforcement action"). Out of the eight chapters in *PKO*, one paragraph in Chapter I ("The Nature of Peacekeeping") is dedicated to explaining "enforcement." It begins by stating that this type of operation "would almost certainly be blocked" by a UN Security Council veto and that Article 42[28] "is unlikely to be invoked in the foreseeable future." It refers to the Korea War and the blockade of Rhodesia (1966) as examples of enforcement action. The paragraph ends: "enforcement is not considered further in this pamphlet.[29]

PKO lists only two subcategories for peacekeeping operations: observer missions and peacekeeping forces. The main task of observer missions is for unarmed officers to man observation posts in the observance of armistices and cease-fires. According to this manual, peacekeeping forces are "armed bodies of troops placed under United Nations command by states" who are members of the UN. The troops normally consist of combat arms units in the peacekeeper role, with logistics and communications units providing support to the UN force's headquarters in the field. *PKO* identifies five tasks under the category of peacekeeping: Separation—the separation of hostile forces with the consent of both parties; Inter-positional Force—to secure the withdrawal of opposing forces behind agreed upon lines; Buffer Zones—the occupation or observation of neutral areas marked by cease-fire lines; Areas of Limitation in Armaments—peacekeepers monitor armament levels in agreed areas of reduced armaments; and Supervised Withdrawal—peacekeepers occupy the area withdrawn from and hand over to the other party. It also is not insignificant that UNFICYP (British peacekeeping operations in Cyprus) is the most predominant vignette in *PKO*.[30]

PEACEKEEPING DEFINITIONS AND PRINCIPLES

The British manual offers a curious explanation of peacekeeping: "it has never been officially defined and an attempt to do so might prove unduly restrictive and embarrassing if an essentially empirical activity were to be shackled by immutable terminology." This very statement in a way reveals the British Army's aversion to doctrine and its predilection to "adapt on the hoof." However, *PKO* does offer a general description of peacekeeping as "an operation involving military personnel, without powers of enforcement, established by the United Nations or some other group of states to help restore and maintain peace in an area of conflict." In addition to the cardinal principles of peacekeeping discussed below, *PKO* identifies seven more: negotiation, suggestion, clarity of intention, firmness, anticipation, recognition of the host government's authority, and integration. Notwithstanding the self-evident principles, "recognition of the host government's authority" is corollary to consent—a PK force deploys at the invitation of the host country and can remain there only with that government's agreement.[31]

CONSENT, IMPARTIALITY, AND FORCE

PKO does not list consent as a principle for the conduct of peacekeeping because according to British doctrine consent is a precondition and a continuous condition that must be maintained in peacekeeping. In fact, *PKO* lists consent as a prerequisite for success. A peacekeeping operation should have "the *consent* of the parties to the dispute and of the host countries, and preferably, enjoy wide enough international support, or at least tacit acceptance, to avoid damaging interference." What's more, the manual emphasizes the absoluteness of impartiality—"total *impartiality* and *neutrality* are essential to retain the trust of the parties to the dispute and of the host government." An imprudent word or act, *PKO* explains, which is perceived as favoring one of the parties over the other can result in noncooperation or hostility and may jeopardize the operation. However, of these three variables, the manual dedicates the most words (four pages worth) to the use of force. Moreover, the manual's principle concerning the use of force is not "minimum force" but "avoidance of the use of force."[32]

PKO has a whole section (Section 25) on the *use of force*. Under the header "Dangers of Using Force," the manual emphasizes that unnecessary or illegal force can escalate the level of violence and can create "a situation in which the peacekeeping force becomes part of the problem." It delineates between passive force (means not aimed at physical harm) and active force (means resulting in harm to individuals). It also has subsections on the justification for the use of active force and conditions for the use of active force. The bottom line, though, is *minimum force*—"only the minimum amount of force may be used to stop a threat to life or an aggressive violation. As soon as the attack or violation ceases fire must be stopped."[33]

The British peacekeeping doctrine at the end of the Cold War thus focused exclusively on traditional peacekeeping. There is but one paragraph on enforcement that dismissed it as unlikely and all of the subtasks under peacekeeping are the traditional tasks associated with operations in Cyprus and the Middle East. The remainder of *PKO* is essentially a checklist for performing the other mundane, but necessary tasks, associated with cease-fire line peacekeeping. For example, the manual includes sections on "Taking Over and Handing Over a Observation Post" and "Duties in an Observation Post."

EXISTING AMERICAN PEACEKEEPING DOCTRINE AT THE END OF THE COLD WAR

On the other hand, the official U.S. doctrine that was in use and germane to peacekeeping operations when Somalia began was the 1986 versions of *FM 100-1, The Army,* and *FM 100-5, Operations,* the 1990 version of *FM 100-20, Military Operations in Low Intensity Conflict,* and the January 1993 Center for Army Lessons Learned (CALL) *Special Edition 93-1,* "Somalia," that included an extract from the operations other than war chapter of the December 1992 draft of *FM 100-5, Operations.* The final edition of *Operations* was published in June 1993, just when the situation in Somalia was starting to look like war. The 1986 edition of *FM 100-5, Operations* does not mention peace operations (although it dedicates one paragraph to peacekeeping) and the 1981 edition of *FM 100-20, Low Intensity Conflict* dedicated about one half page to peacekeeping and humanitarian assistance.

However, the 1990 edition of *FM 100-20, Military Operations in Low Intensity Conflict* includes a whole chapter on peacekeeping—with the consent of the parties and a negotiated truce—thus based on traditional (Chapter VI) peacekeeping models. David Segal and Dana Eyre assert that the inclusion of peacekeeping as part of LIC had two deleterious consequences: (1) peacekeeping was marginalized as it was subsumed under LIC—a marginalized mission within U.S. military strategic culture; and (2) once peacekeeping was included in LIC, "it was inexorably defined as a form of conflict, rather than as a form of conflict management or conflict resolution."[34]

PEACEKEEPING CATEGORIES, TASKS, AND LITERATURE

FM 100-1, The Army is not as significant operationally as *FM 100-5, Operations,* but it does belong to the hierarchy of manuals. Its purpose is to explain the constitutional foundations of the U.S. Army and link the Army to national security policy. However, *FM 100-1* is "the progenitor of other manuals" in the Army' doctrine system. Its bottom line is war and it emphasizes the fact that "the shock action and firepower of well supported combat forces is the essence of the U.S. Army." It explains that war fighting—the imposition of our will by force—determines how the Army is equipped, organized, and trained. This manual also states that the Army "must have the capability to operate across the spectrum of conflict." *FM 100-1* does mention LIC and peacekeeping: "low intensity conflict involves military action below the level of sustained combat between regular forces." In addition, it explains that success in LIC "will ordinarily rule out the protracted commitment of U.S. forces." The manual lists peacekeeping as a LIC mission. In an extensive study on Army doctrine, one author offered this footnote to *FM 100-1*: "although the manual does refer to FM 100-5 as the basic operational doctrine that guides the Army in combat, it entirely excludes any reference to *FM 100-20, Military Operations in Low Intensity Conflict.*"[35]

The preface of the 1986 *FM 100-5, Operations* emphasizes conventional military operations but "recognizes that Army forces must be capable of operating in any battlefield environment," including LIC. Thus, the Army's "keystone" manual considered LIC a battlefield environment, and peacekeeping operations as well, by subsuming PKO within LIC category. The first chapter of this manual also makes it unambiguously clear that the mid-1980s Army was hedging on LIC: "while Air Land Battle doctrine (ALB) focuses primarily on mid- to high-intensity warfare, the tenets of Air Land Battle apply equally to the military operations characteristic of low intensity war." Air Land Battle was the Army's doctrine for fighting the Soviets in the Fulda Gap—it was also consistent with the U.S. military's cultural preference for the big war paradigm. However, to overlay the principles of ALB on LIC is as incongruous as using the Weinberger-Powell criteria to achieve success in peacekeeping.[36]

Nonetheless, this manual notes that the increasing occurrence of "war at the low end of the conflict spectrum" requires special task organization, force composition, rapid deployment, and restraint in execution. Moreover, although the authors of this manual did not deem LIC important enough to define, they did list the subcategory missions of LIC that include counterinsurgency (Foreign Internal Defense), peacetime contingency operations, and peacekeeping. About peacekeeping, the manual states that U.S. Army forces will participate in PKO "which support diplomatic efforts to achieve, restore, or maintain peace in an area of armed conflict." Peacekeeping operations, it continues, rely on a high degree of unit and individual discipline and use force only in self-defense. All in all, this manual dedicates one page of 187 pages to LIC. It does, however, dedicate one three-and-a-half-page chapter (Chapter 12) to peacetime contingency operations which are a subcategory of LIC. Chapter 12, however, offers no typology of these operations but only some general planning guidance. *FM 100-5* does direct the reader to *FM 100-20* (LIC) and this manual contained one chapter on peacekeeping and one chapter on peacetime contingency operations.[37]

The very first page of the 1990 U.S. Army/U.S. Air Force manual is revealing in that it juxtaposes quotes by two authors with seemingly incongruous perspectives on low-intensity missions in particular and on the use of the military as a multipurpose instrument of politics in general. After all, it was Casper Weinberger who codified a list of criteria for using force that essentially proscribed any use of force outside the conventional and mid- to high-intensity paradigm:

> The political object, as the original motive of war, should be the standard for determining both the aim of the military force and also the amount of effort to be made.
> —Carl von Clausewitz[38]

> What is important is to understand the role of military forces and the role of other responses and how these fit together.
> —Caspar Weinberger[39]

For American military strategic culture and its approach to LIC, the context of these quotes reveals more than the content: it is ironic and perplexing that quotes by both Clausewitz and Weinberger appear on the very first page of the last Cold War U.S. Army LIC manual. This is ironic because Clausewitz' overarching principle—the subordination of the military instrument to the political object—is rather incongruous with the Weinberger Doctrine, which essentially prescribes to the President when the U.S. military should use force (mid-intensity conflict [MIC]/high-intensity conflict [HIC]) and proscribes when the U.S. military should not be used (LIC). However, the next section is a bit complicated since, although the 1990 *FM 100-20* was the official doctrine for LIC in 1992, the December 1992 draft version of the new post–Cold War *FM 100-5, Operations* was in circulation. This manual set a precedent by dedicating a chapter to LIC, the name of which metamorphosed into Operations Other Than War (OOTW). The guidance in this chapter, then, though not as comprehensive as an entire manual, in some degree superseded (the principles of OOTW supplanted the imperatives of LIC) and in some way complemented the 1990 LIC manual. What's more, the new *FM 100-5* manual's chapter on OOTW was also extracted in and placed in Chapter II (Operations Other Than War—Emerging Doctrine) of a training pamphlet that Fort Leavenworth distributed to the troops in Somalia. The commander of U.S. Forces Somalia (USFORSOM) under UNOSOM II informed me that U.S. Army forces were using the OOTW chapter from the 1992 draft *100-5*.[40]

Among the four operational categories under LIC, the U.S. Army's 1990 *FM 100-20, Military Operations in Low Intensity Conflict* (hereafter *LIC*) identifies peacekeeping operations and peacetime contingency operations. Unlike, the British doctrine, all four of these categories are considered to fall within the spectrum of conflict. Moreover, the typology of "peace-time contingency operations" includes "peacemaking" which was the U.S. Army's pre-*Agenda for Peace* equivalent of peace enforcement. Thus, the doctrine did bifurcate and explain guidance for both traditional peacekeeping (Chapter VI of the Charter) and enforcement (Chapter VII of the Charter). However, in the emerging doctrine (*Special Edition 93-1* and the *1992 FM100-5*, Draft), the five imperatives of LIC migrated and metamorphosed into the six principles of OOTW. In addition, the newer doctrine fuses the four categories of LIC with the typology of peacetime contingency operations to arrive at 13 OOTW activities that "can take place at different times or simultaneously in different places." The 13 activities include peacekeeping and peace enforcement. However, in the absence of a then to be published peace operations manual, this study infers that the principles for peacekeeping (traditional) outlined in the 1990 *LIC* still applied, although the newer OOTW principles overarched all such operations in general.[41]

For example, the 1990 *LIC* manual lists and explains the principles for traditional peacekeeping—these are almost universal and do not differ significantly from the principles found in the British Army's *PKO*. In addition, the *LIC* chapter on peacekeeping explains that the U.S. "may participate in peacekeeping operations under the auspices of an international organization, in cooperation with other countries, or unilaterally." PKO support political efforts to restore, achieve, or maintain peace in areas of actual or potential conflict. *LIC* identifies, but does not define, several forms of peacekeeping operations: Withdrawal and Disengagement, Cease-fire, Prisoner-of-War Exchanges, Arms Control, and Demilitarization and Demobilization. The 1990 manual also explains that the "control of violence in peacekeeping operations requires a combination of techniques." Among these techniques, it lists observation, patrolling, and information gathering.[42]

PEACEKEEPING DEFINITIONS AND PRINCIPLES

Both the 1990 *LIC* doctrine and the emerging OOTW doctrine in *Special Edition 93-1* distinguished between peacekeeping and peacemaking (this term was changed to peace enforcement in 1992 to be consistent with the terminology in *Agenda for Peace*). The 1990 manual explains that, "situations may arise which require deployment of U.S. military forces to impose peace." Although these operations are often called peacekeeping, *LIC* maintains, they are better described as peacemaking. "Peacemaking missions differ greatly in execution from peacekeeping missions." In addition, the chapter on contingency operations explains that the political complexities of peacemaking dictate that the force employed be sufficient but applied with discretion. Thus, in 1990 peacemaking amounted to peace imposition and required the commander to use psychological operations, maneuver, intelligence, and communication to "achieve a decisive concentration of power at the critical time and place." The *Special Edition 93-1* describes peacekeeping as operations that support diplomatic efforts "to maintain peace in areas of potential conflict." Peacekeeping, it states, requires the consent of the parties involved and it deters violence by physical presence. On the other hand, peace enforcement is defined in 1992 as an operation "to restore peace between hostile factions" with or without consent. Peace enforcement "implies the use of force or its threat to coerce hostile factions." Elements conducting peace enforcement, moreover, "cannot maintain their objective neutrality in every instance" and "must be prepared at all times to apply elements of combat power to restore order."[43]

The U.S. doctrine offers two sets of guiding principles for these operations: OOTW principles and the principles of peacekeeping operations found in the 1990 *LIC*. The 1990 imperatives of LIC—unity of effort, legitimacy, perseverance, adaptability, and political dominance—migrated to operations other than war to become objective, unity of effort, legitimacy, patience, restraint, and security. While all of these seem rather self-evident, it is necessary explain the principles that are of more salience in peace operations. *Legitimacy* "derives from the perception that constituted authority is both genuine and effective and employs appropriate means for reasonable purposes." It also states that committed forces must sustain the *legitimacy* of the operation. *Patience* instructs forces to "prepare for the measured, protracted application of military capability in support of strategic aims." It also explains that the Army must balance the desire to achieve objectives rapidly with "sensitivity" for long-term strategic goals. The other principle particularly germane to peacekeeping is *restraint*. *Restraint* dictates that forces "apply appropriate military capability prudently." This principle cautions that excessive force can undermine legitimacy and unhinge the attainment of short and long-term goals.[44]

Although ostensibly less salient in peace operations, the principles of *objective* and *security* merit examination because they seem to reflect American military strategic cultural attitudes about the use force. *Objective* demands that "every military operation be directed toward a clearly defined, decisive, and attainable objective." What's more, the principle of *security* emphasizes that the commander must protect the force at all times, regardless of mission. However, these two principles seem somewhat chimerical in a realm of operations where success is not easily quantifiable and zero casualties may not be possible. They seem to reflect a Powellian cultural continuity stemming from Vietnam and Lebanon, but somewhat out of context in OOTW.[45]

Notwithstanding, the 1990 *LIC* manual did offer a list of separate of principles to guide the conduct of peacekeeping only. In addition to prescriptions about consent, impartiality, and force, which are explained in the next section, Chapter 4 of *LIC* lists Balance, Single Manager Control, Concurrent Action, Unqualified Sponsor Support, and Freedom of Movement as peacekeeping principles. Balance, it states, is "a function of consent" and it refers to the functional, geographic, and political composition of the peacekeeping force. Freedom of Movement simply states that the force should be allowed to move around the buffer zone or area of operation unimpeded. However, the U.S. doctrine also bifurcates its treatment of consent, impartiality, and force, with one approach for peacekeeping and another for peace enforcement.[46]

CONSENT, IMPARTIALITY, AND FORCE

For peacekeeping operations, *consent* is also a pre-condition for success—"the presence and degree of *consent* determine the success of the peacekeeping operation." In addition, *neutrality*, revealingly, is listed instead of *impartiality*. "Neutrality is closely linked with consent" and to preserve it, the force must maintain an atmosphere and attitude of *impartiality*. *LIC* also considers the application of force to be justified only in self-defense—"the ROE normally allow peace-keepers to use force only in self-defense."[47]

For peace enforcement operations, however, the emerging U.S. doctrine looks at these three principles differently, as being more malleable. For example, *consent* is not a prerequisite—the 1992 doctrine states that hostile factions "may not" *consent* to the intervention. Moreover, peace enforcement forces, in all instances, "cannot maintain their objective *neutrality*" and peace enforcement involves the threat or use of force to "coerce" belligerent factions to "cease and desist." Being ready to "apply elements of combat power" to "separate warring factions" is significantly different than the avoidance of force, except in self-defense.[48]

Figure 4.2
British/American PK Typology, 1992

	British Doctrine			American Doctrine	
	MISSIONS	**PRINCIPLES**		**MISSIONS**	**PRINCIPLES**
PK	OBSERVER MSN PEACEKEEPING	Impartiality Avoidance of Force Negotiation Clarity of Intention Suggestion Firmness Anticipation Integration Host govt authority		Disengagement Cease-Fire POW Exchange Arms Control Demobilization	Balance Force in Self defense Consent Impartiality Single Manager Control Concurrent Action Sponsor support Freedom of Movement
PE	Unlikely	NA		Restore Peace Impose Peace Separate Hostile Factions	Objective Legitimacy Unity of Effort Patience Restraint Security

CONCLUSION—A COMPARISON OF THE DOCTRINE AT THE END OF THE COLD WAR

The paucity of peace enforcement guidance in the British doctrine reveals an almost exclusive focus on traditional peacekeeping tasks. However, the dedication of an entire manual to PKO would seem to make this area more significant to the British Army. On the other hand, the 1990 U.S. Army LIC manual and the 1992 OOTW doctrine exhibited a broader range of coverage and tasks in the realm of peace operations. Whereas British doctrine essentially excluded peace enforcement from the discussion, already in 1990 the U.S. doctrine countenanced the use of force to compel peace between belligerents. While U.S. Army doctrine did not consider this war, it did recognize the requirement to use "sufficient force" and discretion. For peacekeeping, both doctrines (*PKO* and *LIC*) treat impartiality as absolute and as synonymous with neutrality. However, in its broader approach to peace enforcement the U.S. doctrine avers that objective neutrality is not always possible.

Moreover, both doctrines emphasize the importance of consent and minimum force during the conduct of pure peacekeeping. However, it is especially salient that the British Army doctrine absolutely excluded PKO from the spectrum of conflict and the U.S. Army doctrine subsumed both peacekeeping (Chapter VI, UNC) and peacemaking [(later changed to peace enforcement in the 1992 doctrine) (Chapter VII, UNC)] under low intensity war, and later, under operations other than war. Moreover, neither of the two doctrines even identified armed humanitarian operations (AHO) as a subcategory mission of peacekeeping or peace enforcement. The U.S. 1992 chapter on OOTW, however, did list humanitarian assistance as a co-category mission under Operations Other Than War. Figure 4.2 depicts the peacekeeping–peace enforcement bifurcation of tasks in the two doctrinal systems. It also compares the two doctrines' sets of guiding principles for operations in this realm.

NOTES

1. Colin S. Gray, "Strategic Culture as Context: The First Generation of Theory Strikes Back," *Review of International Studies* 25 (1999): 63.

2. "Middle-ground" and "gray-area" are only two of a host of terms that generally emerged after the Cold War to describe UN operations in which the amount of forces and way of using force fell between traditional peacekeeping (Chapter VI of the UN Charter) and peace enforcement (Chapter VII).

3. BG (Ret.) Gavin Bulloch, interview by author, Trenchard Lines, Upavon, England, 16 December 1999.

4. John Mackinlay, telephone interview by author, West Point, New York, 16 Mar 2000.

5. John Gerard Ruggie, "The United Nations and the Collective Use of Force: Whither—or Whether" (A paper of the UNA-USA International Dialogue on the Enforcement of Security Council Resolutions, New York, 1996), 6.

6. John Mackinlay, "Peace Support Operations Doctrine," *The British Army Review* No. 113 (August 1996): 6.

7. Ibid.: 7.

8. Ibid.: 6; and Theo Farrell, "Making Sense of Doctrine," in *Doctrine and Military Effectiveness*, Strategic Policy Studies I, Eds., Michael Duffy, Theo Farrell, and Geoffrey Sloan (Exeter, England: Britannia Royal Naval College, 1997), 4.

9. Richard Duncan Downie, *Learning from Conflict: The U.S. Military in Vietnam, El Salvador, and the Drug War* (Westport, CT: Praeger, 1998), 122.

10. Farrell, 4. Rich Rinaldo, interview by author, Newport News, VA, 21 March 2000. Throughout a six-hour interview, Rinaldo explained and provided memoranda to back up the extent of the information exchange between the U.S. Army and British Army during the writing of the two manuals. There was an implicit mandate that both approaches should be "compatible" before the doctrinal manuals went to final print. The comparison of the two manuals and the findings refer to the interview and the memoranda in Chapters 5 and 6 of this study.

11. Marrack Goulding, "The Evolution of United Nations Peacekeeping," *International Affairs* 69 (1993): 458–59.

12. *The Army Field Manual, Volume 5, Operations Other Than War, Part 2, Wider Peacekeeping* (London: HMSO, 1994), C-3.

13. *CFP 300, Canada's Army* (Kingston: Chief of the Canadian Defence Staff, 1995), 5-5; *Emploi des Forces Terrestres dans l'Action des Forces Armees* (Metz: French Doctrine and Training Command, 1996), 0-5; *FM 100-5, Operations* (Washington, D.C.: United States Army, 1993), 1-1; and *Army Doctrine Publication, Volume 1, Operations* (London: HMSO, 1994), 1A-2.

14. Downie, 43.

15. *The Charter of the United Nations* (New York: UN Department of Public Information, 1993), 19–23.

16. *FM 100-5, Operations*, (Washington, D.C.: United States Army, 1993), 1-3.

17. Gavin Bulloch, "The Development of Doctrine for Counter-Insurgency—the British Experience," *The British Army Review* 111 (December 1995): 22–23.

18. Ibid.: 23.

19. Ibid.: 24; Bulloch interview, 16 December 1999; and Gavin Bulloch, telephone interview by author, 9 March 2000, West Point, New York.

20. Anne W. Chapman et al., *Prepare the Army for War: A Historical Overview of the Army Training and Doctrine Command, 1973–1998* (Fort Monroe, VA: U.S. Army TRADOC Military History Office, 1998), 61–62.

21. Gordon Sullivan, "Doctrine: An Army Update," in *The United States Army: Challenges and Missions for the 1990s* eds. Robert L. Pfaltzgraff and Richard H. Shultz (Lexington, MA: Lexington Books, 1991), 83.

22. Chapman et al., 101–2; and Downie, 77–79.

23. Ibid., 102; and Ricky Lynn Waddell, "The Army and Peacetime Low Intensity Conflict 1961–1993: The Process of Peripheral and Fundamental Military Change," (Ph.D. Diss., Columbia University, 1994), 240, 248, and 251–52.

24. Bulloch interview, 16 December 1999.

25. *Design for Military Operations: the British Military Doctrine* (London: HMSO, 1989), cover. Hereafter, this manual is referred to as *BMD*.

26. *BMD*, 21.

27. *The Army Field Manual, Volume I, The Fundamentals, Part 1 The Application of Force* (London: HMSO, 1985), 11–12. Hereafter, *Application of Force*.

28. Article 42 (in conjunction with Articles 25 and 39) of the *Charter of the United Nations* allows the Security Council to authorize "such action by air, sea, or land forces as may be necessary to maintain or restore international peace and security." Article 25 makes SC *decisions* binding on member states and Article 39 authorizes the SC to determine the existence of a threat to peace and to *decide* on measures under Article 42 of the Charter.

29. *The Army Field Manual, Volume V, All Arms Tactics, Special Operations, and Techniques, Part 1, Peacekeeping Operations* (London: HMSO, 1988), xxi, 1-3–1-4. Hereafter, PKO.

30. *PKO*, 1-7–1-10.

31. *PKO*, 1-5, 4-1–4-2; and Bulloch interview, 9 March 2000.

32. *PKO*, 1-13, 4-1–4-2, 5-6–5-10, and 6-16–6-20.

33. *PKO*, 6-16–6-20.

34. David R. Segal and Dana P. Eyre, "The U.S. Army in Peace Operations at the Dawning of the Twenty-First Century," A report prepared for the U.S. Army Research Institute, November 1994, 63–64.

35. *FM 100-1, the Army* (Washington, D.C.: United States Army, 1986), 8–9; and Michael J. Brady, "The Army and the Strategic Military Legacy of Vietnam," (Master's Thesis, U.S. Army Command and General Staff College, 1990), 122–23.

36. *FM 100-5, Operations* (Washington, D.C.: United States Army, 1986), i and 6. Also, see Brady, 127–29. Brady thoroughly traces the post-Vietnam evolution of the three Army field manuals under examination.

37. *FM 100-5* (1986), 4-6, 169–71.

38. *FM 100-20, Military Operations in Low Intensity Conflict* (Washington, D.C.: United States Army and United States Air Force, 1990), 1-1. For the U.S. Air Force, this field manual is designated as Air Force Pamphlet 3-20. Hereafter, *LIC*.

39. Ibid.

40. See Chapter 13 of *FM 100-5, Operations*, Draft (Washington, D.C.: U.S. Army, December 1992) and "Somalia," *Special Edition No. 93-1* (Fort Leavenworth, KS: Center for Army Lessons Learned, January 1993), 7–12. LTG (Ret.) Thomas M. Montgomery, Interview by author, 14 March 2000, West Point, New York.

41. *LIC*, Chapters 1 and 5; and *Special Edition 93-1*, 7–12.

42. *LIC*, 1-6, 4-1, 4-5.

43. *LIC*, 4-10, 5-7; and *Special Edition 93-1*, 11–12.

44. *Special Edition 93-1*, 9-10; and Rinaldo interview. When asked about the overlap between the imperatives of LIC and the principles of OOTW, Rinaldo explained that the imperatives "migrated" to the OOTW chapter in the 1993 *FM 100-5*. When asked about the principles of peace operations, Rinaldo said the principles of OOTW, "as applied to peace operations" guide actions.

45. *Special Edition 93-1*, 9–10.

46. *LIC*, 4-1–4-2.

47. *LIC*, 4-1–4-2.

48. *Special Edition 93-1*, 12.

5

THE AMERICAN MILITARY IN SOMALIA—INTO THE ABYSS

Whoever fights monsters should see to it that in the process he does not become a monster. And when you look long into the abyss, the abyss also looks into you.
—Friederich Nietzsche[1]

If this isn't combat, then I'm sure having a helluva nightmare.
—Major General Montgomery[2]

INTRODUCTION

General Montgomery was the commander of U.S. Forces Somalia (USFORSOM) under UNOSOM II and these words accurately describe the actions of the U.S. soldiers who fought against Mohammed Farah Aideed's militia in Mogadishu during the night of 3–4 October 1993. What's more, to the U.S. soldiers involved in the battle, all of a sudden surrounded by overwhelming numbers of hostile Somali fighters in the labyrinth of shanties and side alleys of Mogadishu, it must have seemed that they were entering the abyss. In fact, the battle in Mogadishu that night represented the most intense light infantry battle experienced by the U.S. Army since Vietnam. Rangers, Delta Force operators, and the infantrymen of the 10th Mountain Division acquitted themselves courageously and meritoriously in the most dire of situations: with the mission gone awry, outnumbered and surrounded by hostile forces, the commandos fought there way out of Mogadishu with their "precious cargo" (a host of Aideed's lieutenants). Moreover, two Delta Force soldiers were posthumously awarded Congressional Medals of Honor, the first such awards since Vietnam, for conspicuous heroism during the battle. Ordinarily, such valor and distinguished service would be publicized and lauded among military and government circles.

However, the battle in Mogadishu was no ordinary combat action: the fighting occurred within the overall context of a UN "humanitarian operation." With 18 of America's best-trained soldiers and several hundred Somali dead, the action that night was considered a debacle—it was clear that both the U.S. military and the Clinton Administration wanted to quickly put this ill-conceived endeavor behind them. Moreover, it also became evident in the United States, that the onus for this debacle would be cast on the UN's overly aggressive approach to multilateralism —something the U.S. should avoid in the future. In addition, within the U.S. military Somalia revived the specter of Vietnam, and instead of "No More Vietnams," the shibboleth "No More Somalias" appeared.

The UN intervention in Somalia clearly conformed to the definition of AHO presented in the introduction: a massive humanitarian impetus; a multilateral action under a UN mandate; and an absence of geopolitical self-interest. The collapse of Somalia accelerated in January 1991 when President Siad Barre was forced to abdicate in the midst of a general uprising. State failure ensued in a civil war that included no less than 13 rival factions vying for power. While a discussion of factional politics is beyond the scope of this study, it is important to note that Aideed's Somali National Alliance (SNA) and Ali Mahdi's Somali Salvation Alliance (SSA) were central to the humanitarian problem because they controlled the Mogadishu area. Possessing a stronger force and convinced of his right to lead Somalia after defeating Siad Barre, Aideed initially opposed any UN political involvement. In a weaker military position, Ali Mahdi welcomed a UN role.[3]

The active UN role in Somalia was impelled by a letter from interim Somali Prime Minister Omer Arteh Ghalib which was dated 11 January 1992. Ghalib's letter asked the Security Council to address the deteriorating situation in Somalia and to "come up with a programme of effective action to end the fighting."[4] In early 1992, this "deteriorating situation" was best described as a lawless collapsed state in which factional fighting and looting blocked economic production and the distribution of food, causing an epidemic famine which was killing hundreds of thousands.[5]

January 1992 marked the beginning of a yearlong series of Security Council resolutions addressing the situation in Somalia, culminating in December with a large-scale U.S.-led AHO. Resolution 733 of 20 January expressed alarm at "the heavy loss of life" and concern "that the continuation constitutes . . . a threat to international peace and security." Moreover, this resolution made a decision under Chapter VII to implement a "complete embargo on all deliveries of weapons and military equipment," although it did not explicitly invoke Article 39 or 41. After noncompliance with a 3 March cease-fire continued to disrupt humanitarian efforts, the Security Council reaffirmed that "the magnitude of the human suffering . . . constitutes a threat to international peace and security" in Resolution 746.[6]

In adopting Resolution 751 on 24 April, the Security Council decided to establish a United Nations Operation in Somalia (UNOSOM I) and to deploy 50 UN observers to monitor the cease-fire in Mogadishu. The Council also agreed in principle to establish a security force to protect humanitarian efforts. In July, Resolution 767 requested that the Secretary-General make use of "an urgent airlift operation" to facilitate the efforts of humanitarian organizations. The Security Council's increasing impatience with the war-lords' disruption of the relief effort was manifest in this resolution: "the Council does not exclude other measures to deliver humanitarian assistance." Although the United States responded to Resolution 767 with an airlift effort, it became evident that even a sustained air effort would not effect a reversal in the deteriorating situation.[7]

In August, the two principal factions agreed to the deployment of a 500-strong security force as part of UNOSOM I. Moreover, on 28 August, the Security Council approved Boutros-Ghali's request to increase the strength of UNOSOM I to 3,500 personnel (Resolution 775). The battalion of 500 lightly armed Pakistanis that comprised UNOSOM I arrived in Mogadishu in September 1992. The battalion's mission was to secure the port, secure food shipments to and from the airport, and escort food convoys in Mogadishu. However, constrained by stringent rules of neutrality and Aideed's control of the airport and port area, the Pakistanis remained ineffective. Due to the scale of the disaster and the impediments presented by the factions' power struggles, UNOSOM I proved incapable of managing the catastrophe.[8]

By late November 1992, however, the magnitude of the catastrophe induced President Bush to offer U.S. troop support. As a result, on 3 December, the Security Council "determined that the magnitude of the human tragedy caused by the conflict in Somalia, further exacerbated by the obstacles being created to the distribution of humanitarian assistance, constitutes a threat to international peace and security" (S/RES/794). Conspicuously absent in the resolution were any reference to refugee flows and any explanation of how intrastate starvation constituted such a threat. Resolution 794 also recognized the "unique character" of the situation, acting under Chapter VII, it authorized member states "to use all necessary means to establish as soon as possible a secure environment for humanitarian relief operations in Somalia." The deployment of the Unified Task Force (UNITAF) in December 1992 marked a significant increase in the commitment of forces—37,000 well-armed troops, including U.S. Marines.[9]

Although the coercive effect of UNITAF's presence compelled the Somali leaders to sign a general cease-fire agreement in Addis Ababa on 8 January 1993, the UNITAF operation focused mostly on the removal of heavy weapons to establish a secure environment; light weapons were removed only in areas which directly threatened UNITAF facilities. Moreover, although UNITAF attempted to remain politically neutral while conducting humanitarian security missions, its forces were involved in combat with pro-Aideed factions in February, causing Aideed to accuse UNITAF of undermining his political power. Thus, when the UNOSOM II transition began in March, some anti-UN sentiment among Aideed's allies already existed.[10]

Acting under Chapter VII of the Charter, Resolution 814 of 26 March 1993 authorized a UNOSOM II force consisting of 28,000 troops and expanded the mandate for the use of force. The resolution directed the force commander "to assume responsibility for the consolidation, expansion, and maintenance of a secure environment throughout Somalia." It also authorized UNOSOM II to "take appropriate action against any faction that violates or threatens to violate the cessation of hostilities" and "to seize the small arms of all unauthorized armed elements."[11] Manned with a smaller force and supported by a more aggressive mandate, the UNOSOM II leadership immediately alienated Aideed, leading to an escalation in violence.[12]

When UN Special Representative Jonathan Howe renounced UNOSOM support for an Aideed-sponsored peace conference in May, Aideed suspected that his political power was being undermined. Moreover, when day and night patrolling was reduced in south Mogadishu because of a lack of personnel, Aideed seized on the apparent weakness of UNOSOM II. On 5 June 1993 Aideed's militia ambushed a Pakistani detachment, killing 24 soldiers, and prompting an emergency session of the Security Council. Resolution 837 of 6 June 1993 strongly condemned the attacks against UNOSOM II and reaffirmed the authorization "to take all measures necessary against all those responsible for the armed attacks." Supported by a broad mandate, UNOSOM II began to conduct combat operations against Aideed's faction, in essence taking sides in the conflict. On 17 June, UNOSOM II forces conducted an attack against an Aideed stronghold, resulting in heavy UN casualties. In retaliation for the 17 June UN losses, Howe offered a $25,000 reward for Aideed's capture. In the subsequent escalation in fighting, on 12 July, UN forces conducted an attack helicopter raid against Aideed's command center, killing 54 Somalis.[13]

The broad Chapter VII mandate notwithstanding, the October 1993 raid in Mogadishu marked the culmination of UN combat against Aideed. In August, UNOSOM unleashed commandos of the U.S. Special Operations Command with orders to capture Aideed. The ongoing war against Aideed ultimately came to a head on 3 October, when an ill-fated commando raid against Aideed resulted in the death of 18 U.S. soldiers and approximately 500 Somalis. Moreover, as a result of the increased focus on defeating Aideed, the relief activities of this humanitarian operation were reduced by 50 percent in Mogadishu. As a result of the October debacle, the U.S. and most European countries withdrew their forces from UNOSOM II in early 1994. Although UNOSOM remained in Somalia until March 1995, most security and political objectives were abandoned during the summer of 1994 in the face of renewed factional infighting.[14]

Somalia clearly provided a strong moral impetus for action. Vivid television scenes depicting starving women and children, coupled with statistics that indicated 3,000 daily deaths, all contributed to a sense of international moral indignation. The fact that greedy warlords were impeding humanitarian relief further outraged the public. Moreover, Somalia's post–Cold War strategic insignificance seemed to indicate that the motive was purely humanitarian. Nonetheless, one year of chaos and starvation elapsed in Somalia before the UN passed its first resolution; almost two years elapsed before the United States was willing to support the effort.[15] The UN/U.S. humanitarian operation in Somalia ran afoul and deteriorated into a combat situation for myriad and complex reasons. However, this section simply aims to determine if and how the U.S. military strategic cultural characteristics identified in Chapter 3 manifested themselves in Somalia during UNITAF (Unified Task Force) operations and UNOSOM II (UN Operation Somalia II). Richard Duncan Downie maintains that changes in the Army's cultural preferences are reflected in both changes in published doctrine and evidenced in the way LIC/OOTW are conducted. Having said that, the second section examines operations in Somalia for continuity or change[16]

While history, geography, and preferred formation all contribute to cultural preferences, this section examines the traits that are more observable in the short term: (1) civil-military relations concerning force and political-military integration during operations; (2) a propensity for overwhelming firepower and maximum force; (3) an aversion to casualties; and (4) an over reliance on technology.

CIVIL-MILITARY RELATIONS: GOOD INTENTIONS DOWN A ROAD TO OOTW HELL[17]

It would be the Provide Comfort Drill again—secure the area, feed the people, and get out without getting tangled up in local political squabbling. Except this time the Americans were plunging into Somalia—a real hellhole, a graveyard for do-gooders and optimists, teeming with bad actors and stocked to the gills with weapons and ammunition.[18]

When examining the civil military aspects of the decision to send troops to Somalia, two things stand out. One is that the impetus for the decision was almost purely moral—could the sole super power stand by and watch millions starve, just weeks before Christmas? Second, Powellian (in an Uptonian way) doctrine prescribed how and how much force would be applied to resource the political aim of humanitarian relief—it was the first Chapter VII authorized humanitarian relief operation. Only the American paradigm of war, fused to a humanitarian cause, could lead to the emergence of the term "armed humanitarian operations"—this is almost as oxymoronic as coupling the Weinberger Doctrine with LIC. However, the U.S. military would lead the mission and it went in armed for bear—with overwhelming and credible force and an exit strategy identified before the first chalk was airborne. However, the Weinberger-Powell criteria, when applied to a failed state's complex humanitarian emergency, are like applying a band-aid to a sucking chest wound.[19]

Although the military initially opposed a major intervention, the deputies of the Joint Chiefs of Staff came up with three courses of action, from minimal to maximal. The third option was the strongest one and it entailed a U.S.-led multinational task force spearheaded by the U.S. Army and Marines, "modeled on Desert Storm and Provide Comfort." Bolger asserts that most in uniform, moreover, agreed that Somalia was a better option for intervention than Bosnia. "By agreeing to the more manageable of the two schemes, the generals and admirals could expect the usual

Bush permission to shape the effort to match military preferences." This is just what happened, according to Bolger. Two things were clear: there would be a massive show of force at the outset to preempt, dissuade, or crush resistance; and the mission would be limited to providing humanitarian relief only. This was the Powellian "all or nothing" approach of decisive force.[20]

Robert Oakley's comments confirm this attitude about the use of military force: "the initial operation was an adaptation of the Weinberger-Powell Doctrine for peacekeeping: dominant force; clear, limited mission; exit strategy (hand off to UN); and strong public support." [21] Oakley echoes this conviction in his book: "The will and ability to use overwhelming force to back a peacekeeping operation—as the Weinberger-Powell Doctrine recommends—offers the greatest possibility of successfully completing a peacekeeping mission and minimizing *casualties* on all sides."[22] On the other hand, during the UNITAF phase, there was much more civil military integration. During both UNITAF and UNOSOM II, the military was essentially in the lead because of its resources, but during UNOSOM II the effort to integrate civil, military, and humanitarian organizations declined. Oakley asserts that UNITAF: "employed combined military, political, information (public information and psychological operations), and humanitarian means to reduce Somali opposition and gain support at home, exercising restraint when possible, hitting hard when need be, and never breaking off dialogue—even with the nastiest warlord."[23]

What's more, the UNITAF leadership's creation of the Civil-Military Operations Center (CMOC) has been generally regarded as innovative and sound: CMOCs have been used in most peace operations after Somalia. According to Allard's study, "one of the most important initiatives of the Somalia operation was the establishment" of the CMOC. Established by the UNITAF leadership in December 1992, it became the central coordinating modality for U.S. forces, other major multinational contingents, and humanitarian organizations. Through this interagency medium, UNITAF coordinated the activities of all the elements in the Somalia effort. For example, coordinating military security for food convoys was done through the CMOC. An added benefit of the CMOC was the broadening of contacts between the civilian and military components, ultimately resulting in CMOCs in each humanitarian relief sector (HRS). Another salient point Allard observed was that the CMOC served as the nexus to the UN Humanitarian Operation Center (HOC), thereby providing a single focal point for relief operations countrywide.[24]

The fundamental importance of maintaining a dialogue with the different clans also led to another key UNITAF innovation: a "Combined Security Committee" that allowed the UNITAF military commander (Johnston) and key members of his staff to meet frequently with Aideed and other key clan leaders. This forum proved especially useful in gaining and even forcing cooperation with UNITAF mandates, such as weapons cantonment. LTG Johnston recounts the purpose of that dialogue: "Aideed and Ali Mahdi were often unhappy with the message we would send from time to time, but for the most part (they) complied." Oakley sums up his thesis on civil-military coordination: "good military-civilian coordination from the outset is essential for success, including the identification of clear, realistic objectives and the mobilization and implementation of combined military-civilian resources to activate them."[25]

However, under UNOSOM II civil-military integration declined significantly. LTG Thomas Montgomery observed of UNOSOM II, "political, humanitarian, and military strategy were not integrated." The military command, his report notes, developed concepts of operation "without an overarching political strategy from its civilian leadership." According to Montgomery, political strategy did not come out until May, two months after the transition to UNOSOM II, and "it reflected little of the reality of the resource constraints of the military and humanitarian division."[26]

The positive aspects of civil-military integration under UNITAF notwithstanding, again Oakley's book helps summarize the problems with applying Weinbergerian precepts to peace operations:

Between the Operation Restore Hope landings in December 1992 and February 1993, however, little high-level consideration was given to the longer-term issues of peacekeeping in Somalia. The pragmatic Weinberger-Powell doctrine of intervention, designed to achieve limited, specific objectives with the support of overwhelming force if needed, had been well understood by the Bush team.[27]

Thus by applying the Weinberger criteria—which were designed to guide the military to victory in mid- or high-intensity conventional conflicts, but were designed to avoid LIC/OOTW—the U.S. military exhibited a tendency to conduct operations in Somalia in a half-measured way, but inclining toward maximum force.

PROPENSITY FOR MAXIMUM FORCE: CROSSING THE MOGADISHU LINE

A senior U.S. staff member has intimated that, despite the principles of operations other than war, the U.S. military is intuitively uncomfortable about participating in missions in which it cannot rely on overwhelming force to achieve success: "You've got to maintain some of that old war fighting approach where victory was when you were standing there with your foot on your enemy's chest."[28] Responding to U.S. Defense Secretary William Perry's 1994 demands for a more robust and punitive NATO response to Bosnian Serb transgressions, the former UNPROFOR Commander, British General Rose remarked "bombing is a last resort because then you cross the Mogadishu Line." General Rose was referring to the October 1993 fighting battle that occurred in Somalia after an expanded Chapter VII mandate induced the U.S.-dominated UN operation to sacrifice its impartiality by taking sides. General Rose's comment also reflected the extant disagreement between the British and the Americans over peacekeeping doctrine: the Americans were again inclined to mix peacekeeping and peace enforcement in the same theater while the British were averse to the prospects of such a dangerous deviation from their traditional peacekeeping doctrine. Furthermore, the imprudent and excessive use of force by U.S./UN forces clearly placed those forces in the middle of an ongoing civil war. However, Oakley agrees: "the U.S. and the UN made Aideed the enemy by UN Security Council Resolution 837; after a no-warning helicopter gun ship attack on a peaceful meeting of some 200 senior members of Aideed's clan on 12 July 1993, the U.S. became their enemy."[29]

Donald Daniel and Bradd Hayes consider the 12 July attack helicopter raid to be one of the most controversial attacks by the U.S. Quick Reaction Force (QRF). "The effect of this raid on the Somalis was electrifying." This excessive display of force made Aideed sympathizers out of Somalis who had not previously supported him. Daniel and Hayes claim that Aideed "began to assume mythical proportions to many in the country." After examining this raid and the subsequent escalation of force, with concomitant Somali casualties and damage, the thought "Anti-WHAM" struck me instantly. This means that this kind of force, used in an operation other than war context, is the antithesis to winning hearts and minds. Just as Arc Light and napalm strikes had been recruiting aids for the Viet Cong during the Vietnam War, so to, it seems, had AH-1F TOW missiles and AC-130 40 millimeter chain guns, fired in the densely populated slums of Mogadishu, made enemies of theretofore neutral Somalis.[30]

Some vignettes from Bowden's book *Black Hawk Down* help capture the impact of a maximum-force approach in a humanitarian operation. Bowden spent some time in Somalia talking to Somalis who had been in Mogadishu that summer.

He had deep wounds that were still healing from an American helicopter attack three months earlier, on July 12—months before the Rangers had come Farah and the others in his clan had welcomed the UN intervention the previous December. It promised to bring stability and hope. But the mission had gradually deteriorated into hatred and bloodshed. Ever since July 12, the Habr Gidr had been at war with America.[31]

His wounds had nearly healed in the three months since. Now, as the armada of American helicopters roared overhead he was reminded of the shock, pain, and terror. The sight filled him and his friends with rage. It was one thing for the world to intervene to feed the starving, and even for the UN to help Somalia form a peaceful government. But this business of sending U.S. Rangers swooping down into their city killing and kidnapping their leaders, this was too much.[32]

Women walking the streets would have their colorful robes blown off. Some had infants torn from their arms by the powerful updraft [rotor wash]. On one raid, a mother screamed frantically in flex cuffs for nearly a half hour before a translator arrived to listen and to explain that her infant had been blown down the road by landing helicopters.[33]

Even LTG Montgomery, the U.S. forces commander under UNOSOM II, conceded that the increasingly forceful responses to the Somali National Alliance (SNA) after the 5 June ambush of the Pakistanis were consistent with our military culture: "it was a normal reaction to the Pakistani ambush—do something—kick some ass." Kicking some ass, however inappropriate to humanitarian relief, is just what the Quick Reaction Force (QRF) started doing in the summer of 1993. Of the July raid, reporter Marguerite Michaels observed: "Blaming Aideed, the U.S. has led UN forces in an aggressive bid to flush him out, culminating in a daylight attack on a meeting of Aideed's top commanders on Monday. At the end of a 20-minute barrage of missiles and cannon fire from U.S. helicopter gun ships, dozens of bodies lay scattered around the demolished villa."[34] LTG Montgomery has also stated clearly that after the 5 June SNA ambush and other attacks against UNOSOM II on 5 July, the U.S./UN command "basically began a period of counter operations to protect the force and to deny Aideed's militia the opportunity to continue 'guerrilla operations' against the UN." Almost revisiting the history of the Vietnam War, the *Montgomery Report* explains that the counter-guerrilla operations were initially aimed at the weapons cantonment sites, followed by "search and clear" operations to drive the enemy out of their enclave in South Mogadishu, near the UN forces headquarters.[35]

Moreover, closer to the tip of the spear in Somalia, Major General Garrison had this to say when asked about the October raid by the Senate Armed Services Committee: "Speed, surprise, and overwhelming firepower are key to our method of operation. TF Ranger was never pinned down. We decided to stay with the helicopter pilots that were pinned inside their aircraft. The Rangers could have fought their way out at any time, if they had to decided to do that."[36] Mats Berdal observed that the excessive force applied by the attack helicopters and special operations forces were conceived solely by the U.S. civilian and military leadership, which was the driving force behind UNOSOM II.[37]

> If we go into the vicinity of the Bakara Market, there is no question we'll win the gunfight. But we might lose the war.
>
> —Major General William Garrison[38]

This overemphasis on force at the tactical level, to the detriment of strategic aims, seems to hearken back to the U.S. approach to counterinsurgency in Vietnam, where it won many battles but lost the war. In fact, in an interview, Robert Oakley stated candidly: "it was just like Tet." His reference alludes to the Tet Offensive in 1968 when the Viet Cong launched concerted attacks against the cities of South Vietnam but was decimated in the ensuing battles. However, the scope of the Viet Cong attacks against South Vietnam's cities so shocked America that Tet was a strategic victory for the North Vietnamese and Viet Cong because it undermined domestic support for the war. Likewise, although TF Ranger accomplished its raid, captured its "precious cargo," and killed hundreds of Somalis in the process, it was a Pyrrhic tactical victory because the shock of American dead, as explained below, unhinged the Somalia policy.[39]

Nothing is more likely to rapidly destroy consent and compromise impartiality than the unrestricted use of force during an AHO operation. According to Charles Dobbie, "the misuse of force risks destabilizing peacekeeping operations and causing an uncontrolled and violent transition into peace enforcement." Dobbie also maintains, "an effective concept must offer guidance as to what is permissible, where the boundaries lie, what alternatives to the use of force might exist, and what principles should guide its application." However, the need to maintain consent does not rule out the use of force in this context. Consent may actually help to marginalize opposition and render it vulnerable to the use of force. If a strong consensual climate exists, force may be used against a marginal and unrepresentative opposition without jeopardizing operational-level consent.[40]

Although many aspects of using force require consideration that goes beyond the rules of engagement (ROE), ROE significantly influence the degree to which impartiality and consent are preserved by restraints on the use of force. Kenneth Allard has asserted that because the use of force must be perceived as supporting the ends for which the operation was begun in the first place, ROE embody two of the most important principles governing peace operations—restraint and legitimacy.[41]

The different approaches to ROE adopted by UNITAF and UNOSOM II reinforce this point. The ROE in effect for UNITAF and UNOSOM II comprised three components: the proper use of force; the confiscation and disposition of weapons; and the treatment of civilians detained by military forces. The most critical issue involved the use of force and the circumstances in which it was authorized. With laudable simplicity, the UNITAF ROE were presented to the troops in bumper-sticker form. Derived from UNITAF's ROE on self-defense and minimum force, they listed four basic "no's": no technicals, such as trucks carrying mounted machine guns; no banditry; no roadblocks; and no visible weapons. Moreover, since crew-served weapons (like those mounted on trucks and labeled the technicals) were considered a special threat, regardless of whether the crew demonstrated hostile intent, UNITAF commanders were authorized to use "all necessary force" to confiscate them.[42]

However, Marine Lieutenant General Robert Johnston (UNITAF Commander) clarified that this did not equate to "shoot on sight:" he directed commanders to challenge and approach the technicals, using all necessary force if the weapons were not voluntarily surrendered. Similar methods were used in confiscating arms caches. These rules, coupled with the presence of UNITAF's credible and robust combat power, resulted in few challenges to forcible confiscation efforts, and extraordinarily few acts of violence directed against UN/U.S. Forces.[43]

When UNOSOM II officially replaced UNITAF in May 1993, these ROE were initially left unchanged. However, after a further expansion of the mandate in June, the mission changed, resulting in an escalation of the use of force and Fragmentary Order 39. Issued by the UNOSOM II Commander, the order stated: "Organized, armed militias, technicals, and other crew-served weapons are considered a threat to UNOSOM forces and may be engaged without provocation." This rule was unambiguously linked to crossing the consent divide and abandoning impartiality. Subsequently, U.S./UN forces became increasingly involved in larger-scale combat operations. Notably, the more aggressive conduct of U.S.

forces and the implementation of these aggressive ROE were manifest, especially to the local population. While other national contingents emphasized restraint and more graduated responses before applying deadly force, the U.S. forces stressed aggressive enforcement.[44]

The difference between a restrained approach and an overly aggressive approach underscores the inextricable nexus between the use of force, impartiality, and consent. It also underlines the importance of carefully considering decisions that change these parameters. Clearly complex and more easily arrived at after the fact in academia, these decisions must balance the frequently competing demands of restraint and the security of the force. Accordingly, commanders should avoid rash or ill-advised actions that inadvertently cause a degradation of the level of consent.[45]

As events in Mogadishu demonstrated, humanitarian operations cannot succeed when confronted with entrenched and widespread opposition. Moreover, the forcible elimination of one of the principal factions is not a practical or effective method of fulfilling the purpose of AHO. Without the broad cooperation and consent of the majority of the local population and the leadership of the principal ruling entities, success in such a complex environment is simply not a tenable or realistic prospect. The risks involved and the combat power required for an approach that abandons a broad consensual framework render impractical most operations that might be mounted in such a context. Maintaining dialogue and cooperation with the locals and the de facto leadership is essential for any prospect of success. Succinctly stated, maintaining operational-level consent is a prerequisite for the successful conduct of AHO.[46]

Once the nature and requirement for consent has been identified as the critical component, a sound approach to armed humanitarian relief requires that consent to be interpreted and applied doctrinally. After a force is introduced into a failed-state situation with some consent of the involved parties, that force's operational conduct should seek to preserve the consensual divide. The UNITAF operation rather successfully preserved operational consent by maintaining a dialogue with the key leaders. On the other hand, with the advent of UNOSOM II, the lack of dialogue and the escalation of discriminate force irrevocably breached the operational consent boundary. Dobbie illumines: "If perceived to be taking sides or using force in a crass, unfocused way that alienated support, the peacekeeping contingent would reduce its status to that of one of the parties to the conflict, prejudicing its ability to control events and losing its legitimacy and credibility as a trustworthy third party, thereby setting at risk its own security."[47]

To be certain, as evidenced by the battle in Mogadishu, the forces (U.S.) of UNOSOM II essentially joined the conflict and became part of the problem they were there to relieve. What's more, UNOSOM II forces became entangled in activities that were irrelevant to their overall purpose. For example, as a result of an increased focus on fighting Aideed, relief operations in Mogadishu were curtailed by 50 percent during the early fall. According to Dobbie, "such a situation would almost certainly result in a loss of popular support, an attendant loss of control and an unrestricted escalation upwards in the ambient level of violence, heightening political tension and foreclosing opportunities for resolving the conflict." Dobbie is also correct in warning that crossing the consent divide may also be to cross a Rubicon. After UNOSOM II unambiguously crossed the tactical and operational consent divides, there was no chance of getting back. The only remaining alternatives were either exiting the theater or escalating to war.[48]

Likewise, impartiality is inexorably linked to consent. Commenting on the situation in Somalia, Richard Connaughton wrote: "as a rule, states should stay clear of civil wars but, if they are drawn in, it is essential that they remain impartial. If they lean to one side or another, they risk spawning an armed alliance against themselves." Similarly, Cedric Thornberry observed: "without impartiality, the primary virtue, a UN peacekeeping operation will self-destruct."

The requirement for impartiality bestows a unique status on the armed humanitarian. According to Dobbie, "if he values his impartiality he is not at liberty to take sides in disputes or to initiate actions that will engender large-scale hostile reaction from the majority of the population amongst whom he works." In fact, as demonstrated by the results of abandoning impartiality in Somalia, in a multi-faction conflict where the contingent may be heavily outnumbered, survival can depend on preserving perceived impartiality. This also means that the traditional principles (the principles of war) that ordinarily influence soldiers' actions cannot be applied in their entirety to AHO. In addition to being largely irrelevant to AHO, by compromising impartiality, the application of such principles might also prove perilously destabilizing. [49]

CASUALTIES

One American observer even remarked, "the enthusiasm of the nation to take an active hand in crafting a new international order through the agency of the UN and multilateral operations, never strong to begin with, died along with 18 of America's soldiers on the streets of Mogadishu." Few would argue that America seems to have issues about casualties in general; concern over casualties in peace operations is even more acute. Also, few would refute the fact that the 18 deaths, coupled with the shocking media images of slain soldiers, in Mogadishu on 3-4 October 1993 contributed to the decision to jettison the Somalia operation. Four days after the ill-fated raid, President Clinton announced the end of American involvement in Somalia, "ostensibly because of the public's adverse reaction to the casualties." Moreover, the sacking of Les Aspin as a result of Somalia made it clear to the policy community, that because of the public's sensitivities, there was a very low threshold for casualties.[50]

Eric V. Larsen argues that public support had fallen even before the 18 deaths in Mogadishu—"the Congress was both increasingly vocal in it opposition to the mission and already moving to limit the operation." The ambush of the Pakistanis on 5 June and the subsequent escalation of violence led the public, the media, and political leaders to pay more attention to Somalia. By late June, 42 percent of the public believed that the U.S. military would get mired down if it undertook attacks against Aideed. By mid-September, 57 percent of the public surveyed thought that America should stop active military involvement, and 52 percent believed that the U.S. was too deeply involved in Somalia. The deaths of 3–4 October came as a shock and "resulted in dramatic increases in congressional and other political activity and media reporting." After that, about two out of three polled "consistently expressed a willingness to withdraw even if the situation in Somalia deteriorated after the withdrawal." According to Larsen, U.S. interests in Somalia did not justify increasing or even maintaining the commitment to most members of the public. Moreover, almost 40 percent favored an immediate withdrawal.[51]

Another author traces the beginning of casualty wariness to the Korean and Vietnam Wars, where one lesson learned was "it was politically risky, if not suicidal, to preside over any limited conflict that could not be won quickly, with relatively few casualties." During those two conflicts, both the White House and the Pentagon exerted pressure to minimize combat losses down to the lowest echelons of command. As both conflicts became stalemates it became more difficult to justify friendly losses: "a heavy reliance on air power, precision firepower, and mobility, and increasingly stringent standards for acceptable friendly-to-enemy casualty ratios, came to distinguish the American way of war." After and as an outcome of Vietnam the renewed American military's doctrine and the Weinberger doctrine were in harmony—"move fast, strike hard, and finish rapidly." Moreover, the sledgehammer approach of overwhelming force was validated in Panama and the Persian Gulf, giving rise to the new bumper sticker of the American military—"decisive victory and minimum casualties."[52]

Others have argued that the decisive victory in the Persian Gulf War, at minimal cost, only reinforced this "notion of casualty-free operations." "Pentagon pictures showing the effects of smart weapons led people to think that we really can win with technology." One can argue that after the Persian Gulf War, casualties must remain low even in defense of vital national interests. Charles Stevenson asserts that Washington elites accept as gospel the notion "that public reluctance to tolerate casualties among our all-volunteer force is much higher than when draftees bore the brunt of the fighting." A U.S. Army colonel and fellow at the U.S. Institute of Peace observed that the "low pain threshold for peace operations evolved from a low pain threshold for military operations in general, including combat operations." In his 1992 Decisive Force corollary to the Weinberger Doctrine, then Chairman (JCS) Colin Powell emphasizes "decisive force to overwhelm our adversaries and thereby terminate conflicts—swiftly with a minimum loss of life." Likewise, in *Defense Strategy for the 1990s*, Dick Cheney has stated, "our response to regional crises must be decisive, requiring the high-quality personnel and technological edge to win quickly and with minimum casualties."[53]

The Battle of Mogadishu raised the concern for American casualties to a new level. However, it is also important to dispel a myth about casualties—it is not necessarily a popular aversion to casualties but an elite perception and anticipation of a potential public outcry over casualties. A recent study at the Army War College found that casualties are mainly a perceptual issue with the core leaders of U.S. military strategic and political culture rather than with the public. Although casualty aversion seems to be the accepted conventional wisdom among elected politicians and among the country's foreign policy elite, it is not always so among the public. Citing Steven Kull's recent work on the topic, retired Army colonel and a former member of the NSC staff, Don Snider avers that the U.S. public will tolerate casualties if it is convinced there is a consensus among political leaders that the endeavor is in the national interest; and if that consensus is considered strong enough to see the operation through to a successful conclusion. According to Snider, "the elite consensus was obviously missing" in the case of Somalia and, as a result, the Clinton administration's inability to achieve consensus resulted in a policy held "hostage" to public backlash when the soldiers died. Even more alarming, is Snider's implication that senior military officers also bought into the "zero-casualties" myth.[54]

A scholar of rhetoric at UNC Chapel Hill arrived at inferences similar to those of the Army War College study. According to Cori Dauber, "the fact that pressure seems to come from elites in anticipation of public pressure which may or may not occur appears not to have entered debate." This has evolved into the specter of "another Somalia," meaning another mission where casualties create the political pressure to withdraw. The question remained to be answered is whether the politicians' statements about casualties are real, or just instrumental. Dauber contended, that in public debate, the tolerable level for casualties during humanitarian operations had become zero.[55] Dauber provides some revealing and pithy sound-bytes that corroborate this assertion:

> Is it worth one more American funeral to be in Somalia for another six months? I say the answer is no.
> —Phil Gramm, *Capital Gang*, 16 October 1993

> I have to tell you, in all sincerity, that I don't believe the entire country of Somalia is worth one American soldier's life.
> —Larry Joyce, *Larry King Live*, 14 October 1993

According to Dauber, if the operation is not deemed to be clearly in defense of vital national interests, then "[insert country name here] is not worth a single American life." Larsen's study finds that perceived costs and benefits are as or more important than casualties in determining and eroding support. He cogently elucidates that Somalia is exactly the kind of operation that has: "historically suffered from a low willingness to accept costs—prolonged interventions in complex political situations in failed states characterized by civil conflict, in which U.S. interests and principles are typically less compelling, or clear, and in which success is often elusive at best." [56]

Somalia was a fulcrum for the post–Cold War casualty question. It caused the inchoate Clinton administration to reassess its approach to multilateralism under the auspices of the UN Charter and to issue a policy directive (Presidential Decision Directive 25) reflecting its "new" approach to peacekeeping. PDD 25 is essentially a migration of the Weinberger criteria for overwhelming force into the realm of peace operations. These criteria are best articulated in the 1995 *National Security Strategy of Engagement and Enlargement*. On page 12, the *NSS* states that the military is generally not the best tool for humanitarian emergencies but under certain conditions the use of U.S. forces may be appropriate "when the risk to American troops is minimal." On page 13, the same strategy outlines questions to ask before committing forces: "is there a clearly defined, achievable mission?" "what are the potential costs—both human and financial of our engagement?" The last questions in the strategy address the need for public support and exit strategies. However, as Cori Dauber has emphasized earlier in Chapter 3, when you combine the Weinberger doctrine (which is designed to avoid activities other than war) with calls to "do something" for humanitarian reasons, the result is a half-measured approach.[57]

TECHNOLOGY

It was a state-of-the-art military force. Already circling high above the target was the slickest intelligence support America had to offer, including satellites, a high-flying P-3 Orion, and three OH-58D observation helicopters, which looked like the bubble-front Little Bird choppers with a five-foot bulbous polyp growing out of the top. The observation birds were equipped with video cameras and radio equipment that would relay the action live to General Garrison and the other officers in the Joint Operations Center (JOC) back at the beach. Moviemakers and popular authors might strain to imagine the capabilities of the U.S. military, but here was the real thing about to strike.[58]

The quotation above describes Task Force Ranger elements as they prepared to execute the raid in Mogadishu on 3 October 1993. Although studies that explicitly examine the role of America's predilection for technology during the operations in Somalia do not exist, it is possible to infer some generalizations by examining what and how technology was applied during this humanitarian intervention. As a precursory note, one author argues that "our national aversion to bloodletting" will increase expectations that the cost of war can be borne by money and technology. According to James Gentry, high-tech gizmos such as robots, sensors, and unmanned aircraft are best suited for high-intensity war but are of little use in counterinsurgency and peace operations. After all, one only needs to ask Robert McNamara's whiz kids from the Vietnam era how difficult it is to harness technology to defeat pre-industrial and semifeudal insurgents.[59]

In fact, although the U.S. forces under UNOSOM II were smaller in number (about 4,300), they had some of the most lethal and high-tech equipment available to light fighters. One of the oldest systems in their inventory was the AH-1 Cobra attack helicopter. Though a Vietnam vintage machine, this helicopter was very lethal—armed with TOW anti-tank missiles, a 20 millimeter Gatling gun, and 2.75

inch rockets. The U.S. Air Force's AC 130 Specter is deadly enough to vaporize a city block in Mogadishu. What's more, the OH-58D was another example of advanced technology—the ball on top holds thermal sights, a TV camera, and a laser range finder, which can be used to designate for Specter or artillery. This helicopter can detect and identify single humans at ranges up to ten kilometers, at night. Add the 160th Special Operations Aviation Regiment's (SOAR) aircraft—MH-60s, MH-6s, and AH-6s—and that amounts to some serious technology and firepower. [60]

One lesson-learned report highlighted the role of such technology: "during periods of darkness, laser-equipped night vision scopes were used by forward observers and forward air controllers as their primary means of marking targets." It concluded that the Forward Observers Ranging and Marking Scope was a great asset for identifying and marking targets. In addition, the report noted, the OH-58D's lazing capability was an invaluable asset because it enabled "the ground commander the flexibility to employ a wide variety of munitions with surgical precision." In a discussion about minimizing danger to friendly troops and limiting "collateral damage" to civilians, the report emphasized the use of the following high-tech weapons: laser-guided munitions or "direct-fire weapons such as the AC-130 105mm, 40mm, 20mm cannons and the AH-1F fired TOW." However, as a quintessential example of technological asymmetry, the Center for Army Lessons Learned stated that the Somalis even used kites and slingshots as air defense weapons: "on one occasion a rock from a slingshot went through the cockpit of a scout aircraft that was traveling at 90 knots." The same report explained that units conducting operations against a "low technology force" must not rule out unorthodox methods of air defense.[61]

There is a problem, however, with a reliance on asymmetry of technology—a cunning adversary will always seek to find the Achilles heel of the technologically superior force. According to both Rick Atkinson and Mark Bowden, Aideed and some of his commanders had figured out that weakness: "the Americans greatest technological advantage—the helicopter—had to be neutralized with barrage fire using rocket propelled grenades." Moreover, Bowden adds, "to Aideed's fighters, the Rangers' weakness was apparent. "They were not willing to die." What's more, the helicopter pilots of the 160th SOAR whose moniker was "Night Stalkers" had forfeited one of their principal technological advantages—night operations. TF Ranger's Delta planners realized that speed was also essential for success. Consequently, each mission was built around a "template" with helicopters, Rangers, and Deltas operators performing the same functions for every raid. Despite the fact that the task force varied the times of the missions and conducted bogus "signature flights" (false insertions) to keep Aideed's forces off balance, by October the task force had established a pattern or "footprint." Even the commander of TF Ranger, Major General William Garrison, captured it very simply: "you can have all the grand theories about warfare that you want, but ultimately there are only four options: up the middle, up the left, up the right or don't go."[62]

However, according to Atkinson's article, Aideed's SNA had been forming a template of its own: hundreds of rocket-propelled grenades (RPG) had been smuggled into Mogadishu. The Somali commander, Giumale, who oversaw the 3-4 October battle "tried to adapt the lessons learned from years of clan warfare and from extensive reading on guerrilla insurgencies, particularly in Latin America." He knew the American special-forces were considered elite but he thought they had underestimated the SNA militia, which had the tactical and psychological advantage of fighting in their own backyards. One of Giumale's subalterns, a Colonel Aden, observed "if you use one tactic twice, you should not use it a third time," and the Americans already had done basically the same thing six times. Operations to snatch Aideed, which culminated in the October battle, also attest to the difficulty, even with high-tech equipment, of finding a single human target in an urban slum.[63]

CONCLUSION

Restraint is an acquired skill, but it is the *sine qua non* of peace operations.
——Kenneth Allard[64]

The purpose of this chapter has been to discern how U.S. military strategic cultural preferences about the use of force manifested themselves in the American military's first Chapter VII armed humanitarian operation in the post–Cold War era. If it were necessary to generalize the U.S. role in Somalia in one sentence, it would be that maximalist and conventional attitudes about the use of force led the U.S. military to abandon the OOTW principle of restraint, and thus legitimacy. Once again, the OOTW principle of restraint offers some prudent guidance: "the use of excessive force could adversely affect efforts to gain and maintain legitimacy and impede the attainment of both short- and long-term goals." [65]

As a result of direct and collateral deaths and damage, the American military alienated and electrified a large part of the Somali population in Mogadishu. AC-130 Specters and AH-1 Cobras don't win hearts and minds any better than Arc-Light strikes do. After 5 June 1993, the American military went to war against Aideed's clan in what essentially became a counter-guerrilla effort—an asymmetric conflict. In this situation, Aideed's forces needed to identify and exploit their conventionally superior adversary's weak points: the hubris of a hegemonic military on the heels of a great victory, a military cultural reliance on the silver bullet—superior technology; and an aversion to casualties on the part of military and civilian senior leaders. Henry Kissinger's pithy maxim helps to capture the conundrum with asymmetry: "the guerrilla wins if he does not lose; the conventional army loses if it does not win." Again a strategic paradox presented itself: the SNA had unlimited aims (rule of the country) and limited means (a pre-technological militia armed only with machine guns and RPGs), but a willingness to die; the Americans, on the other hand, had unlimited means (TF Ranger and technology) and limited aims (restore order in Somalia), but an unwillingness to die.[66]

Figure 5.1 recapitulates the military strategic cultural characteristics and offers generalizations about how those characteristics manifested themselves during operations in Somalia.

Cedric Thornberry once said that "peacekeeping is no substitute for policy" in reference to a similarly challenging mission—UNPROFOR.[67] This quote points to another lesson from the U.S. military in Somalia—the need to match means with ends. If the mandate is aggressive, having robust and credible force to enforce it is not necessarily a bad thing, as long as the principle of restraint is followed. However, the formulation of mandates must take better account of how proposed courses of action will be put into operation. The mandate/resource mismatch that inhered in the establishment of UNOSOM II, but not in the creation of UNITAF, underscores this problem. Resolution 794 (UNITAF), invoking Chapter VII, authorized member states "to use all necessary means to establish as soon as possible a secure environment for humanitarian relief operations in Somalia." [68]

Although UNITAF possessed significant combat power, its mission statement reflected specific guidance and restraint: "when directed by the NCA . . . will conduct joint/combined military operations in Somalia to secure the major air and sea ports, key installations and food distribution points, to provide open and free passage of relief supplies, provide security for convoys and relief organization operations, and assist UN/NGO's in providing humanitarian relief under UN auspices. Upon establishing a secure environment for uninterrupted relief operations, USCINCCENT terminates and transfers relief operations to UN peacekeeping forces."[69]

On the other hand, also invoking Chapter VII, Resolution 814 of 26 March 1993 authorized a UNOSOM II force comprising 10,000 fewer troops and expanded the mandate for the use of force. The resolution directed the force commander "to assume responsibility for the consolidation, expansion, and maintenance of a secure

Figure 5.1
American Military Strategic Culture in Somalia

Characteristic	Manifestation
Civil-Military	Powellian Decisive Force drives how force applied—Chapter VII PE. Military resource leads/drives throughout but CMOC (UNITAF) was outstanding innovation to integrate.
Force	UNITAF: Robust, credible, and overwhelming w/restraint. UNOSOM II: Deadly force used maximally and partially. War.
Casualties	Catalyst for withdrawal and impetus for request for more force—armor request. Escalation of violence, culminating in October, triggers outcry for immediate withdrawal. Somalia isn't worth 1 American.
Technology	Asymmetry of Technology: U.S. AC-130, OH-58D lasers, SOF birds; SNA sling shots, kites, and innovate with RPGs (lessons from Afghanistan). SNA target technology to inflict maximum damage.

environment throughout Somalia." It also authorized UNOSOM II to "take appropriate action against any faction that violates or threatens to violate the cessation of
hostilities" and "to seize the small arms of all unauthorized armed elements."[70]
Manned with a smaller force and supported by a more aggressive mandate,
UNOSOM II faced an untenable situation at the outset.[71]

Moreover, the UNOSOM II mission statement read as follows: "When directed, . . . Force Command conducts military operations to consolidate, expand,
and maintain a secure environment for the advancement of humanitarian aid, economic assistance, and political reconciliation in Somalia." It seems clear now, and
it should have been understood then by the Security Council, that expanding and
consolidating security throughout Somalia requires more, not fewer resources,
than does securing ports and providing convoy security. However, once the politically alienated Aideed recognized the tenuous situation of UNOSOM II, his militia ambushed a Pakistani detachment in June 1993. This prompted the Security
Council to ratchet up the mandate without increasing the force's capabilities. Resolution 837 authorized UNOSOM II "to take all measures necessary against all
those responsible for the armed attacks." Not only had UNOSOM II unambiguously crossed the Rubicon and gone to war, but it joined the fray with an insufficient military capacity.[72]

If restraint is not applied when formulating mandates and devising mission
statements, it will certainly not be manifest during the execution phase. AHO can
fall under either peacekeeping or peace enforcement but neither, at least in the
U.S. emerging doctrine, are considered war. Even when authorized to use Chapter VII force, the principles of consent, impartiality and minimum force, though
not absolute, are still relevant. In the *Supplement to An Agenda for Peace*,
Boutros-Ghali observed: "In the cases of Somalia and Bosnia, peacekeeping operations were given additional mandates that required the use of force and therefore could not be combined with existing mandates requiring the consent of the
parties, impartiality, and the non-use of force."[73]

During Johnston and Oakley's leadership, UNITAF made a conscious effort to
continue dialogue and maintain the perception of impartiality among the faction
leaders. Moreover, the importance of preserving operational consent through dialogue underpinned Oakley's approach and led to a key UNITAF innovation: a
"Combined Security Committee" which enabled Johnston and key members of his
staff to meet frequently with Mohammed Aideed and other key clan leaders. This
vehicle proved especially useful in gaining and even imposing cooperation with
UNITAF mandates, such as weapons cantonment. Even still, UNITAF's commitment to impartiality extended to the punitive application of force. According to
Oakley, if UNITAF blew up one of Aideed's caches in south Mogadishu, Johnston
would order the troops to find a reason to destroy some site in Ali Mahdi's sector
in the north.[74]

Conversely, when the Howe team arrived with UNOSOM II, it proceeded to
marginalize and then alienate Aideed, jeopardizing operational consent. In addition, regular dialogue between the U.S./UN representatives and the faction leaders

was almost nonexistent. The security committees that Oakley had deliberately nurtured rarely convened after the UNOSOM II transition. After an attack against UNOSOM II forces by one of Aideed's allies in May, the Howe team (Gosende) began to consider removing Aideed from the scene. The loss of consent, as well as the real and perceived partiality, was a harbinger to the escalation of violence that occurred between June and October 1993.[75]

The subsequent escalation in force need not be recapitulated here. However, it is important to reiterate that a strong consensual framework at the operational level can facilitate the use of minimum necessary force. When the purpose is humanitarian, the main effort should not be the use of force but the application of nonviolent military capabilities. For example, psychological operations (PSYOPS) play a critical role in AHO because it can influence attitudes and perceptions to promote, protect, sustain, and transmit consent. It is important to note that the PSYOPS units in Somalia departed with UNITAF. Interestingly, PSYOPS helicopters were the first elements to enter Port-au-Prince during the 1994 intervention in Haiti.[76]

Another problem that plagued UNOSOM II was a very convoluted chain of command arrangement. Unity of command is a time tested axiom of military but under UNOSOM II there were essentially three chains of command that were not necessarily communicating to each other in a timely manner. The three de facto chains of command were the U.S. Forces Somalia (USFORSOM) under UNOSOM II command, the U.S. 10th Mountain QRF Task Force under the control of Central Command (CENTCOM), and the U.S. Special Operations Command (SOCOM), which commanded and controlled Task Force Ranger. According to Kenneth Allard, the problems with unity of command in Somalia add another lesson to Murphy's laws of armed combat: "if it takes more than ten seconds to explain the command arrangements, they probably won't work."[77]

Indeed, choosing indicators of success are particularly important. For example, in the context of AHO, these indicators should not normally be expressed in terms of enemy killed, warlords captured, or objectives destroyed; if they are, this is itself an indicator that the operation has changed in ways that should call into question both the mission and the mandate. More germane and realistic measures of success would be a reduction in the level of violence and an increase in the numbers of children being fed and hydrated. The opposite was true in Somalia by October 1993.[78]

In a 1983 study prepared for TRADOC, Kupperman and Associates found that the least likely conflict to occur—high intensity conventional conflict in Europe—"nevertheless dominates Army thinking, training, and resource allocation." Even so, the predominance of a big war paradigm was a bit more justifiable when the Soviet bloc was still a threat. A "European-war-only" predilection becomes unjustifiable in the face of massive structural change and concomitant smaller scale contingencies. Ten years after the Kupperman Study the U.S. Army still didn't seem to institutionalize one of the report's key conclusions about the LIC role:

It will be important to establish new and very different measures of success in this role . . . winning such a war means not losing lives, not killing indigenous people, and only occasionally creating disturbances connected directly to the desired image of a guerrilla force that cannot be dislodged and that can operate at will in the countryside.[79]

A description of Task Force 2-14's (10th Mountain Division) five-month rotation in Somalia, which included the battle of 3 and 4 October 1993, highlights the contrast between doctrine required for OOTW and actual (combat) operations:

TF 2-14 experienced more sustained combat in Somalia than any unit in the Army since the Vietnam era. Multiple combat operations were conducted at Task Force through company team level. By the end of its tour, the Task Force had been awarded: 413 Combat Infantryman's Badges; 31 Combat Medic Badges; 32 Purple Hearts; four Silver Stars; 12 Bronze Stars with "V" Device; and 12 Army Commendation Medals with "V" Device.[80]

Finally, the UN must be prepared to withdraw or abstain from intervening in situations where AHO cannot be supported by a framework of operational-level consent. Even though the UN Security Council has been criticized for its selective and inconsistent application of Chapter VII measures, sound counsel is provided by a Sun-Tzu maxim: "those who try to be strong everywhere, are strong nowhere." To use the terminology of Thomas Weiss, in choosing where to conduct humanitarian operations, the UN will need to conduct "triage": to focus efforts in areas that can be saved rather than deploying forces piecemeal with little effect. By way of a postscript, the quotes below seem to capture the essence of the American military's approach to missions outside its preferred paradigm of war. [81]

Any good soldier can handle guerrillas.
> —General George H. Decker (1961)[82]

Well-trained, combat-ready, disciplined soldiers can easily adapt to peacekeeping or peace enforcement missions.
> —Major General S.L. Arnold (1993)[83]

Stupidity is defined as doing the same thing over and over while expecting different results.
> —Strom Thurmond[84]

NOTES

1. Friedrich Wilhelm Nietzsche, *Beyond Good and Evil*, Book IV, trans. Helen Zimmern (1886), 146 in *Bartlett's Familiar Quotations* (Franklin Electronic Bookman, 1998).

2. Kenneth Allard, *Somalia Operations: Lessons Learned* (Washington, D.C.: National Defense University Press, 1995), 63.

3. Terrence Lyons and Ahmed I. Samatar, *Somalia: State Collapse, Multilateral Intervention, and Strategies for Political Reconstruction* (Washington, D.C.: The Brookings In-

stitution, 1995), 30 and 77; and John L. Hirsch and Robert B. Oakley, *Somalia and Operation Restore Hope* (Washington, D.C.: United States Institute of Peace Press, 1995), 19.

4. United Nations, SCOR, S/23445, 20 January 1992, 2.

5. Lyons and Samatar, 7.

6. United Nations, Security Council, S/RES/733, 20 January 1992; and United Nations, Security Council, S/RES/746, 17 March 1992.

7. United Nations, Security Council, S/RES/751, 24 April 1992; United Nations, Security Council S/RES/767, 24 July 1992; and Hirsch and Oakley, 25.

8. United Nations, Security Council, S/RES/775, 28 August 1992; Hirsch and Oakley, 26, 27 and 41; Lyons and Samatar, 32–33.

9. Lyons and Samatar, 23; United Nations, Security Council, S/RES/794; Rajendra Ramlogan, "Towards a New Vision of World Security: The United Nations Security Council and the Lessons of Somalia," *Houston Journal of International Law* 16 (Winter 1993): 251.

10. United Nations, SCOR, S/25168, 26 January 1993; Hirsch and Oakley, 77; and Lyons and Samatar, 41.

11. United Nations, Security Council, S/RES/814, 26 March 1993; and United Nations, SCOR, S/25354, 3 March 1993, par. 57.

12. Hirsch and Oakley, 115–16.

13. Ibid., 116–21; and United Nations, Security Council, S/RES/837, 6 June 1993.

14. Hirsch and Oakley, 116–21; Lyons and Samatar, 60; United Nations, Security Council, S/RES/954, 4 November 1994.

15. Kofi Annan, "UN Forces Withdraw from Somalia," *Foreign Policy Bulletin* 5 (May/June 1995): 36.

16. Downie, 122.

17. This title was paraphrased from a passage in Daniel P. Bolger, *Savage Peace: Americans at War in the 1990s* (Novato, CA: Presidio Press, 1995), 274.

18. Bolger, 284.

19. The reference to Christmas was taken from Daniel P. Bolger, *Savage Peace*, 280.

20. Ibid., 281–83.

21. Robert Oakley, Lecture to West Point class "Contemporary Military Thought," West Point, New York, 29 April 1999.

22. Hirsch and Oakley, 162.

23. Oakley Lecture.

24. Allard, 69–70.

25. Allard, 73; and Oakley Lecture.

26. *United States Forces Somalia After Action Report* (Carlisle, PA: U.S. Army Peacekeeping Institute, June 1994), 14. Also referred to as the *Montgomery Report*.

27. Hirsch and Oakley, 151.

28. Major General John Ellerson, *Inside the Army*, November 1993, 13 in John Mackinlay, "Improving Multifunctional Forces, *Survival* 36 (Autumn 1994): 155 and Endnote 28.

29. "Patience and Bloody Noses," *The Guardian*, 30 September 1994, 27; and Oakley Lecture.

30. Donald C.F. Daniel and Bradd C. Hayes, *Coercive Inducement and the Containment of International Crises* (Washington, D.C.: United States Institute of Peace Press, 1999), 102–3.

31. Mark Bowden, *Black Hawk Down* (New York: Penguin Books, 1999), 71.

32. Ibid., 74.

33. Ibid., 75.

34. Marguerite Michaels, "Peacemaking War," *Time*, 26 July 1993, 48.

35. *Montgomery Report*, 16.

36. "Congressional Hearing Summary," Senate Armed Services Committee: 12 May 1994 U.S. Military Operations in Somalia (Washington, D.C.: U.S. Army Congressional Activities Division, 13 May 1994), 4.

37. Mats Berdal, "Whither UN Peacekeeping," *Adelphi Paper 281* (London: Brassey's, 1993), 73–74.

38. Quoted in Rick Atkinson, "The Raid That Went Wrong," Washington Post, 30 January 1994, A1.

39. Robert Oakley, interview by author, West Point, New York, 29 April 1999.

40. *The Mohonk Criteria for Humanitarian Assistance in Complex Emergencies* (Washington, D.C.: The Task Force on Ethical and Legal Issues in Humanitarian Assistance, March 1994), 3; and Charles Dobbie, "A Concept for Post–Cold War Peacekeeping," *Survival* 36 (Autumn 1994): 135.

41. Allard, 37.

42. Ibid., 36.

43. Ibid., 37.

44. Ibid.

45. Ibid., 38.

46. Dobbie: 125.

47. Ibid.: 130

48. Ibid.: 130–31.

49. Richard Connaughton, "Interests, Conscience, and Somalia," December 1992 in Dobbie: 133; and Cedric Thornberry, "The Lessons of Yugoslavia" (Paper presented to a Center for Defense Studies Seminar, King's College London, December 1993) in Dobbie: 133. Dobbie: 139.

50. Edward Foster, *NATO's Military in the Age of Crisis Management* (London: Royal United Services Institute for Defence Studies, 1995), 13; and Don M. Snider, John A. Nagl, and Tony Pfaff, *Army Professionalism, the Military Ethic, and Officers in the 21st Century* (Carlisle, PA: Strategic Studies Institute, 1999), 23.

51. Eric V. Larsen, *Casualties and Consensus: The Historical Role of Casualties in Domestic Support for U.S. Military Operations* (Santa Monica, CA: RAND, 1996), 67–70.

52. Karl W. Eikenberry, "Take No Casualties," Parameters 26 (Summer 1996): 113–15.

53. See James Gentry, "Military Force in an Age of National Cowardice," *Washington Quarterly* 21 (Autumn 1998): 181–82; and Charles A. Stevenson, "The Evolving Clinton Doctrine on the Use of Force," *Armed Forces and Society* 22 (Summer 1996): 511–12. Also, see Colonel Michael W. Alvis, "Understanding the Role of Casualties in U.S. Peace Operations," *Landpower Essay Series No. 99-1* (Arlington, VA: the Association of the U.S. Army, January 1999), 4–5. *National Military Strategy of the United States* (Washington, D.C.: U.S. Department of Defense, 1995), 10; and Dick Cheney, *Defense Strategy for the 1990s: The Regional Defense Strategy* (Washington, D.C.: GPO, January 1993), 15.

54. Snider, Nagl, and Pfaff, 24–25.

55. Cori Dauber, "Poisoning the Well: The Weinberger Doctrine and Public Argument Over Military Intervention," (unpublished paper, UNC Chapel Hill, September 1998), 38–39.

56. Dauber, 38–39; and Larsen, 50–51.

57. Stevenson: 511–25; and *National Security Strategy of Engagement and Enlargement* (Washington, D.C.: The White House, Februrary 1995), 12–13; and Dauber, 40–42.

58. Bowden, 11.

59. Gentry: 184–86.

60. For troop strengths, see *United States Forces Somalia After Action Review* (Carlisle, PA: U.S. Army PKI, June 1994), 7.

61. "U.S. Army Operations in Support of UNOSOM II," *Lessons Learned Report* (Ft Leavenworth, KS: U.S. Army CALL, 1994), I-6-6, I-6-2, and I-5-6.

62. Atkinson, A1; and Bowden, 109–11.

63. Atkinson, A1.

64. Allard, 62.

65. Restraint is explained in *Special Edition 93-1* on page 9.

66. The hubris comment comes from Bolger, 267. The commander of U.S. forces in Somalia, Thomas M. Montgomery essentially states that the UNOSOM II became a counter-guerrilla operation: "the command basically began a period of counter operations to protect the force and to deny the USC-SNA the means to continue guerrilla operations against the UN." See the *Montgomery Report*, officially titled *United States Forces Somalia After Action Report* (Carlisle, PA: U.S. Army Peacekeeping Institute, June 1994). For a discussion of the SNA's deliberately asymmetric approach, see Rick Atkinson, A1. The tactical commander who oversaw the battle "tried to adapt the lessons learned from years of clan warfare and from his extensive readings on guerrilla insurgencies, particularly in Latin America. For an original discussion of asymmetric conflict, see Andrew Mack, "Why Big Nations Lose Small Wars," in *Power, Strategy, and Security: A World Politics Reader*, ed. Klaus Knorr (Princeton, NJ: Princeton University Press, 1983), 128–30 and Henry Kissinger, "The Vietnam Negotiations," *Foreign Affairs* 47 (January 1969): 214.

67. Foster, 13.

68. United Nations, Security Council, S/RES/794; and Berdal, 31.

69. Allard, 16.

70. United Nations, Security Council, S/RES/814, 26 March 1993; and United Nations, SCOR, S/25354, 3 March 1993, par. 57.

71. Hirsch and Oakley, 115–16.

72. Allard, 19; and United Nations, Security Council, S/RES/837, 6 June 1993.

73. Boutros Boutros-Ghali, *Supplement to An Agenda for Peace* (New York: United Nations Press, 1995), 9.

74. Allard, 73; and Susan Rosegrant and Michael Watkins, *A Seamless Transition: United States and United Nations Operations in Somalia—1992–1993* (Cambridge, MA: Harvard University, 1996), Part 1, 23.

75. Rosegrant and Watkins, Part 2, 3–4.

76. Dobbie: 145.

77. Kenneth J. Allard, "Lessons Unlearned: Somalia and Joint Doctrine," *Joint Forces Quarterly* Number 9 (Autumn 1995): 105.

78. Allard, 32.

79. Robert H. Kupperman and Associates, Inc., *Low Intensity Conflict, Volume I: Main Report* (Washington, D.C.: U.S. Army TRADOC, 1983), vi and 33.

80. David C. Meade, MG, USA and William David, LTC, USA, "Restore Hope, Somalia 1992–1994," (Unpublished Draft Article, Fort Drum, NY, May 1994), 1–2. Major General Meade was the commander of the 10th Mountain Division and LTC David was the commander of Task Force 2-14 during its rotation in Somalia. In 1992, as the U.S. Army started to think about peace operations doctrine, then Brigadier General Meade directed CLIC to stop studying peace operations because "if we study it, we may have to do it." Rich Rinaldo, Telephone Interview by author, West Point, New York, 16 March 2000.

81. Robert A. Fitton, *Leadership Quotations from the Military Tradition* (Boulder, CO: Westview Press, 1993), 77; and Thomas G. Weiss, "Intervention: Whither the United Nations," *The Washington Quarterly* Vol. 17, No.1 (Winter 1994): 124.

82. This Decker quote is fairly ubiquitous and is stated without citation in Andrew F. Krepinevich, *The Army and Vietnam* (Baltimore, MD: Johns Hopkins University Press, 1986), 37. Decker is known for his resistance to the Kennedy directive to develop sound counterinsurgency doctrine. This quote reveals the importance he gives to fighting insurgencies as well as his ignorance of history and guerrilla warfare. Implicit in this statement is the notion that an Army trained, organized, and equipped to fight the Soviet hordes in the Fulda Gap cam easily defeat ideologically driven insurgents in an asymmetric conflict.

83. MG S. L. Arnold, "Somalia: An Operation Other Than War," *Military Review* 73 (December 1993): 35.

84. Quoted in Allard, "Lessons Unlearned: Somalia and Joint Doctrine:" 109.

6

The British Army in
Bosnia—Adapting on the Hoof

INTRODUCTION

This chapter has as its purposes the examination of British Army operations under UNPROFOR (Operation Grapple) for military strategic cultural continuity or change: did the British preferences and attitudes about the use of force (identified in Chapter 2) manifest themselves in Bosnia? As is the case more often than not, historically, a paradigm change drove new policies and new operations and initially there was a doctrinal lag in both militaries. The British Army had to "adapt on the hoof" in Bosnia because it faced a new genre of operation for which it had no doctrine in 1992. Bosnia also represented an armed humanitarian operation in the midst of ongoing conflict. The section asks the same questions about the British Army in Bosnia as the previous chapter did about the U.S. Army in Somalia. First, did civil military relations reflect civilian direction or military prescriptions about the use of force and were the civil military components of the operation integrated? Second, did the British Army manifest a predilection for a minimalist use of force? Third, what role did British casualties play in the British Army's approach to Bosnia? Finally, did the British rely heavily on technology to perform the mission in Bosnia. Before answering these questions, however, this introductory section provides a historical overview of peacekeeping operations in Bosnia.[1]

An explanation of why Yugoslavia disintegrated the way it did, and consequently, an explanation of why Bosnia imploded into an inferno of internecine interethnic conflict in the spring of 1992 is beyond the scope of this chapter. A comprehensive explanation is beyond the scope of even a single book and it could easily fill a tome. The tragedy that played out in Bosnia Herzegovina was not monocausal and a host of respected scholars and practitioners have made significant strides toward explaining it. In addition, this author has studied it extensively in order to teach it to undergraduates in a distilled and cogent way. However, risking oversimplification, Bosnia Herzegovina descended into hell because of bad leaders, bad history, and bad demographics, coupled with a declining economic situation. One can also add an intervening factor to these causes—the foibles of the international community.[2]

One look at the mosaic-like map of pre-war Bosnia reveals why the violence was most pronounced there: it had the worst demographics of all the former Yugoslav republics—a case of terminal heterogeneity. In Bosnia, anything less than a circumspect and democratic focus on civic nationalism and human rights would have caused problems. But instrumental perfidy and the espousal of ethnic politics by ambitious local leaders in the Balkans guaranteed that Bosnia Herzegovina would burn. Before Bosnia Herzegovina spiraled into its inferno, its population comprised 43.7 percent Muslims, 31.4 percent Serbs, 17.3 percent Croats, and 5.5 percent Yugoslavs.[3]

> The Balkans are not worth the bones of a single Pomeranian grenadier.
> —Otto von Bismarck[4]

While perhaps not the exact thoughts on the minds of Western diplomats in 1991 and 1992, the basic tone of this 19th century quote most likely captures the attitudes of the leaders of the Western powers that possessed the capabilities to curb the violence in the Balkans: who was willing to put their soldiers in harm's way to stop a conflict that did not seem to impinge on their vital national interests? Certainly, the United States was not interested in deploying troops to Bosnia in 1992. Moreover, key Western powers, such as Britain and France, were willing to do something; but neither exhibited the will or capacity to stop the war. A contemporary but no less prescient comment was offered by British Field Marshall Dick Vincent, the Chairman of the NATO Military Committee, in 1992 when British troops were first deployed to join the UN Protection Force (UNPROFOR) in Bosnia: "once you put your hand in this mangle you'll never get it out." According to Durch and Schear, the role of UNPROFOR proved to be the most frustrating and complex operation ever embarked on by the UN, to include Somalia. This was mainly because UNPROFOR peacekeepers were deployed into an environment where peace was conspicuously absent—an ongoing three-sided ethnic conflict.[5]

Furthermore, UNPROFOR's multifaceted mandate (s) in Bosnia was the end result of UN Security Council efforts to reconcile the sometimes incongruent national objectives of its four engaged permanent members—Britain, France, Russia, and the United States. As a result, UN military forces ambled into Bosnia neither to impose peace nor to monitor a cease-fire, but to keep the population alive while diplomatic efforts proceeded to find a resolution to the conflict. Since a large part of UNPROFOR's mission was to escort the delivery of humanitarian relief, "unlike most UN operations some of its forces were always on the move." UN forces often encountered threats that changed unpredictably because Bosnia was an active conflict zone where tenuous central political control of undisciplined local paramilitary groups was more often the rule than the exception. In particular, operations in Bosnia stressed command, control, and communications more so than any previous UN peacekeeping operation.[6]

UNPROFOR operations also tax any effort to provide a clear and distilled account of British Army operations in Bosnia—the amorphous nature and long duration of UN operations there places any lucid explanation at risk of getting lost in a quagmire. Therefore, to lend concision and clarity to this short historical overview, this section is broken into three parts: a discussion of UNPROFOR's four chronological phases and of the Security Council resolutions germane to them; a recapitulation of the British Army's role in those four phases; and a summary of UNPROFOR's successes and problems. For its examination of the four phases of UNPROFOR activities, this section relies for its organization on William Durch's and James Schear's four-phase outline in *UN Peacekeeping, American Politics, and the Uncivil Wars of the 1990s*. Durch and Schear organize UN operations in Bosnia into these four phases: Phase I—Aid to Sarajevo; Phase II—Escort of Humanitarian Relief; Phase III—Protection of Safe Areas; and Phase IV—Weapons Exclusion Zones.[7]

HISTORICAL OVERVIEW OF THE CONFLICT

Aid to Sarajevo

Two months after the Bosnian Serb forces began attacking Sarajevo, Cedric Thornberry, UNPROFOR's Director of Civil Affairs, negotiated an agreement between the Bosnian Serbs and the Bosnian Government on 5 June 1992 to open the Sarajevo airport for humanitarian purposes under UN control. UNPROFOR would establish and run a security corridor for aid convoys between the airport and the city. On 8 June, the UN Security Council (UNSC) adopted Resolution 758 that implemented the airport agreement. At the end of June, and subsequently in mid-July, the UNSC passed Resolutions 761 and 764, which increased the UN presence in Sarajevo to one battalion, then two battalions, respectively.[8]

Escort of Humanitarian Relief

On 13 August 1992, two months after the Sarajevo airport was opened, the UNSC passed Resolution 770 in response to media accounts of kidnappings, torture, murder, and concentration camps in Bosnia. These accounts attributed responsibility to the Bosnian Serb forces. Invoking Chapter VII of the UN Charter, Resolution 770 called "upon States to take nationally or through regional agencies or arrangements all measures necessary to facilitate in coordination with the United Nations delivery by relevant United Nations organizations and others of humanitarian assistance" to Sarajevo and to other parts of Bosnia Herzegovina wherever it was needed. This resolution essentially gave organizations like NATO and UN member states the go ahead to act as they deemed necessary to deliver aid to the population. Two weeks after the resolution passed, NATO offered troops to

UNPROFOR for escorting humanitarian relief convoys in Bosnia. On 10 September 1992, the UN Secretary General proposed that these units be subsumed within UNPROFOR to operate under traditional peacekeeping rules of engagement. The UNSG also recommended that UNPROFOR's tasks would be to support the UN High Commissioner for Refugees, (UNHCR) efforts to deliver humanitarian relief and to provide protection at UNHCR's request. In addition, the Secretary General proposed that the forces could be employed to protect convoys of released civilians, if the International Committee of the Red Cross (ICRC) so requested, and if the Force Commander considered that the request was practicable.[9]

Without invoking Chapter VII, on 14 September 1992, the UNSC adopted Resolution 776, which endorsed the Secretary General's recommendations and authorized an enlargement of UNPROFOR's mandate to protect humanitarian relief convoys in Bosnia. This same resolution established a separate Bosnia Herzegovina command within UNPROFOR. It also authorized the deployment of five infantry battalions and a transport battalion. UNPROFOR was to be deployed in four or five zones in which an infantry battalion group would operate, including a civilian staff "to undertake political and information functions and liaison with the UNHCR. Again, UN forces would adhere to traditional peacekeeping rules of engagement. UNPROFOR was authorized to use force in self-defense, including scenarios in which armed individuals attempted to obstruct the execution of the mandate by force.[10]

Durch and Schear, however, offer some valuable insight about the consequences of this resolution: "Resolution 776 maintained the fiction, invented thirty years earlier for another UN operation a continent away in the Congo, that impartial intervention was really non-intervention and should be viewed as such by the local parties." They argue that aid to the civilian population is essentially aid to the enemy in a conflict where civilians and their homes are the principal targets, notwithstanding the fact that aid was delivered to all sides. Whenever and whatever external resources are injected into and ongoing war, those resources will be political leverage, subject to local unit commander's decisions and whims to constrict or expand the flow of aid as political necessity dictated.[11]

In a February 1993 report to the Security Council on UNPROFOR, the Secretary General stated that operations in Bosnia had been marked by a tendency on the part of the Bosnian government to blame UNPROFOR for a host of shortcomings. Mainly, the criticism had been leveled at UN forces' failure to carry out tasks that it had not been mandated, authorized, equipped, or manned to fulfill. Moreover, efforts to protect humanitarian convoys throughout Bosnia had been consistently impeded by obstruction, hostile fire, mines, and the refusal of the factions on the ground, especially, but not solely, by the Bosnian Serbs, to cooperate with UNPROFOR. Even so, the report noted that 34,000 tons of relief supplies had been delivered to an estimated 800,000 recipients in over 100 locations throughout the Republic. UNPROFOR was also successful at keeping the airport open in the face of hostile military action against humanitarian aircraft.[12]

Subsequently, in passing Resolution 816 on 31 March 1993, the UN Security Council directed that the flight ban announced over Bosnia the previous October would be imposed with force. UNSCR 816, invoking Chapter VII of the UN Charter, authorized Member States to use "all necessary means," in close coordination with the Secretary General and UNPROFOR, to enforce the flight ban through national or regional arrangements. What's more and in accordance with NATO's December 1992 decision to support peacekeeping operations under the UN on a case-by-case basis, on 8 April 1993, the North Atlantic Council (NAC) decided that NATO air forces would carry out Resolution 816. NATO staffs in Vicenza planned and coordinated the operation (Operation Deny Flight) that involved fighter aircraft from the United States, the United Kingdom, France, Turkey, and the Netherlands. Also, on 8 April, the German constitutional court ruled not to oppose the participation of German aircrews in airborne early warning aircraft (AWACS) support operations over Bosnia and outside the traditional NATO area.[13]

Although the tactical military impact of the NAC's decision was initially minimal, the decision was the harbinger of a significantly expanded NATO role out-of-area as well as a potential and partial escalation in the use of force. Moreover, this UN Resolution was the first to authorize the use of military force in Bosnia in situations other than self-defense: it was a significant stride across the threshold between Chapter VI and Chapter VII. It was also a landmark decision because, in addition to projecting NATO forces beyond the traditional interpretation of Article 6 of the Washington Treaty, it manifested a significant NATO transition from the role of collective self-defense against an armed attack (Article 5) to a regional security role under the UN.[14]

Protection of Safe Areas

In March 1993, an intensification of the fighting in eastern Bosnia resulted in heavy losses of life and in the further obstruction of humanitarian relief convoys in the area. Most of the refugees were flooding into Srebrenica to escape the onslaught of the Bosnian Serb forces. In March and April, the situation in and around Srebrenica deteriorated rapidly as 30 to 40 people died daily as a result of exposure, starvation, or military action. It became clear that Srebrenica was going to fall to Bosnian Serb forces and UNPROFOR could do nothing to stop the offensive. The UNSC had authorized UNPROFOR to deploy a company of Canadians to Srebrenica to secure regular deliveries of aid. However, General Mladic would not let the Canadians through.[15]

What was more shocking and more catalyzing, however, was when news reached Sarajevo on 12 April that an intense artillery attack near Srebrenica had killed 56 people in less than an hour—some of the victims included school children that had been playing soccer. Louis Gentile, the only UNHCR official in the town, witnessed the carnage and reported the following to his head office in Belgrade:

Fourteen dead bodies were found in the school yard. Body parts and human flesh clung to the school yard fence. The ground was literally soaked with blood. One child, about six years of age, had been decapitated. I saw two ox-carts covered with bodies. I did not look forward to closing my eyes at night for fear that I would relive the images. I will never be able to convey the horror.[16]

The day after Srebrenica fell and in an atmosphere of international opprobrium, the UN Security Council adopted Resolution 819 on 16 April 1992. UNSCR 819 invoked Chapter VII of the UN Charter and declared Srebrenica and its surrounding territory to be a "safe area" which should be "free from any armed attack or any other hostile act." It also demanded the immediate withdrawal of Serb paramilitary forces from the areas surrounding Srebrenica as well as demanding the cessation of armed attacks against the town. According to Silber and Little, what the term "safe" meant was left vague. They argue, however, that the resolution avoided the term "safe haven" because this term had a precise definition in international law that implied immunity from armed attack for all refugees in the town. Nonetheless, Silber and Little aver that this mandate pushed UNPROFOR across another critical threshold because it was the first time the international community morally—though, not in any real sense, like providing additional forces to back up the mandate—committed itself to the protection of one side in the war against the other.[17]

Theretofore, UNPROFOR had been limited exclusively to the delivery of humanitarian aid and the provision of "good offices." Moreover, in Resolution 824 of 6 May 1993, the UN Security Council subsequently declared that Zepa, Tuzla, Bihac, and Gorazde and their surroundings were also to be treated as safe areas. The declaration of safe areas, however, created a paradoxical mix of peace enforcement and peacekeeping which resulted in the worst case of both scenarios: "it failed to provide the protection it appeared to offer; and at the same time it aligned the UN, symbolically, with one side in the conflict." It was also the first step down a slippery path that would draw Western powers into the conflict in an incremental and ad hoc way—an eventuality they had all pledged to avoid. In choosing a short-term fix to a long-term problem, the UN had burdened itself with responsibilities it was not capable of fulfilling. When Boutros-Ghali called for 34,000 additional troops for UNPROFOR to protect the "safe areas," member states only came up with 7,000.[18]

A month later, on 4 June, the UNSC passed Resolution 836. This resolution added to the ends-means mismatch already inherent in UNPROFOR's mandate and it increased the difficulty posed by the chimera of partiality and peacekeeping. Once again invoking Chapter VII, the Security Council expanded UNPROFOR's mandate again—it authorized the Force "to deter attacks against the safe areas, to monitor the cease-fire, to promote the withdrawal of military or paramilitary units other than those of the Government of the Republic of Bosnia and Herzegovina, and to occupy some key points on the ground." What is more, these tasks were added to the tasks UNPROFOR had already been mandated to carry out. In addition, the UNSC authorized UN forces to take necessary measures acting in self-defense, including the use of force, in response to artillery or armed incursions into the safe areas or in the case of any deliberate obstruction of UNPROFOR's freedom of movement or of humanitarian relief convoys. Moreover, UNSCR 836 also authorized member states, acting nationally or through regional arrangements, by the application of air power, to take all necessary measures "to support UNPROFOR in the performance of its mandate" in and around the safe areas.[19]

In practice these resolutions were construed as authorizing UNPROFOR to take action if its forces in proximity to the safe areas were subject to attack—this action could include calling on NATO for close air support. But, neither UNPROFOR's leadership nor its major troop contributing states interpreted the resolutions to charge the operation with responsibility for defending the safe areas or to give NATO the green light to do so. Notwithstanding, according to Durch and Schear, by focusing on the Serbs and by demanding their withdrawal and not the withdrawal of Bosnian Government forces, the Security Council gave UNPROFOR a mandate that was unambiguously partial. However, the UN neither provided the means to fulfill the new partial mandate, nor did it rescind the previous mandates authorizing the impartial delivery of humanitarian aid. As a result, UNPROFOR entered a new, more tenuous, phase elegantly described herein: "What had merely been a trip through the Twilight Zone for UN forces became an increasingly Orwellian exercise in which safe areas were not safe, protection was afforded to food but not people, and the vicious customs of war in the Balkans were condemned without consequence to perpetrators."[20]

Subsequently, NATO did respond to the UN authorization for "regional arrangements to use air power in support of UNPROFOR." In August 1993, the NAC agreed to conduct close air support operations (CAS) to protect UNPROFOR dispositions. This announcement triggered debates in 1993 and early 1994 which revealed the seams in the UN-NATO nexus and highlighted the difficulty which inheres in placing Chapter VI forces into a Chapter VII environment. Britain, France, and Canada, with troops on the ground, opposed the use of NATO air power and insisted that a UN special representative should be in charge of any peace implementation force. The United States, on the other hand, strongly advocated air strikes and refused to countenance anything other than NATO unity of command. These debates and the resultant failure to effect progress on the ground, testified to the difficulty of trying to use UN and NATO procedures at the same time. It would be difficult to realize the advantages of NATO's military leverage without overcoming the shortcomings of the UN's decision-making process.[21]

For the reminder of 1993, although NATO had the mandate to use air power and lots of people were talking tough about bombing, not much happened. There were essentially two reasons for this inaction. First, there was a great deal of concern for the safety of the outgunned and outmanned UNPROFOR battalions scattered around the safe areas. Second, the UNPROFOR commanders were reluctant to give bombing a go because whatever it did it probably would not be enough. According to Major General Lewis MacKenzie, "you start backing them into a corner and start bombing them and you've got yourself a major problem, a long term problem." Concisely put, the problem would be 13,000 UN soldiers in Bosnia Herzegovina surrounded by over 100,000 very unhappy Serbs.[22]

Weapons Exclusion Zones

However, as proved to be the case for most of the war, the Bosnian Serbs were their own worst enemies when it came to international public relations. On 5 February 1994 the Serbs mortared a highly congested market place in Sarajevo, killing 68 civilians and wounding many others. In response to this egregious Bosnian Serb attack, on 6 February 1994, Boutros-Ghali stated in a letter to the UNSC that the mortar incident made it necessary to prepare for the use of air strikes in accordance with UNSC 836. The Secretary General also asked NATO's Secretary General to obtain the NAC's authorization to launch strikes against Bosnian Serb artillery positions threatening Sarajevo. On 9 February, NATO issued an ultimatum to the Bosnian Serbs that demanded that they withdraw or place under UN control all heavy weapons located within 20 kilometers of Sarajevo. The ultimatum further stated that any heavy weapons remaining inside the "exclusion zone" after 10 days would be subject to NATO air strikes, conducted in close coordination with the UN Secretary General.[23]

In the interim, the recently appointed UNPROFOR Commander, General Sir Michael Rose, supplemented the NAC's ultimatum with assertive negotiations on the ground. The 100 NATO tactical air controllers who were previously deployed into the theater remained postured to observe targets for the NATO combat aircraft that filled the skies overhead. As the Serbs considered NATO's ultimatum, the UNSC also convened four times between 14 and 15 February 1994. Security Council members welcomed NATO's decision to use force (air) and acknowledged that such force was already authorized by extant Security Council resolutions. Members highlighted the need for precision and caution; they also stated their concerns that UNPROFOR might become a target of retaliatory measures as a result of the air strikes. Nonetheless, on 17 February the Bosnian Serbs agreed to withdraw all their heavy weapons from the exclusion zone within two days. By 20 February, the UNPROFOR Commander and NATO reported that the Serbs had complied with the ultimatum. As a result, the UNSC recommended that air strikes not be carried out.[24]

However, although the Security Council never issued another resolution in 1994 to explicitly authorize air power to enforce the exclusion zone around Sarajevo, it did increase the authorized strength of UNPROFOR by 8,250 troops on 11 March 1994 and by 3,500 on 31 March 1994. Thus, the UN increased UNPROFOR's strength to monitor the exclusion zone without changing the operation's mandates. At the end of March 1994, the Bosnian Serbs launched an assault on Gorazde, with indiscriminate shelling that led to many civilian casualties. In response to events in Gorazde, on 22 April 1994 the North Atlantic Council

(NAC) authorized air strikes against the Bosnian Serb forces around Gorazde if they didn't cease the attack and withdraw their forces back three kilometers from the city center. On 23 April, UNPROFOR and the Bosnian Serbs agreed to establish a 20-kilometer heavy weapons exclusion zone around Gorazde and to deploy an UNPROFOR battalion into the city (3-kilometer radius).[25]

On 9 May 1994, the UN Secretary General submitted a report to the UNSC with the purpose of clarifying the "safe areas" concept. He articulated three overarching principles to guide the implementation of the safe areas: (a) the principal purpose of the areas was to protect people, not territory, and the UN forces protection of these areas was not intended to make them a party to the conflict; (b) the implementation of the safe area mission should not detract from the original mandates (providing humanitarian assistance and to contributing to the peace process); and (c) the mandate must take into account the Force's resource limitations. Notwithstanding, after UNPROFOR and NATO began to threaten the use of force to compel Bosnian Serb compliance with exclusion zones, however, it became very difficult to maintain an impartial image among the Serbs. And Durch and Schear emphasize this point: "this attempt to graft tasks that required the application of coercive force onto a mission conducted under peacekeeping rules of engagement did not work very well." However, it did fit with the emerging British wider peacekeeping doctrine called "just enough force to accomplish the mission but not so much as to make one look like an American."[26]

The exclusion zone regime, coupled with an indecisive use of air power, made UNPROFOR's predicament more untenable and turned any notion of impartiality into an illusion. When Boutros-Ghali updated the Security Council on 17 September 1994, he addressed some of the difficulties UNPROFOR faced. Noting that the significant constraints on the Force's ability to carry out the safe area task remained unchanged, the Secretary General also advised that the exclusion zones around Gorazde and Sarajevo were difficult to enforce, expensive in terms of manpower, and not sustainable indefinitely. Moreover, Boutros-Ghali explained, the UN forces were very vulnerable to any determined effort to take hostages and remove weapons because UN personnel were widely dispersed at weapons collection points. The Secretary General's account also acknowledged that "enforcement of weapons exclusion zones placed additional strains on UNPROFOR as an impartial force. Nonetheless, on 30 September 1994, UNSC Resolution 947 extended the mandate of UNPROFOR to 31 March 1995.[27]

However, the early fall of 1994 also witnessed a deterioration in the security environment in Bosnia Herzegovina. The frequency and lethality of sniper attacks increased in the Sarajevo safe area, notwithstanding an antisniping agreement. The extent of heavy weapons attacks against the city center and suburbs also increased. The Bosnian Serb forces also targeted UN forces, resulting in fatalities and casualties. In August and September, NATO planes conducted air strikes on two occasions to hit Bosnian Serb heavy weapons in violation of the Sarajevo exclusion zone. What's more, heightened Serb intransigence and hostility toward UNPROFOR was prevalent throughout Bosnia. The Serb forces closed a key humanitarian route into Sarajevo, significantly impeding the aid effort into Sarajevo as well as northern and eastern Bosnia. Frequent attacks on the Sarajevo airport caused it to close frequently. In addition, obstruction of and attacks on the humanitarian aid workers were reported in Gorazde, Tuzla, and Srebrenica. Widespread violations of human rights also continued throughout the conflict zone. In response to the latter, the UN Security Council adopted Resolution 941 on 23 September, demanding "that the Bosnian Serb authorities immediately cease their campaign of ethnic cleansing."[28]

Subsequently, in October 1994 the Bosnian Government forces launched an offensive operation against the Bihac pocket. However, the Bosnian Serb forces eventually repulsed the attack and launched a counteroffensive in November, in concert with Krajina Serb forces across the border in Croatia. All UNPROFOR and diplomatic efforts to stop the attack on Bihac failed. What was worse, on 18 November the Krajina Serb forces violated Bihac's safe area status by launching an air attack in which napalm and cluster bombs were dropped on southwest Bihac. On 19 November, moreover, the Krajina Serbs, while bombing a town 10 miles north of Bihac, crashed an airplane into an apartment building, killing several people and wounding many more. In response, the UN Security Council passed Resolution 958 on 19 November 1994. By referring back to UNSCR 836, UNSCR 958 essentially authorized NATO to use air power to protect all safe areas and to enforce exclusion zones.[29]

On 21 November, NATO aircraft bombed the airstrip where from the air attack was launched (Udbina in Krajina). The strike took caution not to strike any of the aircraft or facilities—it only cratered the runway. On 23 November, in response to missiles fired at NATO aircraft, 20 NATO aircraft targeted two Serb air defense sites. The Bosnian Serb forces began shelling the town of Bihac on 25 November; and although UNPROFOR called for NATO close air support, the planes were unable to attack without risking casualties to civilians and UN forces. Apparently in retaliation for NATO air strikes, the Bosnian Serb forces took 450 UN personnel in the Bihac area hostage. According to Durch and Schear, this episode undermined, rather than buttressed, UNPROFOR's credibility and its capacity to maintain the exclusion zones. It also highlighted the rifts in NATO between the advocates of bombing (United States) and the proponents of impartial peacekeeping (France, UK, etc.). The United States wanted to conduct a full-scale air campaign against the Serb transgressions on the Bihac safe area. However, states with troops on the ground reeled at America's willingness to put the UN Force's troops in jeopardy while at the same time the United States was unwilling to put its combat soldiers in the mud.[30]

This lack of consensus on the use of air power between London, Paris, and Washington was best symbolized by "the Mogadishu line," a term coined by LTG Rose and explained in the previous chapter. The Europeans were unwilling to support an offensive/coercive air campaign (peace enforcement) while they had vulnerable peacekeepers on the ground. This would pull them across the Rubicon (Mogadishu line) of consent and impartiality. It would mean, essentially, that

UNPROFOR had taken sides. However, to the Bosnian Serbs, NATO's use of air power to enforce exclusion zones and to protect safe areas had to have put UNPROFOR across that line by the fall of 1994. Nonetheless, as a result of former President Jimmy Carter's mid-December visit to Pale and Sarajevo, the warring factions signed a cessation-of-hostilities agreement (COHA) that declared a four-month cease-fire.[31]

However, by the time the COHA approached expiration, all sides were preparing to win a decision by force, including UNPROFOR. British General Rupert Smith took command of UNPROFOR in January 1995 and he brought a more forceful approach to the job. In addition, the renewal of hostilities and the perpetration of more egregious acts against civilians during the period from March 1995 until August 1995 helped precipitate an escalation in the use of force by UNPROFOR as well as a significant augmentation in the amount of forces available to LTG Smith. It also witnessed an unambiguous transition from peacekeeping to peace enforcement, culminating in NATO Operation Deliberate Force in August and September 1995. As the British Army forces were a significant part of UNPROFOR's build up, these events are addressed in the short summary below and in the answers to the four central questions.[32]

The Role of the British Army in Bosnia

From October 1992 until August 1995, the British Army had at least one battalion (regimental) battle group deployed with UNPROFOR. Moreover, as the Force's mandates continued to expand, so to did the size of the British contingent. Even before the establishment of the Rapid Reaction Force (RRF) in the summer of 1995, the size of the British element had grown to three battalion-size battle groups, plus combat support and combat service support elements. In terms of raw numbers of troops, the British contingent averaged around 3,200 to 3,500 until June 1995. In response to 33 British troops taken hostage by the Bosnian Serbs on 31 May 1995, the British contribution rose to over 8,000 troops, making it the single largest contributor to UNPROFOR. Moreover, after the cessation of hostilities, the British Army continued to play a big role in IFOR and SFOR.[33]

The British Army gave the name Operation Grapple to its role in Bosnia and it rotated regiments in and out on a six-month basis. As a result, by the fall of 1995 the British had conducted six half-year cycles with UNPROFOR, referred to as Operations Grapple 1-6. Moreover, the last two top UNPROFOR commanders, whose tenure was roughly one year, were British officers—LTG Sir Michael Rose in 1994 and LTG Rupert Smith in 1995. Before the summer of 1995, however, all of the British battalion groups that rotated into Bosnia were entrusted with essentially the same sets of tasks, changes to the mandate notwithstanding. The tasks were convoy escorts, route reconnaissance, information reconnaissance, route marking, patrols, and mobile pillboxes and observation posts. The British Army, as well as other UNPROFOR contingents went into Bosnia as peacekeepers but in the absence of peace. As a result, British forces were required to retain their impartiality and the consent of the factions to the extent possible, even though fire was exchanged many times.[34]

Furthermore, British Army regiments embarked on Operation Grapple without any written doctrine on how to do armed humanitarian operations—the only extant doctrine was the 1988 peacekeeping manual. However, according to an officer personally involved with training the 1st Cheshires (the first British battle group in Bosnia), the British trainers at Sennelager Training Center (STC) relied quite a bit on principles learned during the Northern Ireland (NI) experience. The regimental post-training reports (PTR) also reveal a heavy NI influence. Moreover, due to the size of the British Army, units rotating out of Northern Ireland, found themselves training up for Bosnia six months later. The comments of Corporal Jones (Royal Welch Fusilier Regiment) illuminate the importance of this shared experience. When asked about the sniping problem in Bosnia, Fusilier Jones replied: "we're used to that type of patrolling; we're used to being fired at." In addition, Jones considered duty in Bosnia easier than NI, until British hostages were taken in May 1995 at Gorazde.[35]

What the British Army hadn't derived from NI, or from maneuver operations in the Persian Gulf War (Operation Granby), it made up as it went. In addition to standard weapons and gunnery training, the 1st Cheshires were trained on convoy drills, checkpoint procedures, reaction to fire, and reaction to ambush. Every company of the Cheshire Group was also run through this scenario: occupy a forward operating base; escort a convoy; react to hostile fire; and negotiate through a simulated Serbian checkpoint. It was a potpourri of tasks, combining the NI experience, knowledge of peacekeeping in Cyprus and elsewhere, and common sense. The STC crew also developed a training package to increase the number of snipers in the Cheshires, an essential task in an environment where discriminate force would be critical. However, the first train-up was rushed by an early deployment date, though it was subsequently postponed. As a result of the 1st Cheshires' experience in Bosnia, the tasks "booby trap detection and handling" and "survival in built-up areas" were added to the pre-Bosnia train-up for subsequent battalion battle groups.[36]

1st Battalion, Prince of Wales Own Regiment of Yorkshire (1 PWO) followed the Cheshires, and 1 PWO was subsequently replaced by the 1st Battalion, Coldstream Guards for Operation Grapple 3. Initially, each battle group was supported by an artillery regiment as well as an engineer regiment. However, after Gorazde was declared an exclusion zone in April 1994, the British added an Operation Grapple Augmentation Force (OGAF). As a result, the British forces in Bosnia grew to brigade (-) size: two battalions, armored reconnaissance elements, logistical support, and an armor brigade headquarters. Furthermore, with the deployment of the 24th Airmobile Brigade and the establishment of the RRF in the summer of 1995, British forces expanded to almost the size of a combat division. Until Operation Deliberate Force in August 1995, however, the experiences and challenges of all the British Army units were very similar. They faced ambushes, mines, constant and random sniping from all sides, capricious and drunken intransigence at checkpoints, and shelling (although the shelling wasn't usually intended for the British posts). Add to this inclement weather, booby traps, treacherous mountain roads, and top-heavy armor vehicles, and one gets the idea that Bosnia was almost as fun as Somalia.[37]

As one example, the British Army was also responsible for keeping the road from Split on the Dalmatian coast to Sarajevo open—a three-hour trip along a 125-mile highway during peacetime. However, during the war humanitarian relief convoys were forced to use a 250-mile secondary road over the mountains. Filled with natural and manmade hazards every mile, the trip took two days. 1 PWO and other regiments, based 50 miles north of Sarajevo, shuttled through the mountains and valleys to escort UN convoys on this mountain route. On almost every trip, what's more, someone would open fire on the UN convoy. If the British troops could locate the sniper, they would fire back. Once a British soldier was shot dead on the main street of Gornji Vakuf as he was driving his Warrior (infantry fighting vehicle) to pick up a woman wounded during some fighting.[38] Another snapshot of the British Army's experience in Bosnia is provided by excerpts from the Gorazde Force's September 1994 Direct Targeting Incidents Report:

05 Sep 1030	C/S engaged by 4 rounds single shot 20mm from CP230324
08 Sep 1526	16 artillery rounds were reported in the town. Camp to state Red.
11 Sep 2100	2 rounds small arms were fired hitting the wall opposite the guard room. No rounds were returned.
14 Sep 1930	Saxon engaged by sniper fire having broken down during resupply of OP 11. 1000 rounds returned. 1 UN casualty—Private Jones, B Company.[39]

Notwithstanding the difficulty in remaining impartial under such conditions, British soldiers in Bosnia performed their mission honorably and tenaciously. During the period October 1992 through December 1995, the British Army deployed at least 10 infantry battalions, engineer assets, elements of Royal Artillery, logistical support elements, reconnaissance elements, and special forces to support UNPROFOR in Bosnia. They all conducted themselves professionally in meeting the demands of humanitarian aid in very difficult and frustrating conditions. According to one British Army report, some of the key successes in Bosnia were setting up effective liaison with representatives of the factions and developing negotiating techniques that enabled convoys to get through checkpoints where combatants had demonstrated belligerent behavior.[40]

The briefing also pointed out that all vehicle commanders exhibited resolve and patience when they dealt with tense and difficult situations, under strict rules of engagement. "Maintaining an impartial stance, at all levels, enabled UK troops to achieve a highly successful relationship with warring factions in areas of responsibility." Notably, the report observed that a great amount of the success in Bosnia was attributable to the very important lessons from Northern Ireland experience. Although less sanguine, but certainly fair, Durch and Schear considered UNPROFOR's record mixed. On the humanitarian relief side, UNPROFOR did a reasonably decent job, despite political and military obstruction. Moreover, the Sarajevo airlift was the longest-running effort of its kind in history. The airlift delivered approximately 175,000 tons of food and relief supplies while the convoys got another 90,000 tons through. However, UNPROFOR never had the combat power to execute the safe-areas design. Protection of the populations in the safe areas relied on the hope that the warring factions would abide by UNSC edicts based on their moral force. By late August 1995, with more robust forces in less vulnerable dispositions, "humanitarian intervention had metamorphosed into peace enforcement." The next four sections examine how British military strategic cultural preferences were manifested in Bosnia.[41]

CIVIL-MILITARY RELATIONS: DO SOMETHING, MUDDLE THROUGH

> Britain has insisted throughout that the UN Protection Force is not a "war-fighting machine" and has been emphasizing the need for a negotiated settlement.
>
> Malcom Rifkind (1995)[42]

An examination of British civil military relations in the context of Bosnia shows a large degree of harmony. The quote above, marking a period of confusion and transition to a more aggressive approach, in response to the fall of Srebrenica, testifies to the more limited and less forceful approach of the previous three years. From the outset of the mission in Bosnia in 1992, both the British and French governments adopted a limited approach and committed a limited amount of troops. The concept, good or bad, was to insert impartial peacekeepers into an ongoing conflict to deliver humanitarian aid while the diplomats worked toward a negotiated settlement. However, in May 1994 the UN's Civil Affairs Adviser who was involved with UNPROFOR in its early stages, later remarked rather presciently that "peacekeeping is no substitute for policy." It seemed that Cedric Thornberry had recognized that the insertion of peacekeepers into an area anything but peaceful was a tenuous proposition.[43]

Nonetheless, the British, the French, and other European troop contributors supported a concept of operation in Bosnia that approximated traditional peacekeeping because it relied on consent of the parties, impartiality, and a minimal use of force in self-defense, or to protect humanitarian relief supplies. Even though the UN Security Council invoked Chapter VII in several of its many resolutions, the British government and senior British officers vehemently opposed any use of force, on the ground or in the air, which smacked of peace enforcement or offensive action. The adoption of each incongruous and ill-advised Security Council resolution may have seemed like good politics at the time but "the cumulative effect of piling half-measure upon half-measure" ultimately produce a seriously flawed concept of operation. Moreover, each government knew what it did not want to do, but neither did they have any viable strategic solutions. All the resolutions were the outcome of tortuous negotiations among the Permanent Five and others—as a result the resolutions reflected the "lowest common denominator of world opinion."[44]

As a result, the escalatory resolutions authorizing "all necessary means," first to protect the safe areas, then to enforce the exclusion zones, didn't amount to much more than bluffs that the Bosnian Serbs were consistently willing to call. As for the seemingly contradictory legal and diplomatic nature of the corpus of UNSC resolutions, British Foreign Secretary Malcolm Rifkind explained that, although the British government had gone along with a number of these developments with "with great reservations and reluctance," it had also "identified the lines beyond which we would not go."[45] According to Rifkind, those lines were:

the need to retain the dual-key system [for authorizing air strikes] until the Americans were on the ground; the need for the UN to remain non-partisan in its attitude to the crisis; the need to ensure the continuation of the arms embargo, and not to start supplying one side or the other with military equipment; and the need to press for a diplomatic dimension particularly involving the United States, and not believing the UN could somehow enforce a military solution as the ultimate solution.[46]

Another British scholar labeled the United Kingdom's policy in Bosnia as "pusillanimous realism." British resistance to a more forceful intervention stemmed not so much from concerns about the complex nature of the conflict but from the lack of political will in Britain, or elsewhere, to deploy the requisite force to stop the war. Thus, Britain's initial assessment of what to do was similar to France's— restrained and conservative. In terms of British security policy and global status, "the objectives were to ensure a prominent role and to prevent commitments being made by partners and allies that would be impractical or unacceptably costly." As a result, the United Kingdom continued to emphasize a consensual approach to dealing with the warring factions.[47] In 1993, British Foreign Secretary Douglas Hurd based his defense of the British policy on the lack of international political will: "The only thing that could have guaranteed peace with justice would have been an expeditionary force. . . . And no government, no government has at any time seriously proposed that. And that I think is a line which should run through any analysis because it cuts out so much of the rhetoric which has bedeviled this."[48]

Thus, the British approach exhibited one key feature—the deliberate reluctance to commit ground forces to war in the former Yugoslavia. According to James Gow, "Hurd and the UK Government were backward at going forward." Instead of leading the international community and persuading the United States to act, British policy-makers "shrank from more decisive action—and where their counterparts were more enthusiastic, sought to place any possible use of force in a soundly reasoned context." However, there were two other factors that influenced UK policy—Northern Ireland and the role of the U.S. Because of the perceived parallels between Northern Ireland and Bosnia—both were seen as intractable ethnic conflicts—the notion emerged that it would be imprudent to sign up for a NORTHERN IRELAND II. While the deployment of British troops in Northern Ireland was considered a security exigency, a similar commitment to Yugoslavia should be avoided. On the other hand, without the commitment of American ground troops, any proposal for a peace imposition role was considered ill conceived. The European troop contributors just did not have enough combat power to avoid a debacle.[49]

Thus, British policy, as well as the UNSC resolutions that it endorsed, called for the British Army to intervene, but not in a manner that would be perceived as taking one side over the other. To do this, the British Army was required to use minimum force and to operate in such a way that the warring factions continued to consent to its presence in Bosnia. To be fair, though, the approach of the British Army in Bosnia was in response to a dual chain of command: it was the means (along with other national contingents) to carry out both UN mandates and British policy. British policy, however, was also shaped by that government's commitment to work with its European allies and to placate the U.S., to some degree. How did the British Army respond to this mission and was its response consistent with its organizational preferences for similar such operations? The statements and actions of LTG Sir Michael Rose, the British UNPROFOR Commander in 1994, generally echoed the policy makers: do not get dragged into a war with an unending commitment. Specifically, not crossing the consent breach and remaining impartial were viewed as the way to achieve this negative aim.[50]

In fact, it was LTG Michael Rose who coined the "crossing the Mogadishu line" metaphor to defend the British approach in Bosnia as a better path than the one the Americans slipped down in Somalia. The second half of 1994 witnessed heated arguments between the U.S. and the Europeans over the correct course in Bosnia. The U.S. favored a more robust and coercive use of air power whereas the British and other UNPROFOR contributors argued for a more restrained and impartial use of force. After the failure of the UN and NATO to deter the Bosnian Serbs at Gorazde in April 1994, Rose became the most vocal and visible opponent of any concerted use of coercive air power in Bosnia, saying that UNPROFOR was not "in the business of going to war in order to bring about the conditions of peace."[51]

Not only was Rose a vociferous opponent of crossing the consent line, but he was even out in front of policy when it came to statements to the media. Both during his command and after, even after British policy began to support a more robust use of force, LTG Rose remained wedded to the notion of "not crossing the Mogadishu line." For example, in September 1994, Rose commented: "If someone wants to fight a war here on moral or political grounds, fine, great, but count us out. Hitting one tank is peacekeeping. Hitting infrastructure, command and control, logistics, that is war, and I'm not going to fight a war in white-painted tanks."[52]

Moreover, a more polemical columnist described Rose as the reincarnation of Neville Chamberlain: "Sir Michael Rose's repugnance at war making when UN havens become war zones symbolizes Britain's least fine hour." In September 1994 Rose clashed with NATO over proposed air strikes that might have endangered British troops on the ground. In late September, Rose went so far as to warn that allied air power might be used against the Bosnian Government's Army. He also accused the Bosnian Muslims of contriving images of horror for the world in order to generate a tougher response.[53] In response to a question on the air strikes and the Bihac pocket, in November 1994 Rose said the following:

> We are not here to fight a war for any side. We are here as peacekeepers. The countries that have sent their troops here have done so voluntarily and they want to see those peacekeepers back in their own country, having done a good job of work. And it may be a disappointment, but it would have been a cruel illusion if we had ever said that the peacekeeping force here in Bosnia Herzegovina was ever able to defend or protect a piece of territory.[54]

However, the British government lauded LTG Rose's statements to the media. This in itself is indicative of the consonance between civilian policy and the military approach. Furthermore, LTG Rose remained wedded to an impartial and consensual approach to peacekeeping. In a November 1995 speech to the friends of the Imperial War Museum, Rose extolled the concept of wider peacekeeping as marking enormous progress in the previous three years. According to Rose, he had been thinking about the new missions in the middle ground while he was the commandant of the Staff College, just before he took command of UNPROFOR. It is also interesting to note that Rose had an office call in the late fall of 1993 with the single British author who was then writing the doctrine for wider peacekeeping. This meeting took place not long after the battle of Mogadishu, and it was this same author who later used the metaphor "Rubicon" to characterize the line between consent and nonconsent. Nonetheless, during his discussion at the Imperial War Museum, Rose also asserted that for the new peacekeeping missions you "need people who understand what is required on the ground." In Rose's view, the British Army has people that are very good at peacekeeping because they are extremely experienced at peacekeeping in this much more dangerous and tumultuous environment.[55]

British Army commanders, down to the battalion level, also echoed an approach to Bosnia similar to Rose's and to that of British policy makers. Colonel Alastair Duncan, the commander of 1st Battalion, PWO during Operation Grapple 2 stated, "it was someone else's war and I was there to prevent strife if I could, but only where possible." He also emphasized the importance of remaining impartial, even if actively impartial. Duncan compared the need to be even-handed with the act of walking on a tight-rope (a metaphor that later appeared in the British peacekeeping doctrine): "it was a pretty long and difficult tightrope, people were pushing it with sticks trying to push me off and to make matters worse somebody was also shaking the wire." An academic offered another salient explanation why the British Army adopted a limited and nonpartisan approach in Bosnia—to preserve the organizational essence of the British Army.[56]

According to Rod Thornton, the British approach in Bosnia that was subsequently codified in the 1994 doctrinal manual *Wider Peacekeeping* "was a military doctrine that seemed designed to excuse the military organization for its inaction, rather than being a guide for action itself." In other words, Thornton argues, *Wider Peacekeeping* had a specific purpose, other than explaining a sound way to do operations in the gray zone—that purpose was to convince the British public and a host of other agencies that the British Army's approach in Bosnia was the correct one. The British Army did this in order to avoid risk and maintain its organizational health. However, this was not prescriptive in the same way that the Weinberger-Powell criteria had been in the context of Somalia. The British Army was not trying to prescribe the right approach to its British civilian masters because civil-military relations were already harmonious on Bosnia. Instead, the British Army was trying to justify its actions to the public, domestic and international, as well as any other actors who were pushing for more robust force. It was trying to maximize its autonomy and re-establish expertise in the context of a new mission environment.[57]

Moreover, the main threat to its organizational essence was an expansion of the limited operation in Bosnia—this might jeopardize the British Army's ability to carry out its core tasks in Northern Ireland and Germany. Mission creep might have involved the British Army in an intense conflict that it was not well disposed to carry out. Moreover, according to Thornton, "while resistance to the new role was clear, the situation seemed manageable so long as the Army was involved in merely escorting convoys." However, in order to preempt calls from all quarters (especially the United States) for more aggressive and robust action in Bosnia, Rose, and subsequently British doctrine, advocated a stretched or marginally adapted version of peacekeeping—still maintaining consent, impartiality, and minimum force as inviolate principles. *Wider Peacekeeping* also highlighted the difficulties of moving from peacekeeping to peace enforcement (the Rubicon) and it challenged the notion of the "do-something brigade." As Thornton cogently explains, the doctrine "was not needed for the escort of convoys but it was needed to explain why the mission should not go beyond escorting convoys."[58]

A corollary focus of this section, however, is the integration of civil and military components of UNPROFOR in the British Army's area of operation. Generally, there were problems with this. Many of these problems, however, may be attributable to the amorphous nature of UN operations, which involved many agencies, operating over a wide area in Bosnia. There was also no evidence of a structured Civil Military Operations Center (CMOC) in the British Army sector. One report noted that interagency relationships were never formalized, resulting in a lack of coordination and a duplication of effort that frustrated military operators. What's more, the nature of the peacekeeping function in UNPROFOR meant that military forces were given an expanding number of support tasks aimed at facilitating the operations of Non-Governmental Organizations (NGOs) and other components. This relationship was complicated on all sides. Problems result when peacekeepers have to work within "overlapping chains of command at the military-civilian interface, often ill-coordinated, with disparate agendas and making diverse security demands." On the other hand, both the UN and NGO civilian agencies, which increasingly depended on the military for protection, found their neutrality and freedom of movement threatened by association with politically compromised peacekeeping forces.[59]

The 1st Battalion, PWO post-operational report, for example, observed that civil-military integration was a problem. "Coordination between UNPROFOR and the multitude of organizations operating in central Bosnia is poor." The report explains that there had been significant redundancy of effort among the various military, aid, and NGO agencies that negated or hindered progress. There were even incidents of civilian agencies operating in 1 PWO's area of operation without coordinating or informing the battalion leadership. This lack of coordination also contributed to a lack of military information (intelligence in the innocuous vernacular of the UN) that would have been useful for planning operations to avoid hazards. This problem was exacerbated when the UN Bosnia Herzegovina Command (BHC) stopped issuing daily information summaries. Finally, the report recommended more frequent military information conferences in order to facilitate liaison and coordination between the diverse agencies operating within the battalion's area of operation.[60]

Another post-operational report noted the coordination problems with the UN military observers (UNMO): "the UNMO organization has been superimposed upon battalions, creating two structures conducting liaison within one AOR and working with different commanders." This led to confusion on the part of local commanders because it ran counter to the basic military principle of unity of command. This also contributed to conflicting reports of the same events, adding to confusion. Notwithstanding repeated efforts to coordinate UNMO activities with those of the British Army units, the UNMOs deliberately followed a separate line. Finally, the report recommended that the UNMO teams collocate with unit headquarters and that they report to battalion commanders, with a communication link to the sector UNMO headquarters.[61]

PROPENSITY FOR MINIMUM FORCE: DRAWING THE MOGADISHU LINE IN THE MUD

The gray zone was not starkly defined by Rubicon lines and consent divides, and military forces were not suddenly plunged into it by inadvertently crossing a 'line in the sand.' In the confusing realities of having to operate in the gray zone, the Rubicon line was more like a Ganges delta, to be unwittingly crossed and re-crossed without any noticeable change in the state of the peace process.
—John Mackinlay[62]

The British Army, for almost three years, certainly exhibited an approach that emphasized minimal force in self-defense, consent, and impartiality. To be sure, thus far, this book has also demonstrated that a predilection for minimal force in intrastate conflicts is a characteristic embedded in British military strategic culture. Moreover, the British Army's experience in Northern Ireland, though in many ways different than Bosnia, represented the most recent and the most widely experienced model for intrastate policing in the midst of ongoing conflict. Many of the post operational reports and articles refer to Northern Ireland or to a degree of reliance on principles applied in Northern Ireland in Bosnia because of the absence of doctrine.

Nonetheless, it is not possible to make an irrefutable assertion that British behavior in Bosnia was exclusively a result of organizational preferences. This is because leaders and policy makers in the British Government wanted the Army to take a limited and minimalist approach—to do what it could to ameliorate the suffering without getting involved in a three-sided imbroglio. By examining the context, the statements by key leaders, and articles by other experts, this section will show that cultural preferences about the use of force were an influence—as a lens, or filter, through which the "correct" approach was advocated. The irony is, however, that for all the vitriol about the "Mogadishu line," the British Army had in fact crossed it (along with the rest of UNPROFOR) well before the mission in Bosnia deliberately metamorphosed to a peace enforcement mode in August 1995.

A degree of cultural continuity is manifested by the fact the rules on the use of force were generally based on the Northern Ireland experience. Many of the British Army post-operational reports as well as the regimental journals compared the use of force in Bosnia with the Northern Ireland experience. For example, one article compared the force used at checkpoints to the control of checkpoints in Northern Ireland. Moreover, while the approach emphasized minimum force, it did not proscribe the immediate return of pretty robust small arms and machine gun fire, in response to attacks on British soldiers. Another regimental journal noted that, "rounds have been returned but all have shown commendable restraint in the face of intense provocation." Excessive force was to be avoided because that could precipitate the loss of impartiality and consent. Impartiality did not equate to neutrality, it meant that force could be used to respond to groups attempting to obstruct the British soldiers who were carrying out their mandated tasks. Once again, though, in Bosnia LTG Rose was the most visible and vocal proponent of minimum force.[63]

According to Rose, "only a minimum level of force can be used to achieve a specific aim." In addition, before using force warnings must be given, collateral damage must be avoided, and any use of force must also be timely, proportional, and relevant. A peacekeeping force, Rose maintains, can only operate with the consent of those forces that control the territory. Thus, peacekeeping forces must remain noncombatants, impartial. Rose also posited that, adding more firepower into the equation at a later date cannot change the basic rule that forces engaging in such operations "have to act within the limits prescribed for the use of force in any peacekeeping mission." The unambiguous lessons from Bosnia and Somalia, Rose has contended, is that to "confuse the strategic roles of war fighting and peacekeeping, will risk the success of the mission and also the very lives of the peacekeepers and the aid workers themselves." In Rose's view, the same principle of minimum force also applies to the application of air power. Other commanders in Bosnia also supported this minimalist approach to force. For example, one explained that "military force is a very blunt instrument" and once force is used you cannot go back, "there are always ramifications."[64]

Similarly, as late as November 1994 a brigadier who had commanded British forces in Sector Southwest in Bosnia was absolutely convinced that the approach codified in the emerging wider peacekeeping doctrine—minimum force, consent, and impartiality—was the correct one. Brigadier A. P. Ridgway reported that he stood "four square behind the position taken by General Rose against the wider use of air power and the lifting of the arms embargo." He emphasized impartiality as the "key issue." Only if British forces were seen to be impartial, Ridgway maintained, would they receive the consent of the parties, and "without such consent peacekeeping operations become impossible." According to Ridgway, whenever the UN engaged in even a degree of enforcement action, the "tenuous nature" of consent was repeatedly demonstrated. Even the bombing of a single tank would precipitate significantly restricted freedom of movement and other difficulties that lasted for several weeks and impeded operations. Finally, Ridgway maintained that a "more extensive use of enforcement measures would undoubtedly place the security of our widely dispersed and lightly protected forces at considerable risk."[65]

Nonetheless, a RAND assessment of operations in Bosnia, noted the mismatch between the amount of force authorized under Chapter VII of the UN Charter and the employment of ground forces suitable only for Chapter VI (peacekeeping). As a result, the UN mandate was insufficiently fulfilled, despite NATO assistance. Even when UNPROFOR and NATO tried a more coercive approach in early 1994, UNPROFOR's role became ambiguous. "On several occasions, UNPROFOR troops engaged in combat while using white-painted vehicles." UNPROFOR soldiers were placed in an unnecessarily dangerous and incongruous predicament—they "survived and even prevailed because the opposing troops behaved ineptly." The report drew the fundamental conclusion that coercive action and traditional peacekeeping are mutually exclusive and should not be mixed. Essentially, the report found that coercive action was incompatible with humanitarian relief operations because UNPROFOR was unable to protect the widely dispersed humanitarian aid workers from an opponent who demonstrated a willingness to affect retribution against UN troops as well as aid personnel.[66]

By 1995, however, the commander of British forces in Sector South West, Bosnia, asserted that the Northern-Ireland-based ROE were no longer applicable to Bosnia—they were too equivocal. According to Brigadier Pringle, a simple set of more robust and flexible ROE were required to reflect the changed circumstances in the theater (the then pending increase in forces—Rapid Reaction Force [RRF]) in order to avoid the humiliation of British forces. Thus, as a consequence of the problems stemming from mixing peace enforcement in the air with "impartiality" and "consent" on the ground, by June of 1995, the British Army and UNPROFOR were ready to switch to quasi-peace enforcement. Once the RRF was approved on 16 June, General Rupert Smith came up with the concept of white and green echelon forces. On the one hand, the white 1st echelon forces were the troops in place who were conducting peacekeeping and humanitarian tasks in white-painted vehicles and wearing blue helmets. On the other hand, the green 2nd echelon forces were the RRF troops whose helmets and tanks were camouflaged and ready for battle. If the white forces were threatened or attacked, the green forces would come to the rescue. Pringle's post-operational report validated this transition—"the posture of the Op Grapple deployment has gone through a significant switch from white bespoke peace support operations toward a more 'green' conventional approach."[67]

Forces in Bosnia did not transition to full peace enforcement until Operation Deliberate Force began on 28 August 1995, after the Gorazde force had been extracted, and after other vulnerably dispersed UNPROFOR units redeployed out of Serb-controlled areas. In part, the catalyst for the transition was the international opprobrium leveled at UNPROFOR for "doing nothing" when Srebrenica fell in July, coupled with the 25 July 1995 mortar attack on a Sarajevo market place. However, even by that time both the British approach and the wider peacekeeping doctrine that codified it were discredited. According to a post-operational report from the summer of 1995, wider peacekeeping was beginning to cause a loss of UNPROFOR credibility in the eyes of the local population and UNPROFOR was "beginning to feel impotent." Peace enforcement, the report explained, brought the Serbs to the negotiating table and gave the troops a renewed sense of purpose. By June 1995, other British officers at the RRF planning cell in Zagreb were not particularly enamored of the academic warnings about "crossing the Rubicon between peacekeeping and peace enforcing" that were emanating from the British Ministry of Defense.[68]

Thornton's study arrives at another conclusion about the British Army in Bosnia and about wider peacekeeping in particular. After the passage of time and due to potentially humiliating experiences in Bosnia, *Wider Peacekeeping* came to be perceived as too risk averse. The risk of being embroiled in an inter-ethnic war was supplanted by the image of an impotent NATO and an impotent British Army. The British Army took pride in its ability to do imperial policing and OOTW, but now it appeared to shrink from its responsibility to effectively conduct a new OOTW, armed humanitarian operations. The British Army came to see *Wider Peacekeeping* for what it essentially was—a short-term solution for a specific problem—how to avoid being pushed into more aggressive action in the civil war. However, by 1995 the British Army risked damage to its reputation and to its autonomy if it failed to contribute to a solution in Bosnia.[69]

CASUALTIES: "THE KING'S SHILLING"

While in England, this author asked several academics and military officers about casualties and what role casualties played in the British Army's operations in Bosnia. The most common response was some variant of an explanation in the context of Northern Ireland—the British public was conditioned to casualties as a consequence of the thirty-year commitment there that resulted in over 2,000 casualties. However, one former British officer explained the casualty question in the context of an ageless aphorism—"when you take the King's shilling, you accept the consequences." This expression dates back to the 17th century and the new model Army—it refers to the method by which the dredges of British society were recruited (impressed into the army). Recruiters would scour the bars to find potential soldiers and entice them into signing up by buying them beers. At the bottom of the pint was a shilling—if the citizen drank the beer and took the shilling, he accepted the consequences of being a soldier in the British Army.[70]

Richard Connaughton also pointed out that the British Army only had one casualty-free year between the end of World War II and the end of the Cold War. When queried about casualty aversion and force protection in Northern Ireland, a British officer with five tours in Northern Ireland, commented "we never adopted the view that we needed to minimize casualties." It also seems that the very difficulty of finding an accurate figure for the number of British soldiers killed or wounded in Bosnia is revealing—while all armies seek to avoid casualties, the British Army and public does not seem to get to worked up over them. Moreover, the Ministry of Defense did not even keep an accurate tally of killed and wounded British soldiers over the 30 years it spent conducting MACA in Northern Ireland. However, most officers and academics cite over 2,000 casualties of which over 600 were killed—about a battalion's worth.[71]

Nonetheless, as of 20 March 1995, the UN listed the total casualties for UNPROFOR to be 1,366. Of this total, 149 were fatalities, 54 of which were caused by hostile action. The total number of casualties for UNPROFOR, due to hostile action, was 557. For the same period, there were 378 casualties and 35 fatalities as a result of hostile action in Bosnia Herzegovina Command. However, the only post-operational report that addressed British casualties was the 1994 British Forces Commander's report. It noted that 12 British soldiers had been killed as of November 1994, 11 of which were killed in 1994, the same year that LTG Rose was the UNPROFOR Commander. Even so, the British Army stayed the course, casualties notwithstanding, and it continues to serve in Bosnia today.[72]

In 1995, a journalist offered an observation about the British Army and casualties: "Unlike Americans these days, British leaders seem neither afraid to send them [British troops] into danger nor particularly shocked at what happens sometimes when they go." Although the British and the Americans both have all-professional militaries, the British have one with a "stiff-upper-lip attitude." Another British brigadier offered an explanation of the role of casualties: "what seems not well understood nowadays is that war or operations other than war are a risky business, and taking part implies accepting the possibility of casualties." Nonetheless, a British brigadier also emphasizes that unnecessary casualties must always be avoided. That being said, Denaro states that it must be made unambiguously clear that achieving the objective is more important "than taking unavoidable casualties." Peace support operations are about accepting risk, with a clear understanding of the cost of the operation.[73]

TECHNOLOGY

This was the most difficult question to answer. This study did not find any explicit leveraging of technology to minimize casualties. The British Army, however, did innovate with technology a great deal in Northern Ireland in order to counter terrorism. The British created surveillance and countersurveillance equipment, bomb disposal equipment, and riot gear, some of it would also be useful for peacekeeping. For example, in the 1980s in response to Northern Ireland, the British Army developed a new helmet with a detachable riot-control visor. It also devised long-range surveillance equipment. However, this study has not observed any evidence that this technology was used in Bosnia. The British used standard organizational equipment and relied on the U.S. for most strategic reconnaissance assets. As mentioned previously in this chapter, even with available (NATO) air delivered laser-guided precision ammunition, the British forces in Bosnia were reluctant to drop bombs on the Serbs. The British did not employ or ask for either attack helicopters or AC-130 gun ships either.[74]

It is difficult to discern any special emphasis or reliance on technology by the British Army in Bosnia. Although this is a comparative study, the technology question seems to be more applicable to the U.S. Army, an institution of a great power, with intrinsically more resources and technology at its disposal. Perhaps great powers tend to rely on technology more because they can. Nonetheless, the British Army did have state-of-the-art systems available for use in Bosnia. For example, by the summer of 1995 when the mission seemed to be moving toward peace enforcement, British forces in Bosnia had Warrior Infantry Fighting Vehicles, Saxon Armored Personnel Carriers, artillery, and the 24th Airmobile Brigade (equipped with attack, lift, and observation helicopters).[75]

CONCLUSION

Figure 6.1 depicts some generalizations about the manifestation of British military strategic cultural characteristics in Bosnia. After examining statements by policy makers and military practitioners, it seems that the civil and military preferences were congruent: do something but not enough to get sucked into the war. Nonetheless, it was not difficult for the British military to be responsive to its civilian masters, since a minimalist approach to force seemed to reflect continuity in the British Army's attitudes about intrastate emergencies. Since impartiality and consent were contingent on the use of minimum, and not robust or excessive force, it seemed logical for the British Army to be a proponent of those principles as well. It cannot be overstated that the experience in Northern Ireland—the most recent and far-reaching frame of reference—had a significant influence on how the British Army conducted operations in Bosnia. This is particularly true since the British

Figure 6.1
British Military Strategic Culture in Bosnia

Characteristic	U.K. - Bosnia
Civil-Military	Policy and Military in harmony—policy limited to doing something but not getting dragged into the war. Military echoed and pursued absolute impartiality/consent until summer 1995.
Force	Minimalist force: initially self-defense, then in defense of mandate.
Casualties	Exhibits willingness to take casualties—conditioned by NI experience. Not inured to casualties, however. LTG Rose expressed concern about casualties.
Technology	Undetermined: Did not over rely on technological solutions (i.e., air power or attack helos) but employed organic systems (Warriors/Saxons) to protect with effect.

Army embarked on operations in Bosnia without any doctrine for that type of operation.

The relevance of Northern Ireland is also underscored by comments in post-operational reports and journals. For example, one journalist observed: "the ability to cope with this type of operation without extensive specialist training is a testament to the value of existing leadership training and, in particular to the experience of deployment to Northern Ireland where junior NCOs are given a lot of responsibility in relation to their rank." As far as casualties are concerned, the British Government and the British Army seem willing to stay the course in the face of unavoidable casualties. This "stiff-upper-lip" is also, in part, attributable to a long-term commitment to Northern Ireland where casualties became a common occurrence. Furthermore, a view of casualties consistent with the "King's shilling" aphorism possibly reflects a better cultural understanding that soldiers sign up to go in harm's way—that is their profession. Finally, it seems that technology is not much of a factor—there was no evidence of an explicit reliance on technology to leverage a special advantage, or to minimize casualties.[76]

As a postscript, Dick Betts offered the following observations about the safe area concept in Bosnia. The "safe areas" and weapons exclusion zones in Bosnia were islands surrounded by hostile forces. They represented messy territorial anomalies in what was essentially a Serb conquest. It should have been no surprise that the Serbs were waiting, ready to pounce on the pockets, and willing to test the resolve of the international community. Moreover, in the end, many British officers found the wider peacekeeping approach to be pretty useless in the context of Bosnia.[77]

NOTES

1. The expression "adapting on the hoof" comes from Gavin Bulloch—he used it to describe the British Army's approach in Bosnia under UNPROFOR. Gavin Bulloch, telephone interview by author, West Point, New York, 9 March 1999.

2. Among the works explaining the breakup of Yugoslavia are Lenard J. Cohen, *Broken Bonds: Yugoslavia's Disintegration and Balkan Politics in Transition*, 2nd ed. (Boulder, CO: Westview Press, 1995); Misha Glenny, *The Fall of Yugoslavia* (New York: Penguin Books, 1993); and Richard Holbrooke, *To End a War* (New York: Random House, 1998).

3. The ethnic composition of Bosnia is from Lenard J. Cohen, "The Disintegration of Yugoslavia," *Current History* 91 (November 1992): 374.

4. Quoted in Henry Kissinger, *Diplomacy* (New York: Simon and Schuster, 1994), 621.

5. Field Marshall Dick Vincent quoted in Tim Ripley, *Operation Deliberate Force* (Lancaster, England: Centre for Defence and International Security Studies [CDISS], 1999), 71; and William J. Durch and James A. Schear, eds., *UN Peacekeeping, American Politics, and the Uncivil Wars of the 1990s* (New York: St. Martin's Press, 1996), 232.

6. Durch and Schear, 223.

7. A discussion of the four-phase chronology can be found in the Durch and Schear chapter entitled "Faultlines: UN Operations in the Former Yugoslavia," 227–32.

8. Ibid., 227.

9. United Nations, Security Council, S/RES/770, 8 June 1992; Durch and Schear, 228; and "The United Nations and the Situation in the Former Yugoslavia," Reference Paper Revision 4 (New York: UN Department of Public Information, 30 April 1995), 6, hereafter, "UN and SITFY."

10. United Nations, Security Council, S/RES/776, 14 September 1992; "UN and SITFY," 6–7; Durch and Schear, 228.

11. Durch and Schear, 229.

12. *The Blue Helmets: A Review of UN Peacekeeping*, 3rd ed. (New York: UN Department of Public Information, 1996), 523–24, hereafter, *Blue Helmets*.

13. Tony Mason, *Air Power: A Centennial Appraisal* (London: Brassey's Ltd., 1994), 172; United Nations, Security Council, S/RES/816; and "UN and SITFY," 13.

14. Mason, 173; and *NATO: Facts and Figures* (Brussels: NATO Information Service, 1989), 377.

15. *Blue Helmets*, 525; Laura Silber and Allan Little, *Yugoslavia: Death of a Nation* (New York: Penguin, 1997), 269–75; and United Nations, Security Council, S/RES/819, 16 April 1993.

16. Silber and Little, 269–70.

17. United Nations, Security Council, S/RES/819, 16 April 1993; and Silber and Little, 274.

18. United Nations, Security Council, S/RES/824, 6 May 1993; and Silber and Little, 274–75.

19. United Nations, Security Council, S/RES/836, 4 June 1993; and *Blue Helmets*, 525–26.

20. Durch and Schear, 230–31.

21. Alexander Moens and Christopher Anstis, *Disconcerted Europe* (Boulder, CO: Westview Press, 1994), 238; and *NATO's Role in Peacekeeping*, Basic Fact Sheet No. 4 (World Wide Web NATO Gopher, October 1994).

22. MacKenzie quote is from John M. Collins, *Balkan Battlegrounds* (Washington, D.C.: Congressional Research Service, 1992), 22, cited in Daniel P. Bolger, *Savage Peace* (Novato, CA: Presidio Press, 1995), 357.

23. "UN and SITFY," 22; Mason, 179.

24. Mason, 180; and *Blue Helmets*, 529–30.

25. Durch and Schear, 232; and *Blue Helmets*, 532.

26. "UN and SITFY," 28; and Durch and Schear, 240–44.

27. *Blue Helmets*, 533–34; and United Nations, Security Council, S/RES/947, 30 September 1994.

28. "UN and SITFY," 34–35; and United Nations, Security Council, S/RES/941, 23 September 1994.

29. *Blue Helmets*, 535; and United Nations, Security Council, S/RES/958, 19 November 1994.

30. "UN and SITFY," 35–36; and Durch and Schear, 244.

31. "UN and SITFY," 39. LTG Rose used the term "Mogadishu line" to conjure up memories of Somalia where U.S. forces were seen as taking sides against Aideed's militia. Rose used it to vigorously defend his approach in Bosnia, which emphasized impartiality and consent—see John Darnton, "UN Buildup in Bosnia Eyes 'Mogadishu Line'," *New York Times*, 6 June 1995, A18.

32. Ripley, 102–9.

33. The terms regiment, battle group, and battalion will be used interchangeably. Battle group is the most accurate since it connotes the equivalent of a U.S. battalion task force. However, most of the British regiments are really one-battalion regiments since the other battalion in each regiment is militia. Also, see Ripley, 115–18; and "UN and SITFY," 51.

34. *Operation Grapple 1, Post OP Debrief B Squadron 9/12L* (Herford, UK: RAC Gunnery Wing, 26 July 1993), 4. The author knows the names and cycles of the six Grapple operations as a result of sifting through most of the British Army's Post Operational (Post OP) reports from the Tactical Doctrine Retrieval Cell at Trenchard Lines, Upavon, UK.

35. Major Anthony Trevis, interview by author, West Point, New York, 14 April 2000. Tony Trevis is currently assigned to West Point as the British Exchange Officer. During the fall of 1992, he was assigned to the G3 Training shop of the British 1st Armor Division in Germany. Also see Operation Grapple PTRs for Operations Grapple 1-6; and Christopher S. Wren, "At Risk, British Troops Keep Watch," New York Times, 30 May 1995, A6.

36. Trevis Interview; and Operation Grapple FTX Memorandum, 1st Battalion Prince of Wales Own Yorkshire Regiment (1 PWO), Osnabruck, Germany, 11 March 1993.

37. There is not one coherent and distilled source or report that captures British Army rotations in Bosnia. The unit names and force compositions were obtained from the PTRs and Post Op reports compiled by the Tactical Doctrine Retrieval Cell at Trenchard Lines, Upavon, UK. Force composition data was also verified in Ripley, 335–40.

38. John F. Burns, "British Army's Job in Bosnia: To Keep Risky Lifeline Open," New York Times, 23 August 1993, A3.

39. *Operation Grapple 5 –1st Battalion The Royal Gloucestershire, Berkshire, and Wiltshire Regiment (RGBW)/BRITBAT 2 Post Operational Report* (North Yorkshire, UK: 1 RGBW, 31 March 1995), C-1. The Saxon is a four-wheeled armored infantry personnel carrier whereas the Warrior is a tracked infantry-fighting vehicle with a 30mm gun and a co-axial machine gun. The Warrior is the British equivalent of the U.S. Bradley Fighting Vehicle.

40. Charles I. Wyatt, *Operation Grapple*, Outline Briefing (London: British Army, 27 November 1995), par. 11.

41. Ibid.; and Durch and Schear, 250–52.

42. Ian Black, "Rifkind Patches up Rift with France," *The Guardian*, 17 July 1995, 8. This assertion was cited in the context of a series of Malcom Rifkind quotes defending British policy in Bosnia over the previous three years. Rifkind was the British Foreign Secretary at the time of the article.

43. Edward Foster, *NATO's Military in the Age of Crisis Management* (London: Royal United Services Institute for Defence Studies, 1995), 13.

44. Ripley, 44–45.

45. Ibid.

46. Ibid., 45.

47. James Gow, *Triumph of the Lack of Will* (New York: Columbia University Press, 1997), 175, 179–82.

48. Interview by Channel 4 TV, "Diplomacy and Deceipt," *Bloody Bosnia*, 2 August 1993, Media Transcript Service, M2578, 4, cited in Gow, *Triumph of the Lack of Will*, 179.

49. Gow, 181–82, 176, 179–80.

50. Ibid. See pages 174–82 for a discussion of UK policy in Bosnia.

51. See Foster, 15 for the debate on air power. There are various explanations for the unambiguous change in LTG Rose's approach but there is general agreement that the change occurred after Gorazde. When Rose took command of UNPROFOR he was enthusiastic about a more assertive role—this had worked well—showing positive results—when the UN and NATO issued the February 1994 ultimatum to enforce the Sarajevo exclusion zone. However, former SACEUR General (Ret.) George Joulwan said that Rose seemed spooked by the downing of the British Harrier and the death of a British soldier at Gorazde. General Joulwan also inferred from a conversation he had had with the AFSOUTH Commander at the time, Admiral Jeremy Boorda, that Rose had held the Bosnia Serb military, though thugs, in higher regard than the Bosnian Muslims. One reason for this was that the Serbs acted like a conventional and traditional military, with full color guard posted when Rose visited their headquarters. On the other hand, James Gow argues that Rose reassessed his approach because he learned at Gorazde that he could not rely on air strikes from his political superiors at the UN, when he really needed them. When Rose had requested urgent air strikes to stop a heavy onslaught at Gorazde, the Secretary General's Special Representative, Yasushi Akashi, refused permission. See James Gow, *Triumph of the Lack of Will*, 149–50.

52. Quoted in Roger Cohen, "UN General Opposes More Bosnia Force," *New York Times*, 29 September 1994, 7.

53. William Saffire, "Robust or Bust," *New York Times*, 28 November 1994, 17; and Roger Cohen, "British Commander in Bosnia: In a Quagmire and Sniped At From All Sides," *New York Times,* 25 September 1994, 14.

54. The Macneil/Lehrer Newshour, PBS-TV, 29 November 1994 in *Current News Supplement*, U.S. DOD, 1 December 1994, A2.

55. Joel Brand, "Rose Considered Showing Air Strike Plans to the Serbs," *The Times*, 16 January 1995, 12; and General Sir Michael Rose, speech to the Friends of the Imperial War Museum, 16 November 1995, IWM Sound Recording Archives, 16866; and Charles Dobbie, telephone interview by author, West Point, New York, 12 April 2000. Dobbie wrote the British *AFM, Wider Peacekeeping*.

56. Colonel Alastair Duncan, "Operating in Bosnia," *The RUSI Journal* 139 (June 1994): 15–16.

57. Rod Thornton, "Peace Support Operations and the Health of the Military Organization: The Role of Doctrine," (Unpublished Paper, University of Birmingham, UK, March 2000), 2–3, 15.

58. Ibid., 13, 15–16; and *Army Field Manual Volume 5, Operations Other Than War, Part 2 Wider Peacekeeping* (London: HMSO, December 1994), Chapter 4.

59. *Lessons Learned Bulletin Number 1* (Upavon, UK: TDRC, 1993), 5–6; and A. B. Fetherston, O. Ramsbotham, and T. Woodhouse, "UNPROFOR: Some Observations from a Conflict Resolution Perspective," *International Peacekeeping* 1 (Summer 1994): 195.

60. *BRITBAT End of Tour Report* (Vitez Camp, Bosnia: 1st Bn, PWO, October 1993), 3–5.

61. *Post-Operational Report—Operation Grapple 4* (Vitez, Bosnia: 2nd Battalion, Royal Anglian Regiment, 30 October 1994), 5–6.

62. John Mackinlay and Randolph Kent, "Complex Emergencies Doctrine: The British are Still the Best," *The RUSI Journal* 142 (April 1997): 42.

63. *Post-Tour Report—Commander's Review of Operation Grapple 6* (Paderborn, Germany: HQ, 20th Armor Brigade, 9 November 1995), 7; "Humanitarian Role in Bosnia," *Castle: Journal of the Royal Anglian Regiment* 9 (December 1994): 32; and "1st Battalion [PWO] News," *The White Rose* 35 (December 1993): 18.

64. Lieutenant General Sir Michael Rose, "A Year in Bosnia: What Has Been Achieved," *The RUSI Journal* 140 (June 1995): 23–24; Sir Michael Rose, *Fighting for Peace* (London: The Harvill Press, 1998), 364; and Duncan: 16.

65. *Operation Grapple 4—End of Tour Report* (Gornji Vakuf: Commander Sector Southwest, UNPROFOR, 2 November 1994), 4.

66. Bruce Pirnie, *An Assessment of Peace Operations in Bosnia* (Santa Monica, CA: RAND, September 1994), 47.

67. *Post-Tour Report—Commander's Review of Operation Grapple 6* (Paderborn, Germany: HQ, 20th Armor Brigade, 9 November 1995), 2,7.; and Ripley, 132–33.

68. *Operation Grapple 6, Post-Tour Report,1st Battalion The Devonshire and Dorset Regiment* (Barker Barracks, UK: 1 D&D, 20 November 1995), 4; and Ripley, 132.

69. Thornton, 26.

70. Anthony Forster, interview by author, Manchester, England, 19 December 1999; and Richard Connaughton, telephone interview by author, West Point, New York, 1 April 2000.

71. Connaughton interview; and Trevis interview. Trevis explained that in March 2000, the *Daily Telegraph* ran the casualty lists after its own research revealed more accurate figures than MOD.

72. "UN and SITFY," 50; and *Operation Grapple 4—End of Tour Report*, 12.

73. Brigadier A.G. Denaro, "Peacekeeping with the UN," *The British Army Review* Number 113 (August 1996): 27; and Craig R. Whitney, "Bad News They Can Manage," *New York Times*, 11 June 1995, Section 4, page 3.

74. Trevis interview.

75. *Post-Tour Report—Commander's Review of Operation Grapple 6*, Enclosure 2, Task Organization.

76. A.C. Wild, "Grappling with Unfamiliar Problems," *The Infantryman: The Journal of the British Infantry* (1994): 96.

77. Richard K. Betts, "Delusions of Impartiality," *Current* Number 370 (February 1995): 32; and Theo Farrell, "Making Sense of Doctrine," in *Doctrine and Military Effectiveness* (Exeter, England: Britannia Royal Naval College, 1997), 4.

7

STRATEGIC CHANGE AND DOCTRINAL OUTCOMES FOR PEACE OPERATIONS

The military man is the most conservative creature on earth. It is really dangerous to give him an idea because he will not adopt it until it is obsolete and then will not abandon it until it has nearly destroyed him."

—JFC Fuller[1]

INTRODUCTION

The aim of this chapter is to examine and compare the first post–Cold War doctrine on peace and armed humanitarian operations. As is more often the case than not historically, a paradigm change drove new policies and new operations and initially there was a doctrinal lag in both militaries. According to Richard Duncan Downie, structural change and external pressure, coupled with internal consensus for change within militaries, lead to doctrinal change. Did the first doctrinal outcomes of the British and American armies reflect cultural continuity or change, and how much do the doctrines reflect military strategic cultural preferences about the use of force? This chapter contrasts the doctrine and Chapter 8 assesses the degree of continuity or change.[2]

Both Britain's and America's national security policies recognized the sea changes that attended the collapse of the Soviet Union. Both sets of post–Cold War doctrines derived from and were nested to the new strategic principles outlined in those national strategies. To see national security strategy drive national military strategy, and consequently, to observe those strategies catalyze doctrinal change is a good thing—this is how it is supposed to work. However, the aim here is to determine how much doctrinal change occurred in light of massive structural change in the international environment and to observe to what degree cultural predilections, or "ways of war" prevailed. It is first necessary to examine the new national strategic guidelines: for the British government these were reflected in "Options for Change" and parliamentary debates; for the United States, they are articulated in the *1991 National Security Strategy* and the *1992 National Military Strategy.*

For the British there was no one document entitled "Options for Change." The term and the concept simply seeped into the strategic vernacular as the term de jour of the post–Cold War period. The British Government began the process of responding to the new security environment during the spring and summer of 1990. The first discernable time that the more innocuous term options for change appeared as "Options for Change" was in the British parliamentary defense debates on 18 June 1990 when the British Minister of State for the Armed Forces referred to the "Options for Change" review. The actual review process was captured in a in a document entitled *Defence Implications of Recent Events* which was published on 11 July 1990. However, according to the Defence Librarian at the UK Ministry of Defence Whitehall Library, "if anything is to be considered as the basic document for 'Options for Change,' " it was a 25 July 1990 statement on defense policy made in the Commons by the British Secretary of State for Defence, Mr. Tom King.[3]

Defence Implications highlighted the possibility that regional or national conflicts could threaten European stability. It also identified the potential problems that stemmed from the disintegration of the Soviet bloc as: "the re-emergence in Europe of national tensions which produce local or regional instability, particularly in areas such as South East Europe where ethnic conflicts fester." In addition, the report stated that recent events made possible the transfer of military assets from "continental defence to a wider role." A section labeled Wider Commitments explained the potential for commitments outside the NATO area and in the "wider world outside Europe." More importantly, however, Defence Implications explicitly addresses peacekeeping: "this role may well grow, not necessarily exclusively under United Nations auspices." It identifies the possibility of European peacekeeping forces for "deployment in troubled areas of Europe" and states that the peacekeeping role is likely to expand.[4]

What's more, Secretary of State for Defence Tom King's statement in Options for Change emphasized the need for a force structure "appropriate to the new security situation and meeting our peacetime operational needs." King indicated that the new aim was smaller and better equipped forces, flexible enough to contribute both in NATO and elsewhere. His statement concludes by justifying changes to enable Britain to continue to make a contribution to NATO as it adapted to the changes in the security landscape. The entire Options for Change process that culminated in *Defence Estimates 1991: Britain's Defence for the 1990s* process was also captured and distilled in a House of Commons Library Background Paper entitled "UK Defence Policy: Options for Change." In this report Mr. King was quoted as referring to the emerging security situation as a "galloping situation" that was "more dramatic and more comprehensive than people faced whether at Versailles or Yalta."[5]

Likewise, U.S. national security documents also reflected adaptation to the new security challenges. In the preface of the 1991 *National Security Strategy of the United States* President George Bush, echoing his August 1990 Aspen Institute speech, underscored the extraordinary potential of creating a "new international system in accordance with our own values and ideals, as old patterns and certainties crumble around us." After Bush identified some of the dangers in the world— ethnic antagonisms, religious tensions, lingering authoritarianism, and so forth— he emphasized the need for America to remain engaged to "help create a new world in which our fundamental values not only survive but flourish." Among objectives and interests (after the implicitly vital interests), the *National Security Strategy* identified as an objective strengthening the United Nations to make it more effective "in promoting peace, world order and political, economic, and social progress. In the "Relating Means to Ends" section, this document underscored the new vitality of the UN—"it was beginning to act as it was designed"—and its role in "improving the human condition and ameliorating suffering" would continue to attract U.S. resources and leadership. Even more salient, the strategy envisioned a constructive role for the United States in "assisting with elections and the return of displaced persons, as well as with peacekeeping."[6]

Nonetheless, either by default or design, the 1992 U.S. *National Military Strategy* omits any reference to the term "peacekeeping." However, it is otherwise clearly and logically linked to the *National Security Strategy*—it translates grand strategy into military strategy. In the preface of *The National Military Strategy of the United States,* General Powell explained that the strategy justified a "reduced yet appropriate military capability" that would serve the United States for the 1990s. The *NMS* also states that it is the implementation document for the new regionally focused strategy described in the *National Security Strategy.* The introduction essentially mirrors the national strategy in identifying the diverse threats of the new strategic landscape, and the second section lists again the national interests and objectives found in the *National Security Strategy.* The Chairman then translated these into the four military strategic foundations of *Strategic Deterrence and Defense, Forward Presence, Crisis Response,* and *Reconstitution.*[7]

Among the missions listed under *Forward Presence* was humanitarian assistance. In addition, the *NMS* identified collective security and decisive force as two of eight strategic principles. The principle of collective security focused on interstate aggression and burden sharing through formal alliances or ad hoc coalitions. It specifically refers to the Gulf War and the role of the UN. This circumscribed view of collective security (conventional interstate response), moreover, was not incongruous to either the preferred U.S. paradigm of war or to the principle of decisive force, also referred to as the "Powell Corollary" to the Weinberger Doctrine. The principle of decisive force is a bumper sticker for success in America's favorite kind of war (conventional)—"decisive force to overwhelm," "terminate conflicts swiftly," and with "minimum loss of life." This is a great approach to winning conventional wars, but it didn't seem to acknowledge the possibility that operations other than conventional wars—peace operations and asymmetric conflicts, for example — might be more widespread in the 1990s.[8]

However, in the Adaptive Planning section, the *NMS* did identify humanitarian aid and promoting peace as day-to-day tasks to build military and alliance readiness. Moreover, under *Forward Presence* operations, it identifies Humanitarian Assistance and Conflict Resolution as missions: the U.S. military will increasingly be deployed at home and abroad to provide humanitarian assistance and disaster relief. In fact, it even alludes to armed humanitarian operations with an explicit reference to northern Iraq, it states, "in some cases, they [U.S. forces] must also be prepared to engage in conflict in order to assist and protect those in need." However, in the next paragraph on Conflict Resolution, the document seems to reiterate the Weinberger criteria in their entirety: it links crisis responses to vital interests; it qualifies that a commitment of force must be as a last resort; it addresses swift and decisive action; and it underscores the need for clear, measurable, and attainable military objectives. Thus, the implementation document for national strategy offers prescriptions on how to use force to win conventional conflicts. The *NMS* also emphasized the need for CINCs to have "a broad spectrum of capabilities." Also, not out of strategic character, the conclusion of the document highlights the importance of high-technology weapons, and the "edge" they afford.[9]

THE BRITISH POST-COLD WAR PEACE OPERATIONS DOCTRINE

Subsequently, the two national militaries began to generate new doctrine to meet their new national security guidance. The British doctrinal process resulted in two new doctrinal publications germane to peace operations: the British Army published *Army Doctrine Publication Volume 1, Operations (ADP Volume 1)* in June 1994 and *Army Field Manual Volume 5, Operations Other Than War, Part 2 Wider Peacekeeping* (hereafter, *Wider Peacekeeping*) in December 1994. *ADP Volume 1* is the keystone and overarching manual to guide British Army operations. Its equivalent in the U.S. Army is *FM 100-5, Operations*. In its foreword, *ADP Volume 1*, highlights the "profound changes in the security environment" brought about by the events of 1990 and the collapse of the Soviet bloc. *ADP Volume 1* "provides an authoritative guide to the conduct of operations, including operations other than war, and sets out the basis of how to think about operational problems, not what to do about them." However, *British Military Doctrine*, the 1989 cornerstone British Army manual discussed in Chapter 4 and the equivalent of the U.S. Army's *FM 100-1, The Army*, was not re-published with the first series of British Army post–Cold War doctrinal manuals.[10] This is explained in the foreword to *ADP Volume 1*:

ADP Volume 1 provides the link between the essentially timeless content of the *British Military Doctrine* and the tactical level Army Field Manual series, which describes how the doctrine should be put into practice. Specifically, it endorses and develops the manoeuvre approach to war-fighting proposed in *BMD*.[11]

This section examines the doctrinal foundations for conflict and operations other than war. The British doctrine defines conflict as a situation in which violence is either ongoing or threatened. Violence is not necessarily manifest, although the risk or threat of violence is implied. Conversely, after violence has erupted, diplomacy and other nonviolent activity can continue. A state of conflict may exist either between states or within states. The British also categorize conflict into two broad types, based on causation: interest-based conflict and value-based conflict. *ADP Volume 1* describes an interest-based conflict as one that arises from a dispute over resources, trade, or international status. Normally, this type of conflict will be manageable by resolution around a negotiating table. Therefore, efforts to achieve conciliation between the parties will be primarily diplomatic or political, with the military acting in support, as required.[12]

Value-based conflicts, on the other hand, arise from territorial, religious, or ethnic disputes. Such disputes tend to be entrenched and thus conciliation attempts are generally less successful. Since the dynamics of deeply ingrained values and beliefs operate within such conflicts, peaceful instruments of dialogue will be quickly used up. *ADP Volume 1* explains, "one or both parties are then likely to resort to the use of force in seeking to conclude the conflict solely on their terms." Moreover, British doctrine states that in situations where diplomatic or political efforts have failed, military intervention will often be required to conduct actions in support of terminating the conflict.[13]

PEACE OPERATIONS CATEGORIES, TASKS, AND LITERATURE

The British define operations other than war (OOTW) as military operations that are carried out in conditions of conflict other than war. *ADP Volume 1* explains that during such operations, military efforts will probably be subordinated to political activities. Moreover, it states, these operations are aimed at preventing conflict, resolving or terminating conflicts before they escalate to war, or assisting with the rebuilding of peace after war or conflict. The British subsume peacekeeping, wider peacekeeping, peace enforcement, limited intervention, and counterinsurgency within OOTW. These operations are further classified into two subcategories: (1) operations in which British forces are combatants; and (2) operations in which the British are a third party to the conflict.[14]

The first category of operations includes peace enforcement, counterinsurgency, and limited intervention. According to *ADP Volume 1*, these operations are similar to war fighting and, therefore, they are guided by the doctrinal principles of war. On the other hand, the second category covers peacekeeping and wider peacekeeping, operations undertaken in the role of a third party. As such, the impartial status of peacekeepers precludes predicating this type of operation on the identification of an enemy. British doctrine treats this second category of operations separately with a different set of doctrinal imperatives and principles to guide the use of force.[15]

PEACE OPERATIONS DEFINITIONS AND PRINCIPLES

British doctrine describes "humanitarian-relief operations" as operations that aim to meet the needs of refugees, residents, or displaced persons. These operations may be conducted autonomously by the military or in support of civilian aid agencies. Moreover, *Wider Peacekeeping* subsumes the following activities within humanitarian relief: the protection of relief workers and supply deliveries; and the establishment, support, and protection of safe havens. Humanitarian-relief operations may also encompass logistical and administrative activities to support humanitarian-relief efforts. For the purpose of this analysis it is also important to note that the British place humanitarian relief operations within the broader category of "wider peacekeeping."[16]

ADP Volume 1 defines wider peacekeeping as "the wider aspects of peacekeeping operations carried out with the consent of the belligerent parties but in an environment that may be highly volatile." British doctrine therefore devised the category of wider peacekeeping to address the broader aspects of peacekeeping, or "gray-area" operations, which have emerged in the post–Cold War era. However, *Wider Peacekeeping* explains, wider peacekeeping rests within the broader category of peace-support operations as a whole, but it is not related to the conduct of peace enforcement. It explains how to conduct wider-peacekeeping operations without being drawn into a peace-enforcement role either inadvertently or reluctantly. British doctrine trifurcates peace-support operations into three subcategories: peacekeeping, wider peacekeeping, and peace enforcement. In addition, it unambiguously asserts that wider peacekeeping and peace enforcement stand apart. On the other hand, wider peacekeeping and traditional peacekeeping are closely related activities.[17]

Consequently, wider peacekeeping, and concomitantly, humanitarian operations, are carried out under an entirely different set of doctrinal principles than are peace-enforcement operations. Another important categorical distinction lays in the fact that in a peace-enforcement context, British forces are considered combatants whereas they play a third-party role when conducting wider peacekeeping. Peace enforcement implies a predilection to use force and entails the identification of an enemy. Moreover, force packages deployed for wider peacekeeping are not likely to be suitable for peace enforcement. British doctrine acknowledges that "wider-peacekeeping operations represent a dynamic area of doctrinal development and there is as yet no unanimous international agreement on the definitions of terms or categories of activity."[18]

Nevertheless, the British spell out a host of conditions which are likely to be present in a wider-peacekeeping scenario: numerous parties to the conflict; unruly factions which are not responsive to their own authorities; ineffective cease-fires; the absence of law and order; gross human rights violations; the potential for local armed opposition to friendly forces; the presence and involvement of large numbers of civilian organizations; the collapse of civil infrastructure; the presence of large numbers of refugees; and a poorly defined area of operations. Wider peacekeeping, therefore, is likely to be conducted in conditions of civil war or insurgency.[19]

In fact, according to *Wider Peacekeeping*, there is a broad range of possible military tasks required by wider-peacekeeping operations. These operations may be authorized by either a Chapter VI or a Chapter VII UN mandate. In certain cases, British doctrine maintains, a reinforced military capability, including heavy weapons and field artillery, might be needed. However, wider-peacekeeping situations will require resolution by negotiation rather than termination by force. Therefore, much like peacekeeping, military efforts will be intended mainly to create or support the conditions in which political and diplomatic activities may move forward. The notion of victory or defeat is not appropriate to wider peacekeeping. The British measure success by the speed with which the multifunctional effort, as a whole, progresses toward the achievement of the UN mandate.[20]

This mind-set underpins the British principles for wider peacekeeping that are explained below. *Legitimacy* obtains from the cognizance that the purpose and conduct of the wider-peacekeeping operation are just. Thus, the higher the degree of legitimacy conferred upon the peacekeeping force by the international community and the belligerents, the greater is the probability of success. Therefore, it is essential that military forces act in accordance with international law and the UN mandate. According to British doctrine, a perceived failure to act accordingly can diminish the force's legitimacy, authority and, eventually, its operational effectiveness. Legitimacy also helps ensure broader participation by the international community and nongovernmental organizations. *Wider Peacekeeping* cautions commanders against conduct that might undermine the perceived legitimacy of their forces.[21]

Credibility depends upon the force's perceived capacity to carry out the missions assigned to it. The British maintain that credibility is an important psychological factor that is determined by three elements: resources, execution, and the concept of operations. Sufficient means must be effectively engaged in executing a realistic concept of operation. *Wider Peacekeeping* explains, "it is a question of striking a balance between being strong enough to pursue the concept without being over provocative." Credibility is enhanced by displaying an unambiguous capability as well as the demonstrated will to use it. Therefore, flagrant violations of the mandate should be answered correctly and promptly. Credibility will require adequate forces that can escalate or de-escalate their operations as needed.[22]

The principle of *mutual respect* informs the wider-peacekeeping force to obtain and sustain the respect of the various factions. Respect, moreover, should be mutual and the deployed contingent must respect the laws, customs, religions, and culture of the host nation. Forces should also display respect and patience for the problems and the perspectives of the belligerents, when possible. *Wider Peacekeeping* explains that if nourished, mutual respect will contribute to the promotion of cooperation, which is so essential to a consensual framework.[23]

Finally, British wider-peacekeeping doctrine was guided by the principle of *transparency*. Since it important that the force's actions are not misconstrued by the belligerent factions or by the general population, the purpose of operations should clearly be conveyed locally and operationally. Unannounced conduct is susceptible to misinterpretation and unwarranted accusations that the force is pursuing a hidden agenda. British doctrine warns that such misunderstandings can prove perilous during periods of increased tension. Therefore, it maintains, the belligerent parties should be apprised as much as possible of missions and aims of the UN force, consistent with the extant requirements of operational security. Thus, transparency is a very beneficial characteristic of these operations. An inability to achieve transparency can breed suspicion, and it may prevent the development of confidence and undermine the prospects for future cooperation.[24]

CONSENT, IMPARTIALITY, AND FORCE

After analyzing the tasks and the range of environments in which wider peacekeeping might be carried out, the British conclude that the practical exigencies of wider peacekeeping require a large amount of local cooperation. Moreover, this degree of cooperation relies on the presence of *consent*. According to British doctrine, wider peacekeeping is most likely to succeed if friendly forces are able to persuade the belligerent factions of a link between compliance and mutual advantage—that all parties concerned have something to gain from inclusion in the peace process and something to lose from resistance to that process. The British doctrine also maintains, operations cannot succeed in the face of ingrained and extensive opposition. Coercive pacification is not an option with the level of forces normally earmarked for a peacekeeping operation.[25]

Thus, the British assertively maintain that pragmatism and historical lessons dictate that wider peacekeeping tasks firmly belong within a category where the maintenance of *consent* is a principal guide to operational activity. The British doctrine contends that placing these missions in some new category is doctrinally deceptive because this would imply that peacekeeping principles might be safely abandoned in place of a doctrine inclined more towards war fighting. According to the British perspective, an approach that takes little or no account of the need to preserve *consent*, also offers little chance of practical success.[26] The impartial status of forces conducting wider-peacekeeping operations signifies that there are no enemy forces. Therefore, *Wider Peacekeeping* posits, the standard principles of war are not directly applicable to wider-peacekeeping operations. This does not mean that such principles should be abandoned or that wider peacekeeping will not enjoin the highest professional military standards. However, the British identify a different conceptual approach and a particular set of principles that are designed for the environment of wider peacekeeping. Since wider-peacekeeping operations rely on local cooperation, the promotion and sustainment of *consent* is the key to success. Even if coercion seems to be a viable short-term option, it will foster hostility and resentment, creating risk and instability that may eventually prove to be detrimental. This doctrine states that wider peacekeeping is a conflict-resolution undertaking where objectives are attained by persuasion rather than coercion.[27]

Impartiality is also a critical principle that derives from the British doctrinal explanation of the consent guideline. According to *Wider Peacekeeping*, "without *impartiality*, there can be no prospect of preserving the confidence and cooperation of conflicting factions." This idea of *impartiality* is as much a case of perceived *impartiality* as it is of genuine *impartiality*. It is not sufficient for wider-peacekeeping forces only to behave impartially, their behavior must also be construed as impartial. Just as *consent* is not likely to be absolute, *impartiality* may also turn out to be imprecise and fragmented, in practice. In fact, the British maintain, *impartiality* will be continually challenged in most wider-peacekeeping contexts.[28]

British doctrine further maintains that the actual or perceived loss of *impartiality* may have very momentous consequences. In the best case, they maintain, a loss of *impartiality* will probably result in the elimination of any trust that a wider-peacekeeping contingent may have built with the local factions, thereby circumscribing the alternatives available to the force for resolving the conflict. In the worst case, the British explain, a loss of *impartiality* could impel an escalation to peace enforcement, thereby leading to extensive and increased violence with a commensurate increase in military and civilian and military casualties. *Wider Peacekeeping* asserts that commanders should apply the principle of *impartiality* as a significant determinant of all conduct and planning, to include decisions on the use of force.[29]

Impartiality does not necessarily equal the nonemployment of force. According to British doctrine, force may be employed against aggressors to protect the mandate. However, employing force with the deliberate aim of helping or punishing a particular faction would clearly jeopardize *impartiality*. Once *impartiality* is compromised, the risk of destabilization seriously increases, also putting the success of the operation at risk. Therefore, commanders should always strive to demonstrate and preserve *impartiality*.[30]

Minimum force is the British wider-peacekeeping principle that governs the use of force and assists commanders in making decision on the use of force. British doctrine defines "minimum necessary force" as "the measured application of violence or coercion, sufficient only to achieve a specific end, demonstrably reasonable, proportionate and appropriate; and confined in effect to the specific and legitimate target intended." The amount of force used should be appropriate and proportional to the specific conditions. *Wider Peacekeeping* maintains that the level of force employed should not exceed that which is reasonable and necessary for the situation. Moreover, it explains that restraint and discipline will be required to control force in this fashion. The preemptive use of force and reprisals are not appropriate in a wider-peacekeeping context.[31]

This is because the long-term consequences of employing force might differ significantly from the short-term effects. In other words, an inappropriate use of force that nonetheless achieves a tactical victory can result in a long-term strategic failure. *Wider Peacekeeping* illumines, "the use of force in a wider-peacekeeping environment is likely to have profound repercussions that go beyond the demands of the immediate tactical situation." Thus, many parts of the overall operation will probably be affected. In the long run, the use of force is apt to trigger a like response and it may increase tension, jeopardize the perceived *impartiality* of the wider-peacekeeping force, and escalate the overall level of violence. The injudicious use of force, then, may entangle the force in a damaging long-term conflict that is not relevant to the operational aim. Moreover, collateral damage tends to undermine civil affairs efforts and aggravate the indigenous population.[32]

THE AMERICAN POST-COLD WAR PEACE OPERATIONS DOCTRINE

On the other hand, the U.S. Army produced three doctrinal manuals in the first post–Cold War series of manuals relevant to peace operations: *FM 100-5, Operations* in June 1993; *FM 100-1, The Army* in June 1994; and *FM 100-23, Peace Operations* in December 1994. *FM 100-1* links national military strategy to the system of Army doctrine. A salient point, however, is that this version of *The Army* reflects only those objectives listed under the interest of survival in the *National Security Strategy* and the *National Military Strategy*. In the introduction, *FM 100-5* states that it reflects "Army thinking in a new strategic era" and it recognizes that the end of the Cold War has changed the nature of the threat, and thus the strategy of the United States. Finally, there were two incongruities that characterized this series of U.S. Army manuals. First, *FM 100-1*, the U.S. Army's cornerstone manual and the foundation document for the operational doctrine laid out in *FM 100-5*, was published after *FM 100-5*. A discussion with the author of *FM 100-1* revealed that this was simply a bureaucratic lag—the Army just didn't get the manual out on time. The other apparent incongruity was the asynchronous nature of the U.S. peace operations doctrinal process: the U.S. Army started thinking about doctrine for these operations before they gained any prominence in national military strategy. In mid-1992, the U.S. Army Strategic Fellows working at the Army War College were tasked to study issues relating to peacekeeping and peace enforcement. The fellows briefed their study to the U.S. Army TRADOC Commander in December 1992 and TRADOC began developing a peace operations manual in January 1993. Given that the 1992, *National Military Strategy* did not mention peacekeeping, it seems that TRADOC was actually anticipating an expanded role for peace operations in view of world events.[33]

Since there was close collaboration between British and American doctrine writers in developing their keystone doctrinal manuals (*ADP Volume 1* and *FM 100-5*), it is no surprise that the United States' doctrine also separates operations into three categories: peacetime, conflict, and war. Applying all elements of national power, the U.S. seeks to achieve its strategic objectives in these three milieus. *FM 100-5, Operations* states that conflict "is characterized by hostilities to secure strategic objectives" whereas war entails the employment of force in "combat operations against an armed enemy." During peacetime, on the other hand, the U.S. aims to influence international events and those actions that routinely occur between and among states. This manual also emphasizes that the U.S. Army's principal focus is war fighting even though the use of Army forces during peacetime helps "keep the day-to-day tensions between nations below the threshold of conflict."[34]

Although the environment of war is linked to military operations in war and combat, the manual depicts operations other than war as requiring either combat or noncombat operations, or both. This is because, according to *FM 100-5*, operations other than war can occur during times of conflict or during times of peace. This manual expounds, "the states of peacetime, conflict, and war could all exist at once in the theater commander's strategic environment." For this reason, the U.S. Army must be able to conduct *full-dimensional operations*. "This means employing all means available to accomplish any given mission" across the full spectrum of military operations in war and in other than war. The bottom line to the first chapter, nonetheless, is that the "Army must be capable of achieving decisive victory." *FM 100-5* defines 'decisive victory' as applying overwhelming combat power "to win quickly with minimum casualties."[35]

PEACE OPERATIONS CATEGORIES, TASKS, AND LITERATURE

The final version of *FM 100-5* has a more comprehensive operations-other-than-war chapter than did the *Special Edition* extract discussed in previous Chapter 4—these sections will avoid repeating explanations already addressed there. In addition, *FM 100-23, Peace Operations* applies the principles of OOTW specifically to peace operations. Although the 1993 *Special Edition* did not define OOTW, for example, the final edition of *FM 100-5* does define operations other than war as "military activities during peacetime and conflict that do not necessarily involve armed clashes between two organized forces." It also states that doctrine for war complements OOTW. Some of the same principles apply to both environments, modified to meet different situations. OOTW may be long in duration and their direction may shift during the course of their campaign. OOTW are aimed at promoting regional stability, achieving democratic end states, retaining U.S. influence, and providing humane assistance.[36]

FM 100-5 also explains that OOTW "will not always be peaceful actions." Opponents may resort to aggressive acts or fighting in order to undermine U.S. purposes. However, "the use of overwhelming force may complicate the process toward the Army's stated objectives." In addition, victory in operations other than may be very subtle. Among the 13 "activities" in OOTW, the manual lists humanitarian assistance, peacekeeping, and peace enforcement. U.S. doctrine, however, does not delineate between combat roles and third party roles as British doctrine does—there are either combat operations or non-combat operations. For those operations involving combat, the principles of war apply. The figure on page 2-1 does not make clear whether peacekeeping or peace enforcement operations are combat or non-combat, although both operations fall in the environment of conflict. What is clear, though, is that the British place AHO within wider peacekeeping and the OOTW category of noncombatant whereas the U.S. doctrine subsumes most AHO tasks within peace enforcement, a combat OOTW operation in the environment of conflict. See Figure 7.2 for a comparison of the categories and principles of peace operations and wider peacekeeping.[37]

Nonetheless, *FM 100-23, Peace Operations* trifurcates peace operations into support to diplomacy (preventive diplomacy, peacemaking, and peace building), peacekeeping, and peace enforcement. However, the manual categorizes armed humanitarian operations under peace enforcement. In its introduction, it explains that peace operations comprise traditional peacekeeping missions "as well as peace enforcement activities such as protection of humanitarian assistance, establishment of order and stability, enforcement of sanctions, guarantee and denial of movement, establishment of protected zones, and forcible separation of belligerents." Although the stated purpose of peace enforcement is to restore peace and support political efforts to achieve a long-term solution, the manual states that it may include combat action. This eventuality, moreover, would require "the successful application of war fighting skills. During peace enforcement, the manual even goes so far as stating that forces may be "engaged in combat with one or more parties to the conflict."[38]

PEACE OPERATIONS DEFINITIONS AND PRINCIPLES

Although many humanitarian missions may take place in permissive environments, *FM 100-23, Peace Operations* maintains, in other instances, hostile forces may try to obstruct humanitarian operations. Therefore, peace operations forces may be tasked to protect relief workers or the relief supplies themselves. This doctrine states that AHO forces must be equipped with weapons that are suitable for the mission. Protection of humanitarian assistance may require the establishment of protected corridors or routes, base areas for air and sea terminals, and secure sites for the final delivery of shipments to the recipients. When the delivery of humanitarian aid takes place in a nonpermissive environment (this military euphemism means it is being obstructed by force—somebody is shooting at you), combat and combat support forces will be required to conduct such operations.[39]

FM 100-23 explains that humanitarian operations may include the following missions: the protection of corridors through which relief supplies are transported; the establishment of lodgment areas that normally contain sea or air terminals; and the security of supply-delivery sites. Additional humanitarian tasks include the provision of health services, the resettlement of dislocated civilians, and the establishment of essential facilities. What's more, when the delivery of relief supplies and aid is opposed, combat forces will be required to carry out such operations. American doctrine also subsumes the establishment and supervision of protected zones within the category of peace enforcement. Peace enforcement, moreover, is defined as "the application of military force or the threat of its use, normally pursuant to international authorization, to compel compliance with generally accepted resolutions or sanctions."[40]

Protected zones may be established as part of a conflict resolution effort. These zones are described as geographic areas that may contain large numbers of refugees or displaced persons that are susceptible to persecution by one of the belligerent factions. Military forces may be tasked with the establishment, supervision, and defense of these zones. Moreover, these operations can entail the provision of large amounts of humanitarian assistance. *FM 100-23* explains: if the existence of a protected zone is threatened by the belligerent party who claims control of that area, forces must be prepared to conduct operations against those parties which threaten the zone. This manual refers to the 1991 protected zones for Iraq's Kurds as a use of force that was "incidental to the provision of humanitarian assistance."[41]

Even though humanitarian assistance is not distinguished as a separate subcategory of peace support operations, American doctrine similarly maintains that it is likely that these missions will be conducted as a concurrent component of almost every peace support operation. What's more, it states, although AHO are usually limited in scope, humanitarian projects will significantly strain the resources required for aspects of peace operations. Nonetheless, in contrast to the other three doctrines, the U.S. doctrinal typology for peace operations subordinates AHO as a mission under peace enforcement. The aim of peace operations, it states, is to attain and maintain a peaceful settlement among hostile parties, rather than termination by force. These operations are designed mainly to create or sustain the conditions in which diplomatic and political activities may proceed. Because traditional military concepts of victory are not appropriate to peace operations, military action must complement political, economic, and humanitarian efforts in "pursuing the over-arching political objective."[42]

Furthermore, U.S. doctrine clearly distinguishes between peacekeeping and peace enforcement. Although both are peace operations, *FM 100-23* maintains, they are not part of a continuum along which forces may move freely from one to the other. A large boundary separates these operations—they are carried out with very different approaches to the principles of consent, impartiality, and the use of force. Moreover, a force designed for peacekeeping generally will not have the requisite amount of combat power to successfully conduct peace enforcement. Conversely, a force outfitted for peace enforcement has ample capability for peacekeeping, in the event the belligerent parties accept its presence. However, *FM 100-23* cautions against using a former peace enforcement contingent to conduct peacekeeping operations in the same mission area because consent and impartiality are impossible to regain, once abandoned.[43]

As explained earlier, U.S. doctrine represents the most forceful approach to AHO because it unambiguously classifies them under peace enforcement. Moreover, the American doctrine offers one set of overarching principles for all OOTW, including both peacekeeping and peace enforcement. To reiterate, both peacekeeping and peace enforcement are categorized as OOTW and conflict. However, in general, these principles reveal an approach to the use of force that is more restrained than traditional war fighting. What's more, although U.S. doctrine acknowledges that each operation is unique, it has six principles to help leaders develop concepts of operation for conducting all OOTW. Five of the six principles remained unchanged from the pre-Somalia draft of *FM 100-5* and the *Special Edition 93-1* discussed in Chapter 4. The principle of *patience* reverted back to *perseverance*, a principle listed in the 1990 version of *LIC*. However, expanded explanations, to link the OOTW principles specifically to peace operations, are included in *FM 100-23*.[44]

Perseverance is the measured and sustained employment of military capabilities in support of strategic aims. *FM 100-23* states that most peace operations require a long-term commitment that requires more than military efforts alone. This is essentially the same as the explanation of patience articulated in the *Special Edition*. The principle of *legitimacy*, however, is defined differently and more thoroughly: it is the willing acceptance by the people of a group or agency to make and carry out decisions, and it stems initially from the mandate authorizing the operation. However, *legitimacy* is sustained by the perception of the indigenous population that the force's actions are legal, moral, and correct. According to *FM 100-23*, this is achieved through operations that "are conducted with scrupulous regard for international norms on the use of military forces and regard for humanitarian principles." Significantly, though, the manual explains that in peacekeeping impartiality is critical to *legitimacy* whereas in peace enforcement "impartiality and *legitimacy* may be harder to obtain and sustain."[45]

American doctrine still defines *restraint* as the prudent and appropriate application of military capability. However, the peace operations manual dedicates almost an entire page to the explication of this principle. *FM 100-23* explains that restraints on levels of violence, tactics, and weaponry characterize the peace-operations environment. Moreover, it states, the application of excessive force may detrimentally affect legitimacy and undermine short- and long-term objectives. "Its use may also escalate tension and violence in the local area and embroil peace operations in a harmful, long-term conflict contrary to their aims." On the one hand, it states that in peace enforcement force may be used to coerce but must be applied with "restraint appropriate to the situation." On the other hand, it explains that *restraint* does not rule out the employment of "sufficient or overwhelming force" when necessary to "establish situational dominance" and to "protect U.S. or indigenous lives or property."[46] The last paragraph under the principle of restraint is illuminating:

The principle of *restraint* will permeate considerations concerning ROE, the choice of weapons and equipment, and control measures such as weapons status. When force is used, it should be precise and overwhelming to minimize friendly and noncombatant casualties and collateral damage. Precision and high-technology weaponry may help reduce casualties.[47]

The last three principles of both OOTW and of peace operations—*objective, security*, and *unity of effort* are also among the U.S. principles of war, with one modification—unity of command was changed to *unity of effort*. What's more, in its introduction to the principles of peace operations, *FM 100-23* states that many tasks at the operational and tactical levels, especially during peace enforcement actions, "may require the focused and sustained application of force." *Objective* is defined the same but it also discusses terms of reference and clarity of mandate, concepts specific to peace operations. Moreover, it lists force protection, rules of engagement (ROE), and relationships with NGOs among issues to consider. Also under this principle is a discussion of "end state," which "describes what the authorizing entity desires the situation to be when operations conclude." The end state is achieved when political objectives are attained or the military hands the effort over to international agencies.[48]

Unity of effort highlights the importance of focusing diverse means to meet a common purpose. According to FM 100-23, it is difficult to achieve *unity of effort* with the host of nonmilitary organizations and the lack of "definitive command arrangements among them." The principle guides commanders to establish a civil-military operations center (CMOC) whenever possible to provide coherence to the activities of all the organizations in the area of operation. In addition to the military, the CMOC should "include the political, civil, administrative, legal, and humanitarian activities involved in the peace operation." What's more, it states, a single competent authority should be identified to legitimize a peace operation. The manual also emphasizes the importance of ensuring that all levels understand the civilian-military relationship. This discussion of civil-military integration and the CMOC stems from the lessons of UNITAF.[49]

Finally, the principle of *security*, as applied to peace operations, deals with force protection. "Commanders should be constantly ready to prevent, preempt, or counter activity that could bring significant harm to units or jeopardize mission accomplishment." In addition, it explains, in peace operations force protection may extend beyond the military to civil agencies and NGOs. For peace enforcement, "security involves demonstrations of inherent military capability and preparedness." Psychological operations and civil affairs efforts also promote security. Moreover, the force's credibility in the international arena, its perceived impartiality and legitimacy, and the mutual respect created between the force and other parties, all contribute to *security*.[50]

CONSENT, IMPARTIALITY, AND FORCE

FM 100-23 identifies *consent, impartiality,* and *force* as "critical variables" of peace operations and also uses these variables to distinguish between peacekeeping and peace enforcement. This demarcation was the result of the American-British doctrine exchange—the British writers strongly opposed any notion of a "continuum" along which the peace force could slide back and forth from peacekeeping to peace enforcement. As a result, the final edition of *FM 100-23* states that peace enforcement and peacekeeping are "not part of a continuum allowing a unit to move freely from one to the other." These two types of operations occur "under vastly different circumstances involving the variables of *consent, force,* and *impartiality.* Another result of the doctrine exchange was the modification of the U.S. "Operational Variables" chart depicted at the top of Figure 7.1—the final U.S. doctrine depicted the distinction as an unambiguous solid black line that should not be crossed. The British critical principles for peacekeeping are shown in the middle diagram of Figure 7.1. The bottom part of Figure 7.1 shows how the first British post–Cold War doctrine drew a solid line between peacekeeping and peace enforcement, going so far as to call the consent line a "Rubicon."[51]

"The crossing of the *consent* divide from PK to PE is a policy level decision that fundamentally changes the nature of the operation." Moreover, the manual explains, any degradation of *consent* may influence the operations unfavorably and commanders should avoid actions that cause a decline in the level of *consent.* In its explanation of *force,* the manual dictates that commanders understand the relationship between *force* and the "desired end state." However, it does state that peace enforcement may entail "very violent combat actions." On the other hand, peacekeeping requires *impartiality* whereas in peace enforcement *impartiality* may "change over time and with the nature of the operation." In peace enforcement an even-handed and humanitarian approach, even when combat operations are being conducted, however, can help improve the prospects for peace.[53]

The bottom line concerning these variables, however, is that they distinguish peace enforcement (and concomitantly AHO) from peacekeeping. "In peace enforcement *consent* is not absolute and *force* may be used to compel or coerce." In peacekeeping, *consent* is a precondition and *force* may only be used in self-defense. Moreover, according to *FM 100-23*, the nature of peace enforcement operations weakens the perception of *impartiality* on the part of the peace enforcement force. The manual captures this distinction cogently: "peacekeeping enjoys high levels of *consent* and *impartiality* and low levels of *force,* while peace enforcement is marked by the reverse."[54]

The U.S. approach to consent, impartiality, and force are particularly important as these factors generally separate peacekeeping from peace enforcement. However, American doctrine does not address these as principles but as variables of peace operations: "the degree to which these three variables are present plays a major role in determining the nature of the peace operation and force tailoring mix." The American doctrine, therefore, also affirms that the use of force, impartiality, and consent are the key discriminators between peacekeeping and peace enforcement. Moreover, the humanitarian related tasks that fall under peace enforcement in American doctrine are the same tasks subsumed within wider peacekeeping in the British doctrine. It seems, therefore, that these doctrines do diverge in their categorization and conceptual frameworks for AHO. The differences and operational implications between AHO as peacekeeping and AHO as peace enforcement are significant.[55]

Figure 7.1
Compare Consent, Force, Impartiality Diagrams WPK/PO

U.S. Critical Variables

Variables	Support to Diplomacy	Peacekeeping	Peace Enforcement
Consent	High	High	Low
Force	Low	Low (self-defense/defense of mandate from interference)	Sufficient to compel/coerce
Impartiality	High	High	Low

British Critical Principles

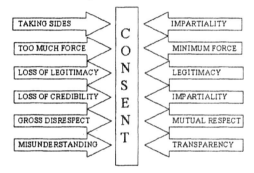

British bifurcation of WPK/PE: consent is the Rubicon

CONCLUSION

> In the modern era, the use or threat of military force is a significant component of comprehensive humanitarian and political solutions.
>
> —Walter Clarke[56]

The purpose of this chapter was to examine and to compare these two militaries' first post–Cold War doctrines for peace and armed humanitarian operations. Corollary purposes were to determine if the first doctrinal outcomes of the British and American armies reflected cultural continuity or change and to see how much they reflected military strategic cultural preferences about the use of force. This aim, moreover, was driven by the ultimate and pragmatic need to understand the implications and lessons for military change during peacetime and for the desire to improve future approaches to AHO. Past failures and disagreements over the correct approach to these operations highlight this need. What's more, the focus on military doctrine is not intended to understate the importance of strategic vision and a politically achieved framework for cooperation. As Mats Berdal has asserted, short-term objectives, such as humanitarian relief operations, "cannot be a substitute for addressing the root cause of internal conflict."[57]

Careful examination of these two doctrines, nonetheless, reveals both convergence and divergence. However, these doctrines diverge in some significant ways, for example, on whether AHO is categorized as peacekeeping or peace enforcement. Nonetheless, in general, these doctrines define conflict similarly although they categorize the types of conflict differently. In various ways, these two militaries differentiate between conflict and war: war is a more violent environment and is explicitly open confrontation between armed forces pursuing vital interests ("a dispute over resources, trade, or international status"). Moreover, war and conflicts short of war are depicted as two different conditions. Nonetheless, the British doctrine places AHO in a third party non-combatant category whereas U.S. doctrine places AHO in the environment of conflict as a combat operation. Moreover, the British doctrine explicitly states that AHO (wider peacekeeping) can be conducted either as a Chapter VI or Chapter VII operation. The absoluteness it ascribes to consent, impartiality, and the use of force clearly makes it a "stretched" version of traditional peacekeeping.[58]

Moreover, the British doctrine states that historical lessons and pragmatism dictate that wider-peacekeeping tasks firmly belong within a category where the maintenance of consent is a principal guide to operational activity. The British contend that placing these missions in some new category is doctrinally improper since this would imply that peacekeeping principles might be safely abandoned in place of a doctrine more disposed to war fighting (this in an implicit reference to both U.S. doctrine and to the American military's experience in Somalia). According to the British perspective, an approach that takes little or no account of the need to preserve consent, also offers little chance of practical success.

However, in contrast to the British, the Americans explicitly place AHO within the category of peace enforcement. Although humanitarian operations are not specifically included in the U.S. typology for peace operations, AHO are defined as subordinate missions of peace enforcement. Moreover, the humanitarian-related tasks that fall under peace enforcement in American doctrine are the same tasks subsumed within wider peacekeeping and peacekeeping in the British doctrine. These doctrines do diverge, then, in some important aspects: the operational ramifications that inhere in the distinction between peacekeeping AHO and peace enforcement AHO are not insignificant. See Figure 7.2 for a comparison of the tasks of wider peacekeeping and peace enforcement as well as a comparison of the principles germane to both.

An analysis of the principles that inform AHO also reveals both convergence and divergence. The way in which the British doctrine addresses consent, impartiality, and the use of force reflects their predilection toward traditional peacekeeping. However, both sets of principles emphasize a restrained and measured application of force, when used. What's more, credibility (legitimacy) and restraint represent a common thread throughout the two approaches. Even the British wider-peacekeeping doctrine, which represents the least coercive of the approaches, maintains that credibility is strengthened by demonstrating the capability and the will to use force. However, the American principles specifically balance the principles of restraint and legitimacy with the security of the force (force protection). Nonetheless, the American principles reveal a preference for decisive force and minimum casualties.

In sum, although there seems to be a veneer of consonance between the two doctrines in their principled and restrained approaches to using force, these doctrines also represent a rather divergent range of typologies. The British approach is at the opposite end of the spectrum from the American approach—the U.S.

Figure 7.2
British/American PK Typology, 1994

| | British Doctrine | | American Doctrine | |
	MISSIONS	PRINCIPLES	MISSIONS	PRINCIPLES
WPK	Humanitarian Relief Guarantee or denial of movement Conflict Prevention Demobilization Military Assistance	Impartiality Mutual Respect Legitimacy Minimum Force Credibility Transparency	Monitoring of Cease-fires Observation Monitoring of truces Supervision of truces	Objective Legitimacy Unity of Effort Perseverance Restraint Security Absolute impartiality *Minimum Force/self-defense* *Absolute Consent* *Absolute Impartiality*
PE	War	Concentration of Force Offensive Action Economy of Force Surprise Selection/Maintenance of the Aim Security Flexibility	Forcible Separation of Belligerents Restore order and stability Protect Humanitarian Assistance Guarantee and Denial of Movement Enforce Sanctions	Objective Legitimacy Unity of Effort Perseverance Restraint Security *Coercive/Appropriate Force* *Consent/impartiality not required*

doctrine unambiguously subsumes AHO within peace enforcement. It also seems clear, that there still remains significant scope for achieving compatibility between these two doctrines. In fact, the concluding chapter will examine some of the progress made toward convergence in the second series of peace operations manuals.

NOTES

1. Cited in Richard Connaughton, "Sea of Troubles," Unpublished manuscript, Dorset, England, November 1999, Chapter 3, page 38.

2. Richard Duncan Downie, *Learning from Conflict* (Westport, CT: Praeger, 1998), Chapter 1.

3. Mavis Simpson, "Options for Change," An unpublished Information Paper, London, UK Ministry of Defence Whitehall Library, July 1991, 2; *Defence Implications of Recent Events*, Defence Committee, Tenth Report (London: HMSO, 11 July 1990), hereafter called *Defence Implications; and Parliamentary Debates (Hansard)*, Volume 177, House of Commons Official Report (London: HMSO, 1990), hereafter called *Options for Change*.

4. *Defence Implications*, xvi, xviii, xxxviii–xxxix.

5. *Options for Change*, 468–70; and , Richard Ware, "UK Defence Policy: Options for Change" (House of Commons Background Paper, London, 4 October 1991).

6. *National Security Strategy of the United States* (Washington, D.C.: U.S. Government Printing Office, 1991), v, 3–4, 13.

7. Colin Powell, *The National Military Strategy of the United States* (Washington, D.C.: U.S. Department of Defense, 1992), preface, 1–2, 5, 6. Hereafter this document is referred to as *NMS*.

8. *NMS*, 8–10.

9. *NMS*, 13, 15–16, 23, 26.

10. *Army Doctrine Publication Volume 1, Operations* (London: HMSO, June 1994), iv; and *Army Field Manual, Wider Peacekeeping* (London: HMSO, December 1994).

11. *ADP Volume 1*, iv.

12. *ADP Volume 1*, 1-3.

13. Ibid., 1-4.

14. *ADP Volume 1*, 7-1.

15. Ibid., 7-2.

16. *Wider Peacekeeping*, 2-2.

17. Ibid., 1-3.

18. Ibid., i, 1-3; and *ADP Volume 1*, 7-1.

19. Ibid., 1-7.

20. Ibid., 1-10.

21. Ibid., 4-8.

22. Ibid.

23. Ibid., 4-9.

24. Ibid., 4-10.

25. Ibid., 2-2.

26. Ibid., 2-4.

27. *Wider Peacekeeping*, 4-1.

28. Ibid., 4-2.

29. Ibid.

30. Ibid., 4-3.

31. Ibid., 4-7.

32. Ibid., 4-3, 4-4.

33. FM 100-5, Operations (Washington, D.C.: U.S. Army, June 1993), vi; *FM 100-1, The Army* (Washington, D.C.: U.S. Army, June 1994), 16; *FM 100-23, Peace Operations* (Washington, D.C.: U.S. Army, December 1994); and see Grant R. Doty, "Peace Operations and the U.S. Army: A Transition," Unpublished paper, Yale University, New Haven, CT, May 1996, 6, 9, 15. Doty interviewed the Strategic Fellows and TRADOC doctrine writers. The Strategic fellows subsequently formed the nucleus of what became the U.S. Army Peacekeeping Institute at Carlisle Barracks, Pennsylvania.

34. *FM 100-5*, 2-0–2-1.

35. Ibid., 2-1, 1-4–1-5.

36. *Special Edition 93-1*,"Somalia"; *FM 100-5*, Glossary-6, 13-0–13-1; and *FM 100-23*, 15-18.

37. *FM 100-5*, 13-0–13-3, 2-1; and *FM 100-23*, 7.

38. *FM 100-23*, iv.

39. *FM 100-23*, 8.

40. *FM 100-23*, 6, 8, 14.

41. Ibid., 9-10.

42. *FM 100-23*, 14, vi.

43. *FM 100-23*, 12.

44. *FM 100-5*, 2-0-21, 13-3–13-8; and *FM 100-23*, 7, 15-18.

45. *FM 100-23*, 18.

46. Ibid., 17.

47. Ibid. This author underlined the word overwhelming.

48. *FM 100-5*, 13-3; and *FM 100-23*, 15-16.

49. Ibid., 16; and Rich Rinaldo, Interview by author, Newport News, VA, 21 March 2000.

50. *FM 100-23*, 16-17.

51. Rinaldo Interview, 21 March 2000; and *FM 100-23*, 12.

52. *FM 100-23*, 13 and Wider Peacekeeping, 2-5–2-13.

53. *FM 100-23*, 12-14.

54. Ibid.

55. *FM 100-23*, 6-12; and *Wider Peacekeeping*, 2-3–2-15 and 4-1–4-4.

56. Walter Clarke and Robert Gosende, "The Political Component: The Missing Vital Element in U.S. Intervention Planning," *Parameters* 26 (Autumn 1996): 37.

57. Mats Berdal, *Whither UN Peacekeeping*, Adelphi Paper 281 (London: Brassey's, 1993), 21.

58. *ADP Volume 1*, 1-3; and *FM 100-5*, 2-1.

CONCLUSION AND
POLICY IMPLICATIONS

INTRODUCTION

The purpose of this chapter is to explain and account for causality, to critique and synthesize this study, and to draw inferences and policy implications for the development of current doctrine and the use of force in peace support operations. To be sure, the development of doctrine is not monocausal and it would be impossible to determine every factor that influenced its development. However, by examining and interviewing central sources this study has tried to "process-trace" key variables and to draw inferences from the statements by core players and from the conduct of the two militaries. This chapter begins with a synthesis of the dependent variable—the first post–Cold War doctrinal outcomes of the British Army and the American Army. The next section summarizes and explains the causal relationships—it traces the relationships between the independent, intervening, and dependent variables. The third section extracts each specific explanatory variable from the causality chart and demonstrates their cause and effect linkages. The subsequent two sections draw generalizations about the two militaries and about peace operations in general. The last section addresses this work's relevance to the Global War on Terrorism and explains implications for the U.S. Army and its transformation process.

TWO DOCTRINES AND TWO PREFERENCES FOR USING FORCE

The previous chapter examined the British and U.S. militaries' first post–Cold War peace support operations doctrines to determine where the doctrine for armed humanitarian operations (AHO) of two relatively compatible military allies converged and diverged. Careful examination of these two doctrines shows convergence and divergence. However, these doctrines diverge in some significant

ways—for example, on whether AHO is categorized as peacekeeping or peace enforcement. Nonetheless, in general, these doctrines define conflict similarly although they categorize the types of conflict differently. In various ways, these two
militaries differentiate between conflict and war: war is a more violent subset of
the broader realm of conflict. In addition, war and conflicts short of war are
depicted as two different conditions.

When it comes to typologies reflecting how to use force, the British subsume
AHO within the category of wider peacekeeping. Moreover, the British doctrine
emphasizes that wider-peacekeeping tasks firmly belong within a category
where the maintenance of consent is a principal guide to operational activity.
The British contend that placing these missions in some new category is doctrinally improper since this would imply that peacekeeping principles might be
safely abandoned in place of a doctrine more disposed to war fighting. According to the British perspective, an approach that takes little or no account of the
need to preserve consent also offers little chance of practical success.[1] One journalist captured the difference in doctrinal approaches succinctly:

The frustrations and anger that have erupted between the United States and Britain have
arisen because the two countries have diametrically opposed views on peacekeeping. The
American peacekeeping slogan is: "Behave or else." The British slogan, even after two
years of endurance in Bosnia, is: "Trust us, we are here to help you."[2]

In contrast to the British, the Americans explicitly place AHO within the category of peace enforcement. Although humanitarian operations are not specifically
included in the U.S. typology for peace operations, AHO are defined as subordinate missions of peace enforcement. Moreover, the humanitarian-related tasks that
fall under peace enforcement in American doctrine are the same tasks subsumed
within wider peacekeeping and peacekeeping in the British doctrine. These doctrines do diverge, then, in some important aspects: the operational ramifications
that inhere in the distinction between peacekeeping AHO and peace-enforcement
AHO are not insignificant.[3] See Figure 8.1 for a depiction of how the two doctrines
approach the variables of consent and force.

In sum, although there seems to be a veneer of consonance among the doctrines
in their principled and restrained approaches to using force, these doctrines also
represent a rather divergent range of typologies. The British approach is at the opposite end of the spectrum from the American approach—the U.S. doctrine unambiguously subsumes AHO within peace enforcement.

It also seems clear that there still is substantial room for achieving convergence
between these two doctrines. What may be surprising, given the diametrically po-
lar approaches to force, is that the U.S. and British doctrine writers conducted a series of meetings during the writing process to exchange ideas and coordinate, with
the aim of creating "compatible doctrine." To be sure, the doctrinal liaison ef-
fected some progress, for example: the Americans dropped the use of a "continuum" of peace operations that the British didn't like because it implied that forces

Figure 8.1
AHO—Two Approaches to Consent and the Use of Force

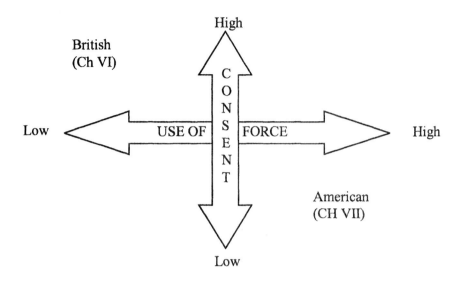

could slide back and forth between peacekeeping and peace enforcement; the British, on the other hand, changed their depiction of the consent line between the operational and tactical levels from a straight line to a curved one, implying that it was less absolute. However, even though there was a December 1994 letter from U.S. Army Chief of Staff, General Sullivan, to the UK Chief of the General Staff, General Guthrie, declaring the differences as resolved and the doctrines as "compatible," it is difficult to see as compatible two doctrines that subsume AHO in two very different categories of operations: peacekeeping (wider peacekeeping) versus peace enforcement.[4]

CAUSALITY: EXPLANATORY VARIABLES AND THEIR RELATIONSHIPS

Figure 8.2 depicts the causal relationship between strategic change, military strategic culture, and the development of peace operations doctrine. The independent variable (see Figure 8.2) was the massive international structural change that resulted in a new national security and national military strategies in the two countries. As a result of an upsurge in peace operations, both the U.S. Army TRADOC and the British Director of Land Warfare (DLW) staff began to think about new doctrine in the latter half of 1992. As a result, both staffs were fully engaged in writing new peace operations doctrines by 1993. In addition, the U.S. and UK doctrine authors were directed to exchange visits in order to achieve some compatibility in their doctrinal approaches.

Figure 8.2
Causal Relationships

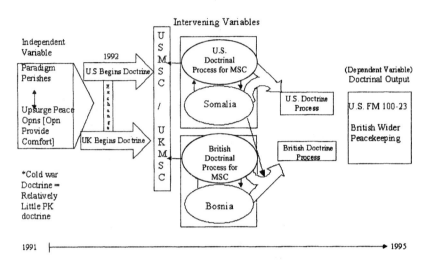

However, in addition to approaching the doctrinal process through military strategic cultural lenses (intervening variable), both militaries embarked on new "gray-area" operations and the doctrinal processes simultaneously. Both case studies, the Americans' in Somalia and the British in Bosnia, also served as intervening variables that fed lessons back into the doctrinal processes. Not only did cultural preferences manifest themselves during operations in Somalia and Bosnia, but, the culturally filtered lessons of those operations fed back into the doctrine. In other words, when the bipolar structure collapsed at the end of the Cold War (independent variable), it impelled an increase in gray area peace operations. This led to the creation of doctrine for these newer operations. The doctrinal processes, however, were influenced by both military strategic cultural preferences and by the culturally filtered lessons of Somalia and Bosnia (intervening variables). Both the British and the Americans, in fact, drew very different lessons from Somalia. The doctrinal processes culminated in late 1994 with the publication of their first manuals for peace operations doctrine for the post–Cold War era (dependent variable). Figure 8.2 uses wide arrows to trace the general flow from independent to dependent variables. However, the single line arrows depict feedback loops by which lessons influenced the doctrinal processes of each military. When asked about influences on *FM100-23*, Rich Rinaldo explained that the UNITAF operation in Somalia had a significant influence on the doctrine's conceptual approach to peace enforcement and humanitarian operations. Likewise, Charles Dobbie, the principal author of *Wider Peacekeeping*, stated that UNPROFOR had had the single most significant influence on the British manual.[5]

It is also salient that LTG Rose defined and described the Briti
UNPROFOR by what it was not—it was not the American approa
ish Army would not cross the Mogadishu line. Thus, although c
doctrinal exchanges occurred throughout the process, the British docu.... .
tially codified an approach that was the obverse of the American approach to
AHO. The two "compatible" outcomes were released in December 1994. However, what was most significant were the interviews with the authors of the doctrine—the authors' statements testify to the influence of core cultural preferences.
These interviews are covered in the next section.

SUMMARY OF EXPLANATORY VARIABLES

Military Strategic Culture

This study defined military strategic culture as a set of beliefs, attitudes, and values within the military that shape collective preferences about when and how military means should be used to accomplish strategic aims. The questions examined
how geography and history shaped these preferences and it derived additional
questions about cultural predilections for civil-military relations, organization,
technology, and casualty aversion. Both armies spent most of the last 200-year period doing constabulary policing and other operations short of war. However, the
U.S. Army devoted most of its intellectual energy after the Civil War emulating
the Prussian military model and thinking about European-style war even though
its U.S. national security did not require preparation for such a war until World
War I. Conversely, the British Army's regiments, the world wars notwithstanding,
remained focused on and engaged in imperial policing. Both Figure 3.1 and the
conclusion of Chapter 3 explain and compare the central characteristics and preferences engendered by the British and American military strategic cultures. Some
of them, as mentioned earlier in this book, are loosely traceable to Cardwell's and
Upton's prescriptions about organization and force.

To briefly recapitulate these characteristics, the British have exhibited a preference for the indirect and pragmatic approach to strategy. The British military has
also accepted and embraced intrastate security, counterinsurgency, and before
that, imperial policing, as normal roles for the British Army. Small wars then have
predominated in the British Army historical experience and they are the institutional tradition. Although the British military has been largely successful in most
of its conventional wars, for political and military cultural reasons the British
Army has viewed its expeditionary role to fight on the Continent as peripheral and
ephemeral for most of its history. In addition, the regiment and the regimental system are deeply embedded in the British military tradition. This characteristic has
also proven somewhat chimerical and problematic: on the one hand, the regimental system has proven responsive and adaptable to the exigencies of intrastate operations; on the other hand, the regimental system was an impediment to preparing
for large-scale conventional conflicts on the Continent. Even after the end of the

industrial era of warfare, attempts to do away with the regiment have met with resistance in the army and with political vitriol in Parliament.[6]

As a corollary to the British Army's experience and ready acceptance of counterinsurgency and constabulary missions as normal roles, the institution has also
embraced a proven corpus of principles pertaining to the use of force in such operations. Consequently, the British Army understands that it should use minimum
force and only when required. The British also display more patience and resolve
when it comes to protracted internal wars—this is explained by a historical tradition of operating in small, independent regiments isolated in distant locations.
British military culture also seems to be more inured to casualties. This is not to
say that the British Army does not try to avoid casualties, only that it does not seem
to be averse to them. Also, partly as a result of a history of making due with limited
resources, the British Army has not come to over rely on technology as a panacea
or substitute for troops on the ground in the fray. From a civil-military relations
perspective, the British political system is more centralized and therefore better
able to exercise control over the military. Consequently, the British Army has been
more responsive as a multipurpose and malleable instrument of the Crown. Finally, though somewhat paradoxically, is the observation that for the most part,
Britain, the European power, eschewed a role in European wars while the non-European power, the United States, accepted one.

Nonetheless, when Britain conducted conventional wars in Europe, it preferred a
Fabian approach. The American military, on the other hand, exhibited a predilection
for big conventional wars with broad-fronted offensives that leveraged its disparate
advantage in numbers and technology. As a consequence of the Civil War and of an
adulation of first the French, then the Prussian model of war, the U.S. Army became
almost exclusively focused on conventional war and massive firepower. Upton and
his disciples, as prophets of the Prussian paradigm, fused it with their concept of total wars of annihilation from the Civil War and proselytized it throughout the profession through institutions and journals. Consequently, any missions or operations not
consistent with the core conventional paradigm came to be viewed as ephemeral and
anomalous. Thus, for about 125 out of the 138 years after the Civil War, the mainstream U.S. Army consistently failed to seriously consider any type of war except a
European-style conventional war. This is in spite of the fact that the U.S. Army has
many more years of actual experience with nontraditional missions than with big
conventional wars. Weigley has observed that when the U.S. Army has had to participate in unconventional or guerrilla wars, "the experiences have soon been dismissed as aberrant." Although the U.S. Army is a product of frontier policing and in
spite of spending the majority of its existence conducting operations other than conventional war, its culture and ethos—evolved in the 19th century—consigned the
very political realm of small wars to the periphery of professional thought. This is
because many officers believed that they should exclude themselves from political
matters and focus on purely military ones.[7]

Moreover, for the better part of the 20th century, the U.S. Army also embraced
the combat division as the central organization because it offered the most utility

in mid- to high-intensity war between industrialized armies. Even at the end of the 20th century, ten years after the Cold War ended, as Army Chief General Shinseki moved the institution toward a more versatile strategic force equipped with medium-weight rapid response brigades, the division remained embedded in the U.S. military culture as much as the aircraft carrier. Since the number of divisions has also been used to justify and conceptualize funding requirements, it will probably outlast its strategic salience just as the two-major-theater-war construct did. Chapter 3 also highlighted that the United States' unlimited resources, values, and political culture converged to create the perception that war is bad; it should be prosecuted as a last resort; it should be waged as a crusade; and maximum force must be used to win swiftly and decisively. Moreover, outside the scope of war as a crusade, in defense of vital interests, a U.S. military cultural emphasis on casualty avoidance and a reliance on the "silver bullet" of technology were discernible characteristics. Finally, Chapter 3 arrived at this notion of an "Uptonian Paradox" as a corollary characteristic of U.S. military strategic culture. Named for Emory Upton because of his influence on the U.S. Army during its professional and intellectual birth, the contradiction stems from the following: the U.S. military ostensibly embraces Clausewitz as the quintessential oracle of war yet it exhibits a Jominian predilection to divorce the political from the military once a conflicts commences. As a part of this paradox, the American military has also demonstrated a tendency to strongly influence the views of its political leaders on when and when not to use the military instrument.[8]

Cultural Manifestations and Lessons

Figure 8.3a compares the manifestations of military strategic characteristics in the two case studies. What seems very evident is that both militaries' propensities for force, the maximalist U.S. approach and the minimalist British approach, contributed to significant problems. The United States became very partial with its excessive use of force against one faction. It also alienated the population it was there to save. On the other hand, the British Army's overemphasis on absolute impartiality and minimum force in self-defense, in the midst of a three-sided war, made the safe area and protection zone concepts untenable. Moreover, although the British strove to maintain consent and impartiality for most of three years, the British Army had in fact crossed the Mogadishu line. Even though General Rose seemed unable to realize this, the February 1994 Sarajevo ultimatum, with the concomitant threat of NATO air power, was an act of coercion, not consensus. Cardwellian underpinnings—a focus on small wars, the regiment, and minimum force—were evident in the British Army's approach in Bosnia. Likewise, Upton's current reincarnation—the Weinberger-Powell Doctrine of overwhelming and decisive force—influenced the U.S. approach during both UNITAF and UNOSOM II. Ironically, neither Uptonian prescriptions nor Cardwellian policy implications stood either Army in good stead in two operations that had much in common.

Figure 8.3a
American and British Military Strategic Cultures in AHO

Characteristic	U.S. - SOMALIA	U.K. - BOSNIA
Civil-Military	Powellian Decisive Force drives how force applied – Chapter VII PE. Military resource leads/drives throughout but CMOC (UNITAF) was outstanding innovation to integrate.	Policy and Military in harmony = policy limited to doing something but not getting dragged into the war. Military echoed and pursued absolute impartiality/ consent until summer 1995
Force	UNITAF: Robust, credible, and overwhelming w/restraint. UNOSOM II: Deadly force used maximally and partially. War	Minimalist force: initially self-defense, then in defense of mandate
Casualties	Catalyst for withdraw and impetus for request more force—armor request. Escalation of violence, culminating in October triggers outcry for immediate withdrawal. Somalia isn't worth 1 American	Exhibits willingness to take casualties —conditioned by NI experience. Not inured to casualties, however. LTG Rose expressed concern about casualties.
Technology	Asymmetry of Technology: U.S. – AC-130, OH-58D lasers, SOF birds; SNA sling shots, kites, and innovate with RPGs (lessons from Afghanistan). SNA target technology to inflict maximum damage.	Undetermined: Did not over rely on technological solutions (i.e., air power or attack helos) but employed organic systems (Warriors/Saxons) to protect with effect

Furthermore, the impact of events in Somalia on the development of both doctrine and on the British Army's approach in Bosnia was significant. The Somalia experience initially impelled both militaries in exactly opposite directions: it caused the British Army to more vehemently oppose any breach of the consent divide, or the Mogadishu line; and it led to the promulgation of PDD 25 in the U.S. national security establishment. PDD 25 codified a fusion between the Weinberger criteria and peace operations policy—Emory Upton meets peace operations. Thus, as a consequence of Somalia, the United States essentially limited its options in peace operations under a UN mandate to only committing military ground forces to operations, with a Chapter VII authorization to use force and when a peace agreement has already been signed. Robust force, robust rules of engagement, and U.S. command are preconditions. Moreover, because the United States is a veto-wielding member of the UN Security Council, in practice this actually means that Uptonian/Weinbergerian criteria have been prescribing overwhelming (Chapter VII) force to the international community as well.

In his book *To End a War*, Richard Holbrooke has called the U.S. reaction to Somalia, "the Vietmalia Syndrome." According to Holbrooke, the scar tissue from the Somalia debacle also significantly shaped the U.S. policy in Bosnia. Although there were fundamental differences between Bosnia and "Vietmalia," any discussion of such differences was unwelcome: "most officials felt they already knew the meaning of Somalia and Vietnam without giving them more than cursory analysis." Most U.S. military leaders would have preferred not to deploy force to Bosnia: they were concerned that the mission would be "fuzzy" and imprecise, like Somalia; and they worried aloud about "the slippery slope" in Bosnia. If they were ordered to deploy, nonetheless, they would do so quickly and successfully.

However, the military would resist taking on any missions beyond "self-protection and the implementation of the military provisions of any peace agreement."[9]

Doctrinal Development and Outcomes

An examination of the 1992 and 1994 doctrines reveals more continuity than change. Figure 8.3b reveals that the British doctrine simply stretched traditional peacekeeping as well as its principles and subsumed the new tasks. The U.S. doctrine, on the other hand, included the new tasks under peace enforcement, a concept that more closely reflected American predilections for over whelming and coercive force. Moreover, three of the six principles for OOTW (which apply to PO also) simply migrated directly from the principles of war. Figure 8.3b depicts the continuity in concepts and principles that were manifest in the evolution of the two doctrines.

Charles Dobbie observed that "we are all prisoners of our heritage" and asserted that because of the requirements of empire, the British were more adaptive and pragmatic on the ground. Moreover, since he was given the task of writing *Wider Peacekeeping* without much guidance or interference, it was his personal military experiences and preferences that influenced his approach—Dobbie had been to Northern Ireland several times and to Oman in the early 1970s conducting counterinsurgency. According to Dobbie, winning hearts and minds is embedded in the British Army beginning with military training at Sandhurst. His perspective on impartiality and consent also stemmed from service in Belfast, where one "needed to reach and communicate with the indigenous people in a friendly and constructive way."[10]

On the other hand, the U.S. author of *Peace Operations* offered an interesting vignette about the embedded nature of minimum force in the British Army: during a U.S.-UK staff exchange when the British were trying to explicate a minimalist approach to force they showed the U.S. officers an excerpt from the movie Ghandi where British soldiers had mowed down a large group of unarmed civilians in Amritsar, India. On the other hand, the U.S. doctrinal process was much more centralized, with lots of input from the Senior Officer Review Group (SORG), comprising retired general officers and Robert Oakley, a true-faith apostle of the Weinberger Doctrine. Rinaldo called their input "senior leader vision" and acknowledged that it represented core military preferences.[11] As an example, here are two SORG comments on a draft of *FM 100-23*:

How do you reconcile the warrior ethic with FM 100-23? You do not want peace keepers to accomplish a peace operations mission. You want warriors to accomplish the mission. You can make warriors peace keepers, but you can't make peace keepers warriors.[12]

Minimum use of force is desired as described in FM 100-23. This is incorrect. The operative word is "appropriate" use of force. Force levels greater than the anticipated need often act as a deterrent to hostile action and can help maintain a benign environment.[13]

Figure 8.3b
Two Doctrinal Typologies: Continuity or Change?

1992

British Doctrine

	MISSIONS	PRINCIPLES
PK	OBSERVER MSN PEACEKEEPING	Impartiality Avoidance of Force Negotiation Clarity of Intention Suggestion Firmness Anticipation Integration Host Government Authority
PE	UNLIKELY	NA

American Doctrine

	MISSIONS	PRINCIPLES
PK	Disengagement Cease-fire POW Exchange Arms Control Demobilization	Balance Force in Self-defense Consent Impartiality Single Manager Control Concurrent Action Sponsor Support Freedom of Movement
PE	Restore Peace Impose Peace Separate Hostile Faction	Objective Legitimacy Unity of Effort Patience Restraint Security

MSC/BOSNIA   MSC/SOMALIA

1994

British Doctrine

	MISSIONS	PRINCIPLES
WPK	Humanitarian Relief Guarantee or denial of movement Conflict Prevention Demobilization Military Assistance	Impartiality Mutual Respect Legitimacy Minimum Force Credibility Transparency
PE	War	Concentration of Force Offensive Action Economy of Force Surprise Selection/Mainten- ance of the Aim Security Flexibility

American Doctrine

	MISSIONS	PRINCIPLES
PK	Monitoring of Ceasefires Observation Monitoring of Truces Supervision of Truces	Objective Legitimacy Unity of Effort Perseverance Restraint Security Absolute impartiality *Minimum Force/self- defense* *Absolute Consent* *Absolute Impartiality*
PE	Forcible Separation of Belligerents Restore Order and Stability Protect Humanitarian Assistance Guarantee and Denial of Movement Enforce Sanctions	Objective Legitimacy Unity of Effort Perseverance Restraint Security *Coercive/Appropriate Force* *Consent/Impartiality Not Required*

From the Rinaldo interview, nonetheless, two conclusions seemed clear: (1) Rinaldo was very conscientious—he studied a vast amount of peacekeeping literature in order to write the best doctrine possible; and (2) the doctrine reflected the experience of Somalia and it incorporated the recommendations of the SORG. However, there are two disquieting footnotes about American doctrine. First, in 1992 when the Center for Low Intensity Conflict (CLIC) began examining doctrine for peace operations, a U.S. Army brigadier general at the Army Staff's Strategic Plans and Policy office with oversight of CLIC told Horace Hunter to stop working on peace operations because, "if you study it, we may have to do it." Second, an infantry battalion commander who recently returned from Kosovo, when asked what doctrine he had followed, commented: "battalion commanders don't have time to read doctrine." He also explained how he measured success in Kosovo: "no casualties, no equipment losses, no civilians shot, and representing the unit well." What is conspicuous in his success criteria is the absence of any focus on the progress of peace building in Kosovo.[14]

On the other hand, Thornton's analysis concluded that *Wider Peacekeeping* was an instrument that allowed the British Army to "stick to current routines or marginally adapt them," by "resisting change in the face of new roles and missions." John Mackinlay, moreover, described wider peacekeeping as a "stretched version" of traditional peacekeeping. In the immediate post–Cold War period, the British were averse to the term "peace enforcement" because it was generally equated to war fighting. In fact, this study's analysis of the British doctrine showed that both the 1988 and the 1994 doctrine defined peace enforcement as war fighting. According to another British officer, this is why there was such a strong emphasis on the consent divide, and on not slipping across the "Rubicon" by default. This may not have been an unreasonable assumption at the time— many British officers felt that this was the main lesson from Somalia. The U.S. decision to abandon any notion of impartiality and to take sides in Somalia against Aideed was "perceived as an inadvertent crossing of the Rubicon between peace-keeping and peace enforcement."[15]

However, even as early as January 1995, one month after *Wider Peacekeeping* was officially released, Wilkinson explained to the British Director of Land Warfare that the basic flaw in the notion of "wider peacekeeping" was "its attempt to stretch peacekeeping doctrine into circumstances where it was no longer appropriate." Moreover, according to Wilkinson, the main lesson of UNPROFOR was that the concept of safe areas and armed humanitarian relief can only be achieved, and "should only be attempted by a force capable of over-matching whatever level of opposition may be offered." This became a recurrent lesson in complex intrastate humanitarian emergencies where states had failed—any prescriptions for maintaining levels of consent in the theater were so problematic to be almost worthless. As a result, almost before the ink was dry on *Wider Peacekeeping*, Wilkinson suggested that crossing the consent threshold did not necessarily equate to abandoning impartiality, and that peace enforcement should be looked at as law enforcement (carrying out the mandate without

prejudice to any party), instead of war fighting. Moreover, the conduct of a sufficiently robust force, as long as it impartially prosecutes its mission, was much
more versatile than a force armed only enough to do peacekeeping. Wilkinson
also explained that an overemphasis on consent would put the peacekeeping
force in a tenuous predicament if consent were withdrawn.[16]

However, the author of *Wider Peacekeeping* said that after what was happening
in Bosnia, the second biggest influence on his work were his discussions with
Glynn Evans at the foreign office's peacekeeping desk. In fact, Dobbie indicated
that he was left alone to write doctrine unimpeded and he based it on what he intu-
ited was the correct way. Moreover, he had seen John Mackinlay's work on second-generation multinational operations (2GMO) and decided to use that as an
example of the wrong approach—he turned it on its head to create *Wider Peacekeeping*. Nonetheless, Dobbie indicated that Glynn Evans was his political backer
at the foreign office. This is interesting as an influence because Evans had been a
big proponent of limiting the British role in Bosnia to "protective support" and she
declared that she had sold some of Britain's closest allies on the concept.[17]

GENERALIZATIONS—CULTURE, CASE STUDIES, AND DOCTRINE

The following are overarching generalizations that can be inferred from this
work:

1. Great powers don't do peace operations or OOTW well. An asymmetry of means,
   coupled with an inherent strategic paradox, makes it difficult to use the right mix of
   force and restraint.

2. Militaries in democracies are multipurpose instruments of their civilian masters.
   During times of relative peace and of low threats to vital national security interests,
   the civilian imperative to "do something" will require the militaries to operate outside their culturally prescribed preferences. It is better to have a well thought out
   conceptual approach (doctrine) to these other missions in order to "do something"
   that has a chance of succeeding.

3. Since a regimental system is effective for small wars, it might be the most appropriate, deployable, and flexible organization for smaller scale contingencies. The British have an advantage since the regiment is embedded in their culture. However,
   although the U.S. Army has created medium-weight Stryker brigades, there is still
   much intransigence about abandoning the division. It is a bit ironic that exactly a
   century ago, the regiment was the central organization of the U.S. Army, as was imperial policing (Philippines) a salient mission. Regimental-sized combined arms
   battle groups would be the most suitable adaptation to technology and to the emerging security landscape.[18]

4. The impact of Somalia on both militaries, both doctrines, and peace operations under the UN cannot be overstated. The "Vietmalia Syndrome" significantly shaped
   the subsequent U. S. approach to peace operations. It also had a significant influence on the British Army's conduct of UNPROFOR. PDD 25 was a direct outcome
   of Somalia—it essentially fused the Weinberger Doctrine to peace operations (a

very incongruous construct). The bottom line of PDD 25 is that the United States will only commit ground troops with a peace enforcement mandate and with robust forces, after a peace agreement has been signed.[19]

5. Large military organizations don't effect innovative doctrinal change well. Innovative change means a significant alteration of military doctrine. However, these doctrines changed incrementally. According to Harvey Sapolsky, "organizational structures that encourage the presentation of innovative proposals and their careful reviews make innovation less likely." This is particularly true of U.S. Doctrine— the SORG and other agencies reviewed several draft proposals of *FM 100-23* before it was finalized.[20]

6. Restraint and the credible and sufficient use of force are the two most important principles for peace operations in the gray zone. The "hearts and minds" of the former warring factions are important in peace operations also. Excessive force does not win hearts and minds.

IMPLICATIONS FOR PEACE OPERATIONS AND OPERATIONS OTHER THAN WAR

Since the first two post–Cold War manuals, the two militaries have achieved much more compatibility on peace operations doctrine. The British doctrine has moved closer in approach to the U.S. doctrine. The British have dropped the wider-peacekeeping concept and adopted "peace support operations." The British doctrine now subsumes many of the gray area missions under peace enforcement, as did the 1993 U.S. manual. Peace enforcement is no longer equated to war fighting. For example, the British doctrine now acknowledges the difficulty of conducting peacekeeping during complex emergencies, or when there is no peace to keep. "The distinction between peace enforcement and other enforcement actions or war will be determined in an examination of the mandate and desired end-state." Even more significantly, the protection of humanitarian operations and the establishment of protected or safe areas are now peace enforcement tasks.[21]

According to Peter Jakobsen, both the British and the Americans have moved closer to the French doctrine, which had all along better articulated principles as well as a sound concepts—*peace restoration operations*—for the new generation of gray area operations. The U.S. Army has again changed the moniker for LIC (OOTW) to *Stability Operations and Support Operations*, the U.S. doctrine in *FM 100-20* emphasizes a credible and sufficient military capability, as well as restraint, for peace enforcement tasks. The British doctrine now calls for the deployment of robust forces operating under a Chapter VII mandate to conduct humanitarian operations. Moreover, both militaries have abandoned any notion of neutrality for an impartial and prudent application of force to protect the prosecution of the mandate.[22]

Peace operations also have implications for military professionalism. According to one British scholar, there is some evidence for the emergence of the soldier-statesman role in the post-modern British military. In the new security landscape, "the soldier-scholar is required to think through the conditions for applying force" in those operations that lie in between war fighting and traditional peacekeeping. Dandeker explains that the most probable military operations lie in this gray area, where much has been learned in the last several years, but where doctrine and experience are still relatively undeveloped. The soldier-statesman's role is becoming more germane because of the complexity of political problems in coalition operations—this is particularly true in operations where there is no threat to vital national interests. Much closer cooperation is required between political and military decision-makers—the result is a blurring of the line between military and political skills, and a challenge "to the traditional ideas of the military professional as an apolitical technician." Dandeker concludes with the assertion that the preparation of military professionals for their roles as soldier-statesmen will require innovation in organization and education.[23]

Don Snider explains that the U.S. postmodern military will likely "focus primarily on peacekeeping and humanitarian missions; to be a smaller, all-volunteer force of professionals, with officers who see themselves as soldier-statesmen rather than as combat leaders or managers of violence; and to enjoy only tepid pubic support." The military's new task is to be able to operate with coalitions in a constabulary role within the context of increased subnational violence and conflict. This is a role that has the military employed in a very limited way for very limited political objectives, often with less than conclusive results. This is a significant change from the war-fighting emphasis of the U.S. military for the last six decades. Although the military acknowledges the possibility of a major-power conflict in the future, there is currently no consensus about when and with whom the conflict might be fought. In view of these two very different roles, and in the absence of clearly articulated civilian priorities, Snider observes that, "it is no surprise that the military is not adapting effectively for either one."[24]

There is, however, a historical vignette that points to the salience of the small war tradition to the future preparation and training for constabulary-type missions.

The small-war army fielded by Great Britain in the nineteenth century was an elite, volunteer force of long-service professionals. Many of Britain's small warriors were recruited locally throughout the British Empire, and most were superbly trained and profited from unexcelled levels of small-unit cohesion derived from a regimental system that more or less kept the same officers and men together throughout their military service.[25]

Britain's small-war army principally comprised light infantry, light cavalry, and light artillery units, with the agility and logistical austerity to enable them to operate effectively in remote and varied operational milieus. Equally significant, according to Jeffrey Record, was a command structure that was characterized by decentralization and the encouragement of junior officer and junior NCO initiative.[26]

Since the small-war environment is not that different from operations other than war (or peace operations), Record's observations about them are germane: the promotion of the values of decentralization, lightness, quality of training, and unit cohesion are no less important for the operations short of war of the future than they were for the small wars of the past. Peace operations in difficult terrain amidst former enemies also argue for specialized, elite, light, cohesive, and tactically versatile forces. In addition, given the United States' ostensible sensitivity to casualties and protracted conflicts, forces must be able to get the mission accomplished at minimal costs. The relevance of these comments is made clear by the ongoing U.S. military operations in Afghanistan and Iraq where U.S. Army forces, with their coalition partners, are conducting protracted counterinsurgency wars against remnant Taliban/al Qaeda fighters and Iraqi former regime loyalist guerrillas.[27]

IMPLICATIONS FOR U.S. ARMY TRANSFORMATION

How is this work relevant to the U.S. Army and its efforts to transform itself? This subject is especially germane to the U.S. military and its allies because the U.S. action in Somalia fundamentally devolved into an urban counterinsurgency, or asymmetric conflict, and asymmetric conflict is the most probable form of conflict that America and its NATO allies face. Four objective facts point to the probability that the U.S. and the west will most likely face an asymmetrically oriented adversary: the western powers represent the countries who have the most advanced militaries (technology and firepower) in the world; the economic and political homogenization among these states essentially precludes a war among them; most rational adversaries in the non-Western world would have learned from the Gulf War not to confront the West on its terms; and, as a result, the U.S. and its European allies will employ their firepower and technology in the less developed world, against ostensibly inferior adversaries employing asymmetric approaches. Asymmetric conflict will therefore be the norm, not the exception. U.S. operations in Afghanistan after September 2001 and in Iraq after the fall of Baghdad certainly attest to the salience of small wars and asymmetric conflicts.[28]

However, the U.S. military's failures in Vietnam and Somalia and the Soviet/Russian military failures in Afghanistan and Chechnya point to another truism about great powers: they tend to fight small wars badly because they embrace and cling to big-war paradigms, to their detriment. The U.S. Army has embraced a big-war paradigm at least since World War I, and more probably since the influence of Emory Upton during the last quarter of the 19th century. This preference for the conventional paradigm became embedded in U.S. military culture over time and by the time of the Vietnam War, this preference shaped the U.S Army so much that it was unable to adapt itself to counterinsurgency, instead preferring to apply a big war paradigm when it was entirely inappropriate. The salience of a continued U.S. military cultural and doctrinal resistance to learning how to do asymmetric conflict to the future of the Army's transformation is evident: the U.S.

Army exhibits a cultural preference for the big war paradigm; culture generally changes incrementally instead of innovatively, and culture hugely influences doctrine and force structure. Thus, the lack of military cultural change that led the U.S. military down the road to debacles in Vietnam and Somalia should help impel and warn the U.S. military that its culture must change more rapidly if it wants to adapt to the increased probability of asymmetric wars. The remainder of this study revisits some of the cultural predilections of the U.S. military and identifies some of the obstacles on the path to transformation.[29]

The U.S. Army remains the principal land force of the sole remaining superpower, and, having been focused against its Soviet competitor's armed forces for almost half a century for a big war show down on the plains of Europe, its orientation is, in essence, conventional and symmetric. The troops of the U.S. Special Operations Command comprise the small portion of U.S. forces that embrace anything close to approximating an asymmetric mindset. Yet even these specially trained warriors look at asymmetric and unconventional approaches through the filters of decades and centuries worth of western military tradition. One need only recall the fact that the most elite of these forces (TF Ranger) had used the same exact template seven times in Mogadishu, making itself very predictable and vulnerable to an asymmetric approach by thugs armed with RPGs. The paradox of the present period is that those forces that are best armed to fight a conventional war—the western militaries—are least likely to fight a war against each other. Moreover, the west and its military forces have generally dominated and monopolized the conventional paradigm of war, usually winning when the east or the south decided to fight according to this paradigm. The philosophies of Jomini, Clausewitz, and Svechin are embedded in the cultures of these militaries. As a result, the West has tended to embrace the direct use of military force, combining maneuver and firepower to mass combat power at the decisive point (this point usually equates to the destruction or annihilation of some enemy force or army).

The problem is that the enemy that we are most likely to fight is one who has for many more centuries embraced a different philosophy of war. Potential adversaries are from Asia and the Near East, cultures who generally embrace an eastern tradition of war. Moreover, the eastern way of war stems from the philosophies of Sun Tzu and Mao. It is distinguished from the western way by its reliance on indirectness, attrition, and perfidy. In other words, the eastern way of war is inherently more asymmetric. Thus, the implication for an army that is transforming itself to meet these new threats is threefold: the U.S. Army must change its military culture, its doctrine, and it must re-examine the utility and relevance of its preferred tactical formation—the division.

American Military Culture and Cultural Change

"No living organization, and the Army is a living organization, can survive without change."[30] The impetus for changing the Army has been manifold: the paradigm shift from Cold-War bipolar system to the post–Cold War unipolar system; the resultant increase in constabulary operations and operations other than war since the 1990s; the conspicuous lack of strategic versatility that was manifest in Task Force Hawk; and finally, the insidious threat that al Qaeda and its sponsors pose to the security of the U.S. homeland. The events on and after 11 September alone have added a new sense of urgency to the impetus for transformation. Since 11 September 2001, moreover, the U.S. Army has been called on to defeat a serious asymmetric threat, relying initially and principally on special operations land forces, to undermine al Qaeda and its Taliban supporters in Afghanistan. In addition, the U.S. Air Force played no small role in defeating the Taliban, in concert with the special operations forces.

The U.S. military prosecuted a very effective and unprecedented strategy against the Taliban regime and al Qaeda in Afghanistan. Combining precision bombing and the employment of Special Forces in an unconventional warfare role, the U.S. military essentially decapitated the oppressive Taliban rule there. However, the U.S. war in Afghanistan is different from the examples of Bosnia and Somalia in one very significant way: the war against terrorism witnesses the use of U.S. military forces in defense of our vital interests—the security and survival of our population is threatened. In this respect, this war has more in common with World War II than it does with Vietnam or Somalia. It is a war as a crusade, against a nonstate actor that attacked and continues to threaten the U.S. homeland. Both the United States and Al Qaeda seem to be fighting to achieve unlimited ends: the United States aims to eradicate the al Qaeda terror network around the globe and the enemy aim seems to be getting the United States out of the Middle East and East Asia. In this case, the U.S. public will probably continue to tolerate casualties and to support a protracted counter-terror war because it is clear that this effort is in defense of vital interests. For this same reason, consensus and resolve to bring this war for the defense of the U.S. homeland to a successful conclusion are also evident among U.S. political leaders.[31]

The war in Afghanistan, however, is distinct in another important way: the first and most successful campaign there saw U.S. special operations troops operating in a pro-insurgent role—the U.S. military was the guerrilla. Being the guerrilla and countering the guerrilla are two very different things. Since the beginning of 2002, however, the U.S. military has been conducting counter-guerrilla operations in eastern Afghanistan. Although the final outcome is yet to be determined, an approach that combines intelligence, small special unit actions, and precision bombing has met with success inside Afghanistan. However, the potential for safe haven afforded to the Taliban and Al Qaeda fighters by the porous and sparsely guarded 1300-mile Pakistani border seems to have been realized since Pakistani national police sources now estimate that as many 10,000 Taliban cadres and 5,000 al Qaeda fighters are hiding in sanctuaries inside Pakistan, with the support of local religious and tribal groups. This situation presents a vexing conundrum: whose forces can and will root out the 15,000 enemy that are being harbored inside a friendly state by and among the 1 percent of the population who are Islamic extremists and the 15% of the population who are anti-American?[32]

If it is at all possible that U.S. forces may enter Pakistan to help that government isolate and eradicate these 10 to 15,000 jihadist guerrillas, there are some lessons from another war in Asia over a quarter of a century ago that can help show the United States what not to do. Vietnam was also essentially a counter-guerrilla war until the United States tried to transform it into something it was not by "Americanizing" (conventionalizing) it. In fact, in 1961 and 1962, U.S. Army Special Forces initially met with some success using proven counterinsurgency techniques (aggressive small unit patrolling, intelligence, winning hearts and minds). By the end of 1962 the Special Forces had recovered and secured several hundred villages from the Viet Cong. Moreover, the U.S. Marines operating in the I Corps area employed similar techniques with their Combined Actions Platoons (CAPs), achieving local success for most of the war. However, when General William Westmoreland's team arrived, it tended to marginalize both the Special Forces and the Marines' CAP program because both were inconsistent with his concept of the U.S. Army's way of war: conventional, lots of firepower, and harnessing technology to "search and destroy."[33]

Likewise, many of the lessons of previous U.S. efforts in the arena of counterinsurgency, particularly some valuable lessons learned in blood and sweat in the Vietnam War, are germane to the counter-guerrilla war in Iraq (Operation Iraqi Freedom), after the fall of Baghdad. This fight, also, is not about "search and destroy," heavy unit sweeps, phase lines, and attrition. It is a war about decentralized, small unit actions, distributed in time and space, in a complex, non-contiguous, and non-linear battle space. First and foremost, the counterinsurgency in Iraq against Ba'athist regime loyalists is about enhancing the legitimacy of the U.S. effort, and the effort of the inchoate Iraqi Governing Council, as well as demonstrating a credible capacity to coerce, discriminately. The integration of the civil and military efforts, actionable intelligence, minimum essential force, small unit actions, protecting the population, and winning the hearts and minds of the population are as important to success in post-Saddam Iraq as they have been to any counterinsurgency effort in history. The USMC Combined Action Program and the limited successes of pacification under the Civil Operations and Revolutionary Development Support (CORDS) organization in Vietnam offer valuable lessons for those prosecuting the war in Iraq. All of these facts combine to offer another catalyst for transformation: if the Army does not adapt to meet the asymmetric exigencies of the emerging security environment, and if the Army does not become more strategically versatile, then the conventional Army risks becoming irrelevant. However, adaptability and innovativeness have much to do with an institution's culture and, often, cultural change is a prerequisite to transformation. For the U.S. Army to really transform, its military culture—the values and attitudes that it embraces about the use of force—must change.[34]

To quickly restate the salient aspects of military strategic culture, military culture is "assessed according to the ideas and beliefs about how to wage war that characterize a particular military bureaucracy." Empirical and measurable indicators include internal correspondence, planning documents, memoirs, and regulations. However, the organizational cultures of the military services are particularly strong because these bureaucracies have a closed-career principle—members spend their careers almost exclusively in these organizations. Because mission identity is an important part of a military's self-concept, military organizations will seek to promote core missions and to defeat any challenges to core-mission functions. Even if other missions are assigned, if the organization perceives them as peripheral to its core mission, then it will reject them as possible detractions from its core focus. Cultural change occurs in terms of "cultural epochs" that normally range in length from just a decade to as long as a century.[35]

In fact, the RAND study cited in Chapter 3 concluded that: "the beliefs and attitudes that comprise organizational culture can block change and cause organizations to fail." These authors explain that culture often originates from successes in an organization's history: what worked in the past is repeated and internalized; what didn't work is modified or rejected. If the organization survives, historically successful approaches are internalized and gradually transformed into "the way we think." The RAND study used a comparative approach: "comparisons with other armies can highlight different approaches to the preparation and conduct of warfare, some of which may be culture based." Finally, this study arrived at two important conclusions: first, cultural change requires a significant amount of time—the study determines five years as the minimum time to inculcate a major cultural change; second, major cultural change must come from the top—leaders at the highest levels must unambiguously back the change.[36]

Having highlighted that militaries do have unique cultures, that cultural change occurs slowly, and that cultural preferences for one type of war may impede adaptation to other modes of war, what generalizations can be drawn about U.S. military strategic culture? First, although insular geography has afforded the United States a degree of cheap security, history and geography have shaped American military culture significantly. Vast land space, hostile indigenous tribes, and a cataclysmic civil war embedded a direct and absolute approach to war. A salient component of this approach was a perceived or real struggle for survival on the new continent dating back to King Philip's War. What's more as a consequence of the Civil War and of an adulation of first the French, then the Prussian model of war, the U.S. Army became focused on conventional war (alone) and massive firepower. Moreover, Sherman, Upton, and their disciples, as advocates of the conventional Prussian model, fused it with their total-war-of-annihilation approach in the Civil War and imbued it in the profession through institutions and journals. As a result, anything outside of the core paradigm came to be viewed as aberrant and ephemeral.

In addition, American political culture, vast resources, and values combine to create the view that war is bad and should only be waged as a crusade to achieve victory swiftly and justly. As a result, the notion of war as a last resort but with maximum force evolved. The U.S. Army for most of this century has also embraced the combat division as the preferred combat formation—this is a "no brainer"—the combat division *was* the most appropriate formation for the U.S. Army's favorite kind of war. Also salient, and topical in the context of peace operations, is a U.S. military cultural over emphasis on casualty avoidance and an overreliance on the "silver bullet," or technology. Finally, the aforementioned factors, coupled with the way and context in which the U.S. Army professionalized at the end of the last century led to what I have called the notion of an "Uptonian Paradox:" the U.S. military ostensibly worships Clausewitz as the principal philosopher/oracle of war on the one hand, but on the other hand it exhibits a Jominian predilection to divorce the political from the military when the shooting starts. U.S. military strategic culture also, while in no way usurping civilian control of the military ultimately, exhibits a tendency to reshape its political masters' views to make those views on war congruent with its preferred paradigm for war. Moreover, Vietnam, Harry Summers' book *On Strategy*, and the Weinberger-Powell Doctrine have all helped perpetuate and exacerbate this tendency of the military to prescribe to the civilian elite "what kind of wars we do and don't do."

The U.S. military's cultural tendency to rely on technology to minimize casualties is particularly salient as, potentially, we can face industrial and preindustrial foes who will employ asymmetry to mitigate our technological advantages. This "silver bullet syndrome" had been exacerbated since the Persian Gulf War, the Powell Corollary, and the antiseptic air campaign against Kosovo. Together these events have created the impression that the U.S. military can harness technology to win decisively without casualties and with a minimum number of troops on the ground. However, America's defeat in Vietnam and the Soviets and Russians defeats in Afghanistan and Chechnya show that technological disparity does not necessarily ensure victory either on the field of battle or at the negotiating table. According to two experts on military policy, the "U.S military policy remains imprisoned in an unresolved dialectic between history and technology, between those for whom the past is prologue and those for whom it is irrelevant."[37]

These same two experts also cogently maintain, "for those who place unbridled faith in technology, war is a predictable, if disorderly phenomenon, defeat a matter of simple cost/benefit analysis, and the effectiveness of any military capability a finite calculus of targets destroyed and casualties inflicted." However, history reveals a very different account—uncertainty, chance, friction, and the fog of battle and of the human mind under stress all seriously constrain our capacity to predict the result. Defeat must be visited upon the minds and the will of the vanquished for it to carry any significance. In asymmetric conflicts, human factors and will are more salient than technological factors in determining victory or defeat—in Vietnam, Afghanistan, Somalia, and Chechnya, adaptive and resolute enemies found ways to mitigate or undermine altogether the advantage of technological superiority.[38]

Military Cultural Change and Doctrinal Change

Doctrinal change is one indicator of military cultural change and incremental doctrinal change reflects an incremental change in military culture. The best work on this subject is still that of Colonel Richard Duncan Downie whose *Learning from Conflict* focused on doctrinal continuity and change as a result of the relationship between a changing security landscape that necessitates change and the military's ability to adapt, based on the timing of its cyclical institutional learning process. More specifically, Downie contended that changes in U.S. Army doctrine can serve as observable measures of institutional learning. Two assumptions underpin Downie's approach: (1) change to an organization's institutional memory is a precondition to institutional learning; and (2) military doctrine is "useful representation of the U.S. Army's institutional memory."[39]

The U.S. Army's "conventional wisdom," as reflected in its norms, SOPs, and doctrine which are widely accepted and practiced, constitutes an organization's institutional memory. To be sure, this conception of institutional memory is very close to the notion of military culture. Institutional memory is "what old members of an organization know and what new members learn through a process of socialization." Institutional memory does not change quickly or easily and it can perpetuate doctrinal continuity even when the doctrine leads to suboptimal performance. Institutional learning is "a process by which an organization uses new knowledge or understanding gained from experience or study to adjust institutional norms, doctrine, and procedures in ways designed to minimize previous gaps in performance and maximize future success." *Learning from Conflict* is salient and relevant because it examines how organizations either learn and act to change their doctrine or don't learn and retain outmoded doctrine. Counterinsurgency and urban operations are not operations about which the main stream (conventional) U.S. Army has evinced a great deal of enthusiasm. However, the U.S. Marine Corps, which is a better incubator for innovative thinking about the unorthodox nature of future war, dedicated an entire battle lab to urban operations, with attendant exercises.[40]

Defense experts also maintain that the U.S. military has not yet fully embraced the notion of fighting in urban terrain because it does not conduct a sufficient degree of experimentation and training to develop and sustain the skills for urban warfare. According to some officials, the U.S. armed forces devote "only a fraction of their training on the complex scenarios of urban combat." Over the last several years, the U.S. Army and the U.S. Marines have made progress at the tactical level, building urban training sites and experimenting with technology that is germane to urban warfare. However, neither the U.S. Army nor the Marines really maintain proficiency in urban operations because they do not spend enough time doing it. Randy Gangle, a retired colonel who works with the urban warfare experimentation laboratory, explains the problem lucidly: "if there is a failure in what we are doing, it's that we don't have enough balance in our training between warfare outside of cities and warfare inside of cities."[41]

Until recently, the U.S. Army doctrine for operations against asymmetric-thinking opponents has been relatively barren. The manual for operations other than war, now called stability operations and support operations (SOSO), was in revision for the better part of a decade and the last time it was issued was 1990. The approved and published *FM 3-07* (SOSO, 2003) includes only one eight-page chapter on Foreign Internal Defense (counterinsurgency) and does not even address counterinsurgency or asymmetric conflict in complex urban terrain. This relatively parsimonious chapter also fails to capture key lessons from the host of counterinsurgency experiences of the 1980s and 1990s. What's more, until 2003, the last Army doctrinal manual for urban operations was published 23 years ago, an indicator of how much importance is attached to these operations by the Army's core elites. The new urban operations manual (FM 3-06) is out and it is quite good. However, while it does capture most of the lessons from Somalia, it does not capture all of the key lessons from the Russians' urban operations in Chechnya. In fact, most heavy forces do not have urban operations as a mission essential task. In addition, the National Training Center, where heavy forces conduct their most intense training, does not even have one mock-up of an urban area.[42]

Doctrinal Change and Alternative Force Structures

Sacred cows make the best hamburger.

—General John Sheehan[43]

According to two military thinkers at the Army War College, "today's debate about the preferred structure of American military forces thus in the end is a debate about the future of war itself." And, a retired military officer know for unorthodox thinking posited, "at a time when the pace of technological and social changes is without precedent in human history, our military is clinging to the past. We are behaving like a blue-collar union in a smokestack industry." What is essential to the future of armored warfare is the ability to erase past expectations and perceptions of what tanks should do and to imagine and envision creative ways to use armor to meet the exigencies of the emerging and future security landscape. Asymmetry is really an afterthought in the tactical realm where full-spectrum dominance sounds neat but where tribal loyalty remains wedded to very conventionally focused training strategies. Before 11 September, mastering, or even acknowledging the asymmetric domain did not "offer opportunities for overwhelming victory associated with conventional warfare because asymmetry in any form is unlikely to ever threaten the nation's survival." However, now it is apparent that opponents who embrace asymmetric methods are as real a threat as any potential conventional opponent. It is also evident that heavy forces coupled to outdated force structures are not the ideal formations for fighting asymmetric warfare in complex terrain. In sum, "the challenges of the changing quality of conflict may require military forces to develop alternative strategies and capabilities, forces structure and design, or innovative applications of military power that today are in short supply."[44]

Today, the division remains the defining organization of the U.S. Army. It was created on a permanent basis in 1914 subsequent to Army Chief of Staff Leonard Wood's experiment with a maneuver division in San Antonio in 1911. The Stimson Plan, named after Secretary of War Stimson, was the catalyst for the establishment of the three-brigade division in the U.S. Army. Stimson first proposed his plan for four maneuver divisions in 1913 to all the general officers that were stationed within the continental United States. "Some of the older ones still had hesitated before so drastic a departure from what they knew." The 1910 *Field Services Regulations* were revised to reflect the new organization; it defined the division as "a self-contained unit made up of all necessary arms and services, and complete in itself with every requirement for independent action incident to its operations." And, although strategic requirements, doctrine, and tactics underwent various changes, eliminating the division for the sake of greater dispersion during the "pentomic era," or to more realistically meet the terrain and enemy situations in Vietnam, was almost inconceivable.[45]

By the 1980s the Army of Excellence (AOE) concept introduced the 'light infantry division' (LID), even though the Kupperman Study had asserted that the Army's organizational [divisional] structure would not permit it to win in a LIC environment. The study had proposed the creation of regionally oriented light infantry brigades to be trained and equipped under a pilot light infantry division training headquarters. In fact the LID was being designed to augment heavy forces even though it was originally conceived as a LIC organization. One author writing in the mid-1980s argued that the light infantry brigade concept clashed with the U.S. Army's large-unit, division and above emphasis. As a footnote to the centrality of the division, Doughty observed that from 1946–1976, the doctrine for the armor and artillery branches seemed almost static. "For most of the period under study, both performed in essentially the same fashion they had in World War II."[46]

"The combat division is the centerpiece of Army war-fighting doctrine and the focus of its operational plans." The RAND study also identified "the centrality of the division" as a distinctive characteristic of U.S. Army culture. This study asserts that the division has long been viewed as the "most prestigious Army assignment and the most sought-after organization in which to command troops." U.S. Army divisions comprise the greater part of its combat power; and to some degree, the Army assesses its state of preparedness by the number of divisions it maintains, especially regular Army divisions. "As an artifact of the industrial age, the division has remained continually in existence since before World War I." Although the Army has periodically redesigned the organization of the division, the division as a concept and an organizing principle remains unaltered. Another author supports this proposition, "recognizing that the development of American military tactics, doctrine, and war fighting organizations for future conflict has been rendered more difficult because the character of the threat is no longer specified, it is not surprising that the Army's Force XXI program has not resulted in any significant change in the war-fighting structure of Army forces since the Persian Gulf War."[47]

In contemporary Army thinking, the division is still the dominant U.S. Army organization that trains and fights as a team—the division combined arms team is still the centerpiece of the U.S. Army's war-fighting structure and doctrine. Even the creation of Force XXI, a truly innovative and forward-looking concept to fundamentally redesign the Army for information-age warfare, implicitly retains the idea of the division as a basic building block. "The very fact that Force XXI testing revolves around brigade, division, and corps operations suggests that test results will explicitly confirm the division's importance." In fact, the cultural resistance to move away from the division to a regimental-sized combined battle group at the end of the 20th century is as strong as was the Army's resistance to transition from regimental operations to divisional operations at the beginning of this century. Macgregor elucidates this problem: "trained and organized for a style of war that has changed very little since World War II, current Army organizational structures will limit the control and exploitation of superior military technology and human potential in future operations.[48]

To the degree that the central role of the Army division stems from cultural preference and resistance rather than a deliberately and comprehensively considered decision, it is likely that the Army may dismiss future changes in technology, the international security landscape, and the national security strategy, if these changes, in fact, prescribe the demise of its organizational centerpiece. With the current division-based force structure, the American Army "continues to reflect the distinguishing features of the industrial age forces that it developed during World War II." Today's Army forces, according to Macgregor, still comprise large industrial era forces capable of massing firepower.[49]

Since a regimental system is effective for small wars, a brigade-size battle group might be the most suitable organization for smaller scale contingencies. The British have an advantage since the regiment is embedded in their culture. However, although the U.S. Army is creating medium-weight and lighter brigades, there is still much intransigence about abandoning the division. A century ago, the regiment was the central organization of the U.S. Army, as was imperial policing (Philippines) a salient mission. Regimental-sized combined arms battle groups would be the most suitable adaptation to technology and to the emerging security landscape.[50] "If one can reduce warfare to the destruction of a few key target sets by small teams of warriors rather than the application of organized violence by large operational formations, military culture would then place more value on the former rather than the latter."[51]

Postscript

The officer corps as the core cultural elite of the U.S. Army must do some serious thinking and innovating about the future of war. "Thinking outside the box" must become a reality not just a popular but meaningless bumper sticker in the Army vernacular. Currently our culture is this "box" and most of our potential or real adversaries know our template—combined maneuver warfare, very mobile armor and airmobile formations, and massing effects with our technological superiority. Moreover, because our military culture has embraced the Jominian-Clausewitzian paradigm of war for so long, it will be hard to break this template. It requires more than just strapping on advanced technology to old systems and old ideas. Industrial and preindustrial opponents who are resolute and cunning will want to fight U.S. forces in complex terrain that undercuts our technological superiority, in urban environments for example. The institutional impetus for change is already here—senior U.S. Army leaders have made it clear that the U.S. Army must transform if it wants to remain relevant.[52]

However, military culture and large centralized and hierarchical institutions change very incrementally. At Fort Hood, where the largest single concentration of armor forces resides, there have been huge strides forward in the area of digital transformation, but there is no manifest change in thinking outside the orthodox and conventional methods of employing these forces. The National Training Center, where most of these forces conduct their annual "super bowl" training event, prides itself as a learning organization but it is not. NTC offers a superb and challenging tactical training environment but it seems to be the cultural Praetorian Guard of a paradigm lost. The box at NTC accounts for much about the orthodox box that Army culture has prescribed for itself—the observer controller group has turned "compliance with the template" into a very lock step series of checking checklists. It is a dangerous thing to transform the current doctrine, which already reflects only incremental and suboptimal change, into dogma. The U.S. Secretary of Defense, the Army Chief of Staff, and senior leaders are now driving change. However, the Army must reach a consensus to transform the organization and its organizational essence, unimpeded by tribal and cultural barriers.[53]

NOTES

1. *Army Field Manual, Wider Peacekeeping* (London: HMSO, December 1994), 2-3-2-4.
2. Michael Evans, "British Army Blueprint on Peacekeeping Highlights Rift with Washington," *The Times*, 30 November 1994, 21.
3. *FM 100-23, Peace Operations* (Washington, D.C.: U.S. Army, December 1994), 6-10.
4. Rich Rinaldo, interview by author, Newport News, Virginia, 21 March 2000; Charles Dobbie, Telephone interview by author, West Point, New York, 12 April 2000; and General Gordon Sullivan, Letter to General Sir Charles Guthrie, 22 December 1994, Washington, D.C.
5. Rinaldo Interview; and Dobbie Interview. Rinaldo and Dobbie were the principal authors of *FM 100-23* and *Wider Peacekeeping*.
6. Hew Strachan, *The Politics of the British Army* (New York: Clarendon Press, 1997), 222-33.
7. Russell F. Weigley, "Reflections on Lessons from Vietnam," in *Vietnam as History*, ed., Peter Braestrup (Washington, D.C.: University Press of America, 1984), 116; and Andrew J. Birtle, *U.S. Counterinsurgency and Contingency Operations Doctrine 1860-1941* (Washington, D.C.: U.S. Army Center of Military History, 1998), 7, 272-73.

8. Richard J. Newman, "Vietnam's Forgotten Lessons," *U.S. News and World Report*, 1 May 2000.

9. Richard Holbrooke, *To End a War* (New York: Random House, 1998), 217–18.

10. Dobbie interview.

11. Rinaldo interview.

12. Senior Officer Review Group, "After Action Report, FM 100-23, Peace Operations," (Fort Monroe, VA: HQ, TRADOC, 15 September 1993), 2.

13. Ibid.

14. Rinaldo interview; and LTC Richard Hooker, Interview by author, West Point, New York, 24 April 2000.

15. Rod Thornton, "Peace Support Operations and the Health of the Military Organization," 14, 23; and John Mackinlay, Telephone interview by author, 17 March 2000; and Phil Wilkinson, "The Development of Peace Support Operations Doctrine," Unpublished draft paper, King's College London, March 2000), 11–12. Wilkinson co-authored the final edition of *Wider Peacekeeping* and he essentially wrote the British military's subsequent 1998 manual *Peace Support Operations.* The newer manual is joint and, significantly, drops wider peacekeeping's absolute adherence to consent and impartiality for gray area missions.

16. Wilkinson, 10–15.

17. Dobbie interview; John Mackinlay and Jarat Chopra, *A Draft Concept of Second Generation Multinational Operations 1993* (Providence, RI: Thomas J. Watson Institute for International Studies, 1993); and Carol Hodge, "Slimey Limeys," *The New Republic*, 9&16 January 1995, 21.

18. The notion of regimental-size battle groups is not new, most notably, Colonel Doug Macgregor has proposed such forces in *Breaking the Phalanx* (Westport, CT: Praeger, 1997), 70–81.

19. For a discussion of PDD 25, see Sarah B. Sewell, Deputy Assistant Secretary of Defense for Peacekeeping and Peace Enforcement Policy, Remarks to "International Peacekeeping 95" Conference, Washington, D.C., 15 November 1995.

20. Harvey M. Sapolsky, "On the Theory of Military Innovation," *Breakthroughs* 9 (Spring 2000): 35, 38.

21. *Joint Warfare Publication 3-50, Peace Support Operations* (London: HMSO, 1998), 1-2, 2-7, 6-11–6-13.

22. Peter Viggo Jakobsen, "The Emerging Consensus on Gray Area Peace Operations Doctrine: Will It Make a Difference?" (Unpublished paper, University of Copenhagen, January 2000), 7–8.

23. Christopher Dandeker, "The United Kingdom: The Overstretched Military," in *The Postmodern Military*, eds. Charles C. Moskos, John Allen Williams, and David R. Segal (New York: Oxford University Press, 2000), 36–37.

24. Don M. Snider, "Postmodern Soldiers," *World Policy Journal* 17 (Spring 2000): 49–50.

25. Jeffrey Record, *Beyond Military Reform* (New York: Pergamon-Brassey's, 1988), 84.

26. Ibid., 84–85.

27. Ibid., 85.

28. See Donald M. Snow, *The Shape of the Future*, 2nd ed. (New York: M. E. Sharpe, 1995), 16–27, 38–52, for a discussion of the probability that western powers will employ force in the third world.

29. For a more thorough explanation of the truism that big powers do small wars poorly, see Robert M. Cassidy, "Why Great Powers Fight Small Wars Badly," *Military Review* 82 (September/October 2002): 41–53.

30. Williamson Murray, ed., *Army Transformation: A View from the Army War College* (Carlisle, PA: Strategic Studies Institute, July 2001), 17.

31. Cassidy: 52.

32. Arnaud de Borchgrave, "Al Qaeda's Privileged Sanctuary," *Washington Times*, 20 June 2002, 19.

33. Andrew F. Krepinevich, *The Army and Vietnam* (Baltimore, MD: Johns Hopkins University Press, 1986), 70–71, 172–77.

34. For an in depth explanation of enhancing regime legitimacy and demonstrating a credible capacity to coerce in a counterinsurgency context, see Larry Cable, "Reinventing the Round Wheel: Insurgency, Counter-Insurgency, and Peacekeeping Post Cold War," *Small War and Insurgencies* 4 (Autumn 1993): 228–62.

35. Legro, "Culture and Preferences in the International Cooperation Two-Step:" 127; and James M. Smith. "USAF Culture and Cohesion: Building an Air Force and Space Force for the 21st Century," *INSS Occasional Paper 19* (Colorado Springs, CO: USAF INSS, 1996), 11–12.

36. James Dewar et al., *Army Culture and Planning in a Time of Great Change* (Santa Monica, CA: RAND, 1996), 2–3, 8, 42.

37. Paul Van Riper and Robert H. Scales, "Preparing for Warfare in the 21st Century," *Parameters* 27 (Autumn 1997): 5.

38. Ibid. David L. Gray, "New Age Military Progressives: U.S. Army Officer Professionalism in the Information Age" in *Army Transformation: a View from the Army War College*, ed., Williamson Murray (Carlisle, PA: Strategic Studies Institute, July 2001), 40.

39. Richard Duncan Downie, *Learning from Conflict: The U.S. Military in Vietnam, El Salvador, and the Drug War* (Westport, CT: Praeger, 1998), 20–24.

40. Downie, 5, 22–25, 34.

41. Kim Burger, "U.S. Joint Ops Urban Warfare Training 'Insufficient,'" *Jane's Defence Weekly*, 2 October 2002, World Wide Web Early Bird.

42. As a side note, some typical responses by Army officers to comments about the difficulty of urban operations and the Russians' defeat in Chechnya is to diminish the importance of those lessons by asserting that the Russians were inept and stupid. However, Army officers in the early 1960s made similar comments about the French defeat in Indochina, writing off the Vietminh victory to French military ineptitude.

43. Quoted in Melissa Applegate, *Preparing for Asymmetry: As Seen Through the Lens of Joint Vision 2020* (Carlisle Barracks, PA: Strategic Studies Institute, September 2001), 15.

44. Van Riper and Scales: 5; Ralph Peters, "The Future of Armored Warfare," *Parameters* 27 (Autumn 1997): 52, 56; and Applegate, 23–24.

45. Weigley, *History of the United States Army*, 334–35; John B. Wilson, *Maneuver and Firepower: The Evolution of Divisions and Separate Brigades* (Washington, D.C.: U.S. Army Center of Military History, 1998), 33–34; and Robert A. Doughty, "The Evolution of U.S. Army Tactical Doctrine, 1946–76," *Leavenworth Paper No. 1* (Ft Leavenworth, KS: U.S. Army CGSC, 1979), 1.

46. Robert H. Kupperman and Associates, Inc., *Low Intensity Conflict, Vol. 1, Main Report*, AD-A 137260 (Fort Monroe, VA: U.S. Army Training and Doctrine Command, 1983), 47; Downie, 75–77; John L. Romjue, *The Army of Excellence: The Development of the 1980s Army* (Fort Monroe, VA: U.S. Army TRADOC Military History Office, 1997), 119; Peter N. Kafkalas, "The Light Infantry Divisions and Low Intensity Conflict: Are

They Losing Sight of Each Other?" *Military Review* 66 (January 1986): 18–27 in *The Army of Excellence*, 119; and Doughty, 48.

47. Dewar et al., 16, 28–29; Weigley, *The History of the United States Army*, 330–40; and Douglas A. Macgregor, *Breaking the Phalanx: A New Design for Landpower in the 21st Century* (Westport, CT: Praeger, 1997), 50.

48. Dewar et al., 16, 28–29; and Macgregor, 62, 227.

49. Dewar et al., 29; and Macgregor, 59.

50. The notion of regimental-size battle groups is not new. Most notably, Colonel Doug Macgregor has proposed the creation of such forces in *Breaking the Phalanx*, 70–81.

51. Gray, 39.

52. This postscript is essentially excerpted from Robert M. Cassidy, *Russia in Afghanistan and Chechnya: Military Strategic Culture and the Paradoxes of Asymmetric Conflict* (Carlisle, PA: Strategic Studies Institute, 2003), 65–66.

53. Cassidy, 65–66.

Bibliography

1st Battalion Prince of Wales' Own Regiment of Yorkshire News. *The White Rose* 35 (December 1993): 10–37.

Adams, Thomas K. "Military Doctrine and the Organization Culture of the U.S. Army." Ph.D. diss., Syracuse University, 1990.

Allard, Kenneth J. "Lessons Unlearned: Somalia and Joint Doctrine." *Joint Forces Quarterly*. Number 9 (Autumn 1995): 105–9.

Allard, Kenneth. *Somalia Operations: Lessons Learned*. Washington, D.C.: National Defense University Press, 1995.

Allison, Graham T. *Essence of Decision: Explaining the Cuban Missile Crisis*. Boston: Little, Brown, and Company, 1971.

Alvis, Colonel Michael W. "Understanding the Role of Casualties in U.S. Peace Operations." *Landpower Essay Series No. 99–1*. Arlington, VA: Association of the U.S. Army, January 1999.

Ambrose, Stephen F. *Upton and the Army*. Baton Rouge, LA: Louisiana State University Press, 1964.

Annan, Kofi. "UN Forces Withdraw from Somalia." *Foreign Policy Bulletin* 5 (May/June 1995): 36–38.

Applegate, Melissa. *Preparing for Asymmetry: As Seen Through the Lens of Joint Vision 2020*. Carlisle Barracks, PA: Strategic Studies Institute, September 2001, 15.

Army Doctrine Publication, Volume 1, Operations. London: HMSO, June 1994. 1995): 105–09.

Army Field Manual, Volume I, The Fundamentals, Part 1, The Application of Force. London: HMSO, 1985.

Army Field Manual, Volume V, All Arms Tactics, Special Operations, and Techniques, Part 1, Peacekeeping Operations. London: HMSO, 1988

Army Field Manual, Volume 5, Operations Other Than War, Part 2, Wider Peacekeeping. London: HMSO, December 1994.

Arnold, MG S. L. "Somalia: An Operation Other Than War." *Military Review* 73 (December 1993): 26–35.

Atkinson, Rick. *The Long Gray Line*. Boston, MA: Houghton Mifflin Company, 1989.

———. *Crusade: The Untold Story of the Persian Gulf War*. New York: Houghton Mifflin Company, 1993.

———. "The Raid That Went Wrong." *Washington Post*, 30 January 1994, A1.

Avant, Deborah D. *Political Institutions and Military Change: Lessons from Peripheral Wars*. Ithaca, NY: Cornell University Press, 1994.

Barnett, Correlli. *Britain and Her Army: 1509–1970*. New York: William Morrow and Company, 1970.

Bartlett's Familiar Quotations. Franklin Electronic Bookman, 1998.

BDM Corporation. *A Study of the Strategic Lessons in Vietnam, Volume III Results of the War*. Washington, D.C.: Defense Technical Information Center, 1981.

Beckett, Ian. "The Study of Counter-Insurgency: A British Perspective." *Small Wars and Insurgencies* 1 (April 1990): 47–53.

Beckett, Ian, and John Pimlott, eds. *Armed Forces and Modern Counter-Insurgency* New York: St. Martin's Press, Inc., 1985.

Bell, J. Bowyer. "Revolts Against the Crown: Tthe British Response to Imperial Insurgency." *Parameters* 4 (1974): 31–46.

Berdal, Mats. "Whither UN Peacekeeping," *Adelphi Paper 281*. London: Brassey's, 1993.

Betts, Richard K. "Delusions of Impartiality." *Current* Number 370 (February 1995): 27–32.

Bi-MNC Directive, *NATO Doctrine for Peace Support Operations*. Brussels: Supreme Headquarters Allied Powers Europe, 1995.

Birtle, Andrew J. *U.S. Counterinsurgency and Contingency Operations Doctrine 1860–1941*. Washington, D.C.: U.S. Army Center of Military History, 1998.

Black, Ian. "Rifkind Patches Up Rift with France." The Guardian, 17 July 1995, 8.

Blue Helmets: A Review of UN Peacekeeping. 3rd ed. New York: UN Department of Public Information, 1996.

Bolger, Daniel P. "The Ghosts of Omdurman." *Parameters* 21 (Autumn 1991): 28–39.

———. *Savage Peace: Americans at War in the 1990s*. Novato, CA: Presidio Press, 1995.

Booth, Ken. *Strategy and Ethnocentrism*. New York: Holmes and Meier Publishers, Inc., 1979.

———. "The Concept of Strategic Culture Affirmed" in Strategic Power USA/USSR. ed. Carl G. Jacobsen. New York: St. Martin's Press, 1990.

de Borchgrave, Arnaud. "Al Qaeda's Privileged Sanctuary." *Washington Times*. 20 June 2002, 19.

Boutros-Ghali, Boutros. *Supplement to An Agenda for Peace*. New York: United Nations Press, 1995.

Bowden, Mark. *Black Hawk Down*. New York: Penguin Books, 1999.

Brady, Michael J. "The Army and the Strategic Military Legacy of Vietnam." Master's Thesis, U.S. Army Command and General Staff College, 1990.

Braestrup, Peter, ed. *Vietnam as History*. Washington, D.C.: University Press of America, 1984.

Brand, Joel. "Rose Considered Showing Airstrike Plans to the Serbs." *The Times*, 16 January 1995, 12.

BRITBAT End of Tour Report. Vitez Camp, Bosnia: 1st Battalion PWO, October 1993.

Brodie, Bernard. *War and Politics*. New York: Macmillan Publishing Company, 1973.

Builder, Carl. *The Masks of War: American Military Styles in Strategy and Analysis*. Baltimore, MD: Johns Hopkins University Press, 1989.

Bulloch, Gavin. "The Development of Doctrine for Counterinsurgency—the British Experience." *The British Army Review* Number 111 (December 1995): 21–24.

———. "Military Doctrine and Counter-Insurgency: a British Perspective." Parameters 26 (Summer 1996): 4–16.

———. Interview by author, 16 December 1999, Trenchard Lines, Upavon, England.

———. Telephone interview by author, 9 March 2000, West Point, New York.

Burger, Kim. "U.S. Joint Ops Urban Warfare Training 'Insufficient.'" *Jane's Defence Weekly*. 2 October 2002, World Wide Web Early Bird.

Burk, James, ed. *The Adaptive Military: Armed Forces in a Turbulent World*, 2nd ed. New Brunswick, NJ: Transaction Publishers, 1998.

Burns, John F. "British Army's Job in Bosnia: to Keep Risky Lifeline Open," *New York Times*, 23 August 1993, A3.

Burroughs, Peter. "An Unreformed Army" in *The Oxford History of the British Army*. eds. David Chandler and Ian Beckett. New York: Oxford University Press, 1996.

Cable, Larry. "Reinventing the Round Wheel: Insurgency, Counter-Insurgency, and Peacekeeping Post Cold War." *Small Wars and Insurgencies* 4 (Autumn 1993): 228–62.

Campbell, Kenneth J. "Once Burned, Twice Cautious: Explaining the Weinberger-Powell Doctrine," *Armed Forces and Society* 24 (Spring 1998): 357–74.

Cassidy, Robert M. "Why Great Powers Fight Small Wars Badly." *Military Review* 82 (September/October 2002): 41–53.

———. *Russia in Afghanistan and Chechnya: Military Strategic Culture and the Paradoxes of Asymmetric Conflict*. Carlisle, PA: Strategic Studies Institute, 2003.

Catton, Bruce, *A Stillness at Appomatox*. New York: Washington Square Press, 1953.

CFP 300, Canada's Army. Kingston: Chief of the Canadian Defence Staff, 1995.

Chandler, David and Ian Beckett, eds. *The Oxford History of the British Army*. New York: Oxford University Press, 1996.

Chapman, Anne W. et al. *Prepare the Army for War: A Historical Overview of the Army Training and Doctrine Command, 1973–1998*. Fort Monroe, VA: U.S. Army TRADOC Military History Office, 1998.

The Charter of the United Nations. New York: UN Department of Public Information, 1993.

Cheney, Dick. *Defense Strategy for the 1990s: The Regional Defense Strategy*. Washington, D.C.: GPO, January 1993.

Childs, John. "The Restoration Army, 1660–1702" in *The Oxford History of the British Army*. eds. David Chandler and Ian Beckett. New York: Oxford University Press, 1996.

Clarke, Walter and Robert Gosende. "The Political Component: The Missing Vital Element in U.S. Intervention Planning." *Parameters* 26 (Autumn 1996): 35–51.

Cohen, Elliot A. "Constraints on America's Conduct of Small Wars." *International Security* 9 (Fall 1984): 151–81.

———. *Making Do With Less, or Coping with Upton's Ghost*. Carlisle, PA: U.S. Army War College Strategic Studies Institute, May 1995.

Cohen, Lenard J. "The Disintegration of Yugoslavia." *Current History* 91 (November 1992): 369–75.

———. *Broken Bonds: Yugoslavia's Disintegration and Balkan Politics in Transition*. 2nd ed. Boulder, CO: Westview Press, 1995.

Cohen, Roger. "British Commander in Bosnia: In a Quagmire and Sniped At From All Sides." *New York Times*, 25 September 1994, 14.

———. "UN General Opposes More Bosnia Force." *New York Times*, 29 September 1994, 7.

"Congressional Hearing Summary." Senate Armed Services Committee: 12 May 1994. U.S. Military Operations in Somalia. Washington, D.C.: U.S. Army Congressional Activities Division, 13 May 1994. Photocopied.

Connaughton, Richard. "Interests, Conscience, and Somalia." Unpublished paper, December 1992. In Charles Dobbie. "A Concept for Post-Cold War Peacekeeping." *Survival* 36 (Autumn 1994): 121–48.

———. "Sea of Troubles." Unpublished manuscript. Dorset, England, 1999.

———. Telephone Interview by author, 1 April 2000, West Point, New York.

Cousens, Richard P., United Kingdom Liaison Officer to the United States Army Training and Doctrine Command. Telephone Interview by author, 10 March 1997, Medford, MA.

Crowe, William J. Jr. "What I've Learned," *Washingtonian* 25 (November 1989): 109 in Christopher M. Gacek. *The Logic of Force: The Dilemma of Limited Force in American Foreign Policy*. New York: Columbia University Press, 1994.

Dandeker, "The United Kingdom: The Overstretched Military." In *The Postmodern Military*. eds. Charles C. Moskos, John Allen Williams, and David R. Segal. New York: Oxford University Press.

Daniel, Donald C. F. and Bradd C. Hayes. *Coercive Inducement and the Containment of International Crises*. Washington, D.C.: United States Institute of Peace Press, 1999.

Darnton, John. "Questions over Mission in Bosnia: Peacekeeper Nations Rethink Aims." *New York Times*, Late New York Edition, 3 June 1995, 5.

———. "UN Buildup in Bosnia Eyes 'Mogadishu Line.'" *New York Times*, 6 June 1995, A18.

Dauber, Cori. "Poisoning the Well: The Weinberger Doctrine and Public Argument Over Military Intervention." Unpublished manuscript. UNC Chapel Hill, 1998.

Davis, Vincent, ed. *Civil-Military Relations and the Not-Quite Wars of the Present and Future*. Carlisle, PA: Strategic Studies Institute, 1996.

Decker, General George H. "Doctrine," *Army* 7 (February 1961): 60–61.

Defence Implications of Recent Events. Defence Committee, Tenth Report. London: HMSO, 11 July 1990.

Denaro, Brigadier A. G. "Peacekeeping with the UN." *The British Army Review* Number 113 (August 1996): 25–27.

Department of History. *Officer's Professional Reading Guide*. West Point, NY: United States Military Academy, 1996.

Design for Military Operations: The British Military Doctrine. London: HMSO, 1989.

Dewar, James, et al. *Army Culture and Planning in a Time of Great Change*. Santa Monica, CA: RAND Corporation, 1996.

Dewar, Michael. *Brushfire Wars: Minor Campaigns of the British Army Since 1945*. London: Robert Hale, 1990.

Dobbie, Charles. "A Concept for Post-Cold War Peacekeeping." *Survival* 36 (Autumn 1994): 121–48.

———. Telephone interview by author, 12 April 2000, West Point, New York.

Doty, Grant R. "Peace Operations and the U.S. Army: A Transition." Unpublished paper. Yale University, May 1996.

Doughty, Robert A. *The Evolution of U.S. Army Tactical Doctrine, 1946–76.* Leavenworth Paper No. 1. Ft Leavenworth, KS: U.S. Army CGSC, 1979.

Downie, Richard Duncan. *Learning from Conflict: The U.S. Military in Vietnam, El Salvador, and the Drug War.* Westport, CT: Praeger, 1998.

Duffy, Michael, Theo Farrell, and Geoffrey Sloan, eds. *Doctrine and Military Effectiveness.* Strategic Policy Studies I. Exeter, England: Britannia Royal Naval Colleg, 1997.

Duncan, Colonel Alastair "Operating in Bosnia," *The RUSI Journal* 139 (June 1994): 11–18.

Dunn, Peter M. "The American Army: the Vietnam War, 1965–1973" in *Armed Forces and Modern Counter-Insurgency.* eds. Ian Beckett and John Pimlott (New York: St. Martin's Press, Inc., 1985

Durch, William J. and James A. Schear, eds. *UN Peacekeeping, American Politics, and the Uncivil Wars of the 1990s.* New York: St. Martin's Press, 1996.

Eikenberry, Karl W. "Take No Casualties." *Parameters* 26 (Summer 1996): 109–18.

Emploi des Forces Terrestres dans l'Action des Forces Armees. Metz: French Doctrine and Training Command, 1996.

Evans, Michael. "British Army Blueprint on Peacekeeping Highlights Rift with Washington." *The Times,* 30 November 1994, 21.

Farrell, Theo. "Sliding into War: The Somalia Syndrome and the U.S. Army Peace Operations Doctrine." *International Peacekeeping* 2 (Summer 1995): 194–214.

———. "Making Sense of Doctrine." In *Doctrine and Military Effectiveness,* eds. Michael Duffy, Thee Farrell, and Geoffrey Sloan. Exeter, England: Britannia Royal Naval College, 1997.

Fautua, David T. "The Long Pull Army: NSC 68, the Korean War, and the Creation of the Cold War U.S. Army." *The Journal of Military History* 61 (January 1997): 93–120.

Fetherston, A. O. Ramsbotham, and T. Woodhouse. "UNPROFOR: Some Observations from a Conflict Resolution Perspective." *International Peacekeeping* 1 (Summer 1994): 179–203.

Fitton, Robert A. *Leadership Quotations from the Military Tradition.* Boulder, CO: Westview Press, 1993.

FM 100-1, The Army. Washington, D.C.: United States Army, 1986.

FM 100-1, The Army. Washington, D.C.: United States Army, 1994.

FM 100-5, Operations. Draft. Washington, D.C.: United States Army, 1992.

FM 100-5, Operations. Washington, D.C.: United States Army, 1993.

FM 100-20, Military Operations in Low Intensity Conflict. Washington, D.C.: United States Army and United States Air Force, 1990.

FM 100-23, Peace Operations. Washington, D.C.: United States Army, 1994.

FM 3-07, Stability Operations and Support Operations. Washington, D.C.: Unites States Army, 2003.

Foster, Edward. *NATO's Military in the Age of Crisis Management.* London: Royal United Services Institute for Defence Studies, 1995,

Forster, Anthony. Interview by author, 19 December 1993, Manchester, England.

French, David. *The British Way in Warfare: 1688–2000.* London: Unwin-Hyman, 1990.

Gacek, Christopher M. *The Logic of Force: The Dilemma of Limited Force in American Foreign Policy.* New York: Columbia University Press, 1994.

Gates, David. "The Transformation of the Army 1783–1815," in *The Oxford History of the British Army*. eds. David Chandler and Ian Beckett. New York: Oxford University Press, 1996.

Geertz, Clifford. *The Interpretation of Cultures*. New York: Basic Books, 1973.

Gentry, James. "Military Force in an Age of National Cowardice." *Washington Quarterly* 21 (Autumn 1998): 179–91.

George, Alexander L. "Case Studies and Theory Development: The Method of Structured, Focused Comparison." In *Diplomacy: New Approaches in History, Theory, and Policy*. ed. Paul Gordon Lauren. New York: MacMillan, 1979.

George, Alexander L. and Richard Smoke. *Deterrence in American Foreign Policy* New York: Columbia University Press, 1974.

Glenny, Misha. *The Fall of Yugoslavia*. New York: Penguin Books, 1993.

Goulding, Marrack. "The Evolution of United Nations Peacekeeping." *International Affairs* 69 (1993): 451–64.

Gow, James. *Triumph of the Lack of Will*. New York: Columbia University Press, 1997.

Gray, Colin S. "National Style in Strategy: The American Example." *International Security* 6 (Fall 1981): 21–47.

———. "Strategic Culture as Context: the First Generation of Theory Strikes Back." *Review of International Studies* 25 (1999): 49–69.

Gray, David L. "New Age Military Progressives: U.S. Army Officer Professionalism in the Information Age." In *Army Transformation: a View from the Army War College*. ed. Williamson Murray. Carlisle, PA: Strategic Studies Institute, July 2001.

Gwynne Jones, Alun. "Training and Doctrine in the British Army Since 1945" in *The Theory and Practice of War*. ed. Michael Howard. New York: Praeger, 1966.

Hackett, John Winthrop. *The Profession of Arms*. London: The Times Publishing House, 1962.

Halperin, Morton H. *Bureaucratic Politics and Foreign Policy*. Washington, D.C.: The Brookings Institution, 1974.

Handel, Michael. *Masters of War: Sun Tzu, Clausewitz, and Jomini*. Portland, OR: Frank Cass and CO. Ltd., 1992.

Haswell, Jock. *The British Army: A Concise History*. London: Book Club Associates, 1977.

Head, William and Earl H. Tilford Jr., eds. *The Eagle in the Desert*. Westport, CT: Praeger, 1996.

Herbert, Paul H. " 'Deciding What Has to Be Done': General William E. Depuy and the 1976 Edition of FM 100-5, Operations." *Leavenworth Paper No. 16*. Fort Leavenworth, KS: Combat Studies Institute, U.S. Army CGSC, 1988.

Hirsch, John L. and Robert B. Oakley. *Somalia and Operation Restore Hope*. Washington, D.C.: United States Institute of Peace Press, 1995.

Hodge, Carol. "Slimey Limeys." *The New Republic*, 9&16 January 1995.

Hoffman, F. G. *Decisive Force: The New American Way of War*. Westport, CT: Praeger, 1996.

Holbrooke, Richard. *To End a War*. New York: Random House, 1998.

Hooker, Lieutenant Colonel Richard. Interview by author, 24 April 2000, West Point, New York.

Howard, Michael, ed. *The Theory and Practice of War*. New York: Praeger, 1966.

———. *The Continental Commitment*. Bristol, Great Britain: Western Printing Services Ltd., 1972.

————. "The Forgotten Dimensions of Strategy." *Foreign Affairs* 57 (Summer 1979): 975–86.

Howe, Jonathan T. "The United States and United Nations in Somalia: The Limits of Involvement." *The Washington Quarterly* 18 (Summer 1995): 49–62.

"Humanitarian Role in Bosnia." *Castle: Journal of the Royal Anglian Regiment* 9 (December 1994): 30–38.

Huntington, Samuel P. *The Soldier and the State: the Theory and Politics of Civil-Military Relations.* Cambridge, MA: The Belknap Press, 1957.

————. "The Evolution of U.S. National Strategy" in *U.S. National Security Strategy for the 1990s.* eds. Daniel J. Kaufman, David S. Clark, and Kevin P. Sheehan. Baltimore: Johns Hopkins University Press, 1991.

Jacobsen, Carl, ed. *Strategic Power USA/USSR.* New York: St Martin's Press, 1990.

Jakobsen, Peter Viggo. "The Emerging Consensus on Gray Area Peace Operations Doctrine: Will it Make a Difference?" Unpublished Paper. University of Copenhagen, January 2000.

Janowitz, Morris. *The Professional Soldier.* New York: The Free Press, 1960.

Jeffrey, Keith. "Colonial Warfare 1900–39" in *Warfare in the Twentieth Century: Theory and Practice.* eds. Colin McInnes and G. D. Sheffield. Winchester, MA: Unwin Hyman, Inc., 1988.

Jenkins, Brian M. *The Unchangeable War.* RM-6278-2-ARPA. Santa Monica, CA: RAND, 1970.

Johnston, Alistair. "Thinking About Strategic Culture." *International Security* 19 (Spring 1995): 32–64.

————. *Cultural Realism: Strategic Culture and Grand Strategy in Chinese History.* Princeton, NJ: Princeton University Press, 1995.

Joint Warfare Publication 3-50, Peace Support Operations. London: HMSO, 1998.

Jones, David R. "Soviet Strategic Culture" in *Strategic Power USA/USSR.* ed. Carl G. Jacobsen. New York: St. Martin's Press, 1990.

Joulwan, General (Ret.) George. Discussion with author, 24 April 2000, West Point, New York.

Kafkalas, Peter N. "The Light Infantry Divisions and Low Intensity Conflict: Are They Losing Sight of Each Other?" *Military Review* 66 (January 1986): 18–27.

Kaufman, Daniel J., David S. Clark, and Kevin P. Sheehan, eds. *U.S. National Security Strategy for the 1990s.* Baltimore: Johns Hopkins University Press, 1991.

Keohane, Robert O., ed. *NeoRealism and Its Critics.* New York: Columbia University Press, 1986.

Kier, Elizabeth. "Culture and Military Doctrine: France Between the Wars." *International Security* 19 (Spring 1995): 65–93.

King, Gary, Robert O. Keohane, and Sidney Verba. *Designing Social Inquiry.* Princeton, NJ: Princeton University Press, 1994.

Kissinger, Henry. "American Strategic Doctrine and Diplomacy." In *The Theory and Practice of War.* ed. Michael Howard. New York: Praeger, 1966.

————. "The Vietnam Negotiations." *Foreign Affairs* 47 (January 1969): 211–34.

————. *Diplomacy.* New York: Simon and Schuster, 1994.

Klein, Bradley S. "Hegemony and Strategic Culture: American Power Projection and Alliance Defence Politics." *Review of International Studies* 14 (1988): 133–48.

Klein, Yitzhak. "A Theory of Strategic Culture." *Comparative Strategy* 10 (1991): 3–23.

Knorr, Klaus, ed. *Power, Strategy, and Security: A World Politics Reader*. Princeton, N. J.: Princeton University Press, 1983.

Krepinevich, Andrew F. *The Army and Vietnam*. Baltimore, MD: Johns Hopkins University Press, 1986.

Kretchik, Walter E. "Force Protection Disparities." *Military Review* 77 (July–August 1997): 73–78.

Kupperman, Robert H., and Associates, Inc., *Low Intensity Conflict, Vol. 1, Main Report*. AD-A 137260. Fort Monroe, VA: U.S. Army Training and Doctrine Command, 1983.

Larsen, Eric V. *Casualties and Consensus: The Historical Role of Casualties in Domestic Support for U.S. Military Operations*. Santa Monica, CA: RAND, 1996.

Layne, Christopher. "The Unipolar Illusion" in *The Cold War and After*. eds. Sean M. Lynn-Jones and Steven E. Miller. Cambridge, MA: MIT Press, 1997.

Lee, Emanoel. *To the Bitter End*. New York: Viking Penguin Inc., 1985.

Legro, Jeffrey W. "Military Culture and Inadvertent Escalation in World War II." *International Security* 18 (Spring 1994): 108–42.

———. "Culture and Preferences in the International Cooperation Two-Step." *American Political Science Review* 90 (March 1996): 118–38.

Lessons Learned Bulletin Number 1. Upavon, England: Tactical Doctrine Retrieval Centre, 1993.

Liddell Hart, B. H. *The British Way in Warfare*. New York: The Macmillan Company, 1933.

———. *When Britain Goes to War: Adaptability and Mobility*. London: Faber and Faber Limited, 1935.

———. *Strategy*. 2nd ed. New York: Praeger, 1967.

Locher, James R., 3rd. "The Goldwater-Nichols Act: Ten Years Later." *Joint Forces Quarterly* 13 (Autumn 1996): 10–17.

Lord, Carnes. "American Strategic Culture." *Comparative Strategy* 5 (Fall 1985): 269–91.

Lynn-Jones, Sean and Steven E. Miller, eds. *The Cold War and After*. Cambridge, MA: MIT Press, 1997.

Lyons, Terrence and Ahmed I. Samatar. *Somalia: State Collapse, Multilateral Intervention, and Strategies for Political Reconstruction*. Washington, D.C.: Brookings Institute, 1995.

Macgregor, Douglas A. *Breaking the Phalanx: A New Design for Landpower in the 21st Century*. Westport, CT: Praeger, 1997.

Mack, Andrew. "Why Big Nations Lose Small Wars" in *Power, Strategy, and Security: A World Politics Reader*. ed. Klaus Knorr. Princeton, NJ: Princeton University Press, 1983.

Mackinlay, John. "Improving Multifunctional Forces." *Survival* 36 (Autumn 1994): 149–73.

———, ed. *A Guide to Peace Support Operations*. Providence, RI: Thomas J. Watson Institute for International Studies, 1996.

———. "Peace Support Operations Doctrine." *The British Army Review* Number 113 (August 1996): 5–14.

———. "War Lords." *RUSI Journal* 143 (April 1998): 24–32.

———. Telephone interview by author, 16 March 2000, West Point, New York.

———. Telephone interview by author, 17 March 2000, West Point, New York.

Mackinlay, John and Jarat Chopra. *A Draft Concept of Second Generation Multinational Operations 1993*. Providence, RI: Thomas J. Watson Institute for International Studies, 1993.

Mackinlay, John and Randolph Kent. "Complex Emergencies Doctrine: The British are Still the Best." *The RUSI Journal* 142 (April 1997): 39–44.

Macmillan, Alan. "Strategic Culture and National Ways in Warfare: the British Case." *RUSI Journal* 140 (October 1995): 33–38.

"Macneil/Lehrer Newshour." PBS-TV, 29 November 1994. In *Current News Supplement*, U.S. Department of Defense, 1 December 1994, A2.

Mariano, Stephen J. "Peacekeepers Attend the Never Again School." Master's Thesis, U. S. Naval Postgraduate School, 1995.

Mason, Tony. *Air Power: a Centennial Appraisal*. London: Brassey's Ltd., 1994.

Matloff, Maurice. "The American Approach to War: 1919–1945" in *The Theory and Practice of War*. ed. Michael Howard. New York: Praeger, 1966.

———. "Allied Strategy in Europe, 1939–1945," in *Makers of Modern Strategy*. ed. Peter Paret. Princeton, NJ: Princeton University Press, 1986.

McDonough, Colonel James R. "Building the New FM 100-5." *Military Review* 71 (October 1991): 2–12.

McInnes, Colin. *Hot War, Cold War: The British Army's Way in Warfare 1945–1995*. Washington, D.C.: Brassey's, 1996.

McInnes, Colin and G. D. Sheffield, eds. *Warfare in the Twentieth Century: Theory and Practice*. Winchester, MA: Unwin Hyman, Inc., 1988.

McNamara, Robert S. *In Retrospect: The Tragedy and Lessons of Vietnam*. New York: Times Books, 1995.

Meade, MG David C. U.S. Army and William David, LTC, US Army. "Restore Hope, Somalia 1992–1994." Unpublished Draft Article, Fort Drum, NY, May 1994.

Mearsheimer, John J. "Back to the Future." In *The Cold War and After*. eds. Sean M. Lynn-Jones and Steven E. Miller. Cambridge, MA: MIT Press, 1997.

Michaels, Marguerite. "Peacemaking War." *Time*, 26 July 1993, 48.

Mileham, Patrick. "Ethos: British Army Officership 1962 – 1992." *The Occasional Number 19*. Camberley, England: Strategic and Combat Studies Institute, 1996.

Mockaitis, Thomas R. *British Counterinsurgency, 1919–60*. New York: St. Martin's Press, 1990.

———. "A New Era of Counter-Insurgency." *The RUSI Journal* 136 (Spring 1991): 73–78.

———. "Low-Intensity Conflict: The British Experience." *Conflict Quarterly* 13 (Winter 1993): 7–16.

Moens, Alexander and Christopher Anstis. *Disconcerted Europe*. Boulder, CO: Westview Press, 1994.

Mohonk Criteria for Humanitarian Assistance in Complex Emergencies. Washington, D.C.: The Task Force on Ethical and Legal Issues in Humanitarian Assistance, March 1994.

Montgomery, LTG (Ret.) Thomas M. . Interview by author, 14 March 2000, West Point, New York.

Moskos, Charles C., John Allen Williams, and David R. Segal, eds. *The Postmodern Military*. New York: Oxford University Press, 2000.

Motley, James B. "U.S. Unconventional Conflict Policy and Strategy." *Military Review* 70 (January 1990): 2–16.

Murray, Williamson. ed. *Army Transformation: A View from the Army War College*. Carlisle, PA: Strategic Studies Institute, July 2001.

Murray, Williamson and Allan R. Millett, eds. *Military Innovation in the Interwar Period.* New York: Cambridge University Press, 1996.

Nagl, John. "Learning to Eat Soup with a Knife: British and American Counterinsurgency Learning During the Malayan Emergency and the Vietnam War." Unpublished Ph.D. diss., Oxford University, 1997.

———. Between 1997 and 1999, John Nagl provided advice and feedback during many discussions concerning methodology and British military attitudes.

———. "Learning to Eat Soup with a Knife." *World Affairs* 161 (Spring 1999): 193–99.

National Military Strategy of the United States. Washington, D.C.: United States Department of Defense, 1992.

National Military Strategy of the United States. Washington, D.C.: U.S. Department of Defense, 1995.

National Security Strategy of the United States. Washington, D.C.: The White House, 1991.

National Security Strategy of Engagement and Enlargement. Washington, D.C.: The White House, 1995.

NATO: Facts and Figures. Brussels: NATO Information Service, 1989.

NATO's Role in Peacekeeping. Basic Fact Sheet No. 4. WWW.NATO.INT, October 1994.

Newman, Richard J. "Vietnam's Forgotten Lessons." *U.S. News and World Report,* 1 May 2000.

Nietzsche, Friedrich Wilhelm. *Beyond Good and Evil.* Book IV, trans. Helen Zimmern 1886, 146 In *Bartlett's Familiar Quotations.* Franklin Electronic Bookman, 1998.

Oakley, Robert. Interview by author, 29 April 1999, West Point, New York.

———. Lecture to West Point class "Contemporary Military Thought," 29 April 1999, West Point, New York.

Olsen, Howard and John Davis. *Training U.S. Army Officers for Peace Operations.* Special Report. Washington, D.C.: United States Institute of Peace, 1999.

Operation Grapple FTX Memorandum. 1st Battalion Prince of Wales' Own Yorkshire Regiment (1 PWO), Osnabruck, Germany, 11 March 1993.

Operation Grapple 1—Post OP Debrief B Squadron 9/12L. Herford, England: RAC Gunnery Wing, 26 July 1993.

Operation Grapple 4 – End of Tour Report. Gornji Vakuf, Bosnia: Commander Sector Southwest, UNPROFOR, 2 November 1994.

Operation Grapple 5 –1st Battalion The Royal Gloucestershire, Berkshire, and Wiltshire Regiment (RGBW)/BRITBAT 2 Post Operational Report. North Yorkshire, England: 1 RGBW, 31 March 1995.

Operation Grapple 6 Post-Tour Report—1st Battalion The Devonshire and Dorset Regiment. Barker Barracks, England: 1 D&D, 20 November 1995.

Paret, Peter, ed. *Makers of Modern Strategy.* Princeton, NJ: Princeton University Press, 1986.

Parliamentary Debates (Hansard), Volume 177, House of Commons Official Report. London: HMSO, 1990.

"Patience and Bloody Noses." *The Guardian,* 30 September 1994, 27.

Peters, Ralph. "The Future of Armored Warfare." *Parameters* 27 (Autumn 1997): 50–59.

Petraeus, David H. "Lessons of History and Lessons of Vietnam." *Parameters* 56 (Autumn 1986): 43–53.

Pfaltzgraff, Robert L. and Richard H. Shultz, Jr., eds. *The United States Army: Challenges and Missions for the 1990s.* Lexington, MA: Lexington Books, 1991.

Pimlott, John. "The British Army: the Dhofar Campaign, 1970–1975" in *Armed Forces and Modern Counter-Insurgency*. eds., Ian F.W. Beckett and John Pimlott. New York: St. Martin's Press, Inc., 1985.

Pirnie, Bruce. *An Assessment of Peace Operations in Bosnia*. Santa Monica, CA: RAND, September 1994.

Posen, Barry R. *The Sources of Military Doctrine: France, Britain, and Germany between the World Wars*. Ithaca, NY: Cornell University Press, 1984.

Post-Operational Report—Operation Grapple 4. Vitez, Bosnia: 2nd Battalion, Royal Anglian Regiment, 30 October 1994.

Post-Tour Report—Commander's Review of Operation Grapple 6. Paderborn, Germany: HQ, 20th Armor Brigade, 9 November 1995.

Powell, General (Ret.) Colin. *My American Journey*. New York, Random House, 1995.

Pye, Lucien W. and Sydney Verba, eds. *Political Culture and Political Development* Princeton, N.J.: Princeton University Press, 1965.

Ramlogan, Rajendra. "Towards a New Vision of World Security: The United Nations Security Council and the Lessons of Somalia." *Houston Journal of International Law* 16 (Winter 1993): 213–59.

Record, Jeffrey. *Beyond Military Reform: American Defense Dilemmas*. New York: Pergamon-Brassey's, 1988.

Rinaldo, Rich. Telephone interview by author, 9 March 2000, West Point, New York.

———. Interview by author, 21 March 2000, Newport News, VA.

Ripley, Tim. *Operation Deliberate Force: The UN and NATO Campaign in Bosnia 1995*. Lancaster, England: Centre for Defence and International Security Studies, 1999.

Romjue, John L. *American Army Doctrine for the Post-Cold War*. Fort Monroe, VA: U.S. Army Training and Doctrine Command Military History Office, 1997.

———. *The Army of Excellence: The Development of the 1980s Army*. Fort Monroe, VA: U.S. Army Training and Doctrine Command, Military History Office, 1997.

Rose, Lieutenant General Sir Michael. "A Year in Bosnia: What Has Been Achieved." *The RUSI Journal* 140 (June 1995): 22–25.

———. Speech to the Friends of the Imperial War Museum, 16 November 1995. Imperial War Museum Sound Recording Archives, 16866.

———. *Fighting for Peace*. London: The Harvill Press, 1998.

Rosegrant, Susan and Michael Watkins. *A Seamless Transition: United States and United Nations Operations in Somalia—1992–1993*. Cambridge, MA: Harvard University, 1996.

Rosen, Stephen P. *Winning the Next War: Innovation and the Modern Military*. Ithaca: Cornell University Press, 1991.

———. "Military Effectiveness: Why Society Matters." *International Security* 19 (Spring 1995): 5–31.

Roy, Ian. "Towards the Standing Army, 1485–1660" in *The Oxford History of the British Army*. eds. David Chandler and Ian Beckett. New York: Oxford University Press, 1996.

Ruggie, John Gerard. "The United Nations and the Collective Use of Force: Whither — or Whether." A paper of the UNA-USA International Dialogue on the Enforcement of Security Council Resolutions, New York, 1996.

Saffire, William. "Robust or Bust." *New York Times*, 28 November 1994, 17.

Sapolsky, Harvey M. "On the Theory of Military Innovation." *Breakthroughs* 9 (Spring 2000): 35–39.

Sapolsky, Harvey M. and Jeremy Shapiro. "Casualties, Technology, and America's Future Wars." *Parameters* 26 (Summer 1996): 119–27.

Sarkesian, Sam C. "The Myth of U.S. Capability in Unconventional Conflicts." *Military Review* 68 (September 1988): 2–17.

Schein, Edgar. "Organizational Culture." *American Psychologist* 45 (February 1990): 109–19.

Segal, David R. and Dana P. Eyre. "The U.S. Army in Peace Operations at the Dawn of the Twenty-First Century." Unpublished report (draft) prepared for the U.S. Army Research Institute for the Behavioral and Social Sciences, 1994.

Senior Officer Review Group. "After Action Report, FM 100-23, Peace Operations." Fort Monroe, VA: Headquarters, U.S. Army TRADOC, 15 September 1993.

Sewell, Sarah B., Deputy Assistant Secretary of Defense for Peacekeeeping and Peace Enforcement Policy. Remarks to "International Peacekeeping 95" Conference. Washington, D.C., 15 November 1995.

Shultz, Richard H. Jr. "Doctrine and Forces for Low Intensity Conflict" in *The United States Army: Challenges and Missions for the 1990s*. eds. Robert L. Pfaltzgraff and Richard H. Shultz, Jr. Lexington, MA: Lexington Books, 1991.

Shultz, Richard H. Jr. *The Secret War Against Hanoi*. New York: HarperCollins Publishers, 1999.

Shy, John. "The American Military Experience: History and Learning." *Journal of Interdisciplinary History* 1 (Winter 1971): 205–28.

Shy, John and Thomas W. Collier. "Revolutionary War" in *Makers of Modern Strategy*. ed. Peter Paret. Princeton, NJ: Princeton University Press, 1986.

Silber, Laura and Allan Little. *Yugoslavia: Death of a Nation*. New York: Penguin, 1997.

Simkins, Peter. "The Four Armies 1914–1918," in *The Oxford History of the British Army*. eds. David Chandler and Ian Beckett. New York: Oxford University Press, 1996.

Simpson, Mavis. "Options for Change." An unpublished Information Paper by Whitehall Library staff. London: U.K. Ministry of Defence, July 1991.

Smith, James M. "USAF Culture and Cohesion: Building an Air Force and Space Force for the 21st Century." *INSS Occasional Paper 19*. Colorado Springs, CO: U.S. Air Force INSS, 1996.

Smith, Richard. "The Requirement for the United Nations to Develop an Internationally Recognized Doctrine for the Use of Force in Intra-State Conflict." *Occasional Paper Number 10*. Camberley, England: Strategic and Combat Studies Institute, 1994.

Snider, Don M. "U.S. Civil-Military Relations and Operations Other Than War." In *Civil-Military Relations and the Not-Quite Wars of the Present and Future*. ed. Vincent Davis. Carlisle Barracks, PA: Strategic Studies Institute, 1996.

Snider, Don M. "An Uninformed Debate on Military Culture." *Orbis* 43 (Winter 1999): 1–16.

———. "Postmodern Soldiers." *World Policy Journal* 17 (Spring 2000): 47–54.

Snider, Don M., John A. Nagl, and Tony Pfaff. *Army Professionalism, the Military Ethic, and Officers in the 21st Century*. Carlisle, PA: U.S. Army War College Strategic Studies Institute, December 1999.

Snow, Donald M. *The Shape of the Future*. 2nd ed. New York: M.E. Sharpe, 1995.

Snyder, Jack. *The Soviet Strategic Culture: Implications for Limited Nuclear Operations*. Santa Monica, CA: RAND, 1977.

———. "The Concept of Strategic Culture: Caveat Emptor" in *Strategic Power USA/ USSR*. ed. Carl G. Jacobsen. New York: St Martin's Press, 1990.

Special Edition No. 93-1. "Somalia." Fort Leavenworth, KS: Center for Army Lessons Learned, January 1993

Spiers, Edward. "The Late Victorian Army." In *The Oxford History of the British Army.* eds. David Chandler and Ian Beckett. New York: Oxford University Press, 1996.

Stevenson, Charles A. "The Evolving Clinton Doctrine on the Use of Force." *Armed Forces and Society* 22 (Summer 1996): 511–25.

Stone, John E. Email interview by author, 26 July 1999, West Point, New York.

Strachan, Hew. "The British Way in Warfare." In *The Oxford History of the British Army.* eds. David Chandler and Ian Beckett. New York: Oxford University Press, 1996.

———. *The Politics of the British Army.* New York: Clarendon Press, 1997.

Strawson, John. "The Thirty Years Peace," in *The Oxford History of the British Army.* eds. David Chandler and Ian Beckett. New York: Oxford University Press, 1996.

Stroup, LTG Theodore G., Jr. "Leadership and Organizational Culture: Actions Speak Louder than Words." *Military Review* 76 (January–February 1996): 44–49.

Sullivan, General Gordon. Letter to General Sir Charles Guthrie, 22 December 1994, Washington, D.C.

Summers, Harry G., Jr. *On Strategy: a Critical Analysis of the Vietnam War.* Novato, CA: Presidio Press, 1982.

Thornberry, Cedric. "The Lessons of Yugoslavia." Paper presented to a Center for Defense Studies Seminar, King's College London, December 1993. In Charles Dobbie. "A Concept for Post-Cold War Peacekeeping." *Survival* 36 (Autumn 1994): 121–48.

Thompson, Loren B., ed. *Low-Intensity Conflict: the Pattern of Warfare in the Modern World.* Lexington, MA: Lexington Books, 1989.

Thornton, Rod. "Peace Support Operations and the Health of the Military Organization: The Role of Doctrine." Unpublished paper, University of Birmingham, England, March 2000.

Travers, Tim. "The Army and the Challenge of War 1914–1918." In *The Oxford History of the British Army.* eds. David Chandler and Ian Beckett. New York: Oxford University Press, 1996.

Trevis, Major Anthony, British Army. Interview by author, 14 April 2000, West Point, New York.

Turabian, Kate L. *A Manual for Writers.* 5 th ed. Chicago: University of Chicago Press, 1987.

"U.S. Army Operations in Support of UNOSOM II." *Lessons Learned Report.* Ft Leavenworth, KS: U.S. Army Center for Army Lessons Learned, 1994.

"United Nations and the Situation in the Former Yugolsavia." *Reference Paper, Revision 4.* New York: UN Department of Public Information, 30 April 1995.

United Nations Security Council. SCOR, S/23445. 20 January 1992.

———. SCOR, S/25168. 26 January 1993.

———. SCOR, S/25354. 3 March 1993.

———. S/RES/733. 20 January 1992

———. S/RES/746. 17 March 1992.

———. S/RES/751. 24 April 1992.

———. S/RES/770. 8 June 1992.

———. S/RES/767. 24 July 1992.

———. S/RES/775. 28 August 1992.

———. S/RES/776. 14 September 1992.

———. S/RES/794. 3 December 1992.

————. S/RES/814. 26 March 1993.

————. S/RES/816. 31 March 1993.

————. S/RES/819. 16 April 1993.

————. S/RES/824. 6 May 1993.

————. S/RES/836. 4 June 1993

————. S/RES/837. 6 June 1993.

————. S/RES/941. 23 September 1994.

————. S/RES/947. 30 September 1994.

————. S/RES/954. 4 November 1994.

————. S/RES/958. 19 November 1994.

United States Forces Somalia After Action Report. Carlisle, PA: U.S. Army Peacekeeping Institute, June 1994. Also referred to as the *Montgomery Report.*

Utley, Robert M. "The Contribution of the Frontier to the American Military Tradition." *The Harmon Memorial Lecture Series Number 19.* Colorado Springs, CO: United States Air Force Academy, 1977.

Van Evera, Steven. *Guide to Methodology for Students of Political Science.* Cambridge, MA: Defense and Arms Control Studies Program MIT, 1993.

Van Riper, Paul and Robert H. Scales. "Preparing for Warfare in the 21st Century." *Parameters* 27 (Autumn 1997): 4–14.

Verrier, Anthony. *An Army for the Sixties.* London: Secker and Warburg, 1966.

Vetock, Dennis J. *Lessons Learned: A History of U.S. Army Lesson Learning.* Carlisle Barracks, PA: U.S. Army Military History Institute, 1988.

Vlahos, Michael. "The End of America's Postwar Ethos." *Foreign Affairs* 66 (Summer 1988): 1091–1107.

Waddell, Ricky Lynn. "The Army and Peacetime Low Intensity Conflict 1961–1993: The Process of Peripheral and Fundamental Military Change." Ph.D. diss., Columbia University, 1994.

Waltz, Kenneth N. *Man, the State, and War.* New York: Columbia University Press, 1959.

————. *Theory of International Politics.* New York: McGraw-Hill, Inc., 1979.

————. "Reflections on Theory of International Politics: A Response to My Critics," in *NeoRealism and Its Critics.* ed. Robert O. Keohane. New York: Columbia University Press, 1986.

Ware, Richard. "UK Defence Policy: Options for Change." House of Commons Background Paper. London: 4 October 1991.

Weigley, Russell F. *Towards an American Army: Military Thought from Washington to Marshall.* New York: Columbia University Press, 1962.

————. *History of the United States Army.* New York: Macmillan Publishing Company, Inc., 1967.

————. *The American Way of War: A History of United States Military Strategy and Policy.* Bloomington, IN: Indiana University Press, 1973.

————. *Eisenhower's Lieutenants, Volume I.* Baltimore: Johns Hopkins University Press, 1981.

————. *History of the United States Army.* Bloomington, IN: Indiana University Press, 1984.

————. "Reflections on Lessons from Vietnam" in *Vietnam as History.* ed. Peter Braestrup. Washington, DC: University Press of America, 1984.

————. "American Strategy from Its Beginnings Through the First World War" in *Makers of Modern Strategy.* ed. Peter Paret. Princeton, NJ: Princeton University Press, 1986.

Weinberger, Casper. "The Uses of Military Power." News Release 609-84. Washington, D.C.: Office of the Assistant Secretary of Defense for Public Affairs, November 1984.

Weiss, Thomas G. "Intervention: Whither the United Nations." *The Washington Quarterly* 17 (Winter 1994): 109–28.

Weyand, General Fred C. and LTC Harry G. Summers, Jr. "Vietnam Myths and American Realities." *CDRS CALL*. Ft Leavenworth, KS: U.S. Army CGSC, July–August 1976.

Whitney, Craig R. "Bad News They Can Manage." *New York Times*, 11 June 1995, 3.

Wild, A. C. "Grappling with Unfamiliar Problems." *The Infantryman: The Journal of the British Infantry* (1994): 94–96.

Wilkinson, Phil. "The Development of Peace Support Operations Doctrine." Unpublished draft paper. King's College London, March 2000.

Wilson, John B. *Maneuver and Firepower: The Evolution of Divisions and Separate Brigades*. Washington, D.C.: U.S. Army Center of Military History, 1998.

Winton, Harold R. *To Change an Army*. Lawrence, KS: University Press of Kansas, 1988.

Wren, Christopher S. "At Risk, British Troops Keep Watch." *New York Times*, 30 May 1995, A6.

Wyatt, Charles I. "Operation Grapple." Outline briefing. London: British Army, November 1995.

Yardley, Michael and Dennis Sewell. *A New Model Army*. London: W. H. Allen and Co., 1989.

INDEX

ABC Conference, World War II strategy, 51, 96

Abrams, General Creighton, 108

Abyssinian War, 37

Aden, 37

Afghanistan, 241, 243

Aideed, Mohammed Farah: opposition to, 156, 157, 159; Somali evaluation, 167–168; Somali warlord, 149, 152, 154, 165

Air force technology, British military, 68

Air Land Battle concept/doctrine, U.S. military, 100, 134, 140

al Qaeda, 241, 243

Algeria, 37

Allard, Kenneth: on CMOC, 154; on unity of command, 168

Allison, Graham, 13

Ambrose, Stephen, 91–92

American army: American War of Independence, 87–88; Beirut, 86, 119; Civil War, 89–90, 97, 98, 105, 110, 231, 232; Cold War, 84, 96–97, 99–100, 110, 130; core roles, 99–103; Dominican Republic, 84; Grenada, 84, 86; Iran hostage rescue attempt, 86; Korean War, 84, 85, 96, 100, 161; military paradigm, 83–87, 120; organization of, 113–115, 249; organizational culture elements, 102; Persian Gulf War, 85, 87, 100, 103, 109, 161, 246; Philippine Insurrection, 83–84, 88, 107; Root reforms, 94; Seminole Wars, 88–89, 93; Somali raid, 149, 156, 163; in Somalia, 129, 131, 151–169; Vietnam War, 83–84, 85, 86, 88, 98–99, 100, 101, 104, 110, 122; Vietnam War lessons, 105–106, 107–109, 113, 119; World War I, 84, 96, 97; World War II, 83, 85, 96, 97, 98, 99–100, 110

American military: American War of Independence, 33–34, 36, 37, 39; casualties, 112, 113, 121, 160–163, 234; Civil War impact, 35, 120; civilian-military relations, 116–120, 121, 234; counterinsurgency doctrine, 134–135; King Philip's War, 87, 94, 120; peacekeeping doctrine, 139–145, 235; and Plains Indians, 37; professional development, 74, 89, 90–92, 116, 121; Somali intervention, 153–154;

ABOUT THE AUTHOR

ROBERT M. CASSIDY, U.S. Army, is a Special Assistant with the U.S. Army Europe Commanding General's Initiatives Group. He is a graduate of the French Joint Defense College. He has served as a brigade operations officer in the 4th Infantry Division during Operation Iraqi Freedom, as squadron executive officer for the 4th Infantry Division's division cavalry squadron, as an assistant professor of international relations at West Point and as a cavalry troop commander in the 82nd Airborne Division. He has a Ph.D. in international security from the Fletcher School of Law and Diplomacy at Tufts University.